COMPUTER GAMES AND TECHNICAL COMMUNICATION

Taking as its point of departure the fundamental observation that games are both technical and symbolic, this collection investigates the multiple intersections between the study of computer games and the discipline of technical and professional writing. Divided into five parts, *Computer Games and Technical Communication* engages with questions related to workplace communities and gamic simulations; industry documentation; manuals, gameplay, and ethics; training, testing, and number crunching; and the work of games and gamifying work. In that computer games rely on a complex combination of written, verbal, visual, algorithmic, audio, and kinesthetic means to convey information, technical and professional writing scholars are uniquely poised to investigate the intersection between the technical and symbolic aspects of the computer game complex. The contributors to this volume bring to bear the analytic tools of the field to interpret the roles of communication, production, and consumption in this increasingly ubiquitous technical and symbolic medium.

Ashgate Studies in Technical Communication, Rhetoric, and Culture

Series Editor: Miles A. Kimball, Texas Tech University

This series promotes innovative, interdisciplinary research in the theory and practice of technical communication, broadly conceived as including business, scientific, and health communication. Technical communication has an extensive impact on our world and our lives, yet the venues for long-format research in the field are few. This series serves as an outlet for scholars engaged with the theoretical, practical, rhetorical, and cultural implications of the field.

Computer Games and Technical Communication
Critical Methods & Applications at the Intersection

Edited by

JENNIFER DeWINTER
Worcester Polytechnic Institute, USA

RYAN M. MOELLER
Utah State University, USA

Routledge
Taylor & Francis Group

LONDON AND NEW YORK

First published 2014 by Ashgate Publishing

Published 2016 by Routledge
2 Park Square, Milton Park, Abingdon, Oxon OX14 4RN
711 Third Avenue, New York, NY 10017, USA

Routledge is an imprint of the Taylor & Francis Group, an informa business

British Library Cataloguing in Publication Data
A catalogue record for this book is available from the British Library

The Library of Congress Cataloging-in-Publication Data has been applied for.

ISBN: 9781472426406 (hbk)

Contents

Part III Getting the Player Involved

Part IV Games in the Professional and Technical Communication Classroom

List of Figures and Tables

Figures

Tables

Notes on Contributors

Jennifer L. Bay is Associate Professor of English at Purdue University, where she teaches undergraduate courses in Professional Writing and graduate courses in Gender and Rhetoric, Community Engagement, New Media, and Postmodern Theory. Her work has appeared in journals such as *College English*, *JAC*, and *The Writing Instructor*, as well as in edited collections.

Melissa Bianchi is a graduate student at the University of Florida in English. She recently finished "Diagnosing the State of Rhetoric through X-Ray Images," in which she demonstrated how rhetorical studies might benefit from a reconceptualization that accounts for visual and verbal communication without the need for a specific subfield for either. By pointing to and demonstrating how procedure (both creative and interactive) can influence the meaning of an imagetext, these X-rays illuminate a space for rhetoric to bridge the gap between visual and verbal analysis.

Samantha Blackmon is an Associate Professor of English at Purdue University with a specialization in Rhetoric and Composition, computers and composition, African-American culture, and lesbian and women's studies. Her research and teaching interests are in Minority Rhetoric and Computers and Composition. Her more recent research project looks at how minority issues play out in the Computerized Writing Environment. She serves as Area editor of *The Writing Instructor* and as a member of the Purdue Advisory Committee for *Modern Fiction Studies*.

Carmen Blandino is an undergraduate at Minnesota State University, where she is studying English and Writing. She has completed a number of internships as an editor and professional communicator and intends to enter this profession upon graduation.

Kyle Bohunicky is a graduate student at the University of Florida, where he does research at the intersection of writing and digital spaces. He has presented on embedded agents in digital humanities. He continues work with computer games as a site to study visual rhetorics, young adult literature, and media ecology.

Jason Custer is a graduate student in Rhetoric and Composition at Florida State University, a Teaching Assistant in the First-Year Composition Program, and Assistant Director of the new Digital Studio location in William Johnston Building.

Dual-wielding a combination of luck and some serious cheat codes, Jason plans to continue his research into how video games and Rhetoric & Composition can inform one another via procedural rhetoric, new literacies, and video game-infused composition pedagogy. He looks forward to finding a supportive outlet for his research into video games. After a lengthy bout of strict Nintendo loyalty, Jason has branched out into PC gaming and is looking forward to bringing his love of all things Valve into the classroom in the spring.

Jennifer deWinter is an Assistant Professor of Rhetoric and faculty in the Interactive Media and Game Development program at Worcester Polytechnic Institute. She teaches courses on game studies, game design, and game production and management. Additionally, she codirects and teaches in the Professional Writing program. She has published on the convergence of anime, manga, and computer games both in their Japanese contexts and in global markets. Her work has appeared in numerous journals, including *Works and Days*, *The Journal of Gaming and Virtual Worlds*, *Eludamos*, *Computers and Composition*, and *Rhetoric Review*. She is the editor for the textbook *Videogames* for Fountainhead. In collaboration with Carly A. Kocurek, she is launching a new book series with Bloomsbury-Continuum on game designers, for which she is writing the inaugural book on Shigeru Miyamoto.

Jeff Greene is an Assistant Professor of Professional Writing at Southern Polytechnic State University where he teaches primarily composition and professional writing courses. His research interests are primarily focused on the intersection of narratology and game studies. He is also is an active author of fiction and nonfiction, and his work can be seen in the *Miami Herald*, *A Capella Zoo*, *Please Don't Magazine*, and more.

Jennifer Grouling is an Assistant Professor of English at Ball State University, where she specializes in Writing in the Disciplines/Writing Across the Curriculum, Writing Program Administration, and Composition Theory and Pedagogy. Her book *The Creation of Narrative in Table-top Role-Playing Games* examines issues of narrative development and coauthorship in face-to-face role-playing games.

Stephanie Hedge recently completed her Ph.D. at Ball State University with a focus on digital literacies. She has taught courses in First-Year Composition, Introduction to Digital Literacies, and Introduction to Rhetoric and Writing. Her recently completed dissertation examines student identity practices in digital writing environments.

Carly A. Kocurek is Assistant Professor of Digital Humanities and Media Studies at the Illinois Institute of Technology and a regional director for the Learning Games Initiative. She researches the history and cultural practices of video gaming in the United States and teaches courses on game studies, media studies, and digital humanities; her current manuscript chronicles the development of early video game culture and gamer identity around the video game arcade during the 1970s and 1980s. Her work has appeared in *Game Studies*, *The Journal of Gaming and Virtual Worlds*, *Syllabus*, *Flow*, and *In Media Res* and in the anthologies *Before the Crash: An Anthology of Early Video Game History* and *Gaming Globally: Production, Play, and Practice*. Kocurek holds a Ph.D. and M.A. in American Studies from the University of Texas at Austin.

A.V. Luce is a Ph.D. candidate in the composition and cultural rhetoric program at Syracuse University. Her research interests include community literacy, sexual literacy, queer theory, social movement rhetoric, and qualitative methods. Her previous publications include the coedited collection *Confederate Girlhoods: A Women's History of Early Springfield Missouri* from Moon City Press and a book review for *Women's Studies and Communication*.

Kevin Moberly is an Assistant Professor of rhetoric, new media, and game studies at Old Dominion University. He has published widely on gaming, new media, and mass culture in journals such as *Eludamos*, *Computers and Composition*, *Works and Days*, and *Kairos*. He has also coauthored several articles and book chapters with his brother, Brent Moberly, about the way that contemporary computer games repackage and commodify the medieval. He is currently working on a book-length project about the rhetorical relationship between computer games, mass culture, and the commodification of the real.

Ryan M. Moeller is an Associate Professor in the Department of English at Utah State University. He teaches courses in professional writing, rhetorical theory, and the rhetorics of technology. His research is focused on how the discourse surrounding emergent technologies affects human agency, especially within the consumer electronics and computer gaming industries. His work has appeared in *Technical Communication Quarterly*, *Kairos*, *fibreculture*, *Game Studies*, *Computers and Composition Online*, *Programmatic Perspectives*, *Works and Days*, and in edited collections.

Marc Ouellette is Managing Editor of *Reconstruction: Studies in Contemporary Culture*. With Jason Thompson, he has edited the upcoming collection *The Game Culture Reader*. He is an award-winning educator whose most recent works in *Semiotic Review*, the *Journal of Literacy & Technology*, and the *International Handbook of Semiotics* combine research and teaching in digital media and its impacts on identity, particularly gender, sex, and sexuality.

Laura Palmer is an Assistant Professor of Information Design & Communication at Southern Polytechnic State University. Her research interests center on people and their interactions with technology. In addition to her work with technical communication and gaming, she is researching social media as it relates to professional communication and public discourse. Her other recent work has explored how social media functions as a site of engagement in higher education. Dr. Palmer teaches courses at both the graduate and undergraduate levels and holds a Ph.D. in Technical Communication & Rhetoric with a minor in Visual Theory.

Christopher Ritter is a Lecturer in the Writing and Communication Program at Geogia Tech. He received his Ph.D. in 2010 from Washington State University, where he studied digital rhetoric, particularly in video games; and he has spent the last three years at Georgia Tech as a Marion L. Brittain Postdoctoral Fellow. His research interests orbit around digital works' persuasive and educational roles in healthcare and social justice. He has taught first-year composition, American literature, multimedia authoring, technical and professional communication, and digital game studies. Currently, his courses teach students the rhetorics of technical communication via service projects for local nonprofits and small businesses. The article written in this collection is in collaboration with a student team in a technical communication class: Sameer Ansari, Scott Daner, Sean Murray, and Ryan Reeves.

Anthony T. Sansone has worked as a web designer and developer, technical writer and trainer, proposal writer and graphic designer for more than fifteen years for both large multinational corporations and small startups. He earned his Masters degree in Technical Communication and Information Design from the Illinois Institute of Technology in 2013. Anthony is a lifelong gamer—PC and tabletop—and plays both regularly with friends and family.

Alyssa Schweigert is a Graduate Teaching Assistant at Ball State University in English with a specialty in Rhetoric and Composition. Her research interests include writing center theory and pedagogy as well as rhetorical interrogations into inequities of power, which she explores in her Pop Culture Association Conference presentation titled "No One Can Speak for Them: A Rhetorical Analysis of the Lakota Ghost Shirt Repatriation."

Lee Sherlock is a Ph.D. student in Rhetoric & Writing at Michigan State University, where he also holds an M.A. in Digital Rhetoric & Professional Writing and a graduate certificate in Serious Game Design through the Department of Telecommunication, Information Studies, and Media. He teaches professional writing and first-year composition at MSU along with work in the Writing in Digital Environments (WIDE) Research Center and Writing Center. His recent scholarship appears in the books *Rhetoric/Composition/Play Through Video Games: Reshaping Theory and Practice of Writing* and *Movies, Music, and More: Advancing Popular Culture in the Writing Classroom*, as well as the *Journal of Business and Technical Communication*.

Eva Grouling Snider is an Instructor at Ball State University, where she specializes in visual rhetoric, digital rhetoric, collaborative writing technologies, writing for the web, and professional writing. She teaches Professional Writing in a knowledge work model. She asks students to grapple with visual design principles, collaborative writing technologies, rhetorical theory, professional writing theory, and the production and publication of real-world documents. Her research involves the effects of gamification in professional writing classes. Her past research includes visual rhetoric and the rhetoric of space, ePortfolios and student identity, and griefing in online games.

Alex Tilley is a recent graduate of Worcester Polytechnic Institute with a dual degree in Interactive Media and Game Development and Professional Writing. His Major Qualifying Project was a fully developed game entitled *Shattered Sky*, for which he and his team developed a dynamic narrative engine to create a sense of rising drama. Additionally, Alex developed extensive playtesting materials and ran a number of usability tests and play tests for this project.

Stephanie Vie is an Associate Professor of Writing and Rhetoric at the University of Central Florida in Orlando. Her research focuses on online social networking and computer games, particularly how these technologies affect literate practices and the composition classroom. She is a reviews coeditor for *Kairos: A Journal of Rhetoric, Technology, and Pedagogy* and a consulting editor for the *Community Literacy Journal* at Michigan Technological University. Her work has appeared in *Computers and Composition*, *e-Learning*, and *Computers and Composition Online*, and her textbook *E-Dentity* (Fountainhead Press, 2011) examines the impact of social media on twenty-first-century literacies.

Josh Zimmerman is a Ph.D. candidate at the University of Arizona in Rhetoric, Composition, and the Teaching of English. Josh's work for both large corporations and small businesses prior to returning to graduate school helped to shape his interest in professional and technical communication. A lifetime of computer games and other nerdy pursuits have shaped that interest into an examination of the spaces where professional communication, computer games, and fandom overlap. He is currently working on his dissertation on computer game development and community management.

Foreword

Judd Ethan Ruggill and Ken S. McAllister

Writing a foreword to an anthology is often a bittersweet thing for scholars. On the one hand, it is a great honor to be invited to introduce a collection of some of the field's most innovative work. Such invitations usually suggest that the writers are sufficiently long in the tooth to assess the quality of the essays within, as well as the volume's place in (and importance to) the field generally. Additionally, the process of writing a foreword is typically far more fun than it is laborious; all the fabulous new ideas the book contains are a joy to read and reflect upon, and these in turn inspire thoughts of future convivialities and collegial exchanges.

On the other hand, it can be hard not to be at least a little envious when writing a foreword. The envy we speak of is not the petty sort to which even the most generous academics are occasionally susceptible. Rather, we mean that deliciously thrilling intellectual envy that scholars feel when they read a colleague's smart work and think "That's great! Why didn't I think of that?" Such envy converts quickly into admiration, edification, and—when the work is particularly insightful—an ongoing engagement with the project and its authors over time. In this ancient and curious asynchronous consummation, envy begets innovation.

However, there is also the more profound and lasting wistfulness associated with not being the one involved in the many close collaborations that anthologies require. The work of building a scholarly community—even the transient kind created within the pages of a multi-author project like this one—is among the most precious and rewarding of all intellectual endeavors. It is the work of pushing a field of study in a comparatively large-scale way, of concentrating a multitude of perspectives and personalities in order to transgress the conventional limits of understanding. As an added bonus, it also happens to be a great way to make friends and cocktail companions.

In the case of this book, our envy (the good kind) is well founded. Editors Jennifer deWinter and Ryan Moeller have assembled an impressive collection of essays on games and technical communication, essays that range from the theoretical to the pragmatic and from the textual to the paratextual. And while some anthologies feel disjunctive at times—when the bonds between essays is left too inchoate, for example—this book is deftly consistent and self referential. Far more than a collection of different ways of seeing, it reads as if the contributors and editors all worked closely with one another to produce a shared vision.

The real value of this book, though, is not what it says or how it says it. It is what its presence as a scholarly artifact and conversation confirms: that beyond the efforts of developers, players, scholars, and students to create and document the work of play—efforts this book's contributors analyze in great detail—computer game play itself is among the most technical and effective forms of communication human beings have yet devised. Consider, for instance, the ease with which players command computers to execute complex calculations and algorithms, catalyzing millions of instructions—rendering these polygons here in this way, using that progression over this amount of time (unless one of a thousand variables interferes with this process, in which case do something else)—with just a few precise flicks of the thumb. Or think about the ways that game software routinely prompt players to make highly systematic decisions and to respond decisively to strategic demands, as when the circumstances of play suddenly change due to new online opponents or a player's idiosyncratic in-game inventory. In cases like these (and many others), the dialogue between game and player is deeply and constantly technical, almost always—and astonishingly—without seeming so. Indeed, at its most sophisticated, computer game-based technical communication is so rapid and well designed that it is not only invisible but pleasurable.

As rich a vein as the dialogue between player and game is for the field of technical communication, it is even more meaningful to the humanities writ large. The advent of computer games and other digital technologies have created a wealth of possibilities for human and human-computer interaction, interaction in which machines regularly function as human playmates, intimates, collaborators, and co-conspirators. This is an inescapable new world, one where the explosive proliferation of new possibilities and problems in the digital domain must be met almost instantaneously by critical analytics and ethical, community-oriented solutions.

For this latter reason in particular, we urge you to read this book, not just with an eye toward what insights it offers about the connections between technical communication and computer games, but also with ears pricked for how the relationship between technical communication and computer games is a microcosm of a vastly more complex scene of cultural exchange, commercial engagement, and human fulfillment. Through the study of games and technical communication, in other words, the intricate and manifold processes by which humanity and technology merge come into sharp focus. This volume provides just such a lens, and it is a finely polished one at that.

Acknowledgments

I would like to acknowledge the Learning Games Initiative for maintaining a robust computer games research collaborative. This group has been influential in shaping how I think about and develop games. I would also like to thank Worcester Polytechnic Institute's Interactive Media and Game Development program. Under the exceptional leadership of Mark Claypool, this undergraduate and graduate program has provided me with both scholarly and pedagogical opportunities in the study and development of computer games. Within that program, I am especially beholden to Dean O'Donnell and Ralph Sutter, who allow me to bounce ideas off of them constantly over drinks. Furthermore, this project would not be in process had it not been for the support of WPI's Department of Humanities and Arts, which houses the Professional Writing degree. So to my colleagues there—Chrysanthe Demetry, Lorraine Higgins, Brenton Faber, Ruth Smith, Kris Boudreau, Constance Clark, and Jennifer Rudolph—all I can say is thank you. And no professional accomplishment would be achievable without personal support, so to Aaron McGaffey, Freya deWinter, and Rowan McGaffey, thank you for providing a foundation.

Jennifer deWinter

This collection would not have seen the light of day without the tireless efforts and dedication of Jennifer deWinter, my coeditor and collaborator. I'd like to thank her for her leadership and commitment to this project. I'd also like to thank Ken McAllister for everything, Judd Ruggill for most things, and Bryan Pearce for some things, and to thank all of them for setting all this in motion years ago at the Alpine Gaming Summit. Another AGS is long overdue. Thanks also to the Learning Games Initiative and the Game Studies, Culture, Play, and Practice area of the Southwest/Texas Popular Culture Association and American Culture Association, many of whose members are represented in this collection, and to my students for helping me always to see the possibilities for future studies in gaming and play. I cannot wait to see you all each year in ABQ.

My kids operate under the (partially true) assumption that my work involves playing computer games all day. They were very disappointed when I told them recently that many of the hours they thought I had been researching games were really spent on this collection. So, to Noah and Jacob, thank you for your endless curiosity and enthusiasm for my work, no matter how mundane it *really* is. You guys rawk. To my beautiful wife and partner, Julie, thank you for everything you do.

Ryan M. Moeller

Finally, both editors would like to thank each of the contributors to this volume—their work has expanded how we think about this topic and challenged us in our own research. A big thanks goes to Miles Kimball, the Series Editor for the Ashgate Studies in Technical Communication, Rhetoric, and Culture, of which this collection is a part. Thank you, Miles, for believing in this project from its earliest conception. And thank you Ann Donahue for shepherding us through the process. Also, thanks to Ashgate's anonymous reviewers for their feedback; you helped us shape this collection into what it is. Finally, a very special thanks to Carmen Blandino, our summer 2013 editorial intern. She has possibly read this volume more times than anyone else. We would also like to thank Emily Petersen for her excellent work on the Index.

Introduction

Playing the Field: Technical Communication for Technical Games

Jennifer deWinter and Ryan M. Moeller

As we introduce this book, we start with a story. It covers multiple years and perspectives, but we intend to shorten it down to about two paragraphs, so here goes: In a research and development section of Nintendo, a number of engineers worked under the codename "Revolution" to develop the Wii, a popular gaming platform that was released in the U.S. during the holiday season of 2006. The team produced technical specifications, internal procedural guides, and any number of supporting documents. Throughout the design process, they tested the system and hardware via rigorous usability standards to ensure that the technology worked. Simultaneously, a group of game developers began to create the vision documents, generate production plans, and write design documents for Wii Sports and other games that would be played on the new game system. They, too, produced a tremendous amount of technical documentation to design, create, test, and then market and support this game. Then the game is released, packaged with the system as the first game that people are likely to play on this new platform. And as marketing ratchets up their communication, and game reviews and walkthroughs are written by professionals and fans, the game development team gets together to write their postmortem—their reflection of what worked and what didn't—to share that with their industry brethren.

So now we turn to Susan and her two children. Susan has just returned from the store, goes to her living room, and opens up the box for her family's new Wii. She sits cross-legged in front of the television, the hardware, controllers, and accompanying game systematically laid out before her as she flips through the booklet, trying to find out how to set up this new system. On page 10, she finds "System Setup" and starts to skim quickly, focusing mostly on the images, but pausing to read the information around the sensor bar. She feels harried, like she needs to hurry up, as her two children have already connected the Nunchuck to the Wii-mote and are waving around this new piece of technology. Once she has the hardware set up, she turns on the system, takes the controller from her children, and starts the process of answering prompts from the Wii system to configure the system to her time zone and space. Once this is done, they are finally able to play their new game, but they don't know how. As soon as *Wii Sports* begins, luckily, they are prompted, shown what to do with the in-game tutorials. And then the fun begins as all of the family moves around the living room, laughing at each other's antics and cheering each other's successes. And as they master this new game, they forget (or have never known about) the thousands of pages of technical documentation that preceded that moment.

This book, then, starts with a simple premise: the computer game industry represents the quintessential intersection between technical and technological innovation and creative activity; as such, the field of technical communication is especially well poised to attend to it, as we hope this collection will demonstrate. In his 2008 *Technical Communication* article "Computer Gaming and Technical Communication: An Ecological Framework," Douglas Eyman makes an argument concerning why the field of technical communication should attend to computer games. Eyman identifies the following three opportunities for technical communicators:

1. market and job opportunities,
2. availability of computer game artifacts for technical communication research, and
3. the theory-building opportunities offered by the affordances of gaming ecologies (248).

Then, in the 2013 inaugural issue of *Connexions: International Professional Communication Journal*, Julia Mason repeats Eyman's call for the articulation of technical communication with games studies. She writes, "Professional communicators and scholars can look to conversations within the field of gaming studies to understand contemporary changes in communication practices, interface design, and technical genres; what job opportunities lie in the gaming industry for professional communicators; and what skill sets these positions require" (175). The intersection is clear, we think. Computer games are highly technical, mediating between designer vision and player experience via circuits and code. And this is where the field of professional and technical communication[1] can contribute to game studies and game industries.

Why Should Technical Communication Pay Attention to Computer Games?

This collection of essays investigates the multiple intersections between the study of computer games and the discipline of technical communication for both research and pedagogical purposes. At the most basic level of this intersection is the simple

---

[1]   We understand that, in many ways, professional and technical communication might be considered separate but related fields. In this collection, we have attempted to address our primary audience as technical communication students, teachers, and scholars; however, astute readers will notice that some authors, by virtue of the classes that they teach or studied, address a more general, combined audience of professional communicators and technical communicators.

observation that games are both technical and symbolic. The gaming industry pushes technological innovation through complex dialectics amongst large and small game developers, hardware developers, distributors, consumers, hackers, Congresspeople, journalists, ESRB raters, parents, IP lawyers, and many others besides. As Ken McAllister argues, "The computer gaming industry is much more than software; it requires factory labor, large manufacturing plants, and massive distribution systems as well. . . . One consequence of the booming gaming industry has been the rapid development of several technologies upon which the evolution of computer gaming depends" (20). McAllister goes on to argue that sales of computer graphics cards have long been driven by the gaming industry, which requires players to upgrade their systems' graphics capabilities to play the newest games. Andy Kessler makes a similar argument in his opinion editorial for the *Wall Street Journal* in which he states that the computer game industry has taken over technological innovation from the military-industrial complex: "Consider the Apple iPhone, often touted as the tech symbol of our era. It's actually more evolutionary than revolutionary. Much of its technology—color LCD displays, low power usage, precision manufacturing—was perfected for hand-held video games like the Nintendo DS and Sony PSP, which sold in the tens of millions." So much of our current technology, from computers to mobile phones, was developed for and by the computer game industry. Computer graphics cards and audio cards have been developed in response to demand—game developers' and players' express desire for photo- and audio-realistic games. The Global Positioning System (GPS), a satellite navigation system developed for the military, has been co-opted by gamers to develop Augmented Reality Games (ARGs), in which players use real-time location to interact with other players and objects and also to participate in geocaching, a treasure hunting game where players use GPS to interact with one another by hiding and seeking caches left for one another. Smart phones, like the iPhone mentioned above, have become gaming platforms in their own right. In fact, several Android tablets are marketed to gamers as gaming platforms. According to *Forbes*, "New research from Gartner shows that mobile app store sales will hit $26 billion globally [in 2013], up from $18 billion in 2012, and that most [two-thirds] of that revenue will come from games" (Olson). Thus, it appears that we are in what Jesper Juul names the casual revolution, a moment in computer game history when everyone is a gamer because of the ease of both gameplay and access (5). As the computer game industry continues to drive technological development and sales, technology users are concurrently using these technologies to play games.

Further, computer games are symbolically communicative, relying on written, verbal, visual, algorithmic, audio, and kinesthetic procedures to convey information. Professional and technical communication scholars are uniquely poised to investigate this intersection between the technical and symbolic aspects of the computer game complex. Johndan Johnson-Eilola argues in "Relocating the Value of Work: Technical Communication in a Post-Industrial Age" that "[we] live and work in an increasingly post-industrial age, where information is fast becoming the more valuable product. Products are still manufactured and purchased, but in a growing number of markets, primary value is located in information itself" (245). He argues that by positioning technical communication as symbolic-analytic work, technical communicators can engage with processes of information and product design "by centering our teaching and research on primary skills for symbolic analysis—collaboration, experimentation, abstraction, and system thinking" (266). The computer game industry presents an ideal site for technical communication research, since it drives technological innovation and production *and* its products use technologies to convey symbolic information. The methods for analyzing these artifacts, referred to by Johnson-Eilola as "collaboration, experimentation, abstraction, and system thinking" (266), have been developed by technical communicators since we began to see our work as being inherently systems-based, situated within organizational and technological complexity.

In "Genre Ecologies," Spinuzzi and Zachry advocate for investigating workplace writing as it is situated within complex ecologies:

> A genre ecology includes an interrelated group of genres (artifact types and the interpretive habits that have developed around them) used to jointly mediate the activities that allow people to accomplish complex objectives. In genre ecologies, multiple genres and constituent subtasks co-exist in a lively interplay as people grapple with information technologies. (172)

Technical communicators and technical communication researchers who employ methods of genre ecologies see organizations and workplaces as complex, networked spaces and work as an activity that connects and produces these spaces. Technical communicators employ methods of data collection and analysis that allow them to intervene and contribute to these activities. In "System Mapping," Moeller and Christensen articulate such a methodology, called genre field analysis (GFA). Based upon McAllister's gamework analysis and genre ecology, GFA allows researchers to identify the various elements of a genre field and to discover moments and spaces where agents can affect change within complex systems:

> [G]enre field consists of the larger networks of influence, structural elements, mediating technologies, and the context surrounding the production or maintenance of any genre, as well as each of the player-agents, genre-agents, transformative locales, and play scenarios that exert force within it. A genre field is very much what Huizinga (1950) called a playground, a sacred space governed by its own rules (p. 14), one that can be studied as separate from its nonattendant influences. (71)

So current methods of research and practice within technical communication offer especially relevant ways of investigating the computer game industry as a complex, symbolic system made up of game developers, interaction designers, hardware manufacturers, and computer game players, each of whom works to make meaning of the various activities in which they participate.

To add to this complexity is recent research in the ways in which computer games proceduralize learning and processes. In his book *Persuasive Games*, Bogost writes,

> *Procedurality* refers to a way of creating, explaining, or understanding processes. And Processes define the way things work: the methods, techniques, and logics that drive the operation of systems from mechanical systems like engines to organizational systems like high schools to conceptual systems like religious faith. *Rhetoric* refers to the effective and persuasive expression. Procedural rhetoric, then, is a practice of using processes persuasively. (2–3)

The idea that processes are rhetorical is nothing new in the field of technical and professional writing. However, with this emphasis on procedurality in games studies comes an ethical critique as articulated by Sicart's "Against Procedurality." Sicart's argument calls attention to the formalist understanding of games as oppressive systems, and game studies as a whole would be better served by remembering players as heterogeneous interlocutors in complex processes. At this intersection, we see a struggle between the ideology of rules (static expressions) and play (free expressions).

Games, then, must balance these aspects with a sophisticated attention to individualized player intention. The field of professional and technical communication has attended to these themes in workplace settings (see Faber; Spinuzzi, 2003 and 2008; and Zachry and Thralls), community settings (see Grabill et al.), and online settings (see Cargile Cook and Grant-Davie; deWinter and Vie; and Slattery). Computer games call upon the analytical tools of the field to interpret the roles of communication, production, and consumption of a technical and symbolic medium that is ubiquitous in the U.S. and many other countries besides.

Further, both technical communication and computer games as educational enterprises share a professional focus on production and application. Both are concerned with industry standards and technologies; both involve project management, teamwork, and software, hardware, and product development; and both have the eventual end-user or player in mind throughout the project lifecycle. For technical and professional communicators, the focus is often on the communicative practices that support these organizational activities, on creating and maintaining effective documents and best practices of design, as well as with (post)humanistic inquiry and interventions. In the computer game complex, the focus is often on managing large creative teams and providing the end-user (that is, the player) with an immersive play experience.

As our story above demonstrates, technical and professional communication contributes to a game project's life cycle at various stages, from proposal writing to documentation to playtesting to walkthroughs. Many commercially released console games are published by multimillion (if not multibillion) dollar companies that can underwrite the production of a $20 million title. Games begin as proposals that must be vetted and sold to publishers willing to develop, produce, and distribute them (see Sansone's and Ritter's chapters in this collection). Once funded, computer games are large-scale development projects that take teams of designers, programmers, artists, animators, writers, producers, and actors many months to produce. Effective product and project documentation as well as effective communication among team members and between the teams and the publisher is critical to this process, especially during the early stages of development. As levels are produced, game designers test their products using a version of usability testing known as playtesting. This testing process produces vast amounts of data in the form of bug notes; video, audio, and gameplay recordings; and focus group and survey data, all of which must be effectively incorporated into the next iteration of the game and subsequent titles. As games are released, computer game producers and fans continue the documentation process by communicating with one another on discussion boards and other media regarding patches and re-releases (see Sherlock's chapter in this collection) and developing walkthroughs, which walk players through each level of the game, as well as aftermarket products, including fan fiction, action figures, game modifications (see Moberly and Moeller's chapter in this collection), and so on. As many of the authors in this collection demonstrate, computer games exist within a complex nexus of artistic, creative, iterative, educational, and technical processes, positioning technical and professional communicators well to examine games as complex cultural artifacts as well as to intervene in critical points throughout the game development lifecycle.

Since its emergence as a field of work and study, technical and professional communication has always been concerned with understanding humanistic interests and agencies among technical processes. In "The Rise of Technical Writing Instruction in America," Robert Connors argues, "For as long as [people] have used tools and have needed to communicate with each other about them, technical discourse has existed" (4). He goes on to trace the emergence of technical writing education from engineering education in the nineteenth century to a full fledged discipline by the end of the twentieth century. As Carolyn Miller argued in her now well-cited 1979 article "A Humanistic Rationale for Technical Writing," "The teaching of technical or scientific writing [requires] more than the inculcation of a set of skills; it becomes a kind of enculturation. We can teach technical or scientific writing, not as a set of techniques for accommodating slippery words to intractable things, but as an understanding of how to belong to a community" (617). Indeed, as several authors in this collection show, the intersection of professional and technical communication with computer game studies in the game space of the classroom allows instructors, at least, to help their students understand how to position themselves as professional, technical communicators within specific communities of practice. Thus, as far as the classroom is concerned, the intersection between professional and technical communication and computer game studies situates students well as game designers and laborers and players, but it also positions games well in our classrooms and in our research.

Yet the argument is not just for games in the classroom or preparing students to join game companies. The exigency for this volume arises not just because games are ubiquitous (and they are) and not just because almost everyone plays them (and they do); it arises in response to the fact that computer games are affecting other technical industries in transformative ways. As computer games become part of our mediated landscape, they enter a dialectic with other media, which facilitates what Bolter and Grusin call a remediation process—a process by which the visual and symbolically coded aspects of one medium affect other media, thereby re-mediating those forms. An easy example that we can point to is the visual interfaces of websites affecting how television news now looks or television news going to the streets and twitter to get comments from people's reactions, remediating social media practices. This is especially important when technical and professional communicators attend to any mediated discourse, and we would argue even more important when considering computer games in this mediated landscape. As computer games gain more market penetration, the semiotics of games transforms other media and practices, remediating our world and our expectations. Thus, games are changing website design, social media design, workplace training, education, experience design, and so on. These changes are sometimes obvious—gamified work or education—and sometimes they are less obvious, such as the transference of visual aesthetics in HCI design.

Professional and technical communication scholars have developed theories and communication strategies for understanding technologies and for addressing the challenges of communicating technologies and technical information. In the introduction to Zachry and Thralls's fabulous collection, *Communicative Practices in Workplaces and the Professions*, Mark Zachry identifies three overlapping issues that communication scholars address: communicative practices are relational to a multiplicity of contingencies in any organization or situation; they are situated in complex ecologies, referred to as "networks, open systems, and rhizomes;" and they may be enacted by people, but they share agency with other "humans, machines, and interfaces" (ix–xi). We think that games studies and play theory have a great deal to offer the field of professional and technical communication in understanding these complex ecologies and how agency is distributed among the various agents who operate within them.

Not only are there ripe possibilities for technical communicators to study games and bring their disciplinary knowledge to bear on this multibillion-dollar industry, there is also an opportunity here to be transformed by play and games. Play denies the seriousness of the workplace while at the same time being deadly serious itself. Indeed, as play theorist Huizinga writes: "The contrast between play and seriousness is always fluid. The inferiority of its play is continually being offset by the corresponding superiority of its seriousness" (8). Play inserts itself, often to the dismay of managers and teachers. And our institutions are trying to tame play, harnessing it in the bridle of education and training. And this works, and there is much to be learned from these attempts. But play and players will invariably disrupt taming processes, desiring instead the carnival, the conquest, and the flow of immersion.

In addition to the lessons that we can learn from play, games too offer rich articulations into technical communication. Games systematize play, providing frameworks for understanding. In many ways, games allow us to scale ourselves to our worlds (as Carlin Wing has said), providing us with a logic for the illogic of human expression—an algorithm for play. This is where computer game designers step in: they design systems of experience. The act of playing those games transforms those systems back into experiences—the experiences of fear, success, and love. Here, we see an opportunity for technical communication to be transformed: we can imagine technologies, not as systematized approaches to defined problems, but rather as systems of human expression. And these systems are at play from design, production, circulation, and consumption. We ask, then: By using the framework of designed experience, how might that change the way that we think about our communication challenges toward internal and external audiences? How might this framework change the motivations behind development? What ethical quandaries might this address, and what new ethical questions might arise? And how might we play in this new landscape? The chapters in this collection are an early attempt to start this conversation, but we could not be exhaustive here. Much like the symbols of humankind, the expressions of play and communication are seemingly infinite in their forms.

About the Collection

In addition to these primary intersections, there are a number of other intersections that this book explores, including the following:

- Games are database-driven: they collect massive amounts of data from players and their interactions.
- Games are procedural: they are rule-based systems that encourage players to test their boundaries. This testing behavior encourages hacking culture and provides insight into mobile and ubiquitous computing, user experience design, and usability.
- Games are used to train workers and students.
- Games are technically produced; they go through a rigorous development process that relies on specialized documentation and testing.
- Gaming cultures provide avenues for community and identity formation for technical and professional communicators to research and participate in.
- Gamification, or the process of turning everyday activities into games in order to compare worker productivity, student learning, or similar intangibles, is fast becoming big business.

Each of the essays in this book addresses one or more of these intersections. We've organized the book into four sections: Connecting Professional and Technical Communication and Game Studies, Industry Documentation and Procedural Guides, Getting the Player Involved, and Games in the Professional and Technical Communication Classroom, although a careful reader will see significant overlap between the parts.

The first part, **Connecting Professional and Technical Communication and Game Studies**, includes two chapters that address the intersections between professional and technical communication and game studies explicitly. In chapter one, "It's All Fun and Games Until Someone Pulls Out a Manual," Greene and Palmer make the claim that there is a professional role for technical communicators to play in game design and development, but they note that the industry is not yet aware of what those contributions are. They present the results of a survey sent to industry professionals that queried their awareness of technical communication and what it offers the industry. Ultimately, the authors call on game developers to consider the value of technical communicators in game development processes while simultaneously reminding those in technical communication that there are valuable opportunities to affect positive change in game development. Following this, Marc Ouellette examines both games studies and professional and technical communication, offering a critique through the lenses of gender studies and queer theory in "Come Out Playing: Computer Games and the Discursive Practices of Gender, Sex, and Sexuality." In examining play as part of the professional institution of computer games, Ouellette notes that the absence of GLBTQ subjectivities speaks to a weakness in both technical communication and games. Indeed, he writes succinctly: "The exclusion, or relegation, of the very topic of gender, sex, and sexuality itself reveals much about the phenomenon" (p. 41). Thus, he sees an opportunity to play with identity and to see through the often nominalizing discourse surrounding technique and technology.

The second part, **Industry Documentation and Procedural Guides**, examines the evolving documentation practices in the game industry for opportunities to inform professional and technical communication practice. In Chapter 3, "Rendering Novelty Mundane: Technical Manuals in the Golden Age of Coin-Op Computer Games," Kocurek is interested in the liminal space created when computer games require new technological skills from arcade owners—but there is no training for those skills. She discusses the emergence of a type of documentation that transforms the "magic" of rarified computers into mundane machines that need regular maintenance. DeWinter picks up where Kocurek left off in Chapter 4's "Just Playing Around: From Procedural Manuals to In-Game Training." Where Kocurek is interested in the owners of arcades, deWinter is interested in the players of those arcade games and tools and instructions that evolved to help them play. Luce, in "'It Wasn't Intended to Be an Instruction Manual': Revisiting Ethics of "Objective" Technical Communication in Gaming Manuals," looks at the ethics of documentation through the case study of *RapeLay*, a Japanese rape simulation game that had a fan-written walkthrough produced for it. She analyzes the authority that fans claim in order to legitimize themselves as experts of content while distancing themselves from the moral and ethical ramifications of that very same content. And finally, Anthony Sansone traces the current shift in practice surrounding game design documents in "Game Design Documents: Changing Production Models, Changing Demands." He starts with a brief analysis of traditional documents and moves through the current documentation needs of Agile production in game companies.

Part III, **Getting the Player Involved**, includes chapters that address how the game industry involves players at multiple levels in the processes of producing and consuming games. Alex Tilley, Carmen Blandino, and Jennifer deWinter turn their attention to what usability testing can learn from a playtesting case study in Chapter 7, "Developing a Testing Method for Dynamic Narrative." They build their case around the challenges that dynamic narratives present to traditional usability testing, using the production of the student-built game *Shattered Sky* as a case study. Then in "Psyche and Eros: Rhetorics of Secrecy and Disclosure in Game Developer–Fan Relations," Zimmerman examines the ways that developers mobilize fans through carefully leaking out "secret" material through YouTube videos and fan access that is closely guarded with Non-Disclosure Agreements. The technical documentation creates desire for unreleased game products, which have commercial and symbolic value. Once the game is released, developers continue to maintain a relationship with the fan communities, a topic that Sherlock takes up in "Patching as Design Rhetoric." Sherlock examines the transformation of patch release notes into game documentation—a practice that arises from the unintentional collaboration between designers, fans, publishers, and so forth. These relationships between developer and consumer are not always so symbiotic. For example, in "'You Are How You Play': Privacy Policies and Data Mining in Social Networking Games," Vie then looks at the ways in which social online games collect player information, disempowering players through metric analysis and subverting them to larger aggressive capitalist mechanisms via the oft-times hidden communications that the company provides players, such as play agreements and terms of service. The last chapter "Working at Play: Modding, Revelation, and Transformation in the Technical Communication Classroom" picks up on this critique of capital. In it, Moberly and Moeller investigate the ideological work that the practice of computer game modifications perform, both for the industry and for the players that engage in this activity, calling the latter, at least potentially, a revelation pedagogy.

Our last section, **Games in the Professional and Technical Communication Classroom**, offers chapters that discuss the implications of situating games in the classroom to various degrees. In "Inhabiting Professional Writing: Exploring Rhetoric, Play, and Community in *Second Life*," Bay and Blackmon ask, "How do we account for interaction that goes beyond discrete literacies—literacies that are more environmental or even spatial?" They see the potential of simulated environments in general and *Second Life* in particular to teach crucial professional skills because these environments provide business contexts that ask students to build, collaborate, and negotiate failure. Bianchi and Bohunicky investigate industry claims that *World of Warcraft* (*WoW*) players make for better laborers than those with advanced business degrees. In "How *World of Warcraft* Could Save Your Classroom: Teaching Technical Communication Through the Social Practices of MMORPGs," they discuss their findings from having their students immerse themselves in *WoW*'s complex genre ecology. They focus specifically on the homologies between business practices and managing a Guild, and they provide a series of assignments and approaches that capitalize on this relationship. Likewise, in "The Three D's of Procedural Literacy: Developing, Demonstrating, and Documenting Layered Literacies with Valve's Steam for Schools," Custer presents his use of game playing and building as a way to teach students layered literacies and procedural rhetoric through developing, demonstrating, and documenting their play and build experiences. Grouling Snider, Grouling, Hedge, and Schweigert, move from discussing using games in class to the actual act of gamifying a class in "Questing through Class: Gamification in the Professional Writing Classroom." In this chapter, they present the results of data collected from a gamified course in technical communication, offering advice and caveats to those thinking of applying ludic or game elements to their course designs. We close this collection with Ritter, Ansari, Daner, Murray, and Reeves, who provide a multivocal reflection of a game design project completed in a service learning, technical writing course in "From Realism to Reality: A Postmortem of a Game Design Project in a Client-Based Technical Communication Course." This chapter offers a nice final punctuation to this volume because it moves us from our opening theories of games to an example of nearly complete industrial practice within a classroom.

The sixteen chapters in this collection provide critical, reflective perspectives on the rich, productive intersections between professional and technical communication and computer game studies. The range of scholars represented in this collection—from associate professors of professional and technical communication to undergraduate students in game design—offers a diversity of perspective that we hope is refreshing and useful in thinking about these intersections. We hope that professional and technical communication scholars and, to a certain degree, game scholars find the research and thinking in this collection to be a starting point for further research into what our interdisciplinary and professionally driven fields can learn from one another.

Works Cited

Bay, Jennifer L., and Samantha Blackmon. "Inhabiting Professional Writing: Exploring Rhetoric, Play, and Community in *Second Life*." *Computer Games and Technical Communication: Critical Methods and Applications at the Intersection.* Burlington, VT: Ashgate, 2014. 211–31.

Bogost, Ian. *Persuasive Games: The Expressive Power of Videogames.* Cambridge, MA: MIT P, 2007.

Bolter, Jay David, and Richard Grusin. *Remediation: Understanding New Media.* Cambridge, MA: MIT P, 1999.

Cargile Cook, Kelli and Keith Grant-Davie. *Online Education: Global Questions, Local Answers.* Amityville, NY: Baywood, 2005.

Connors, Robert J. "The Rise of Technical Writing Instruction in America." *Central Works in Technical Communication.* New York: Oxford UP, 2004. 3–19.

deWinter, Jennifer, and Stephanie Vie. "Press Enter to 'Say': Using *Second Life* to Teach Critical Media Literacy." *Computers and Composition* 25.3 (2008): 313–22.

Eyman, Douglas. "Computer Gaming and Technical Communication: An Applied Framework." *Technical Communication* 55.3 (2008): 242–50.

Faber, Brenton D. *Community Action and Organizational Change.* Carbondale, IL: Southern Illinois UP, 2002.

Grabill, Jeffrey T. *Community Literacy Programs and the Politics of Change.* SUNY P, 2001.

Huizinga, Johan. *Homo Ludens: A Study of the Play-Element in Culture.* London: Routledge, 1949.

Johnson-Eilola, Johndan. "Relocating the Value of Work: Technical Communication in a Post-Industrial Age." *Technical Communication Quarterly* 5.3 (1996): 245–70.

Juul, Jesper. *A Casual Revolution: Reinventing Video Games and Their Players.* Cambridge, MA: MIT P, 2012.

Kessler, Andy. "How Videogames are Changing the Economy." *Wall Street Journal.* 11 Jan. 2011. Web. 7 Jan. 2014.

Mason, Julia. "Professional Writing and Video Games." *Connexions: International Professional Communication Journal* 1.1 (2013): 173–8.

Miller, Carolyn R. "A Humanistic Rationale for Technical Writing." *College English* 40.6 (1979): 610–17.

Moeller, Ryan M., and David M. Christensen. "System Mapping: A Genre Field Analysis of the National Science Foundation's Grant Proposal and Funding Process." *Technical Communication Quarterly* 19.1 (2010): 69–89.

Olson, Parmy. "The Win for Games: They Grab Two-Thirds of App Store Sales." *Forbes.com.* 19 Sep. 2013. Web. 7 January 2014.

Ouellette, Marc. "Come out Playing: Computer Games and the Discursive Practices of Gender, Sex, and Sexuality." *Computer Games and Technical Communication: Critical Methods and Applications at the Intersection.* Burlington, VT: Ashgate, 2014. 35–51.

Salvo, Michael J. "Ethics of engagement: User-centered design and rhetorical methodology." *Technical Communication Quarterly* 10.3 (2001): 273–90.

Sicart, Miguel. "Against Procedurality." *Game Studies: The International Journal of Computer Game Research* 11:3 (2011): n.p. Web. 10 March 2013.

Slattery, Shaun. "Undistributing Work Through Writing: How Technical Writers Manage Texts in Complex Information Environments." *Technical Communication Quarterly* 16.3 (2007): 311–25.

Spinuzzi, Clay. *Tracing Genres Through Organizations: A Sociocultural Approach to Information Design*. Cambridge, MA: MIT P, 2003.

———. *Network: Theorizing Knowledge Work in Telecommunications*. Cambridge UP, 2008.

Spinuzzi, Clay, and Mark Zachry. "Genre Ecologies: An Open-System Approach to Understanding and Constructing Documentation." *Journal of Computer Documentation* 24 (2000): 169–91.

Turnley, Melinda. "Integrating critical approaches to technology and service-learning projects." *Technical Communication Quarterly* 16.1 (2007): 103–23.

Wing, Carlin. "Hitting Walls (v.XXII)." History of Games International Conference. La Grande Bibliothèque, Montreal, Quebec, Canada. June 22, 2013.

Zachry, Mark, and Charlotte Thralls. *Communicative Practices in Workplaces and the Professions: Cultural Perspectives on the Regulation of Discourse and Organizations*. Amityville, NY: Baywood, 2007.

PART I
Connecting Professional and Technical Communication and Game Studies

Chapter 1

It's All Fun and Games Until Someone Pulls Out a Manual: Finding a Role for Technical Communicators in the Game Industry

Jeff Greene and Laura Palmer

The computer game industry and technical communication seem like a perfect professional match. Game development as a process requiring both internal and external documentation plays to the skills of today's technical communicators. With the ability to manage projects, document processes, and work in dynamic team environments, a technical communicator can easily become an asset to any project. Technical communicators are well suited to reconfigure the developer-as-writer model and situate themselves as professionals who can move seamlessly from creating internal artifacts to developing user-centered information products in forms and formats suited to computer game players and their goals.

Yet this ideal match is one that receives little attention in the professional and scholarly publications, and it is a partnership still unrealized in the computer game industry. In 2004, Peterson wrote, in "Why Game Documentation Is Essential to a Satisfying User Experience," that "technical communicators have a place in the multi-billion dollar gaming industry." Peterson predicted that, from his perspective, the video gaming industry would be an area of both opportunity and growth for the profession (6).

Nearly eight years after Peterson's call for technical communicators to be part of the computer game industry, our own piece "It's All in the Game: Technical Communication's Role in Game Documentation" appeared in print. We asked, "Where did these ideas about technical communication, the gaming industry, and documentation go?" and found that this idyllic union between computer game development and technical communication was still missing.

We assumed, in the intervening years since Peterson's article first appeared, this oversight would be addressed. In turn, we believed a quick scan of the "Careers" link on major computer game developers' website would display positions that align perfectly with the competencies technical communicators can offer, especially for developing and managing user documentation. However, what we found in 2011 reflected the reality of 2004; technical communicators were not part of the call to join game development teams. While there are notable exceptions, such as the game development company Prima employing the gamers themselves as technical writers (Luce), the professionalization of technical communication in the field remains stunted. From our perspective, this did not bode well for the future of technical communication and gaming. We wondered then, what jobs would be available?

In 2011, the career positions for technical communicators posted on developers' sites, on job search engines, and even on Gamasutra.com were few at best. If a position existed, the emphasis was typically on very traditional, internal-facing roles for the technical communicators. As a case in point, one gaming company's recent job posting described their technical writing position as centered on developing "technical manuals and documents to describe and provide technical information to internal and external customers" (American Gaming Systems). A natural assumption would be an even split in the internal/external focus; however, the details of the position, as bulleted in the posting, made the internal focus a clear priority:

- Update current documentation to reflect changes due to product evolution, user comments, and design changes;
- Conduct research to determine what engineering changes may affect technical documentation;
- Gather information, organize content, and routinely write reports and correspondence;
- Work with designated reviewers to ensure technical accurateness and pertinence of documentation;
- Create documentation of technical nature, such as set-up guides and user guides, for electronic devices, web-based delivery, and PDFs; and
- Maintain internal technical library including configuration guides, technical release notes, process and procedure guides, and system requirements (American Gaming Systems).

With "user guides" occupying a low slot on the list of duties, the position focuses on very typical and routine types of work. Unfortunately, the technical communicator in this position may not have the opportunity to shine by creating dynamic quick start manuals, strategy guides, and, most relevant today, contextual user tutorials accessible within the game ecosystem (deWinter). While this job advertisement reflected some understanding of what technical communicators can do, it still marginalized what we, and Peterson, see as a vital partnership.

This lack of a tangible intersection between computer game software developers, technical communicators, and documentation practices gives way to compelling questions centered on why technical communication, as a locus of practices and professionals, remains virtually unseen in the gaming industry. As researchers, we wanted to know more about the apparent disconnect between gaming and technical communication; thus, we asked:

- At what point(s) during the development cycle is internal documentation (game design documents, technical design documents) produced?

- At what point(s) during the development cycle is external documentation (manuals, in-game tutorials, etc.) produced?
- Does company size or focus limit roles for writers?
- Does the "technical" in technical communication circumscribe how others see our competencies?
- Are we still subsumed with technical "writer" as the sole descriptor of the profession? Has the broader idea of "communicator" not penetrated the gaming industry's understanding of what we do?
- Does the word "documentation" evoke ideas of only print manuals and guides versus the myriad other artifacts (digital, contextual) technical communicators can and do produce?
- Does the development process/environment—Agile or otherwise— somehow preclude the involvement of technical communicators?

To answer these questions, we reviewed the current literature about development and documentation practices within the gaming industry. Specifically, we examined the typical model of documentation in the gaming industry and the unique writing requirements for computer games. Within these frameworks, we situate key roles for technical communicators and posit their value within a game development company.

Through surveys and interviews, we sought to understand more about game companies, their documentation production practices, and if technical communicators inform and guide the documentation process. Our goal in this work is to establish a greater understanding about how technical communication is considered in game development communities. Our findings situate new roles for technical communicators and demonstrate how a professional communicator can be a valuable member of a game development team.

Double-Duty Documentation: The Importance of Technical Communication in the Computer Game Industry

The stakes for game developers are higher than they've ever been. In the early 1990s, *Doom II* shocked the gaming world with a $200,000 production price tag (Mhatre). Jump to today, where the average top-rated title—commonly referred to as an "AAA" title—regularly costs over twenty million dollars, and it's no surprise that a developer can be ruined by a single underperforming title (Campbell).

Given the high risks associated with game development today, the need for strong internal and external documentation is even more important. According to Rouse, author of *Game Design: Theory & Practice*, solid internal documentation acts as a guide during the production cycle, keeping a team organized and unified in their vision while remaining a powerful reference tool for when a game may be converted to other platforms (356). Likewise, according to Peterson, client-side documentation isn't any less important, performing as a clear gateway to a successful user experience within a computer game title (6).

Many gamers might agree with Peterson: computer games are arguably most satisfying when a player clearly understands a game's rules, fundamentals, and interface. Gamers want to get *into* the game—to fall deeply into the experience through their ability to interact with a game world. Janet Murray, author of *Hamlet on the Holodeck,* describes this sense of "agency" in interactive stories as the "satisfying power to take meaningful action and see the results of our decisions and choices" (126). With agency in mind, tutorials and game documentation take on a far greater role from the perspective of play. Without an understanding of controls and how specific actions might affect the game world, a player may feel lost and lose that all-important sense of agency.

Furthermore, ineffective game tutorials or manuals can add a layer of hindering complexity to a computer game title. Without clear documentation, a computer game may be saddled with a reputation as having an "overly steep learning curve" and this comment (particularly from an influential computer game critic) could hurt a computer game's release, turning away neophyte players and never affording that potential audience a chance to connect with a game. In a competitive marketplace, this can translate into plunging sales and developer bankruptcy.

Moreover, documentation only becomes more important for particularly complicated game genres like grand strategy, 4X, or simulation games such as *Civ V, Galactic Civilizations II, Europa Universalis III,* or *Crusader Kings II.* In these games, players are not only being asked to navigate a complicated user interface, but also to learn multiple detailed systems that simulate everything from strategic warfare to a realistic medieval economy. As Jennifer deWinter asserts in this volume, complex games increase the requirement for "help concerning large-level strategy as well as scene-specific guidelines." With extreme levels of micromanagement and complexity, effective client-side documentation is an absolute requirement for a great user experience (p. 73).

Internal Documentation and the Design Process

From the outset in the game development cycle, internal documentation—concept proposals, game design documents, production manuals, technical design documents, and the like—is being shared, read, revised and re-revised by a vast array of team members in many different roles. According to Rouse, strong internal game documentation describes the game for the team, and it also may be used to schedule several aspects of preproduction and production (358).

In an interview with our team, Uthsav Ahuja, cofounder of Mango Learning, a producer of educational games and mobile applications, shared insight into his development process in respect to internal game documentation as shown in Figure 1.1.

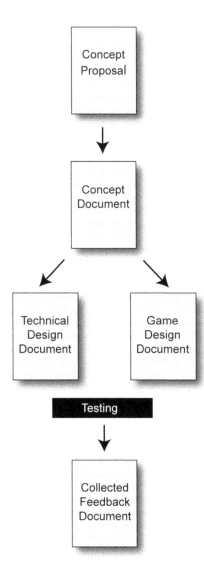

In what Ahuja describes as a "mixture between Agile and waterfall design," game production starts with a concept document (sometimes called a concept proposal), a short document that may be written by practically anyone within the game company, including but not limited to the lead designer. The lead designer inevitably decides what's feasible from the concept, based on access to tools and current technology, and then drafts up a concept document, which is readied for a "green light committee."

The green light committee, which according to Ahuja may be made up of a diverse group of stakeholders including "one or two ops people, one or two people in QA, technical people, and market research," reviews the game. Once the concept document is cleared through the green light committee, the project moves on to preproduction.

A senior producer, senior game designer, one art director, and one technical director carry out the preproduction phase. Two major documents are prepared during this phase: the technical design document and the game design document. The technical director produces the technical design document, which describes the entire technical architecture for the game, serving as a foundation for programming work and a reference point for technical solutions to problems.

Figure 1.1   Workflow for Game
Development
Documentation

Simultaneously, game designers will craft the game design document, an incredibly important text that outlines everything conceptually within a game.

The game design document (or GDD) is the conceptual heart of a computer game, and Rouse explains it as "[a document responsible for] communicating a vision for a game . . . mapping out as much information as possible about how that game will function, what players will experience, and how players will interact with the game-world" (356).

According to Ahuja, the game design document can be several hundred pages and may include sections that detail the game's story, plot, script, game world, characters, genre, target audience, controls, user interface, characters, level design, and many other assets (by no means is this an exhaustive list of what could be included). Shortly after the game design document is produced, an art director gets involved, along with several concept artists. According to Ahuja, this could be "anywhere from 10 to 12 artists" all completing concept art—the purely visual representations that go along with the game design document.

Throughout the process, members of various teams look to the game design document and the technical design document as they track their progress through various milestones in the development cycle. As an example, Ahuja described the "first level milestone" where a single playable level may be produced with the function of testing out a specific game mechanic, an iterative approach common in Agile game development. Ahuja used the example of a first person shooter where "the only thing that will work in the first level will be shooting . . . maybe one enemy will keep spawning in different places and the game mechanic of how you scope, how you select, and how you shoot will be defined in that entire process." The team then reviews this game mechanic and gives it the green light to move forward.

During each milestone, feedback is continually collected from various team members. The team continues to build through milestones until reaching alpha level, where Ahuja says that the game may be "entirely feature complete . . . [as an example] in a car racing game, maybe at alpha, one entire track is complete." At this phase, playtesters are brought in, and even more feedback is collected concerning anything from game-breaking bugs to how fun the game actually is. This continues as the company works toward beta. The team continues to collect feedback throughout the process from multiple sources (including testers), and according to Ahuja, a document is drafted that details the "collected feedback." This document may contain "[up to] 150 points . . . [detailing] what could be fixed before the game goes live and what could be fixed and updated afterwards."

As this process shows, many elements of the game development cycle hinge upon the success (or failure) of an internal game document's ability to communicate a cohesive technical and conceptual vision while also serving as a reference source for the entire team. It would seem, then, that the skills of a technical communicator could contribute greatly to internal game documentation and would naturally complement a design team in this matter.

Client-side Documentation and the Design Process

The importance of solid internal documentation seems obvious when considering the raw complexity involved in coordinating many team members on a project, but as Peterson notes in "Why Game Documentation Is Essential to a Satisfying User Experience," external documentation for the end-user is likely just as important to a satisfying game experience. As discussed earlier in this chapter, external documentation often instructs a user about how to play a game, making the gamer aware of the game's rules and how to best utilize the interface. This satisfying game experience is also connected to the internal documentation, for as Ahuja explains, client-side documentation is "basically excerpts out of the game design document that are collated in a way where the client can actually read them and make sense out of them" and are produced sometimes in alpha when "controls are refined."

At first, it might seem that client-side documentation might only serve the end user, but Andre Henderson, a former character artist/animator at BBMF Americas,[1] describes how multipurpose the tutorial levels actually are in this process. These tutorial levels, after development, would be used for "design pitches to investors" and were often the first "prototype levels that they would show off to potential investors ... to get them to invest in the company."

The Question of Who: Writing and the Gaming Industry

The developer with an interest in and aptitude for writing often performs many of the documentation tasks in software development. However, Scott Ambler, an Agile/Lean documentation practitioner, notes a poignant if not unspoken truth in his web article "Agile/Lean Documentation: Strategies for Agile Software Development." Ambler states "like it or not few technical people have good writing skills" (Section 6, Number 3). He goes on to lament that technical team members, while possessing subject matter expertise, may not have appropriate writing skills, and these skills matter in Agile development, as Sansone illustrates in Chapter 6 of this volume. It may also be the case that technical members do not possess even a basic idea of how to start writing for a project or define what the subject should be. These *ad hoc* writers may be excellent wordsmiths, but they lack formal training for creating materials that, as Ambler says, reflect the needs of an audience that is "much wider than just developers" (Section 6, Number 7).

Those who write game design documents—the internal charter the development team will follow as they create the computer game software—are also a less-than-ideal choice for the role of user documentarian. Damion Schubert, writing in the December 2008 issue of *Game Developer Magazine*, describes many of the errors internal design document writers commit. These errors are not necessarily grammatical, but instead reflect the writers' lack of exposure to writing for audience, purpose, and context. Shubert's assertions about the shortcomings of game design documents derive from what he sees as the "lack of standards" in the industry: "The most common mistake I see in game design documentation is that most of them are way too long, and way too in-depth. Too many designers try to write books, thinking that every word is important. We are, as tradesmen, too

---

[1]   BBMF Americas is a developer and publisher of social and mobile games.

often in love with the sounds of our own voices" (41). While Shubert continues with a discussion about how nonstandardization leads to the creation of what he calls "odiferous game documentation," he clarifies an important fact about writing and documentation. That is, few others on the development team then are suited to taking on writing roles. As an example, the conceptual-creative—the person involved with what Shubert describes as the detailed "history of the weapon factory that devised the Huge Honking Gun"—should not be the individual to develop task-centered documentation for the programmers, project managers, QA testers, and other internal stakeholders. What Shubert calls for, though not by any direct name or title, is the inclusion of an intermediary between the polemics of concept-design and programming-implementation. This position, which Bernadette Longo describes in her 1998 article as the "mediator between technology and what we have come to term 'users,'" is that of the technical communicator (59).

Like Schubert, Sheffield also makes a call for an individual to mediate between the technology and the users in his article, "What Went Wrong?: Learning from Past Postmortems." His call, however, does not directly ask for technical communicators to fill an identified gap. Instead, in his breakdown of development postmortems—those reflective documents that development teams write after a game is released—Sheffield describes circumstances where a technical communicator could have alleviated some of the problems. Sheffield performed a content analysis across three years of game design postmortem articles found in *Game Developer* magazine. He produced a summary of significant problems encountered from a variety of computer game producers. Two of his findings—*communication breakdown* and *lack of technical documentation*—made the top ten of "what went wrong" (7). While both these issues could have been managed by a technical communicator, what remains unknown is: (1) if any of the postmortem companies had a technical writer on staff (unlikely, our research tells us); or (2) if they did not have one on staff, whether the companies understood what technical communicators do and how this individual could have benefited the team.

Unlike Shubert and Sheffield, Scott Ambler in "Agile/Lean Documentation: Strategies for Agile Software Development" makes a clarion call for the inclusion of a professional to handle documentation tasks. The developer-as-writer model occurs commonly in the software industry—the developer with an aptitude for or interest in writing assumes the task of documentarian. While this model can work well, Scott Ambler proposes there are better ways to work, especially with the inclusion of a technical writer. Traditionally, the developer's expertise and knowledge of the topic often make that individual "the best person suited to write documentation." However, there is the option of passing all or part of a system to a technical writer to minimize "the effort on the part of the developer" even if, notes Ambler, this may overburden the writer or, more significantly, introduce errors into the materials (Section 6, Number 3). Ultimately, Ambler concludes that the best scenario is one where "the technical writer and developer work together to write the documentation, learning from each other as they do so" (Section 6, Number 3).

Yet like many, Ambler still sees the "writer" instead of the "communicator" when considering individuals who produce documentation. While his assertion that "technical writers bring a lot to the table when it comes time to write documentation because they know how to organize and present information effectively" is true, he fails to consider what modern technical communicators do and how these competencies could benefit any software development process. Computer games are no exception.

A View to the Gaming Industry

As we noted earlier, the call to make technical communicators part of computer game development teams has been made, though it would appear few have heard or answered. In 2004, Martin Peterson identified new avenues of opportunity for technical communicators and the gaming industry. He asserted that technical communicators today could create far more than only end-user documentation; this body of professionals could help manage a game's internal development and articulate ideas for all members of the team. We echoed Peterson's 2004 sentiment in our 2011 piece, stating that the computer game industry and technical communication belong together. Technical communication's facility with visual design and textual clarity would complement an industry described in 2008 by Schubert as possessing no uniform, standardized way to write, document, or organize information.

This lack of standardization has started to dissipate as the increasing maturity of the profession creates a confluence of the many different entities within the computer game industry. This coming together of different sectors is the result of an increased drive to establish the legitimacy of the industry as a whole. At one end of the spectrum, the International Game Journalists Association (IGJA) formalized *The Video Game Style Guide and Reference Manual* for gaming journalists—the individuals who write articles and reviews about games in popular press magazines. The preface by Hsu of *Electronic Gaming Monthly* told readers in no uncertain terms that "for videogame writing to be taken seriously by adults, it has to be written for adults" (3). Cognizant that many of these writers may not care about the details of proper writing, the authors of the style guide point out that consistency "helps engender trust from readers, and, on a larger scale, lend legitimacy to our industry" (5). At the regulatory end of the spectrum, the maturity of the gaming industry is viewed as part of a strong movement towards professionalization. In the white paper "Survey of Regulatory Practices in the Gaming Industry," authors Bunger Pool, Dudley, and Rucker discuss the evolution and the growth of the industry; they note that "what remains here is a consistent theme of this report, which is the increased level of gaming education and professionalization of the industry itself" (9). In other words, gaming is growing up.

It is at this point that two important facts converge. First, as the computer game industry matures and professionalizes, it will need to consider working with complementary professions. Second, should technical communicators choose to expand their competencies and move into growth areas, the gaming industry is a natural fit. As a profession, technical communicators have evolved beyond the traditional purview of "writer only" and established themselves as having much more to offer. In the updated entry for the profession, the Bureau of Labor Statistics defines a significantly more comprehensive role for technical communication professionals. Technical communication professionals continue to be audience analysts; they assess the situation and develop materials to meet the needs of both internal and external users. However, this profession has grown in such a way that technical communicators are now multi-modal communicators; they work with technologies to "blend text, graphics, multidimensional images, sound, and video" to more effectively meet the needs of the audience. Additionally, because of their work in specialized fields such as science, engineering, or software development, technical communicators may also manage "the flow of information" to support the team or workgroup (Bureau of Labor Statistics). This description extends far beyond Scott Ambler's discussion of a writing-only function.

Yet from a perspective such as ours, we have to wonder where the technical communicators might be in the computer game industry. As Kocurek argues, the manuals that "helped to render novel machines mundane" were vital in the early days of coin-operated games (p. 56). And even today, there are documentation requirements for both internal and external audiences in gaming. However, if older ideas about technical writers as "writers only" still dominate the industry's perception, they might limit the opportunities for growth that Peterson saw back in 2004.

It also may be that technical communicators themselves did not follow Giammona's prescient advice from both 2004 and 2009. In her 2004 article "The Future of Technical Communication," Giammona quoted Ames, who said that as technical communicators, it is necessary to "look at our jobs more expansively, taking a broader perspective" in order to establish true value for the role (353). Giammona, later in the same article, asserted that technical communicators need to become part of "the development and innovation processes" if they want to grow professionally and expand their opportunities (360). In 2009, Giammona continued with her charge for the profession in "The Future of Technical Communication: Remix," where she made the point that technical communicators must repackage themselves so as to create value to an organization (10).

Establishing that value layer both personally and in an organization means technical communicators must respond to changes in industry. As an example, the green gaming movement has seen companies eliminate printed player guides—the creation of which is a small and traditional role for technical writers. Fahey in his article "Ubisoft Does Away With Tree-Killing Instruction Manuals" describes how game developer Ubisoft began an environmental initiative in 2010 to eliminate paper manuals and replace them with in-game instructions (1). Following Ubi's lead, Entertainment Arts (EA) cited environmental reasons and announced in April of 2011 that they too would begin to phase out paper instruction manuals (Villarreal 1).

Rather than seeing the discontinuation of a paper manual as a sign of career obsolescence or discomfiting change, technical communicators need to capitalize on new opportunities. With their expanded set of competencies, technical communicators can fill vital roles—roles that go beyond creating paper-based manuals. Instead, technical communicators can, for both internal and external materials, become part of a dynamic process within the development team.

Specific Requirements of Computer Games

Technical communicators, in their 2012 Bureau of Labor Statistics iteration, bring to the table a significantly more sophisticated and adaptable skill set than most people imagine. For example, technical communicators are trained in writing, design, rhetoric, research, and user experience. Immediately, a technical communicator would understand that the artifacts a computer game player requires differ radically from the norm for other instructional contexts. For a trained technical communicator, the situation of play—what Janet Murray discusses as the user experience of video gaming and the desire for player immersion and agency within the game world—serves to define a particular context for documentation. Additionally, a technical communicator would be aware of the exploratory and experiential approaches to gameplay—particularly as these approaches are coupled with users' pre-existing knowledge—and how those approaches would inform documentation.

The context of use for computer games, coupled with user tasks and goals, means technical communicators need to be adaptable. The types of materials end users require depart radically from the step-by-step procedures or lofty instructional tomes technical writers are stereotypically presumed to generate. For players at home, gameplay is fully immersive experience—gamers all but disappear into the digital world in front of them. This deep engagement with the game, or what Johnson and Wiles, citing Csikszentmihalyi's *Flow: The Psychology of Optimal Experience*, describe as "flow," is a form of user involvement that extends far beyond any daily interaction with technology; rather, the game becomes an extension of reality.

Where are the Technical Communicators, Then? Survey Methods of Study

The unique requirements of computer games and the competencies of technical communicators intersect perfectly as we have demonstrated. Yet game developers still see reassigning a team member to the writing function as a standard course of action. While some mention is made of the role of the "technical writer" in the gaming industry, it's surprising this limited and out-of-date mental model still persists. From our perspective, a role exists for technical communicators, yet such a role remains elusive in the gaming industry; thus, we sought to learn more. To gain additional insight about this disconnect between game development teams and technical communication, we developed and sent a twenty-question survey to the International Game Developers Association (IGDA), the Georgia Game Developers Association (GGDA), LinkedIn game industry communities, and several industry professionals in the computer game industry. The survey gathered information on the respondents':

- Company size, position, years in industry;
- Development platforms and game genres;
- Use of Agile management methods or other methods;
- Explanation of internal/external document process during the development cycle;
- Familiarity with the term(s) "technical communicator" versus "technical writer";
- Insight into the creation of third-party strategy guides such as those created by Prima and Brady Games; and
- Opinions of community-created, crowd-sourced documentation, such as <www.gamefaqs.com>.

The survey also asked respondents a series of open-ended questions about their development and documentation practices. Additional questions focused on respondents' perceptions of technical communicators and what these professionals can bring to the development table.

Findings and Discussion

Our survey respondents were nine industry professionals, working for both small and large companies. Their numbers included producers, developers, 2D/3D artists, and game designers. In terms of experience, the respondents were almost evenly split between relative industry newcomers (1–5 years industry experience) and industry veterans (15+ years industry experience).

The respondents had worked on a number of different platforms, including mobile (iPhone, Android), PC/Mac, and consoles (Xbox 360, PS3, PS2, and others) and had produced games in a wide variety of genres (Casual, MMO, FPS, Adventure, Action, Platformer, Sports and others). Our findings revealed some interesting insights into the role of documentation in the development cycle, among other questions and issues.

Agile Methodology

A majority of respondents stated that they used an Agile management/method (or adaptation) in the development of game products (6 of 9). This echoes a similar finding by Sansone, who notes that Agile-based production is becoming more common. Of those who stated that they used an Agile method, Scrum was overwhelmingly their production method of choice. This makes sense as game development requires adaptability and significant coordination between teams. Of those that didn't use an Agile method, they tended to describe a mixture of methods including "*Ad hoc*," "Waterfall," and "a system based on our backlog and sprint milestones."

Internal Game Documentation

Respondents unanimously agreed that internal design documents (game design documents, technical design documents, etc.) are created "during the development process and refined as the product stabilizes and moves to completion." Yet the question of who writes and edits the internal documentation produced a wide variety of answers with no distribution to suggest any industry standard. Through this survey, it seems that lead designers, producers, technical directors, developers, scrum masters, programmers, and others (even marketing personnel) have a hand in the creation of these documents throughout many phases of the process. Per our early assumptions, dedicated technical writers and/or technical communicators were not listed as contributors to these documents.

Client-side Documentation

Although the professionals were in agreement over the timing of internal design documents, there was far less consensus about client-side or end-user game documentation. Most agreed that client-side documentation or tutorials were created "at the end of the product development" (6 out of 9 respondents), while a smaller number stated that client-side documentation was produced "during the development process and refined as the product stabilizes and moves to completion" (3 out of 9 respondents).

Respondents had a variety of answers for who produces the client-side documentation including game design leads, project leads, and even marketing personnel, but technical writers and/or technical communicators were once again absent from this list.

The Role of a Technical Communicator

Only 2 out of 9 respondents claimed to be familiar with the term "technical communicator." Those two respondents detailed the skills of a technical communicator as those of visual communication, comprehension of audience, analysis, and technical understanding. Most respondents (7 out of 9) saw no difference in what a technical communicator might do versus a technical writer.

Of those that said that they saw a difference, they described that difference (in skills) of a technical communicator as being "comprehension of audience diversity" and "flexibility in design communication and technical breakdown."

Crowdsourced Documentation and Strategy Guides

A majority of respondents (6 out of 9) stated that they had a "very positive" or "somewhat positive" view of community-driven, crowdsourced game documentation such as gamefaqs.com. The rest (3 out of 9) posited no opinion with a "Neutral/No Opinion" choice. Additional comments revealed concerns about accuracy and ownership: "They [crowdsourced documentation] are generally useful to players, although they are often wrong on some details. As long as the host doesn't make it appear that they are official documents from us, this doesn't matter."

Takeaways and Considerations

In his discussion of formats and standards in game design documents, Richard Rouse III, author of the textbook *Game Design Theory and Practice*, exposes a "secret" about internal documentation when he writes, "There is no format! Everyone who writes a game design document just makes up their own format!" This sentiment echoes that of Shubert who lamented the lack of standards across the industry. Although later Rouse admits that there may indeed be "an agreed-upon format [at larger companies] that all of the in-house designers must use for their documents," the real takeaway remains to be that there is no fundamental, standardized format for documentation in the industry. Rouse still urges would-be writers to get their hands on every design document available before writing their own. Further, he also cautions against making a design document that stands out for the wrong reasons by "diverg[ing] too much from other documents in the industry," yet this tenet still allows for a great deal of versatility, creativity, and freedom to get the job done (356). The attitude seems to be if the text communicates successfully to the intended audience, then formats be damned.

According to our survey, this "if it works, it works" attitude seems to prevail in a number of aspects of the game development industry. Both development and documentation methodology seem to vary a great deal from company to company, individual to individual, and purpose to purpose. Which ultimately brings us back to the same questions: Given the complexities, costs, and audience considerations of the game design industry, why aren't more technical communicators present on design teams? Why is this vital task being handled by lead designers, technical directors, and art directors, those individuals with specialized skillsets that may be better applied to other aspects of the development process? Certainly the skill and specialized knowledge possessed by a technical communicator would be particularly advantageous to a design team.

Our survey results only vaguely hint at answers, and the question certainly requires greater study. Since the vast majority of respondents had no familiarity with the term "technical communicator," it could simply be an issue of marketing, where the skill of technical communication and its application hasn't been communicated effectively to the computer game industry. Perhaps industry professionals don't understand how technical communication has evolved past simply writing. The more comprehensive skill set of modern technical communicators, particularly their ability to perform audience analysis and their experience with multi-modal communication, would make them ideal contributors to internal and external documentation. Marketing issues aside, the opportunity for technical communicators to make significant contributions to the computer game industry appears to exist.

What's a Technical Communicator to Do?

If it's all fun and games, but no one is pulling out that manual (instead maybe opting for an in-game tutorial!), can there be any real future for technical communicators in the gaming industry? The answer is yes, but it may require technical communicators to take on roles and functions they haven't previously considered.

One such role might be that of "business analyst"—a position in high demand in 2013. These individuals are responsible for "enabling change in an organizational context, by defining needs and recommending solutions that deliver value to stakeholders" (International Institute of Business Analysis). Many technical communicators already work as project managers; business analyst competencies are one way to expand on that skill set and bring additional value to the profession.

With Agile (and its variations) as a predominant development model, technical communicators would be well served to learn more. Agile offers a development framework that values change, learning, collaboration, reflection, and iteration—all very distinct departures from the traditional, tightly sequenced, and prescriptive model of software development. Where previous linear methods, often labeled as "waterfall," favored staging, separate teams, frozen results, and strict deadline control (Weisert), Agile privileges empirical or exploratory processes that are an optimal model for "research-oriented, high-change . . . and intellectually-intensive" work (Williams). In other words, it embraces the messy, nonlinear nature of creating user products.

While the days of glossy guides, manuals, and flavor text have given way to other ways of engaging with computer games, there is a dynamic place in computer game development for technical communicators. Just as games have moved beyond *Pac-Man*, so have the skills of technical communicators.

Works Cited

Ahuja, Uthsav. Personal interview. 20 Apr 2013.

Ambler, Scott W. "Best Practices for Agile/Lean Documentation." Agile Modeling. 2012. Web. 13 Mar. 2013.

American Gaming Systems. "Technical Writer." Monster. 2013. Web. 21 May 2013.

Bunger Pool, Amy, Robert L. Dudley, and L. Meredith Rucker. *Survey of Regulatory Practices in the Gaming Industry.* n.d.

Bureau of Labor Statistics, U.S. Department of Labor. "What Technical Writers Do." *Occupational Outlook Handbook.* 12 July 2012. Web. 24 May 2013.

Campbell, Colin. "Are AAA Hardcore Games Doomed?" *Imagine Games Network.* July 2012. Web. 23 May 2013.

deWinter, Jennifer. "Just Playing Around: From Procedural Manuals to In-Game Training." *Computer Games and Technical Communication: Critical Methods and Applications at the Intersection.* Burlington, VT: Ashgate, 2014. 69–85.

Fahey, Mike. "Ubisoft Does Away With Tree-Killing Instruction Manuals." Apr. 2010. Web. 23 May 2013.

Giammona, Barbara. "The Future of Technical Communication: How Innovation, Technology, Information Management, and Other Forces Are Shaping the Future of the Profession." *Technical Communication* 51.3 (2004): 349–66.

———. "The Future of Technical Communication: Remix." *Intercom* May 2009: 7–11.

Greene, Jeffrey, and Laura Palmer. "It's All in the Game: Technical Communication's Role in Game Documentation." *Intercom* (Dec. 2011): 6–9.

Henderson, Antoine. Personal interview. 19 Apr. 2013.

International Institute of Business Analysis. "What is Business Analysis?" 2013. Web. 19 May 2013.

Johnson, Daniel, and Janet Wiles. "Effective Affective User Interface Design in Games." *Ergonomics* 46 (2003): 1332–45.

Kocurek, Carly A. "Rendering Novelty Mundane: Technical Manuals in the Golden Age of Coin-Op Computer Games." *Computer Games and Technical Communication: Critical Methods and Applications at the Intersection.* Burlington, VT: Ashgate, 2014. 55–67.

Longo, Bernadette. "An Approach for Applying Cultural Study Theory to Technical Writing Research." *Technical Communication Quarterly* 7.1 (1998): 37–41.

Luce, A. V. "'It Wasn't Intended to Be an Instruction Manual': Ethics, Gaming Guides, and Technical Communication Online." *Computer Games and Technical Communication: Critical Methods and Applications at the Intersection.* Burlington, VT: Ashgate, 2014. 87–106.

Mhatre, Nachiket. "Are Big Budgets Killing the Video Game Industry?" *Tech 2.* Oct. 2012. Web. 29 May 2013.

Murray, Janet. *Hamlet on the Holodeck: The Future of Narrative in Cyberspace.* Cambridge, MA: MIT P, 2001.

Peterson, Martin. "Why Game Documentation Is Essential to a Satisfying User Experience." *Society for Technical Communication Usability SIG Newsletter*. Oct. 2004. Web. 23 May 2013.

Rouse, Richard. *Game Design Theory and Practice*, 2nd ed. Plano: Wordware Press, 2005.

Sansone, Anthony. "Game Design Documents: Changing Production Models, Changing Demands." *Computer Games and Technical Communication: Critical Methods and Applications at the Intersection.* Burlington, VT: Ashgate, 2014. 106–23.

Schubert, Damion. "Writing Better, Shorter System Docs." *Game Developer* (Dec. 2008): 10–12.

Sheffield, Brandon. "What Went Wrong?: Learning from Past Postmortems." *Game Developer* (2008): 7.

Villarreal, Phil. "EA Makes Video Game Manuals An Endangered Species." *Consumerist*. Mar. 2011. Web. 2 June 2013.

Weisert, C. (2003). "There's No Such Thing as the Waterfall Approach! (and There Never Was)." *Information Disciplines, Inc.* n.d. Web. 2 June 2013.

Chapter 2

Come Out Playing:
Computer Games and the Discursive
Practices of Gender, Sex, and Sexuality[1]

Marc Ouellette

Scholars and students of technical communication have a unique opportunity to make an important contribution to the under-examined issues of gender, sex, and (especially) sexuality as they appear in video games. In fact, there are significant confluences between technical communication and gender studies that can be enumerated and elucidated in the process, particularly in terms of agency, performativity, discourse analysis, and the study of technology. In this last instance, the comfort level of technical communicators as users and as producers of technology makes the discipline ideally situated for considerations of LGBTQ-centered texts and, especially, modes of analyses. Here, Herndl and Licona's conceptualization of "constrained agency" from their chapter "Shifting Agency, Kairos, and the Possibilities of Social Action" offers an important area of intersection through an analysis of the ways in which audience, industrial, and institutional expectations can be productive insofar as they occasion rather than foreclose creativity and modes of representation. Constrained agency offers two important areas of intersection in the field of technical communication: first, constrained agency provides an understanding of the ways knowledge is constructed in and through discursive practices. Following from Sedgwick, Weedon, and others, this has become a critical commonplace in gender studies. Second, the products of constrained agency, or the "hit and run" tactics of oppressed groups, reveal player agency at the intersection of theory and practice.

The understanding of the paradox in which constraint actually occasions creativity has been the case within gender studies for some time, especially following Penley's studies of queer archetypes in fan fiction in the 1990s. Compared to other media, computer games provide two further entry points for discussion in terms of the cognitive and affective responses of audiences and the performative requirements of play. In this last regard, the play function of games establishes a context in which creators and users can explore, practice,

[1]   I would like to thank Victor Vitanza and Cynthia Haynes for their assistance with earlier versions of this chapter. Many, many thanks to Alexander Doty for his early support and generous comments.

and rehearse subjectivities not otherwise available in traditional textual forms (Ouellette "Tomorrow We Go Bowling"). Indeed, as Luce and Moberly and Moeller discuss, computer games afford players the opportunity to play with ethics and identity formation, and in the act of engagement, our own subjectivities are imbricated in this process. After enumerating and elucidating these connections between the two disciplines, I consider the ways that practitioners and audiences alike produce queer-centered texts, as well as the ways these arise in unexpected or unintentional ways. I add to Custer's consideration of the intersection among technical communication, game studies, and computer game production in terms of these multiple, layered literacies. As a corollary, then, this chapter will add to the existing definitions and understandings of the multiple literacies involved in technical communication and in game studies.

In this last regard, a particular emphasis needs to be placed on the typical pattern of production upon which technical communication rests. As Williams points out, there is a persistent perception that the field proceeds from what he describes as a "single paradigm—a single discourse—that imbues our discipline with values that favor ends over means and guides how we teach, practice, and conduct research . . . in general, our field is still firmly rooted in what Communication Studies scholars call 'normative' discourse that focuses on expedience, managerialism, and techno-rationality" (430). Williams's premise is that confining the content to normative discourses and emphasizing ends over means may be productive in reaching wide audiences, but it also runs the risk of foreclosing alternatives. Here, it is well worth pointing out that gender and film scholar Doty *insists* on studying mainstream texts and argues that these are more likely and more productive sources for queer readings precisely because they reach wider audiences. In his influential book, *Flaming Classics*, Doty underscores two key points regarding the productive potential of mainstream texts. First, he highlights the ways in which queer readings problematize the assumption that "all characters in a film are straight unless labeled, coded, or otherwise obviously proven to be queer" (2–3). In other words, queer readings need not be confined to texts that are explicitly and exclusively produced by and/or for queer audiences.

Rather, queer readings derive from recognizing the salient codes and discursive practices because these can and do appear in a range of texts, particularly mainstream ones. In a second, related case, Doty asks, "Why do most people still register 'queer' only when confronted with visual and aural codes drawn from a narrow (and often pejoratively charged) range?" (3). In fact, he argues against explicitly focusing on queer characters in part because of the restrictions and the impositions of stereotypes that result. Thus, the readings and the texts are more productive if the characters appear in mainstream productions in large part because of the play afforded by the normative constructions. It is in terms of play within a highly structured, rules-oriented environment that computer games offer the opportunity not only to modify texts but also to enact those modifications, as well as revise, rehearse, and redistribute them. Here, it should be noted that the critical language for interrogating these processes—particularly encoding, decoding, and ex-nomination—derives not from cultural or gender studies but from the shared and foundational concepts of semiotics and discourse analysis. This is important because the two modes of analysis are also related and in turn help to investigate the lacunae in practice as well as in teaching and in scholarship. More importantly, it reflects the impetus to be what Elbow calls "a democratic or egalitarian force to change society," which is deeply rooted in both technical communication and in gender studies (474), a topic in which both Vie and Luce further highlight the role and the tradition of technical communication effecting positive social change through the practices of the discipline.

Playing it Straight: Discourse and Agency

As much as the predominance of normative discourses appears to structure and to condition content within a particularized framework, it also presents locations and instances for explorations in spite of and because of the seeming restrictions. Gender scholar Chris Weedon explains that discourses are "ways of constituting knowledge, together with the social practices, forms of subjectivity and power relations which inhere in such knowledges and relations between them. . . . They constitute the 'nature' of the body, unconscious and conscious mind and emotional life of the subjects they seek to govern" (108). Simply put, discourses enumerate what is acceptable and true at a given moment. Cultural studies scholar Stuart Hall clarifies this sense of discourse in terms of its historical scope. He explains that a discourse consists of "language for talking about—a way of representing the knowledge about—a particular topic at a particular historical moment. . . . Discourse is about the production of knowledge through language. But . . . since all social practices entail meaning, and meanings shape and influence what we do—our conduct—all practices have a discursive aspect" (291). Accordingly, what is "known"—that is, the normative discourse—about a particular topic in a particular period will have an effect on the regulation and on the control of that topic. For example, one might consider the popular, institutionalized view that positions play as the antithesis of work, and further, which posits computer games as mindless pursuits not worthy of study—or worse. In fact, manipulating, subverting, playing despite these kinds of dominant discourses becomes part of the attraction for some players.[2]

However, structures of power need opposition to legitimize their own dominance. Moreover, one of the most salient cognitive and affective consequences

---

[2] For a seminal example of this kind of attraction-repulsion dynamic, see William Warner's "Rambo and the Popular Pleasures of Pain" (1992) for the ways in which academic and media criticisms of the Rambo movies actually enhanced the popularity of the series. Fans of professional wrestling respond similarly to such an extent that World Wrestling Entertainment has actually scripted criticism from women's groups, in particular, in order to attract fans.

of discourses lies in the unstated exclusion of forms and practices of knowledge once a discourse has been established. In this regard, Hall offers two important provisos. First, "every discourse constructs positions from which alone it makes sense. . . . Anyone deploying a discourse must position themselves *as if* they were the subject of the discourse" (emphasis in original, 202). Differing representations are rendered illegitimate in the process.[3] Clearly, then, discourse analysis offers a means of investigating power, historicity, and the potential for social action. This is precisely the point of intersection between approaches familiar within technical communication and those prevalent in gender studies. For the latter discipline, the study of codes and signifying practices instead of the reductive calculus of XX or XY shows that even understandings of these seemingly immutable physiological traits are actually constructed *and understood* in cultural terms.

Sedgwick writes that "modern sexuality itself is so intimately entangled with the historically distinctive contexts and structures that now count as knowledge, that such 'knowledge' can scarcely be a transparent window onto a separate realm of sexuality: rather, it constitutes that sexuality" (8). Thus, Sedgwick concludes that the important task for scholars remains "making clear how fully modern sexuality is already produced through and indeed as discourse" (n.p.). Furthermore, and of particular salience to the present discussion, Sedgwick argues that homosexuality becomes metonymic for discussions of sexuality. This happens because the prevailing assumption, derived from the normative discourse, centres on heteronormativity as the unstated default position. The "coming out" narrative then becomes an unstated requirement according the presumption of heteronormativity; hence, its problematic status in *any* reading that considers queer possibilities. The issue of sexuality as a site of inquiry for differing subject positions and access to power remains unconsidered until and unless homosexuality is raised as a potentiality. For Sedgwick, gender criticism should then "be taken to mean, then, not criticism through the categories of gender analysis, but criticism of them" (n.p.). This is important because the categories serve to structure knowledge and to exclude participants, while more importantly providing opportunities for others. For Doty, this occurs because analysis of the codes and the discursive regimes highlights the "non-straight work, positions, pleasures, and readings of people who don't share the same 'sexual orientation' as the text they are [reading]" (6). In this way, any text can be a site for a queer reading. Here, it is well worth recalling that textual play—pastiche, bricolage, *détournement*, parody, satire, etc.—is an underappreciated cognitive and affective response to video game play. This occurs in and through the game-based manipulations enacted by playing a game and replicates Perron's distinction between gaming and playing and his corollary, gameplaying. The player, in Perron's terms, "knows that the rules of a

---

[3]   When teaching this, I often give "Faculty Club" as an example of a representation that structures knowledge and practice around a set of power relations and privilege. Without it ever needing to say so explicitly, it is well understood that students, staff, and even junior faculty really should not enter. In this way, it reproduces campus power relations.

given game will limit his moves. But he accepts those by playing" (241). Moreover, rule breaking and subversion of cultural and generic codes are key components of many games. For example, the purported lawlessness of the *Grand Theft Auto* games has inspired many players to develop altruistic alternatives by manipulating the built-in firefighter and paramedic routines.

This kind of creative play and manipulation of existing and established discursive constructs provides two key correspondences between technical communication and gender studies, one theoretical and the other its practical application. In a theoretical sense, Herndl and Licona underscore the space of overlap between tactics and strategies from de Certeau's ideas of "hit and run" appropriations of existing texts, which are "ripe for reconsideration as a productive and generative space of action and representation revealing both agentive and authoritative relational practices" (20). However, these are difficult to anticipate and envision during the preparatory stages of text creation, but they do offer additional means of revision, especially because of the participation and the (implicit) collaboration. Where these practices become even more salient is in the interpretive work entailed in consumption, in play, and in the subsequent interventions of players. In the terms of gender studies, we would consider these "crisis tendencies" because of the potential for disrupting and transforming the status quo and impacting future social practice. In video games, the shared space exists in the negotiation between improvisational play and the game's structures (both internal and external). Beyond a given game's rules and procedures, the appropriative texts produced by these interventions depend on fan communities, both authorized and otherwise, and idiosyncratic play, along with paratexts, such as zines, machinima, and mash-ups.[4] Indeed, zines offer an exemplar of a space where the contingency between officialdom facilitating and, quite paradoxically, (de)limiting agency exists and even flourishes. Thanks to the seminal works of Penley, zines and the related genre of slash fiction have been staples of cultural and gender studies for roughly two decades and for precisely the same reasons.

Elsewhere, I have enumerated four readings of representations of GLBTQ characters in video games. In short, these are the explicitly queer, plus three subversive types, each of which relies on a variation of the "hit and run" readings of otherwise straight characters (Ouellette, "Tomorrow We Go Bowling", 35). However, the last three categories prove more productive, in part because explicitly queer texts themselves limit opportunities for intervention, especially in the narrowness of their reach. For this reason, Doty emphasizes, "there is no need for queer canons that are marked as alternative or subcultural because queerness

---

[4]   Zines are unofficial magazines, some of which are called fanzines, produced by fans of given "official" media productions. Machinima is the practice of creating short video productions using the animation provided by video game graphics engines and adding voice tracks to it. Mash-ups are productions that combine sound and video from multiple sources to make a new text. These are a hybrid form of collage. None of these productions is inherently political, despite the obvious challenges of plagiarism, copyright, and ownership.

can be anywhere, in any canon you care to set up" (15).[5] Each of the "hit and run" methods constitutes a cognitive and affective response to constrained agency and the resultant moments of opportunity. For another look at the bottom-up version of the familiar circuit of power, please see Ritter et al. in this collection. While the normative discourse of the core text may limit opportunities for overt displays, the play function all but guarantees that multiple opportunities will flourish. The challenge for those studying the form is to be open to alternative readings to the normative discourse rather than discounting them. Resistance to alternative readings or constructions indicates that these unofficial texts do constitute a threat and an intervention in the complacency of an industry marked by the constrained agency that is (re)produced in and through the normalizing discursive practices, particularly ex-nomination, or the failure to acknowledge the distinguishing sign of dominance.[6]

In the second, or more practical sense, the study of gender, sex, and sexuality can provide a pertinent framework with resonances for studying technical communication. Specifically, Butler's argument that "performance constitutes the subjectivity of the performer" provides a reminder that gender requires a physical enactment adhering to, or departing from, the conditions put forth by the discursive regime that circumscribes that performance (13). The potential for departures from the norm serves as a reminder that each performance is subject to scrutiny and measurement. Both of these are omnipresent in, if not the kernel of, computer games. Whereas the previously cited representations and instances in which computer games provide opportunities for analysis, understanding, and to some extent practice, it is in the last regard that computer games stand out as a location for teaching and study.

These nonnormative, creative readings derive from the inherently rules-based structure of games. To be more specific, Frasca divides the structure of games into two intersecting categories. First, there are the "manipulation rules," which allow the player to have the ultimate say but only within certain confines. For example, some players have made their own altruistic games from the firefighter missions in *Grand Theft Auto*. However, in its reward structure, which Frasca calls its "goal rules," even the game's binary choices have significant potential for unanticipated impacts on the outcome (231). To continue the *Grand Theft Auto* example, the fourth installment of the game rewards players handsomely for siding with an openly gay character and protecting him from homophobic bullies. This productive result of

---

[5]   This is not to say that the queer-themed computer games of Anna Anthropy are not worthy of discussion. In fact, they deserve their own study. Rather, it is the intention of this chapter to show that queer readings are possible for *any* text and to provide the theoretical and practical means for more inclusive mainstream games and understandings of them.

[6]   In the related essay "Gay for Play," I offer a detailed discussion of the ways in which the industry avoids the topics of gender, sex, and sexuality. It becomes apparent in their responses to calls for the greater inclusivity and to paratexts that developers and many established game critics fail to see ex-nominate heteronormativity.

the constrained agency signals potential outcomes produced in and through games that do not necessarily occur with other media forms. Thus, in the next section of this chapter, I offer examples and discussion of how these responses arise in and through computer games and the discursive communities around them. As highlighted earlier, the combination of computer games and the understanding of ex-nomination in its role in the production of normative discourses and readings provides additional modes for revision in the creative process. These are enhanced by the play function and the resultant ability to enact and to interact with the limits and the license entailed in constrained agency.

Out and About: Playing with Constrained Agency

The combination of play and performativity in the presence of perpetual scrutiny and assessment offers very credible means for considering gender, sex, sexuality, and particularly (representations of) GLBTQ characters and themes. At the same time, the proximity of normative and nonnormative readings in games provides technical communicators with greater opportunities and additional skills and resources for understanding GLBTQ issues that affect their work. The recent inclusion of GLBTQ characters in established game franchises provides insights into the development and revision process, while offering potentially prescient practice in the exigencies of constrained agency. Indeed, the way GLBTQ characters have been incorporated into *Grand Theft Auto*, *Jade Empire*, and *Mass Effect*, among others, highlights both the constrictive and the constructive dimensions of constrained agency. Since play forms a necessary component of games' industrial, audience, and institutional expectations, the requisite exploration, adoption of roles, and fantasy creates an environment for examining fully the theoretical and practical manifestations of the paradigm Herndl and Licona enumerate. The exclusion, or relegation, of the very topic of gender, sex, and sexuality itself reveals much about the phenomenon. Intriguingly, the seemingly limitless potential for fantasy and play has had the converse effect on portrayals of gender, sex, and sexuality, so that these have become more rather than less rigid in virtual spaces. Yet the potential for fluid and multiple positions remains. These productive possibilities are tempered, however, by the very real and persistent ex-nomination of heteronormativity, as well as the metonymic status of homosexuality. This is key because these in turn point to foci for revision and occasion the (need for the) agentive interventions listed above.

Admittedly, the study of gender play, game play, and technology can be traced to the explosion of electronic communication in the 1990s. However, a quick glance at research databases shows the bulk of the academic work occurred in a flourish roughly between 1992 and 2002.[7] Further, the work that has been

---

[7]   My own search of Scholar's Portal, Cengage, and Ebsco databases shows very little published work on these subjects in the last ten years. It is well worth noting that the events

done focuses on feminist approaches to gender (sex and sexuality), with GLBTQ questions not yet on the horizon. Even so, the insights prove valuable and instructive. For example, Turkle finds that game play produces an environment that calls for a rethinking of gender play. Turkle suggests that play requires requires "speech, manner, [and] the interpretation of experience" that all conform to the dominant discourses of gender (397). Thus, gender performance demands a small and familiar set of behaviors that stand for the "whatness" of a given formation. In gender studies, this is the very definition of an essentialization, or an enumeration of the irreducible attributes and practices that define a given gender.[8] While acknowledging that *some* essentialization must eventually be made, gender studies scholar Fuss explains that it requires evaluation in terms of "who is utilizing it, how it is deployed, and where its effects are concentrated" (20). Intriguingly, these concerns appear in technical communication scholarships with respect to intercultural communication. For example, Agboka's definition and explication of "heuristic approaches" to analyzing intercultural communication "have sought to foreground the 'thingness' of culture that is definitive in its outlook" (166). Moreover, Agboka stresses that the heuristic approach's "false idea that culture is a set of habits and traits that one can learn and regurgitate in intercultural communication cannot be an effective strategy" (169). The same can be said for easy essentializations of gender, sex, and sexuality. The intent of these reminders is not to deny creativity or to suggest explicit bias on the part of technical communicators and game developers, but to make those deploying the essentializations aware that the conditions of production and the effects of the product remain open to expected and unanticipated responses.

In this regard, no character in contemporaneous computer games more clearly illustrates the salient strategies than Commander Shepard in the critically acclaimed (and almost cultishly followed) *Mass Effect* series. Without naming it as such, popular game critic and reviewer Croshaw hits on the issue of the kind of essentialization involved in producing Shepard. Croshaw reminds viewers that Shepard looks, sounds, and acts like practically every other major game series protagonist. He cites more than half a dozen games and opines that if he made a list it would likely include "70% of all the games ever made." In fact, to the list Croshaw offers, one might add the protagonists from such disparate titles as *Call*

---

and consequences of 11 September 2001, the rapid increase in globalization, and a massive economic recession may contribute to the relegation of gender, sex, and sexuality from research agendas.

   [8] Essentialization need not apply to gender only; it can extend to definitions of cultures, genres, and so forth. However, the key proviso remains grounded in the proviso that all poodles are dogs, but not all dogs are poodles. In other words, there needs to be a recognition that the essentialization favours subjective rather than objective criteria, even if the opposite is believed to be the case. This follows from the position that essentializations are reflective of the ways that gender, sex, and sexuality are produced in and through discourse.

of Duty, *Grand Theft Auto*, *Forza Horizon*, *Heavy Rain*, *Half Life*, and if not for the disco-era mustache, *Interstate '76*. This last is significant because it points precisely to the crux of the dilemma. Croshaw outlines the very contingency of the ex-nomination process; there is no explicit, defined standard but that standard definitely and palpably exists. This is also the very definition of constrained agency. Tweaking one aspect of a character—whether that is the sexuality or the mustache or the accent—does not prove sufficient to encompass the range of possibilities available to players who manipulate and identify with that character through play. Again, the analogue from contemporary technical communication approaches to intercultural text rings true. Zhu emphasizes that "whether it is the creation of a website, a manual, an ad, or a name for a product, [the process] is often inseparable from considering cultural factors and the use of language" (180). Considering these factors avoids reductive essentializations and ex-nominations. Perhaps the best analogue, though, comes from the long and fraught history of the so-called "black" and/or "ethnic" Barbies. Sociologist du Cille puts it best when considering the original and its derivative as "both signs and symptoms of an easy pluralism that simply melts down and adds on a reconstituted other without transforming the established social order, without changing the mould" (338). Furthermore, the location of the object in the context of play reinforces the reinscription through the enactment and re-enactment of the reductive essentializations.

Interestingly, nonacademic commentators show a similar reluctance to accept Shepard, but from the side produced by the ex-nomination of heteronormativity (and masculinity), and in particular the ways (these) discursive regimes exclude alternatives. The effect is that the latter become deviant and unacceptable. In addition, the tweak in the sexuality of Shepard in *Mass Effect 3*, like Mattel's infamous tweak of skin color highlights the tendency towards metonymy in essentializing or in the "heuristic models" Agboka enumerates. When considering the potential effects of what he derisively termed a "full-scale gay romance," Cohen, of the influential game e-zine *Kotaku*, complains about drawbacks rather than opportunities. Foremost among the worries is the threat to the "canon" of *Mass Effect* that the new choice might entail. It should be noted that developing the game on multiple generations of consoles has had a profound impact on the "canon" and on the play of the game. A number of important insights appear, including the obvious metonymic function of homosexuality. Quite simply, Shepard's gender, sex, and sexuality were not issues until the "full-scale gay romance" appeared in the third title, Croshaw's satire notwithstanding. Quite simply, Cohen, like other canonical critics, never mentions that the canon also includes a female version of Shepard when questioning the veracity of a gay Commander Shepard. In a chapter on slash fiction in the *Handbook for Learning in Virtual Environments*, Bury explains, "knowledge of and respect for canon is a form of popular cultural capital" (1160). In other words, the canon forms a discursive regime, which serves to produce and condition knowledge while excluding those who do not conform. Here it is well worth mentioning Gourdin's widely cited survey on diversity in the game industry, produced for the International Game Developers Association

(IGDA), which indicates overwhelmingly negative responses to questions of sexuality, including "who cares about sexual preference," and some declining to participate "as a direct result of this particular question" (15). This is clear evidence of the metonymic dimension of homosexuality, of the taboo surrounding homosexuality, and of the assumption of heteronormativity as a universal default position. More recently, Potanin's essay, "Forces in Play: The Business and Culture of Videogame Production," underscores the reproductive circuit through which young men produce the types of games they grew up playing and still want to play: aggressive, competitive games based on a hegemonic masculine model. Even so, these seemingly systemic biases recall two earlier-mentioned points regarding the queer readings available in mainstream texts, namely the productive potential of such texts provided one acknowledges that assumption and, second, that even the canon can be a site of play and manipulation. As the next point stresses, technical communicators are well situated to make these kinds of interventions.

Further evidence of these obstacles appears in the treatment of the main characters in *Jade Empire* and particularly in the choices that lead to a same-sex kiss. When the choice leads to female characters sharing a kiss, the scene is animated accordingly. However, when the choices lead to male characters showing similar affection, the scene fades to black before contact occurs onscreen. The contrasting treatment reveals more about the discursive structures that condition the games and the gender portrayals in them. The games' canon, for example, can be taken as part of its "procedural rhetoric" (Bogost, ix), or what Aarseth calls its "ergodic," or "work path" dimension (1–2). These are routines that persuade players to act in particular ways and in turn occasion choices that may not reflect the player's own position, as may occur in the previously cited mission in *GTA IV*. What critics of *Mass Effect* are reacting to, then, are the ways in which these routines foreclose and limit choices. It is worth noting, though, that they are also overlooking new possibilities in favour of reverting to the "canon," and especially its dominant discourses. By existing through defined worlds and rules, games inhibit and restrict choice by their very nature. Playing them signals some form of agreement with those limits.

Conversely, the fallout of "constrained agency" can be productive in that it may actually occasion responses. As mentioned earlier, zines and fan fiction are important and influential locations of such responses. Slash fiction, a hybrid from of fan fiction made popular in and through zines, involves the romantic pairing of characters from established stories. The genre takes its name from the "/" between the initials of characters who become lovers when the stories are listed in zines and fan exchanges. As well, stories depicting presumably heterosexual characters have become synecdochal for the form. In encountering the form, Penley recognizes the same "hit and run" tactics of the disempowered that attract users and occasion subsequent machinima, zines, mash-ups, and other texts produced by consumers (139). Moreover, the form illustrates the potential of play, through the manipulation of gender. As a means of using the tendencies and the methods of the dominant culture against itself, it reveals the productive possibilities of constrained agency.

These stand in contrast to the negative attributions to which Cohen clings, along with Gourdin's catalogue of game developers.

A very emblematic example appears on the "April Fools" page of *Gaygamer. net* in 2011. The page features a slash plot of the (then) upcoming *Gears of War 3* installment. The alternate version involves the lead character, Marcus, expressing his love for squadmate Dom. In fact, the cartoonish hypermasculinity of the pair makes them a terrific target for such a move. The new plot represents a reaction to both the constrained agency of the dominant gender order and the potential of game play as a site for enacting the hit and run tactics that Penley and succeeding scholars extol. These alternatives to the normative discourses, however, should not be seen as affirming or excusing the ex-nominating tendency of these regimes. Rather, the following examples point to the need to emphasize the process as opposed to the product of the communication. This is a reminder that gender, games, and writing invoke, involve, and instill performance.

Although she includes computer games as a likely site for slash, Mazar's chapter in *The International Handbook of Virtual Learning Environments* does not include them in her recent examination of the genre. Even so, Mazar offers an early entry point by suggesting that slash/fan fiction offer an exemplary opportunity for projects that stress virtual environments along with multiple and simultaneous subject positions (1142). Likewise, Bury finds "parallels can be drawn between slash communities . . . and virtual learning communities" (1165). The form also lends itself to considerations of process, since it usually involves serial production. As well, any fan fiction author is always already acting in collaboration, experiencing both the affordances and the constraints of the normative material and its rhetorical style. Further, the parasitic nature of the form means negotiating ethical concerns, especially regarding plagiarism and ownership. In addition, Mazar underscores the greater purchase for such exercises afforded by virtual spaces because of the immediacy, the contact, and the need to respond to a "constantly changing" community of practice and readership (1148). Finally, games demand some degree of technical proficiency and comfort with technology. One of the primary impulses for the creation of slash rests in the unacknowledged or unintentional homoerotics and the resulting entry points for identification. For example, the relationship between Capt. Price and his colleague "Soap" in the massively popular *Call of Duty: Modern Warfare 3* is begging for a slash treatment if not a recognition of the canonicity of such a reading given the palpable similarities between their relationship—which hinges on violence, masculine nurturing, homosocial bonding, and death—and its well-documented antecedents in *The Wild Bunch* and *Butch Cassidy and the Sundance Kid*, among others. Games make players part of the process of discovery and manipulation of the text while simultaneously offering all of the benefits Mazar—and countless others—locate in virtual learning environments. This should also apply to new forms like machinima and mash-ups that take advantage of the specific aspects of games, game technology, and the multiple literacies they embody.

Games offer "new" literacies through multiple simultaneous opportunities for consumers to become producers (see Custer, as well as Moberly and Moeller); nevertheless, they also call for a reconsideration of whether or not the emphasis on the new comes at the cost of fundamentals. In particular, the potential for multiple and simultaneous *valid* readings of *any* text seems to be elided in the focus on ends as opposed to means. In this regard, Kellner cautions against assuming traditional literacies no longer matter or are incapable of grasping the ends over means emphasis of neoliberalism. To succeed in virtual environments, Kellner writes, students should be "gaining the skills and knowledge to read and interpret the text of the world and to successfully navigate and negotiate its challenges, conflicts, and crises" (248). Kellner finds that students are learning to produce different forms of media texts, and these reinforce the dominant codes, which indicates that students still a foundation that enables them to critique their participation in these semiological and ideological playspheres. Perhaps this gap explains the absence of Patrick Galloway from *Clive Barker's Undying* on any list of GLBTQ characters in computer games.[9] This character is significant for a number of reasons. As noted game writer Richard Cobbett explains,

> When Dreamworks approached Clive Barker with the original design for what would become *Clive Barker's Undying*, their main character was a tough, hard-headed baldie called Count Magnus Wolfram. "You've got a gay man in charge here," warned an unimpressed Barker. "Bring me someone fabulously sexy. Bring me somebody I want to sleep with." Ten days later, Magnus was gone, *Undying* starred handsome Irish rogue Patrick Galloway, and the games industry had its only major male character to date designed specifically to be sexually attractive to other chaps. (n.p.)

Patrick Galloway was created with GLBTQ audiences in mind, even though straight audiences might not be aware of this fact. Thus, Patrick Galloway resists the metonymic status of homosexuality. He also represents a kind of hit and run tactic insofar as the character is designed to operate without the knowledge of straight audiences. This highlights not only multiple and simultaneous readings but also the fact that gender, sex, and sexuality cannot be easily categorized or encompassed through the mere and singular attribution of one characteristic, nor can the three components be conflated easily. It is well worth mentioning that part of the resistance involved in creating, playing, and enjoying a character like Patrick Galloway derives from the manipulation of the technology and the genre since these are both coded primarily as masculine and/or homophobic.

As much as Patrick Galloway exists in part for GLBTQ audiences, the otherwise unknown existence of such a reading points to another location where games differ from other modes. Not only do games feature the discursive elements outlined above, these occur through the vehicle of play. This aspect foregrounds

---

[9]   There is a Wikipedia page devoted to such a list.

the metonymy of homosexuality through an investigation of the ends over means assumption that texts are fixed, static, and immutable. Here, I am most drawn to Doty's original definitions of queer texts as "a range or a network of non-straight ideas" that come primarily from the reader and which combine with alternative sexualities through the vehicle of the text (xviii). For Doty, subject positions are fluid and multiple so that "you might identify yourself as a lesbian or as a straight woman yet queerly experience the gay erotics of male buddy films" (16).

Game for Anything: Conclusions

As Doty points out, any text can be read this way. This is no different than making a new game from an existing one, in the way rugby and football came from soccer. For computer games, manipulating and changing the text is a built-in attraction that can occur through changes to the source code, new games, or new genres. Some games include designer routines. Others are open source. In fact, manipulations are part of the rules. Thus, the constrained agency imposed by the text and the refusals to accept the reading actually occasion and empower Doty's process. Moreover, he questions the extent to which a text is fixed or even finished. In this instance, games provide a fantastic site of exploration, if only because they rarely produce the same outcome. Indeed, this is one of the central features Aarseth emphasizes in calling for game studies as a distinct discipline. A central part of Aarseth's manifesto is the proclamation that "games are not intertextual . . . games are self-contained" (48). Like a stage play, each session is different. Each session depends on the interaction of text and audience. Computer games enhance this relationship since the audience actually enacts the play.

Computer games, then, provide a unique location for exploration of the multiple and simultaneous cognitive and affective responses to constrained agency. Moreover, these responses are considered in terms of gender, sex, and sexuality—and especially GLBTQ themes; they provide an important series of intersections between technical communication and gender studies. Beyond questions of agency, the set of effects highlights the discursive function in producing gender, sex, and sexuality, as well as the metonymic status of homosexuality. Here, the "hit and run tactics" can be seen most clearly in the often creative ways GLBTQ representations appear in games and elsewhere. Play reinforces these processes through performance, which in turn produces encounters with further layers of constrained agency. These center on the freedom entailed by choice and decision-making functions. The issue of choice is at the heart of any version of game theory, beginning with Johan Huizinga's definition: "the first main characteristic of play [. . . is that] it is free, is in fact freedom" (8). As constrained agency actually produces and occasions possibilities for discursive action—including those enumerated above—so too do the limits of play. For Caillois, these possibilities occur because of the need to "find or continue at once a response which is free within the limits set by the rules" (8). Although they focus on the limits themselves, Vorderer, Klimmt, and Hartman suggest a model based on the process of playing a video game as a "sequence of situations each of which features the player's attempt to resolve the necessity to act by applying (some of) the possibilities to act" (5). What becomes clear, then, is that games provide an occasion for technical communicators to consider more carefully the ways in which gender, sex, and sexuality are represented in theory and in practice. This becomes important because the disciplinary emphasis on the latter makes them ideally situated.

Admittedly, there is not a great deal of information available on queer readings in technical communication scholarship or in that of computer games, let alone a combination of the two. While video games present and offer many new or enhanced opportunities involving multiple and simultaneous literacies, genres, and media, there still needs to be attention paid to some key fundamentals of representation. Thus, the research, teaching, and practice of technical communication—with or without games—should emphasize the ex-nominating tendency, especially during the planning and revising stages of production. Moreover, the new possibilities such as machinima offer only the most recent reminders that texts are not immutable but are in fact subject to negotiations. Games are all about processes, including interacting, performance, practice, rehearsal, and revision. Games incite and instill the productive aspects of the constraint of normative discourses and rules-oriented environments. Technical communicators need to encounter and to explore the ambiguities produced at these moments. Playing with gender not only creates an opportunity for such experiences, while bridging an important gap in the discipline. The encounter with the practice of social action and not just texts that enable work will benefit the discipline as a whole.

Works Cited

Aarseth, Espen. *Cybertext: Perspectives on Ergodic Literature.* Baltimore: Johns Hopkins UP, 1997.

Agboka, Godwin. "Liberating Intercultural Technical Communication from 'Large Culture' Ideologies: Constructing Culture Discursively." *Journal of Technical Writing and Communication* 42.2 (2012): 159–81.

Bogost, Ian. *Persuasive Games: The Expressive Power of Videogames.* Cambridge, MA: MIT P, 2007.

Bury, Rhiannon. "A Critical Eye for the Queer Text: Reading and Writing Slash Fiction on (the) Line." *The International Handbook of Virtual Learning Environments.* Eds. Joel Weiss, Jason Nolan, Jeremy Hunsinger, and Peter Trifonas. Dordrecht, The Netherlands: Springer, 2006. 1151–67.

Butler, Judith. *Gender Trouble: Feminism and the Subversion of Identity.* New York: Routledge, 1990.

Caillois, Roger. *Man, Play and Games.* New York: Free, 1958.

Cobbett, Richard. "Cirque du Strange," Web. 31 May 2007.

Cohen, Drew. "Mass Effect Fans Worry That Expanded Gay Options Will Create Inconsistencies, Alter Canon." *Kotaku*. Web. 17 May 2011.

Croshaw, Ben. "Zero Punctuation: Mass Effect." *The Escapist*. Web. 19 Dec. 2007. 12 Jul. 2013.

Custer, Jason. "The Three D's of Procedural Literacy: Developing, Demonstrating, and Documenting Layered Literacies with Valve's Steam for Schools." *Computer Games and Technical Communication: Critical Methods and Applications at the Intersection.* Burlington, VT: Ashgate, 2014. 247–63.

Doty, Alexander. *Flaming Classics: Queering the Film Canon*. London: Routledge, 2000.

———. *Making Things Perfectly Queer*. Minneapolis: U of Minnesota P, 1993.

———. "'My Beautiful Wickedness': The Wizard of Oz as Lesbian Fantasy." *Hop on Pop: The Pleasures and Politics of Popular Culture*. Ed. Henry Jenkins, Tara McPhearson, and Jane Shattuc. Durham, NC: Duke UP, 2002. 138–57.

du Cille, Ann. "Black Barbie and the Deep Play of Difference." *The Feminism and Visual Culture Reader*. Ed. Amelia Jones. London: Routledge, 2002. 337–48.

Elbow, Peter. "The Cultures of Literature and Composition: What Could Each Learn From the Other?" *The New St Martin's Guide to Teaching Writing*. Eds. Robert Connors and Cheryl Glenn. Boston: Bedford/St Martin's, 1999. 466–78.

Frasca, Gonzalo. "Simulation vs. Narrative: Introduction to Ludology." *The Video Game Theory Reader*. Eds. Mark Wolf and Bernard Perron. New York: Routledge, 2003. 221–44.

Fuss, Diana. *Essentially Speaking: Feminism, Nature and Difference*. New York: Routledge, 1989.

Gourdin, Adam. "Game Developer Demographics: An Exploration of Workforce Diversity." Web. Oct. 2005.

Hall, Stuart. *Representation: Cultural Representations and Signifying Practices*. London: Sage, 1997.

———. "The West and the Rest: Discourse and Power." *Modernity: An Introduction to Modern Societies*. Eds. Stuart Hall, David Held, and Don Hubert. Cambridge: Polity, 1996. 184–227.

Herndl, Carl G. and Adela C. Licona. "Shifting Agency, Kairos, and the Possibilities of Social Action." *Communicative Practices in Workplaces and the Professions: Cultural Perspectives on the Regulation of Discourse and Organizations*. Eds. Mark Zachry and Charles Thralls. Amityville, NY: Baywood, 2007. 133–55.

Huizinga, Johan. *Homo Ludens: A Study of the Play-element in Culture*. Boston: Beacon, 1950.

Kellner, Douglas. "Technological Transformation, Multiple Literacies, and the Re-visioning of Education." *The International Handbook of Virtual Learning Environments*. Eds. Joel Weiss, Jason Nolan, Jeremy Hunsinger, and Peter Trifonas. Dordrecht, Netherlands, 2006. 241–68.

Luce, A. V. "'It Wasn't Intended to Be an Instruction Manual': Revisiting Ethics of 'Objective' Technical Communication in Gaming Manuals." *Computer

Games and Technical Communication: Critical Methods and Applications at the Intersection. Burlington, VT: Ashgate, 2014. 87–106.

Mazar, Rochelle. "Slash Fiction/Fanfiction." *The International Handbook of Virtual Learning Environments.* Eds. Joel Weiss, Jason Nolan, Jeremy Hunsinger, and Peter Trifonas. Dordrecht, Netherlands, 2006. 1142–50.

Moberly, Kevin, and Ryan M. Moeller. "Working at Play: Modding, Revelation, and Transformation in Technical Communication." *Computer Games and Technical Communication: Critical Methods and Applications at the Intersection.* Burlington, VT: Ashgate, 2014. 189–207.

Ouellette, Marc A. "'Tomorrow we go bowling': Covert Intimacy and Homosocial Play in the Grand Theft Auto IV Series." *Learning the Virtual Life: Public Pedagogy in a Digital World.* Ed. Peter Pericles Trifonas. London: Routledge, 2011. 161–77.

———. "Gay for Play: Theorizing GLBTQ Character in Video Games." *The Game Culture Reader.* Eds. Jason C. Thompson and Marc A. Ouellette. Cambridge, UK: Cambridge Scholars, 2013. 47–65.

Penley, Constance. "Brownian Motion: Women, Tactics and Technology." *Technoculture.* Eds. Andrew Ross and Constance Penley. New York: Routledge, 1991. 135–61.

Perron, Bernard. "From Gamers to Players and Gameplayers: The Example of Interactive Movies." *The Video Game Theory Reader.* Eds. Mark Wolf and Bernard Perron. New York: Routledge, 2003. 237–58.

Potanin, Robin. "Forces in Play: The Business and Culture of Video Game Production." Fun and Games '10. Proceedings of the 3rd International Conference on Fun and Games, Leuven, Belgium (Sept. 2010): 135–43.

Ritter, Christopher, Sameer Ansari, Scott Daner, Sean Murray, and Ryan Reeves. "From Realism to Reality: A Postmortem of a Game Design Project in a Client-Based Technical Communication Course." *Computer Games and Technical Communication: Critical Methods and Applications at the Intersection.* Burlington, VT: Ashgate, 2014. 283–306

Sedgwick, Eve Kosofsky. "Gender Criticism: What Isn't Gender." 15 Aug. 1997. Web. 1 Nov. 2013.

Turkle, Sherry. "Tinysex and Gender Trouble." *Sex/Machine: Readings in Culture, Gender and Technology.* Ed. Patrick D. Hopkins. Bloomington: Indiana UP, 1998. 395–416.

Vie, Stephanie. "'You Are How You Play': Privacy Policies and Data Mining in Social Networking Games." *Computer Games and Technical Communication: Critical Methods and Applications at the Intersection.* Burlington, VT: Ashgate, 2014. 171–87.

Vorderer, Peter, Tilo Hartmann, and Christoph Klimmt. "Explaining the Enjoyment of Playing Video Games: The Role of Competition." Proceedings of the Second International Conference on Entertainment Computing. Carnegie Mellon U, 2003.

Weedon, Chris. *Feminist Practice and Poststructuralist Theory,* 2nd ed. Oxford, UK: Blackwell, 1997.

Williams, Sean D. "Interpretive Discourse and Other Models from Communication Studies: Expanding the Values of Technical Communication." *Journal of Technical Writing and Communication* 40.4 (2010): 429–46.

PART II
Industry Documentation and Procedural Guides

Chapter 3

Rendering Novelty Mundane: Technical Manuals in the Golden Age of Coin-Op Computer Games

Carly A. Kocurek

The earliest and most visible commercial success of the computer game industry was the launch of *PONG* (Atari, 1972) as a coin-op machine. Atari founders Nolan Bushnell and Ted Dabney placed the first prototype of *PONG* in a local tavern; within two weeks, the owner had called claiming the machine was broken. When Al Alcorn opened the machine to try to fix the problem, he found it stuffed to choking with quarters. PONG's immediate popularity among bar patrons encouraged Atari and facilitated the sales not only of PONG but also of other coin-operated computer games. Atari's first product was followed into the market by the company's other titles as well as by competitor machines from long-running coin-op outfits like Midway and Chicago Coin and from startup competitors like Exidy. For manufacturers both new and established, and for distributors, operators, and everyone else invested in the coin-op industry, computer games presented an opportunity for innovation, market expansion, and increased earnings.

The strength of this pull is demonstrated by the rapid adoption of the new machines across the industry. Even though computer games cost significantly more than other types of coin-op machines, by the late 1970s, the coin-op industry had heavily reoriented towards computer games. However, at the same time that these machines promised to lure new customers and increase profits, they presented significant challenges for operators and coin-op repair service providers who had to rapidly adjust to a widely dispersed new technology. While advertisements worked to assure distributors and operators that the new machines were reliable and that they would hook customers and increase earnings, operators sought out sources of additional information about the maintenance and repair skills necessary to upkeep the machines. Throughout this transitional period, technical communication in the form of manuals, handbooks, and trade journal articles transmitted knowledge about the new machines and lessened the anxiety surrounding a changing marketplace. The efforts by trade journal publishers in particular demonstrate a rush to fill a gap in companies' efforts to provide adequate documentation for machine operators. However, all these types of documentation shared a purpose. By arming operators with an understanding of the new computer machines as a technology, the technical writing around these same machines minimized their disruptiveness to operators' and repair technicians' existing businesses while facilitating the distribution and deployment of the games. In this way, technical writing served as an essential component of the emergence of computer games in the coin-op industry and helped enable wide access to computer gaming during the medium's earliest period. Manuals, journal articles, and other works of technical communication propagated the technical expertise essential to the operation of coin-op computer games, and in this way, helped render these novel machines mundane.

Post-Pinball Coin-Op Manuals

Coin-op computer games entered into a well-established segment of the entertainment industry in the United States. From the nickelodeons of turn-of-the-century midways to the jukeboxes, pool tables, and cigarette, candy, and soda machines that came after, the coin-op industry has a wide presence, particularly through the industry's development and distribution of cheap amusements. While the coin-op industry is in many ways diverse—it incorporates a variety of machines that provide amusement or sell merchandise—the industry as a whole relies on the appeal of novelty. Manufacturers compete against each other to produce the most exciting or appealing machines, working to distinguish themselves from competitors through innovative design or claims of exceptional reliability. At the same time, distributors and operators attempt to anticipate and gauge public interest in particular types of machines, carefully weighing decisions to adopt particular technologies and hoping to invest only in the machines that will prove to be exceptional earners. The industry's rapid turn toward coin-op computer gaming during the 1970s reflects the industry's longstanding reliance in novelty as a business strategy, but it also reflects significant shifts in the industry as it became focused, at least for a time, on these new machines. This rapid turn was encouraged in part by the machine's quick emergence as top earners, surpassing established earners like pool and foosball tables (Kocurek, 193–97).

The coin-op business operates at several levels. Manufacturers develop machines and sell them to distributors, who sell or lease them to operators, who place them in locations. Operators generally split proceeds from the machines with the owners of the location along an agreed-upon ratio. While sometimes location owners might buy machines outright, this did not become common until well into the 1970s, and trade journal coverage indicated this emerging practice as a disruption of business as usual and a potential threat to the stability of the industry. Indeed, more recent coverage of the industry echoes this sense of uneasiness with location owners doubling as operators ("Inside RePlay"). As an industry often organized around both established businesses at the level of manufacture and family businesses and also at the level of distribution and operation, the coin-op industry is one heavily influenced by longstanding relationships and traditions. It is also, as previously mentioned, a business driven by novelty. This pursuit of novelty leads to innovations both subtle and grand; changes in coin slots are advertised alongside new styles of machines, which can, as in the case of early computer games, effectively present a new medium.

While the coin-op industry is generally organized around novelty, it also relies on the abilities of operators to fulfill multiple roles. For example, the individual or staff running a coin-op operator business would select machines to place, secure locations in which to place them and maintain relationships with location owners, oversee the operation and maintenance of machines once they were placed, and handle the collection income the machines generated. "Operators" could be individuals running a one-man business, or a company with a staff of people with more specialized skills. In either case, operators would be used to being able to handle most aspects of machine placement and operation directly. New technologies both drive the business and present hurdles to operators. Particularly in the case of machines that present significant technological innovation, experienced operators may find themselves scrambling to cultivate the skills essential to overseeing and maintaining machines reliant on new technologies. Computer games as a coin-op technology provided significant opportunities for the business by increasing visibility and profits, but also created just such a disruption.[1]

Operators have a strong financial incentive for overseeing the maintenance of machines directly; any downtime for a machine cuts directly into profits, and outsourcing repairs increases the cost of repairs both in terms of downtime and in terms of paid cost of repairs. This is not to say that all coin-op operators directly employed repair people or were themselves repair people. Those who do not have specialized expertise in machine repair can outsource repairs to specialized services. In either case, however, new technologies can present a sharp learning curve even for the most experienced professionals. Acquisition of such repair skills can be costly in terms of time and money, and they may pose a significant factor for operators assessing whether to adopt a new coin-op technology. While novelty, as previously discussed, may be a significant principle of the coin-op industry, this does not mean that novelties move seamlessly through distribution channels to consumers. Manufacturers must work to educate distributors and operators about new innovations in the industry, and operators and distributors are necessarily careful to consider investments—financial and otherwise—in even the most promising new technologies.

While marketing and advertising efforts may be effective lures, in the case of coin-op computer games, technical documentation was essential to communicating the new technologies employed in the machines and enabling operators to integrate the machines into their business while maintaining efficiency and productivity. The necessity of training through documentation is not unique to computer games, although the specific context of the coin-op industry presents some distinct problems. As demonstrated by Michael T. Peddle's research on workforce training needs at

[1]   Both Zimmerman and Moberly and Moeller discuss other disruptions introduced into the game industry when it relies on labor from players and other non-designers.

the turn of the 20th century, worker adaptability is critical to maintaining not only individual employability, but also productivity and economic growth at the level of industry and at the level of nation (24–26). As a well-established form of technical communication within the coin-op industry, manuals provided a key means of demystifying computer games' inner workings; at the same time, however, the manuals often over-assume the transferability of technical skills initially established for the repair of pinball machines and other preceding coin-op technologies.

Manuals for coin-op machines are generally written for machine operators as the primary intended audience. These manuals, distributed alongside the new machines, much like the manuals that come with toasters and other small appliances, often make this intended audience explicit through labeling as 'operators manuals,' 'operations manuals' or similar. This labeling is evidenced in manuals from a diversity of companies producing coin-op computer games. For example, the manual for Atari's *Breakout* (1976) is labeled as "Operation, Maintenance, Service Manual" ("Breakout"), Exidy's *Crossbow* (1984) manual is billed as an "Operator's and Service Manual" ("Crossbow"), and a number of Konami games from the 1980s including *Jail Break* (1986) and *Hard Puncher* (1988) are labeled "Operator's Manual." This type of labeling reflects the extension of practices around pinball and other coin-op machines. Manuals for coin-op machines generally frame repair and maintenance as central aspects of the operation of the machines and presume that the operator will complete repairs and do troubleshooting in addition to routine maintenance.

This presumption accounts for the technical specificity of the manuals, which are intended for a readership with existing technical expertise that will, in theory, transfer to the operation and maintenance of new machines—even those that present significant technological advances. An assumption of transferable skills exacerbates issues present in many technical manuals, which, as Hans van der Meij has documented, frequently present problem-solving information inaccessibly (151). Early coin-op computer games were often made by established game companies, which had existing standards and strategies for producing manuals. Younger companies like Atari or Exidy entered into this marketplace and so aimed to provide similar resources for customers. Standardization of industry practice in part explains the similarity of manuals across companies. Because of this standardization, the manuals for pinball machines offer a clear precedent for the style and form of coin-op computer game manuals and provide essential context.

Pinball manuals include a diversity of information regarding the machines' technical specifications, and manuals that pre-date the rise of computer games in the coin-op industry demonstrate this as longstanding practice. As can be seen in Figure 3.1, the manual for *Cabaret* (Williams Electronics, 1968) includes diagrams of most of the machine's components, both mechanical and electrical, alongside instructions for adjustments and troubleshooting, and a reminder that "Games Out-of-order cannot earn money" ("Instruction Manual for Cabaret" 12), and manuals for the company's other games from the same period, such as *Jubilee* (Williams, 1970), demonstrate the same standards ("Instruction Manual for Jubilee").

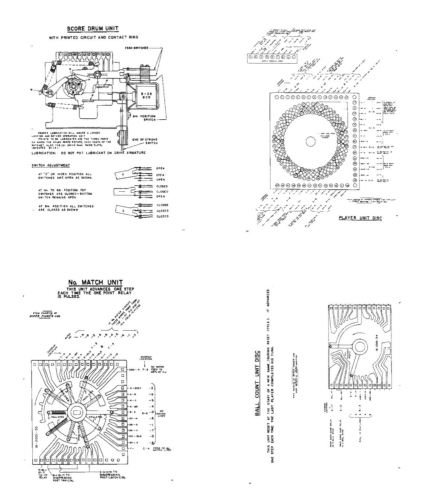

Figure 3.1   Pages 15–19 (pages arranged clockwise beginning with upper left) of *Cabaret* (Williams Electronics, 1968) demonstrate the types of diagrams included in late 1960s and early 1970s pinball manuals

Stern, like Williams, includes detailed diagrams and parts lists in their 1970s pinball manuals ("Lectronamo"; "Magic"). During the late 1960s and early 1970s, Bally Manufacturing produced relatively simple manuals. Even these still include a diagram of the machine and a list of parts alongside detailed instructions for machine adjustments ("#867—'Camelot'"; "#906—'Four Million B.C.'").

While the manuals for pinball games from these three companies are far from uniform, all include diagrams and detailed parts lists alongside basic instructions; the most detailed of these manuals, those produced by Williams, include a troubleshooting guide. All of the manuals cited presume a certain level of technical literacy among users, intended as they are for industry professionals. They demonstrate the role of the operator in maintaining and overseeing the machine. The manuals from Williams make this most explicit, reminding operators, for example, that out-of-service machines cut into earnings and implicitly encouraging them to make repairs quickly; however, all of the manuals figure repairs and maintenance as an integral part of successful machine operation. In offering technical specifications of the machines, the manuals assume existing knowledge and the ability to adapt quickly to new machines based on prior experience.

As aforementioned, manuals for early computer games reflect a continuation of established practices with regards to technical manuals. However, it is noteworthy that the manuals for the new computer games imply that existing coin-op machine operators and repair people were expected to continue to oversee the maintenance of the new machines. The manuals for early coin-op computer games, like the manuals for the pinball machines that preceded them, assumed that those maintaining the machines would have a wealth of existing knowledge. Even as game hardware reflected significant innovations, the manuals treat the technology as clearly explicable and easily serviced by properly trained technicians; there is no acknowledgment that the new computer games might present markedly different challenges than those presented by earlier machines. Game manufacturers billed the new computer games as an exciting new breakthrough for the industry while expecting and facilitating the operation and management of these same machines by established professionals most accustomed to working on pinball machines, pool tables, jukeboxes, and vending machines. This assumption is demonstrated by the types of information covered in the manuals, which frequently include wiring diagrams, technical specifications, and troubleshooting guides alongside or at the exclusion of summaries of the game and descriptions of the game cabinet. Many manuals include little guidance beyond the diagrams, presenting the machine's technical specifications as an adequate explanation on its own.

The documentation for *Centipede* (Atari, 1981), for example, includes instructions and diagrams for a series of diagnostic tests intended to walk the operator or repair-person through the process of identifying common problems (see Figure 3.2). Alongside the detailed directions, however, are warnings, such as, "Do not attempt any convergence adjustments unless you are a qualified color TV technician!" ("Centipede: Diagnostic Tests").

The color television used as a monitor in the cabinet for *Centipede* and for most other computer games at the time would have been a new component for coin-op repair experts to handle, as older types of coin-op machines did not include these types of displays and the monitors presented a variety of serious hazards (Roach, "Owner's Manual: Make Monitor Safety No. 1 on Your List," 88). The potential problems posed by the incorporation of television screens in the games is dispensed with through the brief warning. Some manuals make explicit their assumption of expertise in a range of technical areas. In Sega's 1987 "Introduction to the Owner's Manual" for *After Burner*, the manual details exactly who should be using the manual:

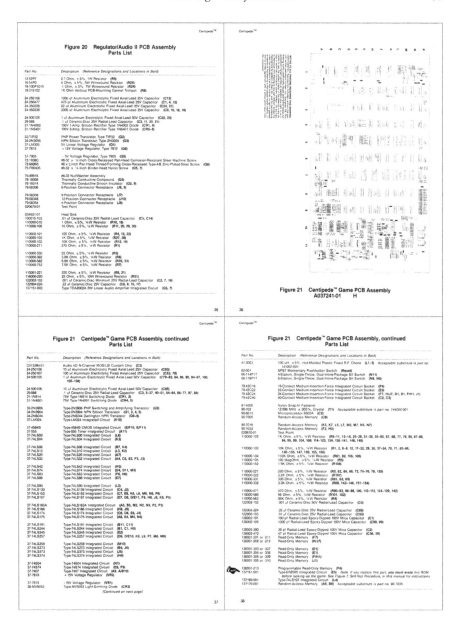

Figure 3.2   Pages 35–38 (shown clockwise beginning with upper left) of the *Centipede* (Atari, 1981) manual, detail of the Printed Circuit Board (PCB) assembly through a technical schematic on page 36 and a parts list that covers the other three pages. The introduction of circuit boards necessitated increasingly complex schematics. (Photo Credit: Jennifer deWinter)

> The manual is intended for those who have knowledge of electricity and technical expertise especially in ICs, CRTs, microprocessors, etc. . . . Should there be a malfunction, non-technical personnel should under no circumstances touch the interior system ("Sega After Burner Owner's Manual" 1).

After this warning, however, the manual includes both detailed wiring diagrams alongside rudimentary listings of parts and cabinet components, suggesting that while the repair technician may need to have technical expertise but not coin-op specific expertise.

The machine operator, then, should in theory be familiar with the external components of the cabinet, many of which are standardized, but may require some guidance in interpreting the inner workings of the cabinet. The manuals as a whole assume an existing familiarity with coin-op machines and their operations. They are intended for a specialized audience of professionals, but the real competency of those professionals with regards to interpreting and adapting to the new technology presented by computer games seems to have been uneven at best. Alternate avenues for repairs, including service offered by manufacturing companies, makes clear that operators were often out of their depth in troubleshooting early arcade games. While outsourcing repairs, either back to the manufacturer or to a third party service, provided one solution to this problem, this approach cut into profits both because they cost more and because they had the potential to significantly increase downtime. Further, even those to whom repairs were traditionally outsourced would have been scrambling to adapt to the new technologies; someone who completed a course in coin-op repair in the late 1960s would have been at the beginning of their career in the early 1970s but would not have received any training in working on computer games while completing their training course. While coin-op repair services that specialized in computer games eventually emerged, this development was not immediate. Today in most major cities in the United States, operators or arcade owners can readily call a specialized repair service with expertise in upright computer games; this was not the case when the machines first developed, and for the reasons previously discussed, contracting repair services outside the operator's immediate staff would have been undesirable. The same culture of novelty and innovation that drives the coin-op business in very real ways also presents special challenges for operators who must rapidly adapt to technological shifts.

Manufacturing Knowledge

Because computer games represented a major technological innovation in the coin-op industry, manufacturers attempting to advertise their machines as cutting-edge innovations in the industry had to simultaneously assure potential customers that the machines would not provide excessive challenges for their technicians or other maintenance staff. Manufacturers responded to these twin challenges in a variety of ways, and the efforts at alleviating anxieties took a variety of forms. Some companies responded by producing more detailed and thorough manuals, which included specific suggestions for troubleshooting and detailed guides to repairs. Others, like Bally/Midway reacted by working to provide additional technical support through supplementary documentation or by offering phone-based troubleshooting assistance. Many stressed the reliability of their machines and advertised their warranties; this strategy was a trademark of advertisements for Exidy's games. Kauffman, the CEO of Exidy, often stressed in interviews that the reliability of Exidy machines was unparalleled. These claims are not accompanied by any specific evidence, but the reassurances indicate the importance of reliability and the manufacturer's awareness of operators' worries about the maintenance of the machines.

The effort to negotiate the dichotomy presented by the insertion of a disruptive technology into a long-established industry—even one primed and fueled by novelty—is often evidenced in trade journal advertisements and articles that alternately express and attempt to assuage operator anxieties. This negotiation is particularly visible in the efforts of trade journals and manufacturers to provide additional resources for education and training. Various types of technical documentation and communication produced during the early period of arcade computer gaming demonstrates the real uncertainty facing experienced professionals while also attempting to alleviate the attendant anxieties. According to Connors, this maneuvering is reflective of the growing sense during the period that technical writing should rightfully rely on a sense of "reader-writer relationship" and that such types of writing could serve purposes beyond straightforward information delivery (343). Almost all technical documentation related to coin-op computer games serves manufacturers by facilitating the adoption of new technologies; the empowerment of operators is an effective sales strategy, a point made by Andersen in her writing on the adoption of Enterprise Content Management (ECM) (70–71). Regardless of motives, technological literacy supported by effective technical communication helps maintain productivity (Fitzpatrick, 48–52). In the initial deployment of coin op computer gaming, technical writing is simultaneously deployed as a means of shaping operator response and facilitating the diffusion of the new technology along established industrial distribution channels.

RePlay Magazine's efforts to provide content relevant to machine repair during the 1980s provides a particularly illustrative example of these efforts. As a major trade journal, *RePlay* covers business trends, new machines, regulations and legal matters, and other news of interest to those working in the coin-op industry. Alongside this industry news, the magazine regularly includes technical content. As with the trade journal's other features, focus shifts dependent upon trends and concerns in the industry. That much of the magazine's technical content during the 1970s and early 1980s focuses on computer games underscores the importance of these new machines to those working in the industry while also suggesting the anxieties and disruptions these new technologies were causing for operators. The material in these articles sometimes reinforces the kinds of information covered in operator's manuals but often offers more detailed information on specific machine components or provides troubleshooting guides for common problems with machines not covered in standard manuals. While the tone and style of this content varies with author, technical articles are generally written in an educational, 'how-to' form and illustrated with diagrams.

For example, *RePlay* ran an occasional feature by Frederick Roach, Director of Education for Nevada Gaming Schools, a vocational school specializing in coin-op repair, which instructs readers in methods for troubleshooting machines by examining the power supply titled "Owner's Manual." In the January 1983 "Owner's Manual" piece, Roach takes on "The Important Power Supply," which he says is the second most important component of any coin-op machine after the player controls (73–74). A second "Owner's Manual" feature from August 1983 also focuses on power supply issues, under the title "Understanding Power Supply Series Reregulators"; by then, Roach was serving as Director of the Electronics Department at the Nevada Academy of Art and Technology (91). Roach's focused approach to common issues with coin-op machines addresses problems operators might see with machines produced by a broad spectrum of companies.

Another series that appeared in *RePlay* during approximately the same time takes a folksier approach while still providing guidance on technical matters. Beginning in May 1983, the trade journal ran a series of pieces written by Frank Seninsky under the title "Frank's Field Findings." At the time, Seninsky ran his own route of coin-op machines, served as president of Alpha-Omega Amusements, Inc. and Alpha-Omega Sales Co., and served as a writer of technical features for several trade publications. The first of Seninsky's pieces for *RePlay*, "Frank's Field Findings or . . . Everything You Always Wanted to Know about Coin Acceptors—Both Metal and Plastic," provides detailed information about adjusting metal and plastic mechanical coin acceptors to avoid tampering, slugs, and other issues, and is illustrated with detailed diagrams of acceptor components (121–24). Seninsky's later contributions display specific attention to problems in maintaining computer games. A July 1983 piece offers "Service Tips for Bally/Midway Games," covering common problems with nine Bally/Midway video titles (134–36), and an August 1983 piece covers "Making 'Roc 'N Rope' Conversions" (94–96).[2]

Roach and Selinsky's technical articles for *RePlay* demonstrate the critical role repair and maintenance plays in the coin-op industry generally, and Selinsky's general focus on computer games indicates both the importance of the machines for the industry and the issues caused by the rapid deployment of this new technology. While the spread of computer gaming presented one kind

---

[2]   Selinsky often consulted with manufacturers in the course of writing his articles, as seen in his quick notes of thanks and sourcing of information; the availability of this specialized advice to Selinsky is evidence of the work manufacturers were doing to ensure satisfaction among operators and demonstrates their interest in and willingness to deploy technical writing as a means of achieving this goal.

of disruption to the business of coin operation, the now-infamous computer game industry crash of 1983 presented another. However, both changes were addressed in *RePlay* in part through the journal's technical content. Selinsky's article on completing a conversion of an existing cabinet provides a particularly excellent example of this process. The article reflects increased availability of and interest in cabinet conversion kits at the time, while including some choice commentary on the necessity of cabinets for operators trying to make the best of a rocky market. In fact, the lead for the piece directly suggests conversion kits as a means of addressing upheaval in the industry while also acknowledging that conversion kits present operators with new, different problems: "With the state of the amusement industry what it is today, more amusement operators are converting their old (useless) computer games, and choosing the conversation that will last more than a week before becoming 'obsolete' is a difficult chore" (94). Selinsky's article both articulates the problem—that choosing a conversion kit that makes a good long-term investment is difficult—and offers a solution—*Roc 'N Rope* is available from a respected manufacturer and can be readily installed. Selinsky's article is a prime example of the way in which technical writing can serve as a solution-oriented approach to industry disruptions.

Conclusion

While coin-op computer game manuals largely treated computer games as an extension of existing technologies, other types of technical communication around the games directly acknowledged the machines' novel characteristics and worked to enable their adoption by established coin-op professionals. Manuals reflect a continuation of technical writing practices established around earlier types of coin-operated games, particularly pinball, and treat the new computer games as a readily intelligible evolution of prior coin-op technologies. By contrast, other types of technical writing about the games, particularly trade journal articles, and even technologically focused advertisements, present efforts to actively educate industry professionals about the operation and maintenance of computer games and render the novel machines familiar. This divergence between the way manuals and trade journals treat the technology of coin-op in some way reflects the machines' position in the industry; they were certainly a disruptive, but they were a disruption to an industry attracted to and fueled by such novelties.

While the coin-op industry thrived on and demanded novel innovations from manufacturers, technological innovations could present distinct problems for operators. Operators confronting new technologies had to not only make critical assessments about the value of the technology and whether or not to adopt, but also to develop strategies for maintaining and operating the coin-op technologies they chose to adopt. Investing in technologies requires significant financial and human resources, and even in the case of an industry driven by new technologies, these costs are a significant barrier to rapid dissemination. During the earliest period of coin-op computer gaming history, technical communication around coin-op computer games worked to explicate the games, and provide operators with a technical familiarity with the machines. By increasing familiarity with a potentially intimidating new technology, technical writers throughout the 1970s worked to make computer gaming seem less disruptive to established business and repair practices and to reassure operators that the benefits of adopting these new machines would far outweigh the drawbacks. In the wake of the computer game industry crash of 1983, technical writing again emerged as a strategy for facilitating industrial transition and easing operator fears.

Journal articles published during the period provide pointers on the repair of electronic and mechanical components of machines, provide insights into the advantages of particular types of coin acceptors, and provide troubleshooting and safety tips. Although these articles address different game titles and touch on diverse technical issues, they work as a body to educate operators about key issues in working with coin-op computer games. This type of practical knowledge is invaluable for operators tasked with overseeing a diverse collection of machines from different manufacturers. Beyond this utility, however, this practical knowledge also serves a more abstract purpose by working to assuage anxieties triggered by rapid technological and industrial change. In the coin-op industry, technical writing is integral both to the operation and maintenance of machines and to the adoption and dissemination of novel technologies. By thoughtfully deploying technical writing, manufacturers, trade journals, and industry leaders ensure that the novelties that drive the coin-op industry are rapidly adapted and transformed from cutting-edge novelties to technologies of daily life.

Works Cited

"#867— 'Camelot': Installation and General Operation Instructions." Chicago: Bally Manufacturing, 1969. Web. 17 April 2013.

"#906— 'Four Million B.C.': Installation and General Operation Instructions." Chicago: Bally Manufacturing, 1970. Web. 17 April 2013.

Andersen, Rebekka. "The Rhetoric of Enterprise Content Management (ECM): Confronting the Assumptions Driving ECM Adoption and Transforming Technical Communication." *Technical Communication Quarterly* 17.1 (2007). 61–87.

"Breakout: Operation, Maintenance, Service Manual." Sunnyvale, TX: Atari, c. 1976. Web. 17 April 2013.

"Centipede: Diagnostic Tests," Sunnyvale, TX: Atari, 1981. Web. 22 April 2013.

Connors, Robert. "The Rise of Technical Writing Instruction in America." *Technical Writing and Communication* 12.4 (1982). 329–52.

"Crossbow: Operator's and Service Manual." Sunnyvale: Exidy, 1984. Web. 17 April 2013.

Fitzpatrick, Bob. "Technoliteracy, Technophobia, and Programming Your VCR." *Training* 31.1 (1994). 48–52.

"Inside RePlay: April 2013," *RePlay Magazine*, 2013. Web. 24 April 2013.

"Instruction Manual for Cabaret." Chicago: Williams Electronics, 1968. Web. 17 April 2013.

"Instruction Manual for Jubilee." Chicago: Williams Electronics, 1970. Web. 17 April 2013.

"Jail Break: Operator's Manual." Tokyo: Konami, 1986. Web. 17 April 2013.

Kocurek, Carly. "Coin-Drop Capitalism: Economic Lessons from the Video Game Arcade." *Before the Crash: Early Video Game History*. Ed. Mark J.P. Wolf. Baltimore: Wayne State UP, 2012. 189–208.

"Lectronamo." Chicago: Stern Electronics, 1978. Web. 17 April 2013.

"Magic." Chicago: Stern Electronics, 1979. Web. 17 April 2013.

Moberly, Kevin, and Ryan M. Moeller. "Working at Play: Modding, Revelation, and Transformation in Technical Communication." *Computer Games and Technical Communication: Critical Methods and Applications at the Intersection.* Burlington, VT: Ashgate, 2014. 189–207.

Peddle, Michael. "Frustration at the Factory: Employer Perceptions of Workforce Deficiencies and Training Needs." *The Journal of Regional Analysis & Policy* 30.1 (2000). 23–40.

Roach, Frederick. "Replay's Owner's Manual: Make Monitor Safety No. 1 on Your List," *RePlay Magazine* (Oct. 1983): 88.

———. "RePlay's Owner's Manual: The Important Power Supply." *RePlay Magazine* (Jan 1983): 73–4.

———. "RePlay's Owner's Manual: Understanding Power Supply Series Regulators," *RePlay Magazine* (Aug. 1983): 91.

Selinsky, Frank. "Frank's Field Findings or . . . Everything You Always Wanted to Know About Coin Acceptors—Both Metal and Plastic." *RePlay Magazine* (May 1983): 121–4.

———. "Frank's Field Findings or . . . Making 'Roc 'N Rope' Conversions." *RePlay Magazine* (Aug. 1983): 94–6.

———. "Frank's Field Findings or . . . Service Tips for Bally/Midway Games." *RePlay Magazine* (Jul. 1983): 134–6.

van der Meij, Hans. "Does the Manual Help? An Examination of the Problem-Solving Support Offered By Manuals." *IEEE Transactions on Professional Communication* 39.3 (1996): 146–56.

Zimmerman, Josh. "Psyche and Eros: Rhetorics of Secrecy and Disclosure in Game Developer–Fan Relations." *Computer Games and Technical Communication: Critical Methods and Applications at the Intersection.* Burlington, VT: Ashgate, 2014. 141–56.

Chapter 4

Just Playing Around:
From Procedural Manuals
to In-Game Training

Jennifer deWinter

Computer games have, from their earliest instantiations, been accompanied with manuals that explain "how to play." It is difficult to overstate the importance of these gameplay procedural guides: computer games are complex algorithms that use goal-oriented design to compel players to do particular tasks in a particular way (see, for example, Galloway, 2004; Bogost, 2007). And these tasks are not necessarily intuitive for players, especially if the game is introducing a new gameplay mechanism, hardware tool, controller configuration, and so on. Kocurek writes about this in her chapter "Rendering Novelty Mundane," emphasizing the importance of training nonskilled workers to maintain expensive cabinet hardware in the early history of arcades. In the world of players, however, this is further evidenced by the fairly limited success of *Computer Space*, the first arcade game released in 1971. While this game came with a complex manual for installation, maintenance, and even some gameplay tips, no such manual or supplementary documentation accompanied the game for players. At this particular moment in history, that type of documentation was necessary since there was no homologous skill set that players could transfer from one game to another, let alone to a new medium (the arcade game). Indeed, as Bushnell, one of the designers of *Computer Space,* admitted in the documentary *Video Game Invasion: The History of a Global Obsession*, "Sure, I loved it, and all my friends loved it, but all my friends were engineers. It was a little too complicated for the guy with the beer in the bar" (quoted in Carr and Comtois).

In response to this design communication challenge, instructions were packaged with games—and continue to be with many games—explaining both the hardware (console set up and controller configuration) and the gameplay mechanisms (jump, dash, collect coins, save princesses, and the like). In addition to these sources, a supplementary market flourished with strategy guides, pay-per-minute help lines, and magazine features that provided walkthroughs and additional strategies. This institutionalized market was then augmented with fan-produced walkthrough guides provided for free on the Internet, playthrough videos and discussions, and discussion forums.[1] While all of these forms of procedural documentation had audience needs and enjoyment in mind, the problem that they each encountered is the need to leave the game in order to play the game. So while the manual still exists (some may say anachronistically), game designers now embed training into their games, teaching players how to play these technologically specialized programs. Meanwhile, players themselves are expanding their voluntary participation across game space (and the work required in games—see McAllister and Ruggill) to participate in supporting other players, especially in online multiplayer games, such as *World of Warcraft*. Within this network of in-game scaffolding, players do not need to leave the proverbial magic circle: on one side, they are provided "just-in-time" training in-game, and often in-narrative, seamlessly. On the other side, players rely on and often eventually participate in a community that is defined by experience in the game. Documentation, then, is both ludic and rule-bound, is both for the individual and for the community. While players "play around" in the game (a strategy that has been studied in people learning other software programs—see, for example, Novick et al., 2009), they are learning the underlying rule structure for both gameplay *and* community participation.

Lessons that can be learned from documenting "how to play" computer games and in computer game spaces are important to study within their own right—this is a culturally important medium generating $25 billion in revenue (ESA) and providing technologically sophisticated and cognitively demanding material for a large and diverse market. Further, lessons derived from these successful strategies can be used to reimagine procedural documentation from other fields as embedded help into already existing processes. In this chapter, then, I discuss the challenges presented to game designers who are interested in maintaining player immersion in game-space. Following this, I explore instances of just-in-time procedural training provided by game designers to teach players how to play the game. Finally, I conclude with a brief discussion of the lessons that technical communicators can take from teaching gamers how to play these complicated systems of computer technologies.

Gameplay and the Magic Circle

In his seminal 1950 work *Homo Ludens: A Study of the Play Element in Culture*, Huizinga wrestles with the seriousness of play, providing an in-depth analytical consideration of the very term. Play, according to Huizinga, occurs in an invoked magic circle—a safe place removed from the ordinary world. Actions in this magic circle are rule-bound and demarcated in space and time, and people who enter the circle do so voluntarily, subjecting themselves to the play or game space. Play

---

[1] These videos are both professionally produced (see Giant Bomb's website) and created by fans of the game who want to help other players or just showcase their own skill (see Luce's chapter in this collection).

contains such elements as "order, tension, movement, change, solemnity, rhythm, rapture" that is later augmented with ritual and spiritual transcendence (17). Thus, the two poles of play's ambivalence are frivolity and ecstasy (21). In many ways, this is the foundation of the difficult-to-define concept of immersion: "All forms of entertainment strive to create *suspension of disbelief,* a state in which the player's mind forgets that it is being subjected to entertainment and instead accepts what it perceives as reality" (Laramée, quoted in Salen and Zimmerman, 450). And while Salen and Zimmerman discuss the fallacy of this position, game designers continue to strive for immersion, for players to be "lost in the game."[2] Thus, when players are unable to understand the rules of the game and what they need to do to succeed, they often become frustrated and leave the game. Sometimes, they leave the game to read an on-line help guide to return and try again; sometimes, they just leave.

Early in computer game history, the arcade industry attempted to respond to player needs by including instructions on the cabinet to explain the controls and elementary gameplay (see Figure 4.1).

Figure 4.1   Arcade Cabinet Play Guide

---

[2]   The "lost in the game" idiom is so prevalent in game design and how people discuss it as a high-level goal that it appears on marketing materials for design companies, such as the company TriLabyrinth: Get Lost in the Game.

Quickly readable instructions on cabinets are nonintrusive and often placed near the controls. The problem that arises with this approach to game documentation is that many people playing the game do not read the instructions for a number of reasons. Some players choose to jump in and start playing, experimenting with the game itself and playing around (in much the same manner that people tend to approach new computer programs). In some instances, the instructions are difficult to find on the cabinet, the printing placed somewhere that people would not necessarily see. And finally, arcades are dark; it's just difficult to see the words in small print. Yet the most important point here is that the directions were outside of the game. If a player struggles at an arcade cabinet, that player cannot pause the game and look at the rules. The player must lose the game before referencing rules, and that's assuming that the player has the motivation to follow up after an already frustrating play experience.

This is akin to the point that Huizinga makes about knowing and accepting the rules of the play-sphere. Wolf offers anecdotal evidence of this, writing,

> while visiting me and trying *Myst* for the first time, a friend of mine randomly clicked on three plaques without knowing what he was doing, and actually stumbled across the right combination that raised the ship. He was not all that interested in the game and did not play for very long. (48)

To extend this example to the case of arcade games, if a player enters a game without an understanding of the rules, then the player cannot appreciate the process of the game even though the goals and outcomes may be clear from the exigency of the game. As the arcade industry continued to evolve, instructions were eventually included on one of the opening splash pages or even on cut scenes. While these started the process of integrating the instructions onto the same plane of the game, the challenged posed to the mythical magic circle remained similar: the instructions were always outside of the game, and players could ignore them or miss them before hitting the start button to play.

As computer games moved from the arcade to the home console, the instruction booklet rose in prominence. Packaged with game cartridges, these instruction booklets provided controller hardware explanations, directions on how to play, narrative overviews, compliance and warranty information, and even space to take notes. The twenty-two-page instruction booklet that accompanies the original 1985 *Super Mario Bros.*, for example, starts with the Nintendo Seal of Quality page followed by the "Object of the Game/Game Description," which defines the goal in a narrative structure: "You are Mario! It's up to you to save the Mushroom People from the black magic of Koopa!"[3] Following this call to action, subordinated on the page, is the following instruction: "Please read this

---

[3]   This emphasis on narrative goal at the beginning of the booklet is particularly noteworthy when compared to the emphasis on the booklet, which is an index of all enemies and their point values.

instruction booklet to ensure proper handling of your new game, and then save the booklet for future reference" (2). However, as anyone who has owned and played a game system probably knows, these booklets do not have long lives. They are often ignored at best or permanently lost at worst.[4] This is evidenced by their rarity in the secondary games market because people lose them early in the product's lifecycle. This both perpetuates the problem identified above with the arcades and creates a demand for additional support services to enhance the in-game experience of play.

As computer games became more complex, players wanted additional materials to help them excel at gameplay. Thus, in the late 80s and throughout the 90s, the computer game complex saw a rise in supplemental help for gamers in the form of pay-per-minute help lines, strategy guides, gaming magazine walkthroughs and strategy highlights, and fan-printed fanzines. Later, with the rise of the Internet, the pay-per-minute telephone helplines disappeared as player-written walkthroughs and forums rose in prominence. While all of these forms of help have significant differences—products of different production models, exigencies, and distribution channels—they all offer players additional procedural information concerning how to play the game. As computer games became more complicated, the need for help concerning large-level strategy as well as scene-specific guidelines increased. As players became 'stuck,' they looked to additional information for help. Again, the help is available to teach and scaffold gameplay, but it occurs outside of the game-space, outside of the magic circle. This suggests a failure of sorts on the part of designers, whose goal, according to Bickford in his book on *Interface Design*, is to keep players "'in play' as long and as deeply as possible" (178). In the best cases, these supplementary help guides extend the magic circle, enabling people to remain in the game universe longer and more deeply. However, in the worst-case scenarios, when players cannot find the exit door to the following level, they must leave the magic circle, only to wade through the murky waters of re-immersion if and when they return to the game. It comes as no surprise, then, that designers started to design tutorials *into* games.

In-Game Tutorials and Just-in-Time Help

Game designers have developed a number of approaches for integrating procedural guidance for players:

- Tutorial Levels: Separate levels that players are encouraged to enter before beginning the linear narrative of the main game. These levels provide

---

⁴   This is not unique to computer game booklets. Mehlenbacher et al. found that people didn't read vehicle owner's manuals, yet they wanted a physical copy rather than merely electronic access. And Novick's already cited work speaks to this as well in technical communication.

short, highly scaffolded, and described procedural guides to new players, focusing especially on movement;
- Integrated Stepped Tutorials: Gameplay stops and players are provided a message or visual representation of gameplay that teaches a new button, combination, feature, or strategy;
- Integrated Narrative Tutorials: Like stepped tutorials, these are integrated into the gameplay or narrative, such as a non-player character asking the player to do something to ensure that the player knows how to control the character or can enact a strategy; and
- Adaptive Messaging: Messages that only appear when players do not succeed or are not employing the best strategy for the situation.

Each of these approaches requires players to be in the game space and subject to the rules of play in those games. Further, while the above list distinguishes between these different approaches, they are often used in combination in contemporary games. Also worth noting before moving on to an in-depth consideration of these approaches is the fact that the other forms of help are still available. Procedural help propagates, providing different types of help and game support to a variety of different audiences and players.

Tutorial Levels

Tutorial levels answer the need to teach players the basic mechanics of the game. In discussing the process of creating their game *Endless Web*, Smith et al. discuss the purpose of the tutorial level: "The first phase of the tutorial teaches the player the controls and core platforming concepts, and requires the player to take the platform hazards tuning portal" (194). These levels are separated from the main game. In some instances, designers let players opt in to the tutorial level by asking them to select it off of the main menu page. In other instances, designers provide the tutorial level as soon as the player starts the main game. When players sign in the first time, they must pass through the tutorial level; however, all subsequent playthroughs do not include the tutorial level. Figure 4.2 illustrates the tutorial level of *Katamari Damacy*, a simple game in which the player roles a ball that picks up objects along the way. The goal is to pick up enough objects to make the ball a particular size, from a few meters to the size of a planet.

    As the game starts, players find themselves in the training level, where the king of the cosmos humorously introduces the skills that the player must perform in the game while he also defines the goals of the game. Once players complete this level, they can move into the actual levels of the game.

    These tutorial levels, when done well, can provide players with both knowledge of the rules and confidence in their own skill when navigating the game environment. In their article "What We Learned Evaluating the Usability of a Game," Lucas and Fulton conducted a player or usability test of a particular game to determine gamer satisfaction. They write, "[b]ecause the initial experience in

Figure 4.2   The Training Level for *Katamari Damacy*

a game is critical to keeping the player interested, our play tests focused on the training level and the first mission level of the game. (The training level introduces players to the various skills required in the game)" (7). The connection between player satisfaction, player understanding, and tutorial levels is taken up by Gow et al. in the discussion section of their article "Capturing Player Experience with Post-Game Commentaries." In this study, players reported significant confusion from their play experiences, which the authors explained as being because "None of the players had played *Rogue Trooper* before, and it was a tutorial level that introduced a variety of game mechanics and controls" (7–8). Yet players were skipping these levels or not paying attention to the lessons. Thus, at the most fundamental level, the ability to enjoy a game is intimately tied to (at the very least) a basic understanding of the controls and goals, which are covered in the tutorial.

Studies from technical communication, however, demonstrate that a reliance on the tutorial level can present important problems, since many users don't read manuals. For example, Ganier found from a study on the use of manuals that, "procedural documents are seldom used the first time the user handles an appliance" ("Observational Data" 407). Likewise, Novick and Ward's SIGDOC conference paper "Why Don't People Read the Manual?" found that "The data and the model suggest that users actually do avoid turning to the documentation if they can otherwise avoid it" (2). And by documentation, Novick and Ward reference both paper documents and the computer program's help system. In the Novick et al.'s 2009 SIGDOC conference paper, the authors once again drive this point home, explaining that computer users would rather play around with the program or go to online help than use documentation. Yet even this willingness to go online is called into question by Paris and Linden's research, which found that "People are usually reluctant to consult help and, typically, they consider on-line help to not be useful" (7). So, too, in games, we see players avoiding help systems and tutorials: in an online forum of Escapist Magazine entitled "Quit

Assuming I'm an Idiot," gamers come out strongly against tutorial levels. This reaction echoes Goodwin's finding in "Emplotting the Reader: Motivation and Technical Documentation": "Pushed hard enough, audience resistance gives way to hostility: The reader closes the manual, despises the writer, forgets the product" (102). Indeed, in his Game Developer Conference talk, Fan, designer for *Plants vs. Zombies*, speaks out emphatically against the tutorial level, calling the tutorial level "unfun" in comparison to starting the game and even creating the visual joke during his talk of replacing the "tutorial" button with the "kill myself" button. In creating *Plants vs. Zombies*, Fan employed a combination of stepped tutorial with adaptive messaging.

Integrated Stepped Tutorial

Stepped tutorials are integrated into gameplay and provide guidance just as the player needs to learn a new mechanic or control. In many ways, this is similar to just-in-time information access. The "just-in-time" idiom comes from supply chain management, ensuring that people receive input materials and commodities right when they need them. This approach cuts costs in the supply chain by eliminating storage while scaling production to need. In information access, "just-in-time" provides information when the context demands it. In his ACM Computers in Entertainment talk, Gee writes, "Good games give information 'on demand' and 'just in time,' not out of the contexts of actual use or apart from people's purposes and goals" (2). And this approach is well supported in educational psychology. Merriënboer et al.'s article "Taking the Load Off a Learner's Mind: Instructional Design for Complex Learning," for example, note that "[p]rocedural information specifies the correct performance of recurrent aspects of learning tasks. It is best presented precisely when learners need it during their work on learning tasks, and it is critical to present split attention effects when presenting this information" (10). This is different than supportive information, which can be presented out of context to provide a framework through which to think of particular tasks. Instead, just-in-time information delivers necessary information within the immediate context of informational need.

   This just-in-time approach, then, is particularly well suited to computer games, which are procedural and goal oriented. Further, as Ganier writes in "Factors Affecting the Processing of Procedural Instructions: Implications for Document Design," "The first step in processing instructions corresponds to setting a goal representation" (16). In computer games, goals are often layered, shifting as shorter goals are met. The context of the game and the information needed, then, shifts as well. Providing just-in-time information requires both a complex understanding of content and an ability to anticipate needed information.[5]

---

[5]   In their paper "User Interactions with Everyday Applications as Context for Just-in-time Information Access," authors Budzik and Hammond present their work on automated just-in-time help: Information Management Assistants. In this article, they provide a

Again, in his Game Developer Conference talk "How I Got My Mom to Play Through *Plants vs. Zombies*," Fan provides what he tongue-in-cheek refers to as the tutorial on tutorials. And the runaway success of *Plants vs. Zombies*—the game set a new iTunes app store record in 2010 by breaking $1 million in nine days—has much to do with its accessibility. *Plants vs. Zombies* is, at heart, a tower-defense strategy game. Players must protect their houses from a continuous onslaught of zombies by collecting sunshine currency to buy and plant defense plants in the yard. The graphics are cute and disguise the fact that this is a fairly complicated game, complete with resource management and strategy. Fan explains that he slowly introduced game mechanics in-game with every other level. This strategy adheres to a number of his core design concepts: he teaches players by having them do something once. If words are needed to explain something, then he keeps the number of words to a minimum and makes the messages as unobtrusive as possible. And probably most interesting, he introduces game mechanics, not every level, but every other level. According to Fan, "if you intentionally stagger the teaching of game mechanics, it's a really powerful tool in teaching players how to play your game." He goes on to explain that the design process was liberated by the production team's decision to not teach everything at the beginning of the game. Further, Fan argues, players are proportionally more willing to invest time learning something the longer that they participate in a game.

Finally, Fan found through the design and testing of his game that they needed to give players more time to play with a new game mechanic before introducing the next mechanic. So while the team originally thought that they would introduce a new zombie in each level, they chose to introduce one zombie every two levels. One level would introduce the new zombie and game mechanic while remaining relatively easy to pass, providing players a safer environment for exploring new material before making the game more difficult and challenging in the next level. This strategy allows players to play around with new game mechanics, exploring the different possibilities allowed in the affordances of that mechanic, before increasing the complexity and difficulty.

Integrated Narrative Tutorials

Integrated narrative tutorials are those offered in the narrative structure of the game by character or environmental feedback. The game does not stop to teach the player a new game mechanic or control. Rather, the lesson is blended into the game so that the player character must respond to stimuli in the environment. In many ways, this is an example *par excellence* of Goodwin's theory of "emplotting" a technical writing reader with narrative structure and the hero's

---

conceptual architecture figure that places "anticipator" and "content analyzer" toward the beginning of the process diagram, and this would be a useful resource for those interested in further study of just-in-time information management. Of particular note for this chapter is the idea of the relevance of active goals to which just-in-time information addresses.

journey to increase connection and investment. According to Goodwin, "a manual must *emplot* the reader, that is, must *create an action-oriented role within a storyline that transforms the reader* from a hesitant, if not reluctant neophyte, into a competent software user" (99–100). A high-profile example of this is the opening tutorial in *Halo: Combat Evolved* (Bungie, 2001), an exclusive launch title for the Microsoft Xbox and run away commercial success that launched the *Halo* franchise.[6] Xbox introduced a new controller that has eleven input buttons, two directional stick inputs, and one directional D-Pad input. Because it was a launch title, the designers of *Halo* had to design a game that showcased the new Xbox hardware and software. However, the hardware was complex and needed to provide the player with scaffolded learning. Designers could have included the hardware information in the booklet (which they did), and they could have included a tutorial level or a stepped tutorial in which they stopped the game and taught the player game mechanics and how to use the controller. Instead of these options, the designers integrated the tutorial directly into the narrative.

The game starts with an opening cinematic that lasts approximately four and a half minutes during which time the player does nothing but watch. A gigantic ship is flying through space, obviously setting up the series as a space opera. The dialogue between the non-player characters (both human and computer intelligence) provides the exposition necessary to establish plot (humans versus an alien race known as the covenant) and provide a clear reason that the player and the player's avatar is newly entering the game: "The Chief" avatar has been in cryostorage and is being unsealed, or "thawed," in response to an impending danger. Scientists are on the deck, managing the activation process. When Chief is activated from cryostasis, the scientists complete a series of tests *with the avatar* to ensure that everything is in good working order.

The dialogue moves from diegetic storytelling to an expanded magic circle that now encompasses the player into the diegesis. The opening tutorial lasts several minutes, so I limit my transcription to the initial moment when the player becomes active in the story and trained to the hardware and game mechanics. As non-player characters announce that they will activate the player's avatar, the music changes to a type of spiritual chanting, and the player sees the avatar that they will play in first-person mode for the remainder of the game. The player is greeted by a military scientist who says, "Sorry for the quick thaw, Master Chief. Things are a little hectic right now. The disorientation should pass quickly." A second voice seconds the first greeting, saying, "Welcome back, sir. We'll have you battle ready STAT." Following this, the military scientist turns back to the player and says, "Chief, please look around the room. I need to get a calibration reading for your battle suit's diagnostics" to which the player must look around using one of the

---

[6]   According to VG Chartz, 6.43 million units of *Halo 1* have sold. The franchise as a whole is a multibillion dollar industry with spinoffs into multiple media, including games, books, comics, machinima, and a newly announced television series to be produced by Steven Spielberg (Goldberg).

input sticks on her controller. At the top left corner of the screen, "use [picture of stick] to look" flashes on the screen. The game will not progress until the player does this.

Once the ability to control looking has been established, the narrative progresses. The military scientist provides positive feedback to the player, saying, "Good. Thank you, sir," after which, the technician announces, "I'm bringing your health monitors online, sir." Once this is announced, a new interface element appears in the top right corner, obviously the health monitor. Once this is finished, the scientist declares, "Vital signs look normal. No freezer burn. Okay, sir. Go ahead and climb out of the Cryo." Once again, the game switches to a cinematic in which the player can see the avatar move from a third-person point-of-view before switching again to the first-person. Now that the avatar is out of the cryopod, the scientist says, "I gave you a double dose of the wake-up stim. Take a quick walk around the cryo-bay and join me at optical diagnostics station the when you're ready." At this time, the player is free to walk around using the directional input, again verbally explained in the top left of the screen. Once the player approaches the scientist, the scientist says, "Stand on the red square, please. I know the ordinance techs usually take care of your targeting sensors, but we're short of time, Chief. Just look at each of the flashing panels to target them. When you lock on, it will change color. Okay, that looks good." The color changes from red to green, providing feedback that the player has done this correctly. Following this first successful targeting trial, the technician character interrupts, saying, "Sir, I'm getting some calibration errors. I'm going to invert your looking pitch so you can see if you like it better that way. Try targeting the flashing lights again. Is that better, or should I switch it back? Okay, try looking up and down again, please. Do you want me to leave it like that or switch it again? Okay, I'll leave the pitch normal, but if you want, you can change it yourself later. I'm ready for the energy shield test now." This presents the player with control over the type of input configuration that he or she might like.

As this test proceeds, an intercom announcement explains that the Covenant antagonists will be invading shortly, and that all hands are needed. Thus, even during the training, the game gives a sense that the narrative is continuing around the player-character. The diagnostics are interrupted by the Covenant invasion, and the player is suddenly thrown into the game without weapons. This design decision teaches the player spatial control in the game before introducing the added complexity of weaponry. Further, it heightens the sense of drama in the game: emergency lights and alarms are going, the sound of the Covenant invaders sound bestial as they eat humans, and the human military is fighting for their lives.

By integrating the tutorial into the game, the designers are attempting to maintain the diegesis of the game-space. Everything that happens (at least verbally) happens in the narrative of the game itself. Returning again to Huizinga's theory of the magic circle—the "temporary worlds within the ordinary world, dedicated to the performance of an act apart"—the move to incorporate the tutorial into the narrative of the game is an attempt to maintain the formation of the magic circle longer, denying the need to reenter the ordinary world (10). And this concern is a real one. Play, according to Huizinga, is inherently labile: "At any moment 'ordinary life' may reassert its rights either by an impact from without, which interrupts the game, or by an offence against the rules, or else from within, by a collapse of the play spirit, a sobering, a disenchantment" (21). By incorporating the tutorial into the narrative, the designers were attempting to seamlessly integrate this into the play experience, not allowing the ordinary world to interrupt the game. The danger that they ran into, however, was the internal collapse of the play space.

The first time people play through *Halo*, the controls and events are entirely new, and the tutorials are all connected into the plot in such a way that it seems ingenious and enjoyable. The second time that players play through *Halo*, they are already experts at the controls and do not need the tutorial. And this is a problem because they cannot skip the tutorial and opt into play. Indeed, players rail against the forced tutorials in online forums and in person, especially those that players cannot skip. Again, in the forum "Quit Assuming I'm Stupid," meganmeave writes, "[w]hat's worse are the tutorials you cannot skip! . . . [I]f you start a new playthrough, you have to play the damn tutorial again. So annoying!" To this thread, tomtom94 adds, "Forced tutorials in any game, any game at all, irritate me beyond belief. They should be OPTIONAL. Particularly if you're playing through a second time." What appears to be consistent on this forum and others like it is the ways in which forced tutorials (which almost all games that integrate the tutorial into the narrative have) break the magic circle, causing frustration with the game.

Adaptive Messaging

Halo pops up messages during its integrated narrative tutorial, providing visual redundancy for the directions provided by NPCs. This is not adaptive messaging; it is a type of messaging that supports stepped and integrated tutorials. Adaptive messaging applies to those messages and hints that pop up *in response* to what the player is doing. In their article "Reflective Middleware for Integrated Network Monitoring with Adaptive Object Messaging," Han et al. discuss the network requirements of adaptive messaging: "The reflective messaging layer customizes messaging protocols to adapt to changing network and system conditions. This is achieved by fine tuning messaging protocols using the information provided by the system monitoring layer and the application communication requirements" (61). In other words, computer programs must monitor actions and link those actions to appropriate informational access needs and communication requirements. This is a more advanced version of the Microsoft Word paperclip avatar who used to notice that you were working on a new document and wanted to know if you needed any help.

Adaptive messaging is, unsurprisingly, very effective in speaking to the audience of those messages; they seem to appear "just for you." Computer systems use designed algorithms to read and categorize user actions, determine success within the defined framework, determine if the user needs to know information to succeed (or be sold something), and provides information seemingly just in time. And this is rhetorically persuasive for all the obvious reasons: users—or in a game's case, players—are the rhetorical audience for all messages. Adaptive messaging ensures that the message meets a certain exigency; further, not only is it kairotic, it is (or at least it feels) personalized, increasing a feeling of ethos wherein the user feels that the messages are tailored to them and their needs increasing a sense of connection. Indeed, Kaptein and van Halteren find that adaptive messages are more persuasive than other forms of messages. In their article, "Adaptive Persuasive Messaging to Increase Service Retention: Using Persuasion Profiles to Increase the Effectiveness of Email Reminders," they write:

> When designers attend individual differences in user response to the use of persuasion principles in persuasive systems, then they will design adaptive persuasive systems: 'systems that select the appropriate influence strategy to use for a specific user based on the estimated success of this strategy.' To be able to build adaptive persuasive systems, designers should create systems that are capable of identifying their users, representing different social influence strategies, and measuring their effectiveness. (n.p.)

Their study bears out this hypothesis: adaptive messaging outperformed other messaging principles, convincing users to respond to the messages that they "feel" are more personalized.

In games, designers can design adaptive messages into their games, providing players an experience appropriate to their particular levels. In other words, experienced players who are able to transfer what they know about gameplay from one situation to another are unlikely to encounter helpful messages. They are doing fine in the game space. Players who struggle, miss opportunities, or use poor strategies, on the other hand, might encounter a series of progressively more pointed adaptive messages as they move through the game. Fan discusses this in his "How I Got My Mom to Play Through *Plants vs. Zombies*," explaining that player mistakes appeared during playtesting, and those mistakes limited the possibility of success in game. The challenge that Fan and his team faced, however, was how to support new players while not alienating skilled players. One approach he used was adaptive messaging. He worked with his team to redesign the game so that players were able to play without interference the first time. If the player made the same mistake (planting the defending plants too close to the zombie starter line, for example), then a message would appear: "One of your peashooters died! Try planting them further to the left!" (see Figure 4.3: *Plants vs. Zombies* Adaptive Messaging).

Figure 4.3   *Plants vs. Zombies* Adaptive Messaging

While this method works to help delineate between skilled and unskilled gamers in a certain genre, it does run the risk of overtly prescribing gameplay, taking the joy away from discovery and mastery. Fan makes a strong point in his talk when he explains that designers are best served when they leave the player room for exploration, for playing games is "better learned through experimentation than through handholding." One way that Fan has approached this is creating adaptive messaging that starts with a warning and moves toward imperatives. For example, in the game *Insaniquarium*, some players could not figure out what to feed the carnivore fish. When the first carnivore fish died, the message "Warning! Your carnivore has died!" pops up on the screen. After the second fish dies, the message "Hint: Carnivores won't eat fish food" appears. It's not until the third fish dies that the directive, "Try feeding small guppies to your carnivores!" tells the player what to do.

Adaptive messaging works well in games that are well playtested; designers can see where players are struggling with the game, what mistakes or alternative strategies that they might be playing, and create messages that speak to those players' particular needs as they need to know it. However, adaptive messaging would prove more problematic in large, dynamic games such as *World of Warcraft*, which must balance the closed system of planned gameplay with the openness and volatility of gamer communities. Add to this the sheer amount of information needed to play *World of Warcraft* as a master player (the *WoW* Wiki is the second largest wiki after Wikipedia), and the information design challenge appears daunting. *WoW* gets around this by having a fairly supportive and welcoming community comprised of players who often meet new players and offer to show them around. This mentorship model, however, cannot be replicated at this time in designed tutorials, yet further research into this area would provide important information concerning the types of information that new players seek versus the type of information that expert players think that they need to pass on. Regardless, adaptive messaging, especially combined with other forms of in-game tutorials, prove a powerful rhetorical method to convey technical information when players need it in order to support the experience of the game and the player's likelihood of success when playing.

Conclusion

Game designers face a number of challenges in supporting players. Computer games are, themselves, complex programs with any number of affordances, both anticipated and unanticipated. Further, players do not always want to play the game as it was intended; they just want to play. Wark's book *Gamer Theory* presents the multiple subjectivities and activities that gamers often exhibit. Not only are there those people who want to play the game according to the rules and win by those rules, there are also those people who want to troll the game by ruining other people's experiences, trifle in the game by just playing around in the game space without engaging in the rules of the game, and be bored by the game by resisting engagement and immersion into the game space. This comes into obvious tension with game designers, who hold a vision and design an experience for the player. Then, of course, this experience can also be disrupted by new hardware (players don't know *how* to use the controller, for example) and new game mechanics (players didn't know that running along the walls was even an option).

In-game tutorials are a way to mediate the complexities between hardware, game mechanics, player desire, and designer vision. The tutorials normalize, in many ways, an approach to gameplay that adheres to traditional motivations: a desire to play well and to win. They can also open up the game space to experimentation, trial and error strategies, and unintentional player strategies, while still providing a scaffold for learning new skills and in-game strategies. This is not to say that the other forms of procedural documentation have been replaced. Like most other technologies, the informational technologies of play diverge and diversify. Further, each mediated form provides an extra part of the gameworld experience, from the feelies—extra content that come packaged with games—to the status and online communities that accompany fan-based walkthroughs. What I intend to emphasize as I end this chapter is that in-game tutorials are an important part of this technical landscape, communicating to players material and immaterial affordances and expectations and helping those players build skills. In other words, by making these tutorials in-game, they are part of the computer-based play experience, within the coded magic circle of play.

Works Cited

Bickford, Peter. *Interface Design: The Art of Developing Easy-to-Use Software.* Chestnut Hill, MA: Academic, 1997.

Budzik, Jay, and Kirstian J. Hammond. "User Interactions with Everyday Applications asContext for Just-in-time Information Access." *Proceedings of the 5th International Conference on Intelligent User Interfaces* (2000): 44–51.

Carr, David, and David Comtois. *Video Game Invasion: The History of a Global Obsession*. Beantown Productions, 2004.

Computer Space. Nutting Associates. 1971. Video Game.

ESA: Entertainment Software Association. 2013. Web. 10 June 2013.

Fan, George. "How I Got My Mom to Play Through Plants vs. Zombies." *Game Developers Conference*. 2012. Web. 28 June 2013.

Galloway, Alexander R. *Gaming: Essays on Algorithmic Culture*. Minneapolis: U of Minnesota P, 2004.

Ganier, Franck. "Factors Affecting the Processing of Procedural Instructions: Implications for Document Design." *IEEE Transactions on Professional Communication* 47.1 (March 2004): 15–24.

———. "Observational Data on Practical Experience and Conditions of Use of Written Instructions." *Journal of Technical Writing and Communication* 39.4 (2009): 401–15.

Gee, James Paul. "What Video Games Have to Teach Us About Learning and Literacy." *ACM Computers in Entertainment* 1.1 (October 2003): 1–4.

Goldberg, Lesley. "Steven Spielberg to Produce Live-Action 'Halo' TV Series." *The Hollywood Reporter*. 21 May 2013. Web. 25 June 2013. <http://www.hollywoodreporter.com/live-feed/steven-spielberg-produce-live-action-526251>.

Goodwin, David. "Emplotting the Reader: Motivation and Technical Documentation." *Journalof Technical Writing and Communication* 21.2 (1991): 9–115.

Gow, Jeremy, Paul Cairns, Simon Colton, Paul Miller, and Robin Baumgarten. "Capturing Player Experience with Post-Game Commentaries." *Proceedings from the Annual International Conference on Computer Games Multimedia and Allied Technologies* (2010): n.p.

Halo: Combat Evolved. Bungie. 2001. Video Game.

Han, Qi, Sebastian Gutierrez-Nolasco, and Nalini Venkatasubramanian. "Reflective Middleware for Integrating Network Monitoring with Adaptive Object Messaging." *IEEE Network* 18.1 (Jan/Feb 2004): 56–65.

Huizinga, Johan. *Homo Ludens: A Study of the Play Element in Culture*. Boston: Beacon, 1950.

Insaniquarium. Popcap Games, Flying Bear Entertainment. 2004. Video Game.

Kaptein, Maurits, and Aart van Halteren. "Adaptive Persuasive Messaging to Increase Service Retention: Using Persuasion Profiles to Increase the Effectiveness of Email Reminders." *Personal and Ubiquitous Computing* (2012): n.p.

Katamari Damacy. Namco, Now Production. 2004. Video Game.

Kocurek, Carly A. "Rendering Novelty Mundane: Technical Manuals in the Golden Age of Coin-Op Computer Games." *Computer Games and Technical*

Communication: Critical Methods and Applications at the Intersection. Burlington, VT: Ashgate, 2014. 55–67.

Lucas, Shannon, and Denise Fulton. "What We Learned Evaluating the Usability of a Game." *Usability Interface: The Newsletter of the STC Usability SIG* 11.2 (2004): 7–8.

Luce, A. V. "'It Wasn't Intended to Be an Instruction Manual': Revisiting Ethics of 'Objective' Technical Communication in Gaming Manuals." *Computer Games and Technical Communication: Critical Methods and Applications at the Intersection.* Burlington, VT: Ashgate, 2014. 87–106.

Mehlencacher, Brad, Michael D. Wogalter, and Kenneth R. Laughery. "On the Reading of Product Owner's Manuals: Perceptions and Product Complexity." *Proceedings of the Human Factors and Ergonomics Society Annual Meeting* (2002): 730–34.

Novick, David G., Oscar D. Andrade, and Nathaniel Bean. "The Micro-structure of Use of Help." *Proceedings of the 27th ACM International Conference on Design of Communication* (2009): 97–104.

Novick, David G., and Karen Ward. "Why Don't People Read the Manual?" *Proceedings of the 24th Annual ACM International Conference on Design of Communication* (2006): 11–18.

"Quit Assuming I'm an Idiot." *The Escapist.* August 2010. Web. 20 June 2013.

Ruggill, Judd E., and McAllister, Ken S. *Gaming Matters: Art, Science, Magic, and the Computer Game Medium.* Tuscaloosa: U of Alabama P, 2011.

Salen, Katie, and Eric Zimmerman. *Rules of Play: Game Design Fundamentals.* Cambridge: MIT P, 2004.

Smith, Gillian, Alexei Othenin-Girard, Jim Whitehead, and Noah Wardrip-Fruin. "PCG-Based Game Design: Creating Endless Web." *Proceedings of the International Conference on the Foundations of Digital Games.* New York: ACM, 2012, 188–95.

Super Mario Bros. "Instruction Booklet." Nintendo. 1985.

VG Chartz. "Halo: Combat Evolved." 22 June 2013. Web. 30 June 2013.

Wark, McKenzie. *Gamer Theory.* Cambridge, MA: Harvard UP, 2007.

Wolf, Mark J. P. *Myst & Riven: The World of the D'ni.* Ann Arbor: U of Michigan P, 2011. *World of Warcraft.* Blizzard Entertainment. 2004. Video Game.

Chapter 5

"It Wasn't Intended to be an Instruction Manual": Revisiting Ethics of "Objective" Technical Communication in Gaming Manuals

A. V. Luce

Trigger Warning: The case study discussed in this chapter deals with virtual representations of rape.

In a 2009 news story for the *Telegraph Online*, Matthew Moore details the events banning a game involving simulated rape from Amazon Marketplace. Further research revealed a gaming guide that explained that the purpose of the game was to play a male avatar who is motivated to finish a thwarted rape—this second attempt, however, entails raping not just the original victim, but her two daughters as well. It was not blogs or news stories that provided the most details but the gaming guide. While the game itself has been banned and taken out of commercial distribution in the United States, YuSaKu's *RapeLay* guide remains, providing not only the story behind the game but also detailed instructions for how to complete the game.[1]

There are two aspects of the gaming documentation that are of particular interest: first, its continued online presence on gaming forums like GameFAQs and Neoseeker, which challenge our disciplinary expectations about *where* technical writing takes place today. Online gaming forums constitute what Kimball describes as, "*ad hoc* online collections of tricks, tips, and cheats—myriad accounts of ways a user can make the institutionally designed world of the game his or her own, if only temporarily" (74). These sites—and contributors who post technical guides on them—complicate our understanding of the daily rhetorical and ethical actions that technical communicators face, particularly in *ad hoc* and extra-organizational technical communities. For technical communicators, the description of *RapeLay* documentation likely brings to mind other infamous examples of ethically

---

[1] YuSaKu has many online handles, and one particular handle is traceable to a Facebook page. On the Facebook profile, YuSaKu is a middle-aged male living in the US. Among his interests are listed games of various forms and anime, further demonstrating his background with Japanese style art and gaming. I will reference sites linked to YuSaKu, like Facebook; however, to maintain the gamer's privacy, I will not provide any information aside from the name he used to publish the guide.

problematic technical situations, such as the *Challenger* disaster, the Intel Pentium chip, and Holocaust engineering (see Moore, 1992; Markel, 1997; Katz, 1992). Scholars in technical communication long have been concerned with identifying and categorizing ethical issues in technical documentation practices,[2] particularly how ethics, rhetoric, and philosophy intersect and inform technical communicators' roles as workers, educators, students, and citizens (see for example Markel, 1997; Dombrowski, 2000). These treatments examine the root of ethics in considerations of right action and obligation to others, and how best we can implement ethical routines into technical practices. However, these cases involve specialists and technical communicators working within organizational conditions in which ethics are expected and communicated as well as either teaching or learning ethical codes of conduct within disciplinary traditions. Cases like the Challenger explosion and the Holocaust are extreme and thus easy examples to use in classrooms because they provide a clear path through ethically treacherous terrain. However, *ad hoc* sites as well as technical rhetors outside of organizational/institutional schemas confront our ethical reflexivity, moving us away from universal ethics and authorship and toward situational, technical contexts.

Second, *RapeLay* provides a more contemporary and complex example for investigation by technical communicators. A central concern for technical communication must not be merely the role technical writing plays in organizational and institutional loci, but the function of technical rhetoric outside of these domains. As Katz advises, in his germinal article "The Ethics of Expediency: Classical Rhetoric, Technology, and the Holocaust," technical communication, as a deeply rhetorical field, constructs and interacts with our conception of technical knowledge: "If telos is politically constructed and ethics are culturally relative, we must realize the role our rhetoric plays in continually creating, recreating, and maintaining not only knowledge, but values as well—including the value of technological expediency through how we teach rhetoric, and how we use it" (271). Thus, I examine how ethics play out in the *RapeLay* guide and demonstrate how noninstitutional examples constitute an excess of agency and authority, ethos, and ethics alike. I argue that many rhetors, both academic and public, can easily argue against the merits of technical communication toward the ends of simulated rape; however, what is more complex and thus not as easily discernible is the point at which that ethics is traceable to any one agent, any one authority, and any one institutional condition. Even though its content is deplorable, *RapeLay* documentation is an excellent case study for technical communication scholars and practitioners; it represents a community of thousands of volunteer technical communicators and the ethics that arise from their activities.

Further, the role of technical communication to mask the unethical in the mundane is perhaps more likely or at the least exacerbated when ethical situations

---

[2]   For further discussion of documentation conventions and functions in gaming, see Kocurek's work on cabinet manuals and deWinter's work on procedural manuals for play in this collection.

are both dispersed online and in the hands of *ad hoc* technical communicators who have not necessarily earned legitimacy through the typical educational and professionalizing processes that most professional technical communicators have. This is a continually relevant aspect of situational ethics for students of technical communication. While the answer may be apparent to readers of this and other work in technical communication, the question remains for the computer gamer with no or alternative training: what training in or awareness of ethical behaviors can we expect technical communicators to have outside of institutions that regulate ethical behavior, especially within social groups with different expectations?

"Do You Dare Play?": Agency and the Rhetorical Evolution of Gaming Guides

Game guides have been produced for many years through more official, institutional channels, appearing as help manuals included with the game cartridge or a larger strategy guide that can be purchased in addition to the game; however, gamers have been in the ad hoc publishing industry since the early days of the Internet. The shift from institutionally published to community-produced guides is in large part due to a transference or replication of technical aspects that are attributed to gaming guides. For example, published guides often feature a formulaic document structure, a gaming version of instructions. Published manuals usually include a table of contents, background on the story that encompasses the game, platform instructions and controls, a walkthrough of main and side missions, details about features of the game (such as character, armor, locations, and the like), credits, and legal statements. Online guides have trimmed the documentation, and modified legal aspects slightly. Often, online guides feature titles and graphics, game and platform information, copyright for the guide writer, table of contents, walkthrough, game controls, alternative missions or cheats, and other guides published by that writer. The overlap of guides is often due to documentation regulation established by online forum sites like GameFAQs or Neoseeker. These documentation standards provide a template for online guides, which create a condition for authority and expertise. Indeed, a large part of the shift from institutional to community-based guides is the structure and forum for guides published by gamers rather than through official companies.

However, the shift from corporate guides to online gaming forums has altered the conditions and nature of authority and agency within guides and walkthroughs. In this migration, technical genres can remain similar, although they are modified for the user and audience who are reading the documents. For example, gaming guides from commercial publishing house Prima[3] feature extensive breakdowns of missions, including controls and explanation of the functions of the game controls and missions as players progress through the game. These manuals are often 150

---

[3]   Prima Publishing is an imprint of Random House.

or more pages in length due to the extensive detailing of the game, section-by-section and action-by-action, as well as extras like rendered art.

Game manuals that accompany game disks developed by corporate writers continue this tradition but in simplified form, often providing a larger schematic for game controls and brief explanations of game chapters and key moments in the game. Current companies like Ubisoft are making manuals condensed, available online, or in digital form only. Publishing houses produce both of these game manual types, either in conjunction with the game release or separately as complete guides for the games. However, Prima, one of the largest guide publishers, revolutionized the guide-writing model by employing gamers as the technical writers. On their company page, an anonymous writer describes the workplace in the following way: "Most of us came to Prima Games with dreams of playing video games for a living" ("About Us"). This use of institutional structures with practical experts is blending the community model (user-driven and specific to the community of the technical genre) and institutional production models.

Textual production models are just one piece of the shift from institutional to community-based technical communication. The Internet, as a simultaneous information delivery system and widely dispersed realm of information exchange, requires thinking about "publishing" and gaming as a broader, more networked distribution paradigm. The shift impacts not just how expertise is constructed but also how differing models of distribution and circulation acknowledge expertise:

> More than anything, the collective intelligence of the Internet has changed how gamers access expert guidance in how to play a game. Websites such as GameFAQS [sic] offer vast collections of user-generated documents that provide hints, tips, and detailed walkthroughs of video games that easily rival anything that traditional publishing provides. Self proclaimed experts produce competing FAQs, sometimes for one title over a variety of consoles such as xBox [sic], PlayStation, or Wii. Ardent gamers engage in lively debates on forums, arguing about which game FAQ is the best. (Greene and Palmer p. 8)

Expertise is no longer primarily defined in relation to or authorized by institutions; in the website forum model, expertise is determined by the gamer and validated by other forum subscribed gamers. Technologies and accessibility to online forums create conditions that are divergent from professional publishing, which Herndl and Licona attribute to the rhetoricality of agency and authority. This means that, "agency is not an attribute of the individual, but the conjunction of a set of social and subjective relations that constitute the possibility of action. The rhetorical performance that enacts agency is a form of kairos, i.e., social subjects realizing the contextualized opportunities for action" (1). Conceived this way, agency is not something that someone can *have* so much as something someone can *demonstrate* through rhetorical procedures and material conditions that are recognized as action. Thus, agency as kairos is the performance of action in the opportune conditions to create or enable action. It is important to keep in mind that action here is discursive in nature, which means, "Agency speaks, then, to the possibilities for a subject to enter into a discourse and effect change" (4). However, to talk about agency as a material and rhetorical process is not to imply that agency is "a set of objective rhetorical abilities of a rhetor, or even her past accomplishments" (7), as that is again a condition of having abilities. Rather than coming to situations always already having agency, often agency is constructed through situations and documents. As silly as it seems, a good example of this is an initiation ritual that Prima Games uses to initiate newbies of the company, which demonstrates how agency is less a personal capacity and more a condition of material and rhetorical circumstance:

> On your first day at Prima Games, we'll decorate your cubicle for you in a fashion that we deem appropriate. Each day, you'll be permitted to remove one item. It doesn't take long for the rookie to realize that it's actually a really tough job—we work with rough, pre-release game builds that freeze up frequently, and the games are constantly being tweaked and balanced. We can spend hundreds of man-hours mapping out all of the collectibles in a game, only to find out that the developer completely re-arranged them at the last minute. ("Our Culture")

The decision about what to remove—an action that appears as personal agency—is actually framed by conditions that both give the newbie the opportunity for action and constraints that keep that action limited and within the culture and tradition of Prima.

Thus, agency in the form of writing gaming guides—or even playing games—is framed by several conditions that influence what and how agency can be constructed and enacted. These conditions include:

- The availability of forums and the criteria and/or restrictions for publishing on major online gaming forums like GameFAQs and Neoseeker;[4]
- The publishing of popular games and first-come-first-serve online guides, meaning that within online forums, guides are more likely to be published and receive popular attention if they are relevant to the release date of the game, popularity of game genres, etc. In the case of more niche market games like eroge[5] and *RapeLay* more specifically, publication is more tangential to release date and reliant more on popularity of the genre;

---

[4] For a more complete look at the GameFAQs online guidelines and Neoseeker publishing requirements, visit <http://www.gamefaqs.com/contribute/> and <http://www. neoseeker.com/contribute/>, respectively.

[5] Eroge is a Japanese-English neologism that combines "erotic" with "game" (Japanese phonetically spells games as geemu). Eroge gaming is defined by Wordpress blogger Hau Omochikaeri as, "a portmanteau of *erotic* game, and as such, all eroge include some erotic content. . . . Eroge goes hand-in-hand with *visual* novels, which are all-ages story-based eroge, akin to Western fiction." It is only on YuSaKu's Xbox Live profile that

- The access to the game being written about (as well as the time to finish it and produce and publish a guide). *RapeLay* was publically accessible through commercial channels until 200X, and available now only through peer-to-peer file sharing sites;
- A familiarity with game genres and game formats enables the writer to write exhaustively about the particulars of games. YuSaKu's familiarity with eroge games and his multiple publications on games in this genre gives him the ethos to attend to the context and particular tasks of the game for his gamer audience; and
- A rhetorical understanding of audience factors in order to instruct gamers on proceeding through the game. For *RapeLay*, this means addressing a range of gamers from newbies to experienced Eroge gamers, as well as attending to the particular controls tied to tasks in *RapeLay* specifically.

In this way, what looks like open access publishing online is actually the performance of ethos and authority amid a web of rhetorical and material factors that enable and constrain YuSaKu's *RapeLay* guide. YuSaKu not only has to navigate access to the game (either before or after commercial and public accessibility) but also the publication standards of the online forum in which he plans to publish. In order to publish, he must understand the rhetorical guidelines and context established by online gaming forums as well as how to construct a document that meets those standards and supports his ethos as eroge guide writer. Agency is not merely the ability to write in this case; it is the ability to write a guide within these myriad constraints that enable public publication while also setting forum standards for guides.

"Self Proclaimed Experts": Authority within Online Gaming Forums

According to Herndl and Licona, "Like agency, authority is realized in contextualized relational practices that define the subject's capacity and the opportunity to function as an authority and/or an agent. We are particularly interested, however, in the slippage between the agent function (as agency) and the author function (as authority)" (20), and I will use the idea of authority as similarly contextualized rather than internalized to consider the role that the guide writer plays in *RapeLay*'s circulation. While Herndl and Licona use Foucault's author function heavily to argue that authorship and authority is a loci that a writer may occupy given the right conditions, I wish to consider instead how conditions arise that allow a gamer to be recognized as an expert technical guide writer. To do so, I turn to the writer of the *RapeLay* guide.

---

he lists interest in eroge gaming. It is perhaps the sexually graphic nature of that style of gaming that has influenced his choice to list this genre of game on some online sites and not others.

YuSaKu, American guide writer and eroge gamer, has published forty-one guides on Neoseeker and twenty-seven eroge-specific guides featuring erotic, sexually mature content ("YuSaKu"). While blogger Hau Omochikaeri advises that not all eroge games are graphic in nature, YuSaKu's listed eroge guides are predominantly for games that involve graphic sexual content, sometimes nonconsensual. The *RapeLay* guide is featured on six gaming sites, including Neoseeker and GameFAQs ("XI Other Works")[6]. The number of guides he has published exceeds his lesser gaming experience, demonstrating that he is more proficient playing and writing the genres that he is interested, mainly eroge, than having a varied gaming background.[7]

While YuSaKu may not meet more traditional technical publishing paradigms by working as an agent of a publishing house or even the hybrid publication house and gamer-as-expert model that Prima Games employs, he does fit within the conditions that grant authority and expertise for *online* game manual writers, a point similar to Kimball's assertion that, "[a]s technology becomes further integrated into our daily lives . . . we should expect to see not only more complex user interactions involving institutional technical communication, but also more technical communication happening outside, between, and through corporations and other institutions" (67). If guide-writing authority is tied to number of publications, then his twenty-plus eroge publications and the usefulness of his guides demonstrate that he is a successful and established guide writer for two of the largest gaming forums in the U.S. In order to publish on Neoseeker and GameFAQs, his guides would need to follow both technical and rhetorical specifications.[8] YuSaKu would need to be familiar with audience expectation for guide details, communicate them through technical language, and do so understanding both game details and information (in this case a Japanese to English patch, torrent network information, newbie lingo, and guide formatting to name a few) and already extant online walkthroughs in order to determine whether he wants to supplement that information. These rhetorical moves not only require a range of information, but also knowledge of community-mandated technical communication specs. In other words, through his published work online, YuSaKu demonstrates an authority and expertise in eroge games specifically and gaming instructional genres more broadly.

While community-based guide forums create opportunist conditions to demonstrate authority and expertise—a channel that might be viewed as less

---

[6]   The *RapeLay* guide that I quote from was originally found on GameFAQs, but at the date of this publication, it is available on Neoseeker, not GameFAQs.

[7]   According to his MyGamerCard profile (no longer available online but accessed in 2009) he has only played 16 games, has a total game score of 2240/17550, and has 132/761 total achievements.

[8]   Specifications for GameFAQs are explained in the sections "Composing Your Guide" <http://www.gamefaqs.com/features/help/entry.html?cat=28> and "Formatted FAQs" <http://www.gamefaqs.com/features/help/entry.html?cat=53>.

"professional" than publishing houses—the community-based model is audience-centered in a different way. Online forums are more interactive for users in terms of feedback: gamers can comment, critique, or endorse guides on a faster timeframe due to accessibility associated with the Internet as opposed to print. The increased interactivity of users/gamers is a blessing and a curse in that it provides writers access to a range of feedback very quickly; it can also, however, lead to flaming and unproductive tangents. Such community interaction is part of the rhetorical nature of online forums, and a characteristic of computer-mediated communication (Hiltz and Turoff, 1993; Gurak, 2001). Professionally published manuals have more detailed guides; however, the gamer does not have the opportunity to comment or seek additional help. In addition, the writer's expertise and agency is also correlational to the audience, and audience reception can negatively affect the writer's ethos and conditions in which s/he can publish guides.

Returning to the case study of *RapeLay*, in a Neoseeker message board thread, a user called UnholyReaver begins a thread titled "least detailed faqs of all time, please help" in which he criticizes YuSaKu's guide for its lack of specific and detailed information regarding in-game mouse controls. UnholyReaver is questioning the usability of the guide for novice gamers, which is the purpose of a guide:

> It's not that hard to put a basic controls section in a faq. The words "Left clicking on screen allows you to move camera, right click on buttons for options" would f-ing TRIPLE the usefulness of your faq.
>
> . . .
>
> Way to give the juicy details without any of the basics.
>
> . . .
>
> How did you get her on the train? Who writes these faqs and never says how to do anything? (UnholyReaver)

To this YuSaKu responds in the following way:

> I wrote it, and for such an undetailed FAQ, it sure is getting some good feedback. It wasn't intended to be an instruction manual. Tell you what, since I'm tired from work, I don't think I'm going to help you
>
> . . .
>
> Normally, I would have done a lot more with the *Rapelay* [*sic*] guide, but there's already a few good question/answer FAQs, and a plethora of information pages on the game, so I didn't want to bother with it. I was under the impression that

the FAQ was received quite well, until I saw your post, calling it the 'Worst detailed FAQ of all time'. (UnHolyReaver)

I will return to the inconsistency of YuSaKu denouncing the technical merits of his own guide, but for the time being, I wish to draw attention to how the debate highlights two distinct levels: usability and forum popularity. UnholyReaver is finding it difficult to navigate the game, so this gamer turned to a FAQ to understand the controls and step-by-step missions. In reading the *RapeLay* FAQ, the gamer did not get the detailed information needed to advance in the game. The gamer then took the complaint online to the question forum and critiqued the posted FAQ while simultaneously asked for additional help.

The other side of that coin is that the community-based technical writer can also respond, as YuSaKu has done. His counterargument is twofold: while he does address issues of usability and detailed description (admitting that he would "have done a lot more"), he also sees guide popularity as a demonstration of guide respectability. His response to UnholyReaver indicates that he had not received any negative feedback previous to UnholyReaver's post. YaSaKu's argument indicates that the FAQ's reception should outweigh a single user's critique. Further, his attack on UnholyReaver as well as his excuse that he had no time to improve it due to his real job, indicates that instead of receiving the critique as constructive user feedback to the usability of the guide, he sees the gamer as being a n00b, that is, a person unfamiliar with particular games or gaming in general.[9] Even though FAQs and guides are intended to assist gamers of every level, YuSaKu's response indicates that there is perhaps a level of expected or desired expertise on behalf of the gamer too, instead of only on the guide writer's end.

This demonstration of expertise and ethos in the rhetorical conditions of online forums echoes other models of technical communication both intra- and extra-institutional. Johnson proposes three types of models to explain the writer and audience interaction in technical genres: users-as-practitioners, users-as-producers, and users-as-citizens. The first two are important to the forum argument above. In the first, users-as-practitioners, the users are seen as "idiots" with some situational cunning, but not the technological savvy that technical writers have. In the second, users-as-producers, users are understood to have knowledge rooted in their experience (61). Johnson argues that user participation is invaluable and necessary to bring about "technological development, dissemination, and . . . an egalitarian process that has its end in the user" (85). This applies to the forum argument in that YuSaKu treated UnholyReaver as user-practitioner with no concrete understanding of basic gaming controls. YuSaKu sees the minimal details of mouse clicking as information that all gamers should have an understanding of, and thus does not need explanation. However, UnholyReaver perceives his role as a user-as-producer in which his previous gaming record gives him the experience

---

[9]   For a discussion of noob culture, see Matthew M. White's "L2P Noob: Examining Tutorials in Digital Games."

to assess what information is needed in guides to assist new gamers to that game. Thus, his critique is the same as Johnson's insofar as he desires more interaction in the guide process because of his gaming background.

YuSaKu is, it seems, attempting to hold onto expertise that is continually shifting and subject to not only the genres and authority of technical communication but also gaming experience, user participation and feedback, as well as shifting gaming technologies. He will validate his own expertise even if it means flaming a fellow gamer and his guide audience. In an online technical economy, such behavior might be warranted, even necessary, to keep one's reputation for expertise and authority intact. More importantly, however, this demonstrates the contingent and rhetorical nature of expertise and authority. Both are not inherent capacities that YuSaKu has, but instead aspects of a technical gamer that he must fashion and defend due to the continually evolving nature of online and collaborative rhetorical conditions. This demonstrates both the productive and problematic aspects of authority/expertise as Herndl and Licona articulate it in that agency is the ability to take action—write a guide in this case—among a complex web of social and rhetorical factors that shape the ability to act and constrain it at the same time.

"It Wasn't Intended to Be an Instruction Manual:" Ethics and Ethos For Online Technical Communicators

Ethos and ethics have always been connected through technical writing. Stephen Katz's "Ethics of Expediency" is perhaps the most astute work to call attention to the ways that technical language has the potential to endorse and mask with authority unethical protocols. Katz traces Nazi technical documentation and the implemented plans to use technology for more efficient extermination of European Jews to what he calls the "ethics of expediency." This ethics, he argues, is appealing for its logical and objective nature. Its allure resides in its ability to be "the only ethic that can be 'measured,' whether that measure be a cost-benefit analysis employed by an industrial engineer to argue for the automation of a plant, or the number of people exterminated in one day—'pure' expediency (undiluted and uninhibited by other ethics) recognizes no boundaries, no degrees of morality or other ethical limits" (266). According to Katz and Winner, the justification for some technology is its own ability to fulfill technical criteria or use (what Langdon calls "technological imperative"), which becomes more important than the principles behind the technology or that the technology represents (264).
On one level, this is certainly the case in *RapeLay*: the computer engineering software is able to replicate more realistic avatars to simulate scenes that are common in Japanese culture, like subway car molestation and rape. Because gaming systems can reflect cultural reality, games are developed on consoles to mimic that reality despite the ethical implications of the act and its simulation.

However, while expediency allows Nazi engineers to distance themselves from the unethical and horrific results of more efficient technology, gamers use guides to immerse themselves into the process of the game and its un/ethical processes. The distance between Just's memo and the mobile extermination units is created and sustained through the objective technical language of his memo, which ideologically separates the act of extermination from the calculations to improve the efficiency of a vehicle. Yet with YuSaKu's guide, the technical breakdown of the game and its tasks is meant to enhance the tasks enacted in the game. This means that gamers turn to guides in order to more effectively go through the tasks and processes that the game environment puts them through. So in the case of *RapeLay*, the gamer has already made the choice to play a game of ethically questionable content. This makes it seem as if the responsibility for the content is on the gamer. Yet the game experience, the full enactment of the rape of both the mother and her daughters, is guided by, well, the guide. YuSaKu is leading gamers through those tasks so as to achieve them—to rape virtual women—as fully as they can.

What we discover through *RapeLay* is something divergent from Katz's technical situation. Rather than use a writers' authority and ethos through technical communication to create a distance from the effects, guide writers like YuSaKu and their audience both are in the thick of the action. Both actions are unethical, but the distance of the writer to the actions means that the guide genre, and even the online context of the writing, has positioned the writer differently. In *RapeLay* guides, the more experience the writer has with the situations in the game, the more effectively he can imbue that knowledge to the gamer. In applying the Katz analogy here, the writer never actually exterminated the Jews but instructs others how to do it more efficiently; however, YuSaKu's instructions are intended to mimic his own experience. Thus, this is a mentorship in executing rape through technical writing, not a delegation of unethical actions so as not to get the writer's hands dirty.

There are complications to the role that YuSaKu plays in the actions of the game and his writing. For example, the spoiler alert to the guide notifies gamers that this game has graphic and disturbing content: "This H-Game is intended for Mature Audiences ONLY!!! It includes THE SICKEST, MOST GRAPHIC-INTENSE RAPE SCENES EVER IN AN H-GAME (Involving controlling a rapist as he sadistically tortures a family). It also contains a hefty ammount [sic] of hardcore scenes, incest, teenage pregnancy, etc." However, the warning is subverted by his tone and innuendo when he tells readers, "if this sort of thing offends you…then go away. Go on, shoo. AND PUT THAT THING AWAY, you'll go blind" (YuSaKu). The warning downplays the implication that the game content is used for sexual stimulation, and the focus is instead on the user/gamer's choice to proceed "at his or her own risk." Just as the onus for the usefulness of the guide was shifted to the audience, here the content of the game is also shifted to the gamer in terms of responsibility.

A further complication is found in the same forum exchange between YuSaKu and UnholyReaver in which the moral and ethical justification of the game is mixed with the technical validity of the guide. I quote the exchange at length in order to show the intermingling of the moral and technical rationality:

5/1/2008

UnholyReaver: Not a new user at all, but uninterested in the politics of bulletin boards. Why raise a rank or whatever? Congrats on being important on the internet, man. God I wish I could post as many times a day as you. If I could do that AND rape girls in games, no one would ever mess with me.

YuSaKu: . . . Now, you just had to take another shot at me didn't you? Don't accuse me of 'getting off' on a rape game. I don't expect you to know this, because you probably haven't read any of my other FAQs, but I am VERY anti-rape. Tell you what, read this: http://www.honestgamers.com/systems/guide. php?guide_id=4438&platform=PC&abr=PC&gametitle=Virgin+Roster++%7E Shukketsubo%7E Especially the part where I denounce rape. I was planning to add a similar disclaimer to the *Rapelay* FAQ, but as I think I've already said, I'm a very busy man. Well, now that you figured out how to click a mouse button junior, why don't YOU go have fun raping an underage girl in a public toilet. Bet you're doing it one-handed. Don't let mommy catch you.

UnholyReaver: . . . I don't write guides and publish them for games that sicken me. The ONLY reason I'd play a game this short with such limited gameplay is to jerk off to it. Real games have hours of detail, progression of skills, customized characters, equipment, multiplayer... this was intended (and you have played as intended, whatever you say. I didn't say you 'got off' to it, you put that in there) to be played one handed.

YuSaKu: . . . I only published the Rapelay guide because I was sick of seeing it on my desktop, and I knew I wasn't really going to mess with it anymore. Last year I had so many projects on my to-do list that were supposed to be done by now: Translation/FAQ for Kana Okaeri, finish off Segment 2/3 of my Morrowind update, begin write-ups for Kamisama Noiutooritsu and Snow Sakura, re-visit Ai Yori Aoshi, ect. I mean I could go on. But one thing bothered me: Nobody had done anything for Rapelay. mean, the game was translated forever ago, but no FAQ. So I did a write-up and left it so I could sketch in stuff later.

UnholyReaver questions the morals of a man who would publish a guide for a game involving rape, and YuSaKu accuses him of the same. Both gamers claim to be playing the game simply because it's there, because they have the time, but without the investment in the content. Indeed, YuSaKu denounces the time he put into the guide, downplaying it as a project he quickly finished to get it off his desktop. Both gamers emphatically reject the sexual stimulus aspect of the game, instead accusing the other of using the game as pornography, which both men deny.

These gamers are responding to the ethical ramifications of this game from an American cultural standpoint.[10] Their debate and even flaming represents a classic shirking of responsibility for the content of the game; while they may hide behind claims that they don't *enjoy* the content, gamers know better. Gamers seek out games to enjoy the content and challenge themselves. Either YuSaKu and UnHolyReaver are a rare kind of gamer that just plays random games that just happen to come across their desktop, or these gamers are obscuring the real issue of the game (its content) by diverting energy toward flaming and technical problems.

For example, the particular phrase, "Way to give the juicy details without any of the basics," carries a heavy weight as UnHolyReaver accusing YuSaKu of failing to deliver the very purpose of a guide, which is to instruct through details; not to tease the reader with the context of the game without the actual help of moving through it. This is betraying the instructional nature of guide writing. More importantly than that, YuSaKu's technical contribution is to turn the system of the game into an experience, and UnHolyReaver has accused him of distilling that experience so that it is unhelpful for the reader, which further severs their connection to the game instead of bringing them closer to it. For a community trying to find assistance with the game, a spoiler guide demonstrates YuSaKu's failure to fulfill his role as a guide writer. This is an insult to his gaming community. This one comment calls into question his ethos as a technical writer and as a trusted gamer that has put himself into the position of guiding other gamers who need help.

When his technical expertise—how well he wrote the guide—is questioned, he defends it and flames his critic. He justifies his stylistic and technical choices, or at the very least, excuses them because of the nature of guide writing as a hobby rather than a professional job. Yet when it comes to his rationality for playing the game, as well as his enjoyment of its content, he rejects the rationality of pleasure and reduces his technical work to merely a project that he wanted to complete and publish with minimal consideration of content or even style. Thus, the technical writer denounces his own work on many levels as well as denounces a rationality of pleasure in the game due to its morally disturbing content. Such denouncement complicates his agency and authority, shifting the conditions that create either category in such a way as to destabilize how either agency or authority *can ever be constructed.*

More to the point, if YuSaKu is keenly aware of his own ethical participation in the production and distribution of facets of *RapeLay*, as his dialogue demonstrates, then why was he compelled to use technical communication to further circulate

---

[10]   Its original distribution was in Japan, with a separate cultural and ethical context. Yet through third-party distribution, the game has become part of a U.S. cultural gaming landscape. I am less concerned with the intended Japanese audience, as the guide was discovered on American forums and has its own ethical responsibilities from a U.S. technical context.

materials related to the game within a third-party, U.S. context? Katz's warning about the dangers of technological rationality and its bedfellow ethics of expediency perhaps provides some guidance toward an answer: "in our culture, the danger is that technological expediency (unlike happiness for Aristotle, which appears to be only a part and result of virtue) can become the only basis of happiness, can become a virtue itself, and so subsume all ethics under it, making all ethics expedients and thus replacing them" (270). If technological expediency—the ability to produce merely for the sake of production quickly and efficiently—is our culture's only form of happiness, then a part of the fault of distribution lies not in the Japanese gaming company that produced the game but in gamers who play it out of enjoyment.

I do not wish to also sidestep the content issue but rather highlight it through the role of technical communication and its writers, who are a cog in the distribution machine. Katz also speaks to this problem, invoking the rhetorical components of technical communication: "In fact, founded on the ethic of expediency and taken to extremes, rhetoric itself becomes a kind of technology, an instrument and an embodiment of the end that it serves" (268). YuSaKu's guide is such an example. His guide is a rhetorical act, as is his enactment of expertise and authority to publish the *RapeLay* guide, all of which carry with it ethically problematic aspects. Although he denounces his role in the distribution of culturally censored materials, he uses technical writing to instruct and guide gamers to and through the game itself. While he may not have created or distributed the game, his role contributes to its distribution and also comes with rhetorical consequences. Just as Katz is concerned with the role of Just's memo in the carrying out of the Holocaust, even though it was not his vision *per se*, I argue that YuSaKu's technical FAQ is a rhetorical means towards an ethically disturbing end.

YuSaKu is able to deny that his guide "was not intended to be an instruction manual" because he has no professional stake in his work. It is not his job, nor is it his main source of income. Despite his pronouncements about rejecting the content of the game, on his guide as well as his LiveJournal and Facebook page, he is an avid *hentai* and eroge fan, which means he values or enjoys these genres. I believe his denouncement of the content of *RapeLay* the game and the minimization of his guide is an attempt to grapple with the very ethics of his craft. He and other gamers like UnholyReaver also demonstrate that discussions of ethical content and rhetorical and technical writing are happening in places where unrecognized technical communication is talking place.

Implications of *RapeLay* FAQ and *Ad Hoc* Technical Communication

Kimball foregrounds his argument by stating that, "we also need to broaden our field of view to account for technical communication as a practice extending beyond and between organizations" (69), and I believe, like Katz, that there is an ethical obligation to do so not merely to celebrate how well technical communication is used by individuals outside of institutions but because people must take responsibility for the varied ways that technical communication is used ethically both within and outside institutions and organizations. This is especially true in *ad hoc* technical communications where either the technical writer is a freelance agent or institutional guidelines are not present to oversee technical specifications. That's not to say that all organizational guidelines are inherently ethical, as many scholars have demonstrated, but it is the case that organizational guidelines are more likely to produce uniform work that is subject to more critical scrutiny by users and writers alike.

Yet in the *RapeLay* guide scenario, this is not entirely true either. GameFAQs and Neoseeker both have technical guidelines for guides and walkthroughs, which can be quite extensive in terms of technical specifications and formatting.[11] Yet the content and ethical or legal issues concerning games goes unchecked in the *RapeLay* guide at least. That YuSaKu has published other *hentai*/eroge guides would indicate that this is more the case than not. Perhaps the spoiler alert featured on most of YuSaKu's *hentai*/eroge guides serves as a kind of professional code of ethics, yet the farcical tone and his willingness to denounce through message board exchanges representations of rape in games highlights that the spoiler alert does not begin to cover the deeper ethical issues in terms of game content.

What the *RapeLay* guide published by YuSaKu offers, then, is a return to Katz's concern that technical communication uncoupled from content can produce not only ethically problematic works but also further segregate technical communication from its rhetorical responsibilities. Moreover, when technical communication is used as an objective vehicle to convey to an audience what seems like mundane tasks, such as playing a game, the ethical content of the tasks can become obscured and justified. Treating technical communication as objective allows us to supplant the virtues that we ascribe to other forms of rhetorical discourse: "In Hitler's rhetoric, expediency is the necessary good that subsumes all other goods, and becomes the basis of virtue itself" (263). When expediency is the virtue of technology and technical communication, as Katz shows through Just's memo to make portable execution of Jews more efficient, then the ramifications can be dire. Further, when we measure rhetoric on its ability to effect its own ends, even disastrous or harmful ones, then we run a similar risk. What Katz wishes us to reconsider is contentment that *any* end of rhetoric is a good end, if that is indeed what Aristotle implies.

From a disciplinary standpoint, the issue I propose with *RapeLay* is less with its content—although I certainly have a long list of issues with the ethics of the game's content—and more with both the orientation and ethical treatment of technical communication and its usefulness in a contemporary study of technical communication in online *ad hoc* sites. When technical communication is treated simply as a vehicle for successful instruction or completion of a task, technical

---

[11] See, for example, http://www.gamefaqs.com/contribute/ and http://www.neoseeker. com/contribute/ respectively.

communication is arhetorical (windowpane rather than discourse) and thus is dismissed from ethical, rhetorical responsibility. Many scholars have demonstrated why treating technical communication as arhetorical is not, nor has ever been, a viable option (for examples, see Miller, 1993; Katz, 2004; Diehl, 2008; Johnson-Eilola and Selber, 2004 and 2013; and Jeyaraj, 2004). Others (Katz, 2004; Cappola and Karis, 2000; and Markel, 2001 to name a few) have proposed that when we treat technical communication as an extension of deliberative rhetoric in which it is merely a means to an end, we run the risk of allowing the following ideologies to persist: Any technical means that produces its intended ends is good, regardless of ethics. Katz argues that treating technical communication as an extension of deliberative rhetoric, in which any effect is productive, is also not ethically viable. YuSaKu's *RapeLay* guide forefronts these issues and demands that the field confronts these potentially troubling situations when they arise.

The treatment of technical communication in this case is not a problem with the discipline but one in which the discipline should take careful note, especially if we want to update our examination of ethics in technical communication outside of organizational loci. A consideration of ethics online will better prepare students for the range of environments in which technical documentation and ethics takes place today. If gamers continue to feel the need to get guides "off their desktops," then guides will continue to be written based on generic elements and technical accuracy of games, regardless of content. Similarly, as long as gaming sites continue to endorse game content like *RapeLay*, then the orientation of technical communication to games will continue to be either vehicular or deliberative. Neither is a productive lens in the end. Further, as long as gamers look for technical documents to assist them in unethical behavior, then technical communication will likely be subject to market rationalism and potentially nefarious ends. These scenarios exclude the *RapeLay* manufacturers for one main reason: the game content board responsible for regulating content in Japan deemed the game market worthy in Japan. I do not feel it is fair to hold Japan to our standards of gaming, as the colonial implications of this are another topic all together. However, the fact remains that U.S. technical writers are producing documents that endorse gaming practices like rape through guides and walkthroughs. While U.S. culture may not have the same ethics of gaming content production (though I'm well aware of the issues of some of North America's gaming content), we do have an ethics of production, in organizational environs at least. Perhaps with more open awareness and conversation between scholastic, organizational, and online loci where technical communication happens, ethical dilemmas like *RapeLay* might produce, and reframe, renewed conversations about ethics and technical communication.

Conclusion and Discussion

RapeLay is a productive case study for technical communication during this moment in the field's consideration of ethics. The field often works through issues of ethics using rhetorical theory, such as Miller, who argues that, "if consensus theory is right, we might expect all rhetoric to be primarily epideictic, to aim chiefly at reinforcing communal values, 'strengthening adherence to what is already accepted,' in the words of Perelman and Olbrechts-Tyteca" (85). As more recent scholarship like Moeller and McAllister's points out, such a stance isn't quite realistic:

> . . . by uncritically adopting Aristotle's conception of rhetoric, which posits that the means of argumentation shift according to the values of a particular audience, Miller implies that technical communication-as praxis must be similarly constrained. Although this is a generally reasonable claim, it becomes problematic when actually applied because, as Steven Katz points out, most audiences for technical communication today have been trained to expect "just the facts." If today's audience for technical communication holds the objective, neutral transmission and reception of information as its highest good, then technical communicators have little opportunity to envision and enact their own sense of a different social good; the rhetor must, to a significant degree, conform to the audience's ethics. (189)

This is both true and not true. Certainly, we can see that gamers are looking for guidance in playing *RapeLay* because they want the full experience of the game. However, that shouldn't give technical writers an excuse to use unethical community values as the roadmap of technical writing. Thus, we need to evolve past Miller to conceive of technical writing not as merely speaking for the community but as challenging the community as well. As Faber reminds instructors about the teaching of technical communication within academia, "If our students are to be empowered citizens, either as emerging professionals or not, they need to understand the social and political contexts of professional work and the ways professional activities play a role in the future development of their communities," meaning the relationship between writer and audience is reciprocal, even cyclical, rather than strictly hierarchical (332).

　If *RapeLay* can teach us anything, it is that we must reconsider our understanding of the place where technical writing happens. The overlap and slippage between institution and community-based technical communication makes the *RapeLay* guide difficult to categorize. What is clear, however, in spite of the complications of the case study, is that further work with the ethical orientations and frameworks for technical communication is needed. Especially in lieu of the shifting nature of technical genres in gaming communities due to rise in online, community sponsored sites that post instructions and guides for a range of games. While not within the domain of the discipline, technical communications should take note of the technical practices that happen in ad hoc situations outside of professional jurisdiction. If we continue to treat technical practices as the domain of the workplace and the classroom and expect conversations to spring from these domains, then we disclose potentially key sites of technical writing not shaped through disciplines, C.E.O.s, professors, managers, or the legal department. These sites are rich for not only their technical practices, but also and more importantly for their reflection of our disciplinary values and ethics.

What I hope RapeLay leaves us with is a renewed sense in the vigilance we should have as technical writers to note how our work is being perceived and replicated in ad hoc domains that value technical communication. Further, I hope this example ushers a return to Katz's work in order to understand how the false objectivity of technical communication and its masking of problematic ethics in mundane tasks does not come about by war alone, but by any situation in which technical communication serves the needs or the community values of instruction or technical guidance. Indeed, as Zimmerman argues in this collection, the community values in video games are often harnessed for profitability—the unexamined ideologies and desires create affordances that must be examined within an ethical framework. We might take these opportunities to further discuss the role of not merely the technical writer but equally the audience in the production of technical documents, especially in instances where we might not like what we read.

Works Cited

Coppola, N.W. and B. Karis. *Technical Communication, Deliberative Rhetoric, and Environmental Discourse: Connections and Directions*. Atlanta, GA: Elsevier Science, 2000. ATTW Contemporary Studies in Technical Communication.

deWinter, Jennifer. "Just Playing Around: From Procedural Manuals to In-Gaming Training." *Computer Games and Technical Communication: Critical Methods and Applications at the Intersection*. Burlington, VT: Ashgate, 2014. 69–85.

Diehl, Amy, Jeffrey T. Grabill, and William Hart-Davidson. "Grassroots: Supporting the Knowledge Work of Everyday Life." *Technical Communication Quarterly* 17.4 (2008): 413–34.

Dombrowski, Paul M. "Ethics and Technical Communication: The Past Quarter Century." *Journal of Technical Writing and Communication* 30.1 (2000): 3–29.

Driskill, Linda. "Understanding the Writing Context in Organizations." Ed. Johndan Johnson-Eilola and Stuart A. Selber. *Central Works in Technical Communication*. New York: Oxford UP, 2004. 55–69.

Enos, Theresa and Stuart C. Brown, eds. *Defining the New Rhetorics*. Thousand Oaks, CA: Sage, 1993. 79–94.

Faber, Brenton. "Professional Identities: What is Professional about Professional Communication." *Journal of Business and Technical Communication* 16.3 (2002): 306–37.

Faber, Brenton and Johndan Johnson-Eilola. "Migrations: Strategic Thinking About the Future(s) of Technical Communication." Eds. Barbara Mirel and Rachel Spilka. *Reshaping Technical Communication: New Directions and Challenges for the 21st Century*. New York: Routledge, 2002. 135–48.

GameFAQs. *Video Game Cheats, Reviews, FAQs, Message Boards, and More.* CBS Interactive Inc., 2013. Web. 20 Feb. 2013.

———. "GameFAQs Help: Composing Your Guide." *Help.* CBS Interactive Inc, 2013. Web. 20 Feb. 2010.

———. "GameFAQs Help: Formatted FAQs." *Help.* CBS Interactive Inc, 2013. Web. 20 Feb. 2010.

Greene, Jeffrey and Laura A. Palmer. "It's All in the Game: Technical Communication's Role in Game Documentation." *Intercom: Society for Technical Communication* 58.10 (2011): 6–9. Web.

Gurak, Laura. *Cyberliteracy: Navigating the Internet with Awareness.* Boston: Yale UP, 2001.

Herndl, Carl G. and Adela C. Licona. "Shifting Agency: Kairos, Agency, and the Possibility of Social Action." *Communicative Practices in Workplaces and the Professions: Cultural Perspectives on the Regulation of Discourse and Organizations.* Eds. Mark Zachry and Charlotte Thralls. Amityville, NY: Baywood, 2007. 133–53.

Hiltz, Starr Roxanne & Murray Turoff. *The Network Nation: Human Communication Via Computer.* Cambridge: The MIT P, 1993.

Jeyaraj, Joseph. "Liminality and Othering: The Issue of Rhetorical Authority in Technical Discourse." *Journal of Business and Technical Communication* 18.1 (2004): 9–38.

Johnson, Norman A. "Anger and Flaming in Computer-Mediated Negotiations Among Strangers." *Decision Support Systems* 46.3 (2009): 660–72.

Johnson-Eilola, Johndan, and Stuart A. Selber, eds. *Central Works in Technical Communication.* New York: Oxford UP, 2004.

———, eds. *Solving Problems in Technical Communication.* Chicago: University of Chicago, 2013.

Katz, Stephen B. "The Ethics of Expediency: Classical Rhetoric, Technology, and the Holocaust." Eds. Johndan Johnson-Eilola and Stuart A. Selber. *Central Works in Technical Communication.* New York: Oxford UP, 2004. 195–210.

Kimball, Miles. "Cars, Culture, and Tactical Technical Communication." *Technical Communication Quarterly* 15.1 (2006): 67–86.

Kocurek, Carly. "Rendering Novelty Mundane: Technical Manuals in the Golden Age of Coin-Op Computer Games." *Computer Games and Technical Communication: Critical Methods and Applications at the Intersection.* Burlington, VT: Ashgate, 2014. 55–67.

Lea, Martin, T. O'Shea, P. Fung and R. Spears. "'Flaming' in Computer-Mediated Communication: Observation, Explanations, Implications." *Contexts of Computer-Mediated Communication.* Ed. Martin Lea. Hertfordshire, England: Harvester Wheatsheaf, 1992. 89–112.

Markel, Mike. "Ethics and Technical Communication: A Case for Foundational Approaches." *IEEE Transactions on Professional Communication* 40.4 (1997): 284–98.

————. *Ethics in Technical Communication: A Critique and Synthesis.* Westport, CT: Ablex, 2001.

Miller, Carolyn R. "Rhetoric and Community: The Problem of the One and the Many." Sage, 1993. 79–94.

Moeller, Ryan M. and Ken S. McAllister. "Playing with Techne: A Propaedeutic for Technical Communication." *Technical Communication Quarterly* 11.2 (2002): 185–206.

Moor, Peter. "Conforming to the Flaming Norm in the Online Commenting Situation." University of Twenty Student Theses. 2007. Web. 2 Jan. 2013.

Moore, Matthew. "*Rapelay* Virtual Rape Game Banned by Amazon." *Telegraph Online.* 13 Feb 2009. Web. 20 Feb. 2010.

Moore, Patrick. "Intimidation and Communication: A Case Study of the Challenger Accident." *Journal of Business and Technical Communication* 6.4 (1992): 403–37.

Omochikaeri, Hau. "Eroge." *Hau Omochikaeri.* Wordpress, 2009. Web. 15 Oct. 2011.

Perelman, Chaïm, and Lucie Olbrechts-Tyteca. *The New Rhetoric: A Treatise on Argumentation.* Notre Dame: U of Notre Dame P, 1969.

Prima Games. "About Us." *About Us.* Random House Inc., 2013. Web. 20 Feb. 2013.

————. "Our Culture." *About Us.* Random House Inc., 2013. Web. 20 Feb. 2013.

RapeLay. Illusion Soft, 2006. PC.

UnHolyReaver. "Least Detailed FAQs of All Time, Please Help." Message Board. *RapeLay.* n.p 24 April 2010. Web. 20 Feb. 2013.

White, Matthew M. "L2P Noob: Examining Tutorials in Digital Games." *Loading… The Journal of the Canadian Game Studies Association* 6.10 (2012): 30–52.

Winner, Langdon. *Autonomous Technology: Technics-out-of-Control as a Theme in Political Thought.* Cambridge, MA: MIT P, 1977. 100–6.

YuSaKu. "Rapelay (Import) FAQ/Walkthrough Final." Neoseeker, 2007. Web. 20 Feb. 2010.

Zimmerman, Josh. "Psyche and Eros: Rhetorics of Secrecy and Disclosure in Game Developer–Fan Relations." *Computer Games and Technical Communication: Critical Methods and Applications at the Intersection.* Burlington, VT: Ashgate, 2014. 141–56.

PART III
Getting the Player Involved

Chapter 6

Game Design Documents: Changing Production Models, Changing Demands

Anthony T. Sansone

Game design documents (GDDs) are a common documentation tool used by game designers to manage the development process. Typically, GDDs describe, sometimes in great detail, a game's story, mechanics, art direction, level design, sound and music, obstacles and rewards. GDDs borrow from similar documentation in other creative endeavors like film and books for authorial treatments and software engineering for development processes. However, game design differs from all of these artifacts; thus, approaching game design in the same way may not produce a quality product. Game design is a fluid undertaking that changes as development proceeds. The need to manage the process while showing respect for and encouraging the creativity of the skilled specialists involved in the process can be challenging. Designing to an unchanging document impedes creativity and holds the team to expectations that may become impractical as developers find problems as they code (see Christensen et al. for more discussion on this). GDDs need to match the technical maturity of the games they produce and of the developers that produce them. Adapting to these needs requires changes not just to the documentation but also to the methodology of designing games.

Many game design studios are already making these changes. Rather than producing full GDDs, many designers draft simplified design vision documents to indicate the core of the game and establish its tone and feel. Development is changing rapidly, and designers are creating progressively more detailed and refined versions of the game that they have actual players try early and often to find out what does and does not work (see, for example, Armbinder, 8; Dormans, 23; Fullerton et al., 248–77; and Sigman, 15). This evolution in game design results in games that are, at least in theory, more enjoyable for the player and profitable for the developers and publishers.

Not a great deal of research has gone into GDDs. Most research touches on them as part of a broader topic, such as game design theory or player experience (see, for example, Tracy Fullerton's *Game Design Theory* or Ulf Hagen's "Design for Player Experience"). In this chapter, I explain the function, difficulties, and possible future of game design documents. In the first section, I explain what GDDs are and what purpose they serve, reviewing and evaluating four GDDs of well-known commercial titles. The second section addresses difficulties and concerns about GDDs; GDDs suffer from low return on investment since the time spent to create, review, maintain, and retain far exceeds the benefit the development team gets from having commissioned it. The third section investigates what methods are now being used in some instances to design and develop games. Many design studios have moved away from prescriptive design documents into a different methodology of iterative development in service of an overarching vision. Throughout this chapter, I argue that there is a disconnect between what is thought to be good design practice and what currently works as best design practice in the industry. Game design now begins with creating a feeling or concept based on the designer's own experiences around which a design vision can be articulated and then communicated to the team. This concise vision then takes form in prototypes that are rapidly built and playtested until a final version emerges.

What are Game Design Documents?

A GDD should determine what elements will create an enjoyable game for the player and how these elements will be delivered. Joris Dormans, in his 2012 dissertation on *Engineering Emergence: Applied Theory for Game Design*, notes: "[GDDs] typically contain descriptions of a game's core mechanics, level designs, notes on art direction, characters and their backgrounds, etcetera. Some advocate lengthy detailed descriptions covering every detail of a game, while others favor brief documents that capture design targets and design philosophy" (44). Bernd Kreimeier, in his 2003 survey of game design methods, explores how game design and GDDs are interwoven. Any consideration of game design methodology must be, by extension, a discussion as to how game design documents should be written and organized. GDDs appear to be a standard methodology to accomplish that organization, yet what constitutes a GDD is often debated. According to Dormans: "Over the years, writing game design documents has become a common industry practice, although no standard emerged that describes how, when or to what purpose these documents should be written" (44). Though GDDs are commonplace, they exist without any objective standard. They can be structured in any way the designer desires and are unique to the project or company. This causes a number of problems, from training game designers to defining design visions. This is made more complicated because companies are idiosyncratic while simultaneously, workers have varied expectations and frustrations with the genre.

These documents, according to experienced game designer Tim Ryan, ideally evolve as a series of related documents: from concept and proposal, to functional specifications and technical specifications: "A game-concept document expresses the core idea of the game. It's a one- to two-page document that's necessarily brief and simple in order to encourage a flow of ideas" (Part 1, par. 13). This describes the game, its key features, genre, and platform. The lead designer drafts the concept document. It requires a key differentiator: a description of what the game apart from its competition. Ryan notes, "Just know that the longer your introduction, the more diluted your vision will seem" (Part 1, par. 19). The game proposal secures game development resources, building upon the concept and serving as the equivalent of a TELOS feasibility study in project management. The proposal describes how the game can be developed. It involves multiple departments, like marketing, legal, finance, and development.

The functional specification is the actual design of the game, ideally written from the player's perspective. Ryan notes that "In other words, what is seen, experienced or interacted with should be the focus of the document . . . . Readers are really just looking to this document to visualize what's in the game, not how it works" (Part 2, par. 19). Functional specs explain the game's features and functions: narrative, player interface, music, sound, art, game mechanics and level design. The technical specification explains how the game will be developed. Written for lead programmers and technical directors, the technical specifications would include details on platform specifications, linked code libraries, application programming interfaces, artificial intelligence, physics, object data, and data flow. Dormans explains that game development has followed the "waterfall method" of software design: complete each step before starting the next, starting with the design document. "This document is typically written before the software is built and frequently is part of the agreement between contractor and client. The waterfall method assumes that all requirements are known and can be recorded before the software is built" (3). This method obviously affects the type of design documents that Ryan is outlining, one in which the designer anticipates the full project toward the beginning and outlines the full scope to each unit of the development team.

In practice, in the GDDs of the four major titles reviewed, none meet this ideal of four distinct and detailed documents. They were, at best, a combination of the first three document types emphasizing the narrative and gameplay. In looking at the GDDs for *Doom*, *Grim Fandango*, *Planescape: Torment* and *Duke Nukem Forever*, I was not able to identify a common pattern, format or methodology, which according to Dormans, has been one of the most common critiques of using GDDs (44). My question, then, is: what effect does so much remediation have of GDDs as artifacts considered to be central and essential to the creation of a product by a variety of artisans and specialists? A film crew knows how to use cameras, lights and microphones; otherwise, its crew members would not have jobs. A film crew needs a director to tell them what he or she wants to create in tone, image and theme. Game designers work in the same way amongst the developers, artists, and sound engineers. They do not need to be told how to code, draw, or record, but they do need to know what effect the designer wants to create for the player. Once the vision is laid out, the team can be let loose to design based on that vision. The results may require later revision, but the more evocative and comprehensive the original concept, the better for the entire design team and the project.

Four Case Study GDDs

The oldest and best known of the games I researched was *Doom*. Designed in 1992–3 by id Software and released on 10 December 1993, *Doom* delivered innovative gameplay: high levels of emotional response, multiplayer gaming, and offered players the opportunity to do some simple game modification. Moberly and Moeller discuss game modifying practices in their chapter in this collection. *Doom* was the first commercial game released online and was circulated as a free limited version via bulletin board systems. Most of these key features of the game are absent from the GDD, which was notably released online (most GDDs whither in vaults, protected by various legal barriers; for more on security and privacy in the game industry, see Zimmerman in this collection). The seventy-nine-page *Doom Bible* spends two pages on detailed physical and character descriptions of five characters never actually featured in the game. Thirteen pages of narrative and location descriptions follow. Creative director and bible author Tom Hall and John Carmack, *Doom*'s developer, disagreed on this narrative. David Kushner notes in *Masters of Doom*, "'Story in a game,' [Carmack] said, 'is like a story in a porn movie; it's expected to be there, but it's not that important'" (128). Most of the *Doom Bible* has no more than a few sentences per page; it was never completed. Hall eventually was fired from id Software for trying to follow a GDD to which no one wanted to develop (135).

Another high profile title, *Grim Fandango* (Lucasarts, 1998) is a film noir homage based on visual elements of the Mexican Day of the Dead holiday. Its GDD quotes Winston Churchill on its cover: "This report, by its very length, defends itself against the risk of being read" (Schafer). The *Fandango* GDD, a "puzzle document," proffers a *dramatis personae* and provides descriptions of every cut-scene for each of the four years (or acts) of the game. Most importantly, it presents all eighty puzzles in the game as scenes from a book and includes the complete resolution of each puzzle, outlining what actions are needed for the subsequent outcome. The GDD also includes concept art throughout, usually illustrating the narrative passage for the specific puzzle.

The delightfully entertaining and profane *Product Review Packet for Planescape: Last Rites* (the game was released as *Planescape: Torment* on 12 December 1999 by Black Isle Studios) comes quite close to the ideal set of GDDs in one document. It includes the vision, proposal, and functional specifications. Although the table of contents promises it will cover the development of the game, I cannot speak to the technical specifications, since the copy to which I have access does not include these. This may be because they were redacted for circulation; the technical aspects of games are some of the most closely guarded secrets of the game industry. The GDD provides a complete plot, full character studies, and a bestiary with concept art. The plot section summarizes the game in a single sentence: "You are a large, fleshy puzzle box with several locks. Find the keys" (Avallone 33). It also describes the feature set concisely to meet the needs of a game proposal. The game's vision is stated clearly:

> *Last Rites* is a violent, irreverent and breathtakingly beautiful RPG set at the crossroads of the multiverse. We intend to create an amusingly eccentric, mindspinning, cliché-breaking power fantasy splashed with visceral moments of breathtaking violence. . . . Set in the TSR world of Planescape, *Last Rites* will be using the Bioware Forgotten Realms CRPG engine as a base for the game, and Interplay artists and designers will supply the Planescape ambiance. (2)

This GDD includes commentary about the GDD from the protagonist's assistant, Morte. The comical asides make the forty-seven-page document a more enjoyable read.

The last GDD details parts of *Duke Nukem Forever* (Gearbox, 2011). *DNF* was in development for fourteen years, after which, it was released to critical derision (Metacritic). The game had stopped production in May 2009 due to the layoff of the entire production team. Three levels from the GDD were published on the web site Voodoo Extreme (Burnes). In the functional specification section, the designer provides descriptions, walkthroughs, and maps of the three levels. Again, it is important to note for the purposes of this chapter that the released game deviated from this GDD after 3D Realms took over in mid-2010 with changes to tone and plot. This serves to illustrate the common disconnect between the design document and the ways in which games change during the production process.

As game design has matured, the need for solid design tools remains. Some have failed to gain acceptance because, as Dormans notes, the return on investment to learn and use the tools can be perceived as excessive:

> Game design documents are generally considered cumbersome and inefficient; they are seldomly [sic] put to good use. Everybody uses game design documents in their own way. For some designers, these documents capture the creative direction early in the development process, while for others they are a tedious requirement of the job of game designer. For the purpose of the discussion here, no generic wisdom to aid the development of design tools can be extracted from the diffuse practice of writing design documents. (64)

These documents fail to help in the design of games because they can be inflexible, they can take away from development time, and they are often incompatible with more recent advances in software design methodology that better meet design and development needs.

The Fluidity of Game Design

Though GDDs are considered a tried and true method for managing development, they have come under some harsh critique for not responding to the fluid nature of game design. Dormans notes that GDDs are written before prototyping and are analogous to requirements documents in software engineering. This parallel falls apart, though, when one considers that requirements documents are written to meet a client's needs. The traditional game design methodology attempts to meet requirements that are not and cannot be fully defined. The concept comes from one or more designers, but those designers are not the final beneficiaries of the product: the players are. As Katie Salen and Eric Zimmerman state in their book *Rules of Play*, a game designer does not create direct meaning for the player. She creates the possibilities in the game, but the player has a part in creating the experience. The player is at least one step removed from the designer (6–7). Moberly and Moeller use Sicart's critique of proceduralism to discuss how players make meaning in games in the ways that they engage and interact with the rules of the game (pp. 190–91).

Being too prescriptive by creating a GDD may limit the design and designer unnecessarily. As Kreimeier notes, "Detailed recommendations . . . on game design document structure might ultimately be self-defeating: by adding more details to the prescription, the maintenance overhead is only increased" (par. 12). In other words, the designers need to account for what will happen during play. That can only happen during iterative playtesting before the game is finished to work out what players *will* encounter, not just what the designer thinks the player *should* encounter.

Dormans finds three major differences between designing games and software applications using traditional methodology that make the transfer of practices from software to game development. First, game design is iterative. A game will change during production regardless of the developer's skill or experience. A game's behavior is unpredictable as certain characteristics only become evident when implemented. Second, games are not created for the same purposes and audiences as most other software. Software is coded to meet certain requirements of the users of that software. As noted previously, this is untrue in game development, so the need to document prior to development is reduced greatly. Third, most games are not built with future development in mind. Games do not need documentation to be drafted to help future developers. Even with a sequel, the game itself often is built from the ground up. This may seem counterproductive on first thought, but the underlying platforms change regularly (five to seven years for consoles [Game-Machines.com], three to five years for computers [Baird, 1]), so the industry's design practices have adapted to account for rapidly changing technology (for more on this process, please see deWinter and Moeller's introduction to this chapter).

In Hagen's paper on "Designing for the Player Experience," his interview with the lead designer at Massive raises the issue of the utility of the GDD: "Earlier, you wrote a 300 page design document and then you thought 'this will be really fun . . . later.' But 50 percent of what you write . . . isn't useful, because it's just a product of the drawing board, you know" (2). A game's design refines itself as it is developed. Something is tried then tested before the results are documented and changes are made. Constant refinement results in ignoring the original GDD as changes are made; thus, the GDD is continually being revised. The return on investment for a lengthy, prescriptive GDD reduces as development continues. Additionally, as

Christensen et al. note, prescriptive GDDs can severely cripple a design team's perceived sense of agency or ability to contribute to a game's development (7). Arguably, the culture of game development, much like other software development, makes the creation, maintenance and utilization of traditional GDDs a potentially futile effort. Time and attention devoted to large documents does not exist in the high turnover/tight deadline environment of large scale game development and is oftentimes unnecessary in smaller development houses.

Changes in Development

Game development has changed since the GDDs I examine in this chapter were published. The preferred software design methodology prior to the early 2000s, the waterfall method, requires development to complete one step in the process before the next step is started. The first step would be to write a design document. While the waterfall method is still used in stable development environments, the introduction of Agile-based production management correlates to a sense of GDDs' decreasing benefits. As suggested by the GDDs examined earlier, they are considered too comprehensive and word heavy, so few people aside from the lead designers read them. In reflection of both the perceived futility of comprehensive GDDs and of the production problems such GDDs present, designers have found other ways to express and communicate the game's design vision (Hagen, 2; Dormans, 44). GDDs could be viewed much like their considered peers at software development companies: software design documents (SDD). Unfortunately, SDDs lack currency in those environments as well. Venolia et al. note that at Microsoft developers each have their own internal understanding of the product and do not rely on documentation. The views on design documents were varied and inconclusive:

> We received conflicting information about design documents for issues within a team. In the interviews design docs were described almost as write-only media, serving to structure the developer's thinking and as an artifact to design-review, but seldom read later and almost never kept up-to-date. On the other hand our follow-up survey respondents reported a different picture of design documents for issues within the team: their feature teams wrote an average of 8.0 documents in the prior year, and kept 51% of them up-to-date. We were surprised with these numbers and can't reconcile them with the results of the interviews. (4)

Software development started to change with the advent of Agile development practices beginning in 2001 (Agile). The Agile Manifesto resulted from a consensus of writing and helping others to write, code based on four main values: 1) individuals and interactions over processes and tools; 2) working software over comprehensive documentation; 3) customer collaboration over contract negotiation; and 4) responding to change over following a plan. Agile development practices throw the practice of "document *then* develop" out the window. It results in more developers working together to make software or, in this case, software-based games. According to Legault and Weststar, 48.4% of their respondents use Agile development practices, indicating that more developers are moving toward Agile methods (9). Dormans goes so far as to claim that documenting designs has lost its appeal (4).

Game development is also less about creating wholly new technologies. As Nathan Martz of Double Fine Games says in his 2012 Game Developer Conference talk, developing technology is very time consuming (49). There are many solid affordable game engines that allow artists and designers to develop assets in a visual environment with minimal programmer assistance. They also give programmers modular extensible framework to build and test games. Engines provide animation, physics, user interface, modeling, animation and many other features that no longer need to be built from scratch (Epic Games). Since the tools allow more rapid development of game features rather than the technology that provides them, explicit and lengthy documentation is arguably less necessary. As game design is a discipline of constantly improvement performed by highly skilled developers, the design and development practices have become more responsive, communicative and iterative.

A New Documentation Method for Game Design

As illustrated above, GDDs in their traditional form do not always best serve the game design community as a design methodology; the return on investment cannot justify their utility to guide the game development process. Another methodology appears to be superseding the practice of comprehensive documentation and waterfall development. In considering what design methodologies could be, Dormans states that they could not replace the vision of the designer: "[T]he best methods do not restrict a designer's vision. Rather, they should enhance it, enabling them to work faster and create better results. Ideally, design methods also facilitate teamwork and collaboration" (22). Hagen found that game design has become designing for the player experience. This has meant, in practice, designing and developing games by considering how they would be played rather than how they could be designed. Designing for the player has come down to four steps: create vision, communicate vision, prototype concept, playtest the code, and build early and often.

Game design cannot start from nothing. While exhaustive documentation covering most possible outcomes has fallen out of favor, this has not resulted in no documentation at all. All game design starts with an idea. When Hagen asks the senior producer at Dice how they find their ideas, he responds: "You close your eyes and think: What do I find fun? It's as simple as that." (2) Game designers call the central concept by different names: "core," "pillar," "guiding light," "hook," or "focus." (Fergusson, 18; Parkin, n.p.; Martz, 30). For the purposes of this chapter, it will be referred to as the game's vision. The vision provides focus for the design and development of the game. In a postmortem of the game *FTL: Faster Than Light*, creator Matthew Davis explains that the vision guided the project and kept the development on track: "We started with a very vague idea for a concept and used that as a guiding light for the entire project. By having one singular focus we were able to abandon everything else that didn't fit in line with that vision" (quoted in Parkin, par. 3). Massive's lead designer emphasizes the personality and enthusiasm of the designer forms the game. According to Hagen, this "vision bearer" could be a single person but is more often than not a small team. With the vision in hand, designers then need to translate it into game design. Mark Cerny, lead architect for the Sony Playstation 4, laid out his method for game design at the 2002 GDC Europe. The "Cerny Method," as he named it, invests time in pre-production to deliver a prototype and a macro design document to drive production (3). This division first captures the creative output, then produces the game. Cerny's method dispels certain myths of game design, especially the planning and scheduling of game creation. Pre-production is chaotic; the core team refines their idea during an "offline" period of time negotiated with the publisher. This results in two deliverables: the first playable version of the game and a macro design document. While the prototype version is not ready for testing, it offers two levels of a publishable quality within the defined game scope, including player and enemy/obstacle behaviors; complete basic technology, art direction and a touch of the game's variety. The macro design, or vision, document defers from traditional GDDs. Cerny argues a 100-page GDD wastes resources. The designers cannot plan for every possible outcome of the game; game design is not like commercial software design with a known set of requirements to meet. Until the vision is defined, no requirements exist to be met. This means that a GDD also deceives and misleads the team by setting the development direction before verifying the fundamentals. A good vision document should tell the team about the characters, special mechanics, level structure, size, count and contents, and the overarching plot structure in about five pages. This document helps keep proper scope: Progress can be tracked during production, feature creep and drop are prevented and creativity is properly circumscribed. As Massive's lead designer explains to Hagen: "You ask yourself: 'What kind of drama should it be . . . what feeling do you want to bring out?' The design documents you create today are very light stuff. It's more a presentation, a thought, it mustn't be a structured document" (2). Micro design documents are created through the development process. They include script, level maps, enemy descriptions and behaviors, puzzles, and special gameplay descriptions with as much detail as needed.

Communicate the Vision

Once the vision document has been created, it needs to be communicated to the rest of the team. The range of development teams varies wildly from one to more than 200, yet no game development team starts at 200. It grows in distinct phases. During the idea or concept phase, the team is rarely more than ten people. This may grow to twenty or thirty in pre-production. According to Hagen, the team grows to meet the demand of building out content and testing the system in support of the vision. Teams may reach 100 to 200 members during production. The numbers tend to drop toward the end of the development, as the team's efforts are primarily focused on quality assurance and testing (4). The team members are not robots on an assembly line. Though the vision is communicated in pre-production, it does not curtail further creativity. Good designers value all input. The lead designer at Dice explains the best work happens when people are creative within the set boundaries (Hagen, 4).

While designers value ideas, brainstorming is not game design. Design involves selecting a few ideas that work best together as part of creative whole. Designers prevent scope or feature creep by communicating the design vision so the team will understand the type, genre, or feel of the game. The vision can be imparted in a variety of ways: playing off of positive emotional responses to other mediums or concepts or finding a phrase that captures it in a nutshell. This is sometimes referred to as the "elevator pitch:" how designers explain the game to someone during a short elevator ride. Done well, this explanation grips the audience in a way that they get it. Hagen relates that the game director at Starbreeze said: "The pitch is often based on other games . . . so, you say something like this: 'Imagine *Knights of the Temple* and *Riddick* . . . but cartoony!'" Sometimes, the essence of a game can be captured in a single word. The designer of *World of Goo*, Kyle Gabler, uses the word "juicy" to convey the feeling of the game they were creating (5).

The senior designer of *Rock Band*, Dan Teasdale, distills his game's vision to what he called the "One Question." In his talk at the 2009 GDC, he explains that changing the design vision into a question to helps make design choices:

> I needed to get everyone to have the exact same design direction in their heads when making the game. . . . Basically, whenever you're asking yourself questions about focus or scope or direction or content, you ask yourself "The One Question." So if you do it right, you instantly have the entire team making the same types of judgment calls. (Teasdale)

The One Question for *Guitar Hero* was "Does it rock?" For *Rock Band*, the One Question was "Is this an authentic band experience?" These questions affected the name of the game itself, as other choices did not properly relate the ideal.

In addition to distilling the design into a core experience question, a vision can be communicated with similes and exemplars. Comparing the designer's vision of the game with an experience or idea the team members already know can bridge the gap in understanding easily. Two examples from Hagen of how to communicate this vision comes from the art director of *Dead Space*. One exemplar is that all of the lights look like dentist chair lights; they evoke a greater feeling of discomfort. An opposite can also communicate the designer's vision. Using *Dead*

Space again, Hagen notes the art direction specifically stated the game should not look like the science-fiction action genre. Even though *Dead Space* takes place on a spaceship in the future, this statement was to remind the developers their game was not *Halo* or *Mass Effect*.

Sometimes relating the tone and aesthetic of a game can only come from nonverbal means. Simple visuals, like concept artwork or photos of similar themes, can capture the feeling of a game. Complex visuals, like animations or videos, can inspire the development team. Teasdale says a 1970s concert video from The Who inspired the experience they wanted to create with *Rock Band*. Another way to communicate the game is to show the prototype developed during pre-production. This specific prototype is commonly called a "vertical slice," which can make other communication options redundant. Regardless, because the teams grow and change constantly, the vision document and prototype are often made available as part of the onboarding process for new employees and reviewed with each new phase.

Prototyping as Part of the Design Process

The value of prototyping comes out during the creation and communication of the vision. The first prototype comes directly out of the vision and pre-production. The lead designer at Massive explains: "The game itself . . . it's very physical. You should be able to play it . . . you develop it by prototyping it, so you don't take any chances" (quoted in Hagen 1). Dahl and Legre prototyped *Mirror's Edge* heavily, going from concept drawings, to pre-visualization, to animation, to character design (15–27). Likewise, Cerny advises building, borrowing or buying whatever technology will allow rapid prototyping at the start (11). Tyler Sigman, in his postmortem on his game *HOARD*, extols the prototyping's benefits. It allowed his team to design, fail, redesign and playtest quickly but not carelessly. The vision was simple: "You are a dragon, collect as much treasure as you can in 10 minutes!" (80). Game mechanics, game balance and fun were worked out through paper and digital prototypes.

Tracy Fullerton et al., in their book *Game Design Workshop*, also advise prototyping immediately after the vision is developed. Prototyping emphasizes gameplay mechanics, to see if everything works and makes sense to the player. In this book, Eric Zimmerman explains that prototyping starts iterative design: design, test, analyze, refine . . . and repeat (Fullerton et al. 16). Sigman states his fundamental rule of game design: more iterations equal a better game and iterations are maximized through prototyping (78). Iterative design relies on the refinement of a prototype into a final product. The best way to refine a prototype is to let people playtest it. They find ways to accomplish tasks or run into problems that the designers never considered. The process of playtesting provides iterative feedback that is captured in the more dynamic design documents. As Tilley et al. note, playtesting differs greatly from standard usability testing. The goal is not to meet rigid, complete requirements for specific audiences, but to stay true to the vision of the designer. Playtesting seeks to gauge if the game meets the goal of play: an enjoyable player experience.

Conclusion

Contemporary design practices have evolved from the traditional, comprehensive design-document-as-bible to be read and followed to more concise expressions of theme, tone, and vision communicated simply and emotionally. The *de facto* methodology to plan and manage game development—the game design document—has been superseded in some companies. The new methodology comes from advances in software development processes and technology. Game design now begins with a vision of what the game should be about based upon the designer's own experiences: a feeling or concept around which a design vision can be articulated. This vision is then communicated to the broader development team through artifacts that encapsulate primary theme of the game. The designers and developers create a prototype of the game, which provides the basics of the game: mechanics, characters and gameplay. Players then test this prototype and the developers iteratively design improved versions of the prototype and the testing starts anew. Documentation, likewise, exists, but it is developed in small chunks and in response to iterative needs. This process continues in rapid succession until a final version of the game is produced.

Many studios and designers have moved to these methods over the past few years because experience had shown they could not account for everything in a comprehensive initial design. This initial design would change as new quandaries came up during development. So, rather than see this as a bug in the process, they deemed it a feature and moved toward this iterative process as the new default. This approach is now being integrated into game development coursework. For example, Ritter et al. explore how iterative development has worked in the classroom and how design documentation impacts this activity in their chapter of this volume. In future studies, more primary research involving observations and interviews with game designers and developers at all levels and departments as well as playtesters would show if this new way of designing works as effectively as everyone thinks it can. Copies of vision documents and older GDDs can be reviewed to provide some form of chronology and perspective on the transition to this methodology happened or how pervasively it is happening now. Finally, inquiries should be made of designers, community managers, and support staff to see if the changes to the business model of gaming with downloadable content (DLC) require yet another change in how games designs are or should be documented.

Works Cited

Agile Alliance. "The Agile Manifesto." Agile Alliance, February 2001. Web. 5 May 2013.

Ambinder, Mike. "Valve's Approach to Playtesting: The Application of Empiricism." *Game Developer Conference, 2009.* 24 March 2009. Web. 6 May 2013.

Avellone, Chris. "Planescape Last Rites Product Review Packet." Black Isle Studios, 12 July 2007. Web. 26 March 2013.

Baird Equity Research. "IT Systems and Networking." *RW Baird.* 15 August 2011. Web. 7 May 2013.

Birdwell, Ken. "The Cabal: Valve's Design Process for Creating Half-Life." *Gamasutra.* 10 December 1999. Web. 5 May 2013.

Burnes, Andrew. *Duke Nukem Forever Development Documents.* Voodoo Extreme. IGN, 11 May 2009. Web. 30 April 2013.

Cerny, Mark. "Methods. Keynote." *Game Developer Conference Europe. 2002.* Web. 4 May 2013.

Christensen, David M., Jason L. Cootey, and Ryan M. Moeller. "Playing In Genre Fields: A Play Theory Perspective on Genre." *Proceedings of the 25th Annual ACM International Conference on Design of Communication.* ACM, 2007.

Dahl, Tobias and Mikael Lagré. "Creating First Person Movement for Mirror's Edge." *Game Developer Conference China 2009.* 11 October 2009. Web. 5 May 2013.

Dean, Paul. "Retrospective: Doom." *Eurogamer. Gamer Network.* 15 January 2012. Web. 30 April 2013.

deWinter, Jennifer, and Ryan M. Moeller. "Introduction: Playing the Field: Technical Communication for Technical Games." *Computer Games and Technical Communication: Critical Methods and Applications at the Intersection.* Burlington, VT: Ashgate, 2014. 1–13.

"Doom Intro." *YouTube.* Google. 7 November 2011. Web. 30 April 2013.

"Doom/Walkthrough." *StrategyWiki.* 9 April 2006–20 October 2010. Web. 30 April 2013.

Dormans, Joris. *Engineering Emergence: Applied Theory for Game Design.* University of Amsterdam. Dissertation (2012). Web. 2 May 2013.

Epic Games. "Features." *Unreal Engine. Epic Games,* n.d. Web. 6 May 2013.

Fullerton, Tracy, with Christopher Swain, and Steven S. Hoffman. *Game Design Workshop.* Burlington, MA: Morgan Kaufmann, 2008.

Hagen, Ulf. "Designing for Player Experience: How Professional Game Developers Communicate Design Visions." Södertörns University, Huddinge, Sweden. 2010. Web. 3 May 2013.

Hall, Tom. *Doom Bible.* id Software, 28 November 1992. Web. 26 March 2013.

Kreimeier, Bernd. "Game Design Methods: A 2003 Survey." *Gamasutra. UBM Tech,* 03 March 2003. Web. 4 May 2013.

Kuchera, Ben. "Why Your Games Are Made by Childless, 31 Year Old White Men, and How One Studio Is Fighting Back." *The Penny Arcade Report. Penny Arcade, Inc.*, 14 April 2013. Web. 2 May 2013.

Kushner, David. *Masters of Doom: How Two Guys Created an Empire and Transformed Pop Culture.* New York: Random House Digital, Inc., 2003. eBook.

Martz, Nathan. "Pitching Perfect Prototypes." Game Developer Conference 2012, 8 March 2012. Web. 5 May 2013.

Metacritic. "Duke Nukem Forever." 14 June 2011. Web. 25 May 2013.

Moberly, Kevin, and Ryan M. Moeller. "Working at Play: Modding, Revelation, and Transformation in the Technical Communication Classroom." *Computer Games and Technical Communication: Critical Methods and Applications at the Intersection.* Burlington, VT: Ashgate, 2014. 189–207.

Parkin, Simon. "Designing Without a Pitch: An *FTL* Postmortem." *Gamasutra. UBM Tech*, 26 March 2013. Web. 3 May 2013.

Ryan, Tim. "The Anatomy of a Design Document, Part 1: Documentation Guidelines for the Game Concept and Proposal." *Gamasutra. UBM Tech.* 19 October 1999. Web. 2 May 2013.

Ritter, Christopher, Sameer Ansari, Scott Daner, Sean Murray, and Ryan Reeves. "From Realism to Reality: A Postmortem of a Game Design Project in a Client-Based Technical Communication Course." *Computer Games and Technical Communication: Critical Methods and Applications at the Intersection.* Burlington, VT: Ashgate, 2014. 283–306.

Salen, Katie, and Eric Zimmerman. *Rules of Play.* Cambridge, MA: MIT P, 2004.

Schafer, Tim, Peter Tsacle, Eric Ingerson, Bret Mogilefsky and Peter Chan. *Grim Fandango Puzzle Document.* LucasArts. 30 April 1996. Web. 26 March 2013.

Sengers, Phoebe. "Autobiographical Design." Proceedings from the Experience-Centred Design Workshop. In Ext. Abstracts, CHI 2006, ACM Press (2006), 1691–4. Web. 5 May 2013.

Sigman, Tyler. "Guerilla Prototyping: A Design Post-mortem of the Arcade Strategy Game HOARD." *Game Developer Conference 2012.* Web. 6 May 2013.

Speyrer, David, and Brian Jacobson. "Valve's Design Process for Creating Half-Life 2." *GameDeveloper Conference 2006.* Web. 5 May 2013.

Stead, Chris. "The 10 Best Game Engines of This Generation." *IGN. IGN Entertainment.* 15 July 2009. Web. 6 May 2013.

Swift, Kim and Erick Wolpaw. "Integrating Narrative and Design: A Portal Post-Mortem." *Game Developer Conference 2008.* Web. 4 May 2013.

Teasdale, Dan. "Dirty Deeds Done Dirt Cheap: Design Lessons Learned from Rock Band (Designer's Cut)." *Game Developer Conference 2009.* Web. 3 May 2013.

Tilley, Alex, Carmen Blandino, and Jennifer deWinter. "Developing a Testing Method for Dynamic Narrative." *Computer Games and Technical Communication: Critical Methods and Applications at the Intersection.* Burlington, VT: Ashgate, 2014. 125–40.

Venolia, Gina, Rob DeLine, and Thomas LaToza. "Software Development at Microsoft Observed: It's About People ... Working Together." *Microsoft, 2005*. Web. 3 May 2013.

"Video Game Consoles." *Game-Machines.com*. XAdvance Web Publishing, n.d. Web. 7 May 2013.

Zimmerman, Josh. "Psyche and Eros: Rhetorics of Secrecy and Disclosure in Game Developer–Fan Relations." *Computer Games and Technical Communication: Critical Methods and Applications at the Intersection*. Burlington, VT: Ashgate, 2014. 141–56.

Chapter 7

Developing a Testing Method for Dynamic Narrative

Alex Tilley, Carmen Blandino, and Jennifer deWinter

Designed for use on task-oriented software such as word processors and account managers, usability is defined by the ISO 9241-11 standard as the "extent to which a product can be used by specified users to achieve specified goals with effectiveness, efficiency, and satisfaction in a specified context of use." It reflects the goals of the task-oriented software designer to create a product such that a user can use it without hindrance, hesitation, questions, or frustration. Each usability criteria (effectiveness, efficiency, and satisfaction) can be evaluated quantitatively; effectiveness can be measured in completion rates and errors, efficiency from time on task, and satisfaction using any of a number of standardized satisfaction questionnaires. As Nacke describes it, usability has concrete, measurable aspects and therefore has a foundation based on numbers. However, when applied to the testing of games and play, this type of usability test does not account for the experiences encoded into the design. Further, this limitation is more highlighted in games that have dynamically generated content. In this chapter, we discuss the tension between usability testing and playtesting through the case study of our game *Shattered Sky,* a game created by Holly Fletcher, Zach Garbowitz, Thane Sanford, and Alex Tilley. This game provides players with a dynamically generated narrative in response to their choices, and the team had to check for user engagement and enjoyment.

From the beginning, the *Shattered Sky* team sought to push the boundaries of computer game technology in order to create a truly dynamic narrative. Set at a diplomatic summit, it cast the player as the leader of a nation plunged into an international crisis, which stood to reshape the world's balance of power. The player's goal: To ensure the player's nation emerges dominant from the summit through political maneuvering, espionage, blackmail, and even murder. While this may sound like standard computer game fare, the technological underpinnings of *Shattered Sky* made it unique in its genre. Instead of weaving a linear or branching storyline, *Shattered Sky* generated a dynamic narrative, giving each non-player character the ability to act and react just as the player could through the power of goal-based AI. Thus, in place of a single storyline, *Shattered Sky* possessed hundreds upon hundreds of potential narratives, ensuring that each playthrough of the game was a different experience.

However, the wide range of potential narratives within *Shattered Sky* proved difficult to test. While traditional linear or branching storylines could be evaluated on a case-by-case basis, the sheer number of possible narratives in *Shattered Sky* was simply so large that such an analysis was impractical. A new evaluation method was required; one that fit *Shattered Sky*'s unusual testing requirements. First, the evaluation method needed to be objective and quantified, in order to be replicable. Second, the evaluation method had to be concise as it must be run on a large number of tests in a relatively short time. Third, it had to determine if a given narrative is both interesting and engaging—in essence, if it is a good story. With these criteria in hand, *Shattered Sky*'s development team began to examine traditional usability testing methods in search of an evaluation method for *Shattered Sky*.

Games, Narrative, and Engagement

In order to design an evaluation system capable of classifying narrative as good or bad, we had to first define narrative. Ip argues that it is important to draw a clear distinction between stories, plots, and narratives, as these are often incorrectly bundled together; therefore, this study will use Abbott's definitions of the three terms, definitions that are reinforced by Ip in game studies. They state that stories are a chain of events, plots are organized events, and narratives are representations of events. Ip puts these definitions in the context of media, claiming "the story is the information about an event or sequence of events (typically linear), the plot being the causation and links between events, whereas the narrative is the unique way in which story is being presented to the audience" ("Part 1" 107). In the context of *Shattered Sky*, narrative is the most important to evaluate for it encompasses story, plot, and how well these two game elements are presented to the player. All of these elements are critical to the success of the game.

Evaluating whether a given narrative is enjoyable is no easy task; each person has their own preferences for what they find to be gratifying. According to McCabe and Peterson in their article "What Makes a Good Story?" the variance in opinion over what is or is not an enjoyable story prevents any story from being tested in such a manner, for there can be no "enjoyability standard" to test the narrative against. To institute such a standard is to privilege one specific definition of *enjoyable* above all others, greatly reducing the effectiveness and usefulness of any resultant evaluation. Thus, the enjoyment of a given narrative cannot be directly calculated without heavily biasing any results. Methods exist by which one can indirectly evaluate enjoyment of a narrative and to gather information on the factors that viewers subconsciously use in determining their levels of satisfaction. Narrative engagement, the ability of the work to occupy the mind of the viewer, is by and large the most influential of these factors and can be directly linked to story enjoyment. Busselle and Bilandzic claim, "narrative experiences that are more engaging [and] result in greater enjoyment and greater effects"

(328). Unlike enjoyment, engagement is a quantifiable concept according to Green and Brock and therefore can be evaluated numerically through the evaluation of its component parts. By framing enjoyment as a derivative of engagement, one can measure an audience's enjoyment of a narrative without many of the problems raised by a direct assessment. In order to document viewers' engagement with a given piece of narrative, we broke engagement down into its component parts: transportation, identification, and flow. Each of these influences the construction of mental models of meaning, the methods by which audience members understand narrative (as described by Graesser, Olde, and Klettke) and thus dictates their level of engagement. By understanding each of these terms and how to evaluate them, we could begin to construct a model to gauge general narrative engagement and thereby narrative enjoyment.

The first step in a good narrative is to seize the audience's attention, to induce such focus on the story that they lose track of their surroundings, time's passage, and ultimately themselves. This process of focus shift, called "flow" by Csikszentmihalyi, occurs as the audience becomes completely entranced with a given narrative to the point that all they wish to do is continue experiencing it. While flow can occur in non-narrative situations, such as playing sports, it is particularly important for immersion in narrative. Gerrig claims that unlike sports or other such activities, stories provide alternatives to the audience's immediate reality, which disrupt the influx of real-world information; the brain can only process a fixed amount of information at any given time. When flow occurs, it is the real world perceptions of environment and self that are discarded, leaving the mind a blank canvas. With no sense of surroundings or self, the audience is open to the alternate realities presented in the narrative. The truths of the presented narrative's world take the place of reality within the mind of the audience, a process dubbed "transportation" by Green and Brock. Gerrig and Rapp claim that this effect is so strong that it requires conscious effort by the audience to disbelieve the realities presented in an experienced narrative, a reaction they describe as "the willing construction of disbelief." Nonetheless, the *degree* to which a given narrative immerses an audience, and thus the engagement it offers, varies greatly from story to story.

While transportation places the viewer within the alternate reality of the story, further components are necessary to maintain this immersion. Identification is one such factor wherein the viewer strongly identifies with a character or assumes his or her position. Cohen describes identification as when a viewer ceases "to be aware of his or her social role as an audience member and temporarily (but usually repeatedly) adopts the perspective of the character" (251). In terms of Segal's Deictic Shift Theory, the audience members switch to the time and location of the narrative, effectively re-iterating Green and Brock's transportation process and keeping them within the subjective world of the story's characters. A well-known example of this can be found in George Lucas's original Star Wars trilogy in the opening scenes of *Episode IV: A New Hope*. While the opening scenes of space combat bombard the viewer with vivid imagery of an alien existence, transporting them in a visual sense, these visuals alone are not enough to prevent willful disbelief among the audience. To prevent this, Lucas introduces the characters of C3PO and R2-D2 to the chaotic scene. These characters' antics allow the audience to immediately identify with them in this otherwise foreign environment, keeping them engaged long enough for the rest of the world to become familiar and enabling identification with characters once deemed strange or incomprehensible.

The relationship between flow, transportation, and identification is one of synergy: a complex fusion of cognitive events that result in narrative engagement. Together, Bilandzic and Busselle claim that these aspects of narrative engagement siphon cognitive and emotional resources away from their previous uses and invest them in an observed story. If even one were to falter, the audience's engagement with the story would suffer greatly for it. Distractions resulting in the loss of flow force real world facts back into the audience's mind, facts that often clash with the truths of the story world. The sense of realism within the narrative vanishes, which in turn decreases narrative engagement according to Hall. Furthermore, since the audience's sense of "being there" is decreased, the degree to which they are transported by the narrative and identify with its characters suffers as well. Anything that detracts from one of these important narrative aspects detracts from all of them.

Play and Dynamic Narrative Assessment

As the *Shattered Sky* development team discovered, the interaction between traditional usability testing and narrative is a complicated one. According to Pagulayan and Steury, many current approaches to computer game testing fail to differentiate computer games from other software products and therefore test traditional usability rather than the goals of the designer. While these traditional usability standards are sufficient for certain aspects of the game, such as the interface and peripherals, they fail to take into account the emotional responses evoked by gameplay. Patrick Jordan claims that such testing relegates player roles to that of users and downgrades games to tools: One simply to be used by the other to achieve a very defined, concrete goal. This completely neglects the enjoyment of the user in reaching that goal, the experiences they have along the way. In a sense, traditional usability cares only about the destination, whereas games focus on the journey.

Shattered Sky's focus on this journey, the actual play of the game, makes it even more difficult to develop a method for evaluating how much players enjoy it. While the narratives found in *Shattered Sky* share many similarities with those found in novels, theater and films, they must contend with one additional narrative influence: that of play. Play fundamentally alters the nature of narratives within its mental space, propagating certain narrative elements while discarding others. The fusion of narrative and play must be treated as a separate entity rather than the sum of its parts and thus requires new models for evaluating the stories it contains.

As with narrative, it is important that one define the concept of "play" before one undertakes an exploration of its complex relationship with stories. Far too often, claims Klabbers, the term "play" is treated as analogous to games or simulations, when in fact it should be treated as an umbrella term for all human activities that fit its unique definition. While not all agree on what that definition is, this paper uses that created by Huizinga in his book *Homo Ludens: A Study of the Play-Element in Culture*:

> Play is a voluntary activity or occupation executed within certain fixed limits of time and place, according to rules freely accepted but absolutely binding, having its aim in itself and accompanied by a feeling of tension, joy and the consciousness that it is "different" from "ordinary life." (28)

According to Huizinga, play does not have a singular definition; rather, it possesses traits that identify it as such. In the context of Huizinga's definition of play, what we need to emphasize here is a fixed temporal and spatial location, a set of governing rules, and a distinct division between play and ordinary life. Through careful measurement of Huizinga's play-traits, the otherwise abstract concept of play can be given qualitative and quantitative form within a specific medium, such as games.

At first glance, the relationship between the characteristics of play and narrative seems to be a purely synergistic one, with various aspects of play assisting in narrative processes. For instance, play's differences from ordinary life imply that some level of narrative transportation is occurring among the players, facilitating engagement with their activity. Similarly, the voluntary nature of play implies a focus on the activity at hand, focus akin to that required for narrative flow. Yet these synergies are the exception and not the rule when it comes to play-narrative interactions. According to Juul, the relationship between play and narrative is best described as complementary, not symmetrical, with play both assisting and detracting from narrative engagement. Within computer games, a small subset of play, this effect is even more pronounced, for they provide the illusion of interactive narrative, a fallacy, Frasca claims, that is born out of games' promise of simultaneously providing player freedom and maintaining narrative coherence. The trouble with games is ultimately their interactive nature—the ability of the player to change the narrative space he or she engages with. For more on this complication, please see Moberly and Moeller's chapter in this collection. Interactivity is a defining aspect of games and can act as both a help and a hindrance to engaging storytelling. The interactivity provided by computer games gives the player the ability to bond with characters on an unparalleled level. The presence of a physical representation of the player, or a representation that the player claims ownership of, serves as a site of continuous identification for the audience. Silverman et al. claim that the on-screen avatar allows fictional characters to stand in for viewers, causing them to slowly accept the avatar as a representation of themselves. Thus, players *become* their avatars rather than simply identifying with them, enabling narrative transportation on a grand scale. According to Rehak, identification in computer games differs from that in literature and film due to the fact that its view is a "present one," one where the audience does not say, "That's what I *see*" but rather "That's what I *do*." This participatory aspect of identification promotes greater levels of engagement than is possible in other mediums.

However, the relationship between games and narrative is not entirely complementary; many aspects of games inherently harm the stories they try to tell. Systems within games often break those game's narratives, producing elements that constantly remind players that they are just that, players of a game. User interface (UI) elements are an excellent example of this, for they provide data the player would not see if they were truly acting as characters within the presented world. This discrepancy, Rehak admits, forces players to constantly flip between the role of participant and observer, making them aware of both themselves and their avatar. It disrupts narrative transportation and identification by forcing the player to exist in a world that is both real and false at the same time, which in turn reduces narrative engagement.

The mechanics of games do far more than dispel the illusion of presence in an alternate world. Bosses must be beaten, puzzles must be solved to progress; these objects serve as temporal roadblocks to story development. Due to these obstacles, the potential emotional response of the player to events in the story cannot be choreographed; there is simply no way to determine when the player progresses to certain narrative points. The interactive element of games introduces an unknown variable into all potential stories crafted within that narrative space: the actions of the player. These actions, Glassner claims, are typically uninformed compared to the professional wisdom of the story creators, resulting in players choosing the blandest, most indistinct middle ground for fear they might disrupt what is to come. In doing so, the player becomes responsible for breaking their own engagement, a risk that cannot be mitigated without the removal of the interactivity that makes game narratives unique. A series of incompatibilities arise in these cases, as we discuss below.

The Incompatibility of Narrative, Play, and Effectiveness

When applied to computer games as a whole, rather than just their interfaces, the usability criteria of effectiveness stands in direct opposition to several tenants of both narrative and play. Defined by Rubin and Chisnell as "the extent to which the product behaves in the way that users expect it to and the ease with which users can use it to do what they intend" (4), the concept of effectiveness makes several assumptions about the nature of the evaluated product that are inappropriate for narrative and play as a whole. First, it assumes that users' external goals are their primary purpose for interacting with the product, and that this will remain true throughout their experience with it. Yet if their goal is to enter a state of play, as is the case in a computer game, this assumption quickly falls through since the goal of the players is then simply to continue within the magic circle of the product. This is similar to Hassenzahl's description of "action model," where goals are determined on the fly and the product becomes an end unto itself. In such situations, blanket assessment of user goals is impossible, for few users share the same goal at any point in time. Second, the rubric of effectiveness implies a level of definition that seldom exists within the realms of play, narrative, and other enjoyable activities. According to Brandtzeg et al., such pursuits are "not seen as the engagement in . . . series of well-defined tasks, achieving well-defined goals. Rather, [they] consist of an interwoven complexity of activities in dynamic environments with several actors and conflicting interests" (56). For instance, the narrative terms of flow, transportation, and identification cannot exist within a vacuum; each concept relies on the others to function in some capacity. To try and evaluate the efficiency of identification, flow and transportation would also need to be evaluated, which would render the evaluation useless since its entire goal is to single out variables in the user experience.

Due to this contradiction and that discussed above, the usability criteria of effectiveness are unsuitable for use in evaluating play and narrative, particularly within the context of a computer game such as *Shattered Sky*. If the user enters the play experience with the goal of simply completing the game, and that goal remains constant throughout the experience, then the game has categorically failed to engage the player. If *Shattered Sky* engages players and thus causes them to assume goals within the game, then efficiency's assumption of a constant external goal is violated and the criterion loses its usefulness. Therefore, the usability criterion of effectiveness is incompatible with the evaluation of dynamic narratives like that present in *Shattered Sky*.

The Incompatibility of Narrative, Play, and Efficiency

The usability criterion of efficiency suffers from many of the same problems effectiveness does when evaluating narrative and play, largely due to the fact it makes similar assumptions. Rubin and Chisnell describe it as "the quickness with which the user's goal can be accomplished accurately and completely" (4). Once again, it incorrectly assumes that the user's external goals are the primary purpose for using the product, and that these goals are clearly defined. In addition, efficiency assumes that hasty completion of goals correlates to positive experiences in the user, a claim that is seldom true within the context of narrative and play. According to Adams and Rollings, such emphasis on quick completion discourages complex planning in favor of brute force solutions, a trait particularly harmful in an intrigue-based game such as *Shattered Sky*. It is important to remember that play is a means unto itself; by Huizinga's definition, it does not have a goal that efficiency can evaluate. For instance, within *Shattered Sky* it is entirely possible for the player to end the game, achieving their external goal of game completion, within the first minute of play. However, this brute force method undermines the internal goals generated by the player within the game, creating a narrative that is neither engaging nor enjoyable. Efficiency is ultimately a poor criterion in testing narrative and play.

The Incompatibility of Narrative, Play, and Satisfaction

While the human-centric nature of the usability criteria of satisfaction allays much of tension between usability, narrative, and play, it cannot escape its work-based origins. Defined by Rubin and Chisnell as the "user's perceptions, feelings, and opinions of the product" (4), satisfaction is the only aspect of usability that humanizes users, treating them as people rather than task-oriented machines. This is certainly an improvement over the concepts of effectiveness and efficiency but not enough to overcome the work-bias inherent in usability standards. Usability's bias translates into skewed models of meaning, models rooted in the same flaws possessed by the ideas of effectiveness and efficiency. According to Blythe and Hassenzahl, satisfaction's flaw is that it aims to prevent pain rather than promote enjoyment, making the fatal assumption that the absence of the former translates to the latter. In doing so, the vast fields of narrative, engagement and play are condensed into the single oversimplified concept of satisfaction, and even this exists solely in terms of work. Ultimately satisfaction and thereby usability as a whole deals with the question "Does it work?" rather than the more important question: "Is it fun?"

Affective Usability, Playability, and Playtesting

Although traditional usability is largely unsuitable for the evaluation of a narrative-based game such as *Shattered Sky*, the field of affective usability shows greater promise. Finucane et al. claim that logic, the favored attribute of traditional usability, is seldom the sole factor in the decision making process. Instead, people use what the researchers deem an affective heuristic, the evaluation of an object's representation based upon positive and negative feelings associated with the object. Thus, while one path may be the logical choice, some might refuse to take it due to negative associations with objects along the way. In the context of a testing environment, this can be disastrous, returning unfavorable results even when the product is sound. Affective usability testing not only helps alleviate tester bias, but according to Hassenzahl, Burmester, and Beu, it also evaluates user enjoyment with the product. Consequently, it seeks to move away from the confines of the ISO 9241-11 standard, instead taking a more user-centric, holistic approach to usability. In so doing, affective usability reduces many of the incompatibilities between narrative, play, and itself.

When applied to games in particular, affective usability testing morphs into methodologies even farther removed from traditional usability concepts. Dubbed playability by Jarvinen et al., these new systems encompass "a collection of criteria with which to evaluate a product's gameplay or interaction." This definition is supported by Fabricatore et al.'s assertion that "playability is the instantiation of the general concept of usability ... determined by ... understanding and controlling gameplay"; in essence, playability is usability tailored to games. The core approach of the method is the same; however, the specifics are altered to suit the interactive medium. For instance, in Jarvinen et al.'s model, playability replaces the rubrics of effectiveness, efficiency, and satisfaction with functional, structural, audiovisual, and social playability, while in Desuvire et al.'s, it incorporates game play, game story, game mechanics and game usability. While these criteria are still subject to the same quantitative testing traditional usability components are, the focus is shifted away from the end goal in favor of the path to said end goal. In short, testing becomes less about the user's destination and more about the journey.

Nevertheless, playability criteria are far from the perfect method for testing a narrative based game such as *Shattered Sky*. Though each criterion covers an important aspect of the game, there are no measures to cover the game as a whole, the general experience as compared to the specific component parts. Neither affective usability testing nor playability testing adequately covers this overall experience. This is where playtesting comes in.

Playtesting is the overall evaluation of a computer game's fun factor, the overall enjoyment of the game. According to former IGDA Chairman Schell, playtesting deals with overarching issues in game mechanics, pacing, narrative and gameplay, allowing designers to test their implementation of the design document, to see if their designs on paper match their designs in practice. While this may seem similar to playability testing, playtesting's scope is quite different: it focuses on the overall game rather than its components. In essence, playtesting deals with a game on a macro level, whereas playability testing deals with a game on the micro level. Of course, given the non-standard nature of most playtesting methods, this is not always the case.

Ultimately, playtesting is primarily a subjective form of testing, utilizing a wide variety of methods to gain valuable insight into the strengths and weaknesses of one's game. There are numerous ways one can conduct playtesting, some of which are informal and qualitative, and others which tend to be more structured and quantitative. And the corporate models for doing so are widely varied, from formal playtesting career tracks to the exploitation of fan communities as free labor (see Zimmerman). Yet according to Fullerton et al., one thing all forms of playtesting have in common is the end goal: how to gain useful feedback from players in order to improve one's game. The methods used to do so should be tailored to the game being tested rather than to a standardized methodology.

Practical Adaptations

Any system developed to test dynamic narrative must evaluate several critical areas while avoiding the computer science bias of traditional usability testing. First, we determined that the testing method must evaluate the flow, transportation, and identification of the tester, for these factors are crucial to an engaging story. Second, the tests must check for tension between gameplay and narrative, for games that emphasize dynamic storytelling require a level of immersion not possible with such conflict. Finally, the evaluation method must integrate the concepts of playability and playtesting to minimize the influence of results-oriented usability testing.

The following ten criteria represent an attempt to fuse traditional usability standards with narrative evaluation standards. They are to be integrated with the post-playtesting questionnaire, focusing the playtester on critical components of successful narrative engagement. This fusion of evaluation criteria coupled with the standardization of traditional playtesting will hopefully result in a superior methodology for evaluating games employing dynamic storytelling. At the very least, it represents a step forward in the way narratives are assessed in interactive media. Following the guidelines that we created to test our game, we discuss the initial results.

1. **The game controls and interface were straightforward and easy to use:** This criterion is based on Rehak's claim that intrusive UI forces the player out of their narrative immersion, forcing them to jump back and forth between reality and the fictional world. In narrative-based games this is particularly unwelcome, as it prevents transportation and reduces engagement. Thus, game designers must assess their current UI and controls to ensure that the interface and control scheme are as unobtrusive as possible.

2. **The game held my focus:** Focus, according to both Csikszentmihalyi and Hall, is essential for maintaining narrative engagement. Players must maintain focus on the game in order to be transported to the narrative world within it. Should focus be lost, real world facts re-enter the mind of the player, breaking engagement and therefore decreasing enjoyment. Game designers must ensure that their products hold the focus of the player such that this does not occur.

3. **I felt immersed in the game world and story:** This statement aims to gauge the player's transportation into the narrative world. Such reality shift, according to Gilbert, causes players to immerse themselves in the game universe in a manner that requires a conscious effort to break. In many ways, this is testing the "vision" of the game—that nebulous concept that designers and development teams define and design into a game (see Sansone for more about the importance of this). Not only does this increase engagement, and thereby enjoyment, but it causes players to overlook small errors in game that would otherwise be obvious.

4. **I identified with the character I played:** Ideally, the player will identify with his or her avatar, the character he or she plays in the game. Cohen claims that this transports the player into the place of the character, keeping

them immersed in the story. This reinforces both transportation and focus, resulting in greatly increased engagement on the part of the player.

5. **I identified with at least one of the non-player characters:** If the players do not identify with their character, they may still gain the benefits of Cohen's identification if they identify with one of the NPCs. Much like R2D2 and C3PO, identifying with minor characters can act as a stabilizer for transportation and focus.

6. **I thought the characters were well-developed, with their own histories, personalities, and goals:** In order for players to identify with characters, they must view them as people rather than synthetic constructs. By analyzing the strength of each character in the game, designers can gauge the game narrative's potential for identification. If players perceive characters as flat or interactions artificial, even the most interesting game can struggle to maintain narrative engagement.

7. **I understood the role of my actions on the development of the story:** There are two purposes to this question: one, it examines whether the playtester understood the story or not, and two, it evaluates the player's feeling of control over the story. Glassner claims that enjoyable choices are informed choices and that the player should understand the implications of their choices when presented with them. Otherwise, the player feels betrayed by the designer, greatly decreasing their enjoyment of the game.

8. **I had a clear goal the entire game:** It is critical that the player have a clear goal to guide their decision making as they play through the game. Adams and Rollings state that players should always have some overarching goal otherwise they will become distracted and irritable. This statement evaluates whether a game successfully provides such a goal to the player.

9. **I felt the conclusion I reached reflected my decisions in the game:** One of the potential pitfalls of games utilizing dynamic narrative is that the non-player characters may decide the fate of the player without sufficient input from said player, making decisions that dictate end-game conditions behind the player's back. Adams and Rollings claim that the players should be aware of the position they are in as they play the game as this allows them to make informed decisions about future choices.

10. **I did not feel constrained by the game:** Running into artificial constraints can easily break narrative transportation, snapping the player back into the reality that they are simply playing a game. Care must be taken to avoid this clash between narrative and play, and this statement evaluates designers' success or failure at achieving this.

We developed a method in which there were two observers during the playtest in addition to entry and post-testing interviews with the players. While additional research is certainly needed, *Shattered Sky*'s testing method shows promise as a story-focused playtesting rubric. Each section of the test performed as expected:

the pre-test weighed the importance of tester responses, the quantitative evaluation provided standardized data on important aspects of the game, and the follow up interview questions put this data in context of player enjoyment and replayability. However, with only fifteen playtests across three builds, sample sizes were not large enough to conclusively prove the success of *Shattered Sky*'s playtesting method. The team of four had only six months to develop a new game, and these limited resources and time accounts for the lack of further iterations. Moreover, given the unpolished nature of the builds tested, most responses to evaluations of story engagement were biased by technical issues. Yet even with these complications, several patterns emerged in playtester responses that speak to the validity of the playtesting method and the need for future research into playtesting (as opposed to usability testing).

Negative Effects of Interface on Narrative Engagement

The first pattern to emerge from *Shattered Sky*'s playtesting was just how severely a clunky interface could disrupt narrative engagement and general game enjoyment. Initial playtests of *Shattered Sky*, which used an unwieldy point-and-click interface, detracted from the identification and transportation elements. The team felt that poor user interface was responsible for these issues, as playtesters reported they were "too busy fighting the controls to care about the story." As a result of this feedback, the controls were changed from the clunky point-and-click mechanic to a much smoother WASD or arrow-based control scheme. This change in hardware interface increased the transportation and identification ratings, correlating with the increase in interface feedback.

Importance of Plot Clarity to Narrative Engagement

The second major pattern to emerge from *Shattered Sky*'s playtesting was how a clear, understandable plot and characters affected player's narrative engagement. McCabe and Peterson are indeed correct when they claim, "People are sensitive to structure, not merely to content, when judging a narrative to be good" (n.p.). Prior to Alpha v3, *Shattered Sky* lacked a proper introduction, thrusting players into the maneuvering of the summit with only a brief explanation from their second-in-command. After adding an introductory meeting in Alpha v3 (which was intended to set initial NPC attitudes and further introduce the player to each character), the change made the earlier drama levels last longer and provided additional time for the player to explore and talk to other characters. Not only did the improved narrative clarity increase their enjoyment of the game, but players also reported that they were much more likely to replay the game as well. One player wrote: "I understood the start of the story and wanted to see how it ended." Through adding more structure, *Shattered Sky* managed to strike the elusive balance between narrative coherence and interactivity described by Frasca. However, this did not completely eliminate the tension between play and narrative within the game, regulating it to other areas of gameplay.

Continued Tension between Play and Narrative

Unfortunately, the third pattern that playtesting uncovered proved to be an unsolvable one so late in the game's development; the game's narrative was being impinged upon by gameplay mechanics. While initially, this sentiment seemed to stem from the difficulty of movement due to poor UI, further testing found this to not be the case. Even in later versions of the game, players professed that they felt the majority of their time was spent hunting down characters to talk to rather than the conversations themselves. They believed that "the game would be much better if you could just teleport to the character you wanted to talk to." Several testers correctly identified that these breaks in conversation reduced drama in the game, resulting in moments of high drama punctuated by periods of inactivity as the player navigated the environment. In a game that hinges on a sense of constant, rising drama, this is detrimental and represented a problem that had to be dealt with at the design level. While there was insufficient time to properly address the continued tension between *Shattered Sky*'s gameplay and narrative, the negative effect it had on players was fortunately overshadowed by their desire to narratively explore the game. One solvency for this in our iterative design process might be to enact the recommendation for person-to-person teleportation. Another option would be to strengthen the environment as a character type, engaging the player-character to interact with the setting more when searching for clues and finding serendipitous usable materials when not talking to non-player characters.

High Replayability

In spite of the bugs, frustrating controls, and unfinished artwork, not a single player reported that they would not play the game again. Even the most critical playtesters, people who openly ridiculed the game while playing, felt drawn to play again. When asked why they would play the game again, most replied that they were curious to see what would happen if they acted differently. A second group wished to see how the game ended, and the minority wished to see how the game changed. It is important to note that several of our playtesters played before endings were implemented; resulting in the answer "I want to see how the story ends." This is because, as Sansone writes, we tested early and often, long before many of the key game components were enacted. However, the majority of players reported at least some sense of curiosity in discovering just how many ways the game could play out. Based on this, it would appear that *Shattered Sky* avoids the problem that Glassner claims is responsible for bland narrative in games: There is no simple, middle ground. Unlike many games, *Shattered Sky* lacks a basic, neutral path through the game; players are forced into making choices, either of their own volition or by the goals of non-player characters. Choices that, by their very nature, inspire curiosity once made because the game engine opens and closes possibilities based on player choices. Players could not help but wonder about what might have been and sought to return to the game to sate this desire.

Conclusion

The ten criteria and the method tests are but a small step towards the integration of traditional usability testing and narrative evaluation. While the *Shattered Sky* development team found them effective at highlighting issues in generated narratives, further examination is required to confirm their generalizability outside the specific needs of this development process. However, it is clear that the growing tension between cutting-edge computer games and standard usability practices necessitates additional research lest player's engagement in these digital narratives fall by the wayside. As advances in AI and procedural generation allow for increasingly variable player experiences, the methods used in evaluating these narratives must similarly evolve. Traditional usability concepts such as efficiency and effectiveness cannot provide sufficient data on user experiences within a dynamic narrative, yet their standardization and ease of application remain useful to even the most branching story. Thus, it is not the methods themselves that need changing but the criteria through which they are applied. Only when we updated these criteria to synergize with the increasingly dynamic narratives told through computer games could we achieve effective evaluation.

Works Cited

Abbott, H. Porter. *The Cambridge Introduction to Narrative*. Cambridge: Cambridge UP, 2002.

Adams, Ernest, and Andrew Rollings. *Game Design and Development*. Upper Saddle River, NJ: Pearson Education, 2007.

Blythe, Mark A., and Marc Hassenzahl. "The Semantics of Fun: Differentiating Enjoyable Experiences." *Funology: From Usability to Enjoyment*. Eds. Mark A. Blythe, Kees Overbeeke, Andrew F. Monk, and Peter C. Wright. Dordrecht, The Netherlands: Kluwer Academic P, 2004. 91–102.

Brandtzæg, Petter Bae, Asbjørn Følstad, and Jan Heim. "Enjoyment: Lessons from Karasek." *Funology: From Usability to Enjoyment*. Eds. Mark A. Blythe, Kees Overbeeke, Andrew F. Monk, and Peter C. Wright. Dordrecht, The Netherlands: Kluwer Academic, 2004. 55–66.

Busselle, Rick, and Helena Bilandzic. "Fictionality and Perceived Realism in Experiencing Stories: A Model of Narrative Comprehension and Engagement." *Communication Theory* 18 (2008): 255–80.

———. "Measuring Narrative Engagement." *Media Psycology* 12.4 (2009): 321–47.

Cohen, J. "Defining Identification: A Theoretical Look at the Identification of Audiences with Media Characters." *Mass Communication & Society* 4 (2001): 245–64.

Csikszentmihalyi, Mihaly. *Finding Flow: The Psychology of Engagement with Everyday Life.* New York: Basic, 1997.

Fabricatore, Carlo, Miguel Nussbaum, and Ricardo Rosas. "Playability in Video Games: A Qualitative Design Model." *Human-Computer Interaction* 17.4 (2002): 311–68.

Finucane, Melissa L., Ali Alhakami, Paul Slovic, and Stephen M. Johnson. "The Affect Heuristic in Judgments of Risks and Benefits." *Journal of Behavioral Decision Making.* 13.1 (2000): 1–17.

Frasca, Gonzalo. "Simulation Versus Narrative: Introduction to Ludology." *The Video Game Theory Reader.* Eds. Mark J. Wolf and Bernard Perron. London: Routledge, 2003. 221–35.

Fullerton, Tracy, Chris Swain, and Steven Hoffman. *Game Design Workshop: Designing, Prototyping and Playtesting Games.* New York: CMP Books, 2004.

Gerrig, Richard J. *Experiencing Narrative Worlds: On the Psychological Activities of Reading.* Chelsea, MI: BookCrafters, 1993.

Gerrig, Richard J., and David N. Rapp. "Psychological Processes Underlying Literary Impact." *Poetics Today* 25 (2004): 265–81.

Gilbert, Daniel T. (1991). "How Mental Systems Believe." *American Psychologist* 46.2 (1991): 107–19.

Glassner, Andrew. *Interactive Storytelling: Techniques For 21ˢᵗ Century Fiction.* Natick, MA: AK Peters, 2004.

Graesser, Arthur C., *Brent* Olde, *and Bianca* Klettke. "How Does the Mind Construct and Represent Stories?" *Narrative Impact: Social And Cognitive Foundations.* Eds. Melanie C. Green, Jeffery J. Strange, and Timothy C. Brock. Mahwah, NJ: Lawrence Erlbaum, 2002. 229–62.

Green, Melanie C., *& Timothy C.* Brock. "The Role of Transportation in the Persuasiveness of Public Narratives." *Journal of Personality and Social Psychology* 79 (2000): 701–21.

Green, Melanie C., Timothy C. Brock, and Geoff F. Kaufman. "Understanding Media Enjoyment: The Role of Transportation into Narrative Worlds." *Communication Theory* 14.4 (2004): 311–27.

Hall, Alice. "Reading Realism: Audiences' Evaluations of the Reality of Media Texts." *Journal of Communication* 53.4 (2003): 624–41.

Hassenzahl, Marc. "The Thing and I: Understanding the Relationship Between User and Product." *Funology* 3 (2005): 31–42.

———, Andreas Beu, and Michael Burmester. "Engineering Joy." *Software, IEEE* 18.1 (2001): 70–76.

Ip, Barry. "Narrative Structures in Computer and Video Games: Part 1: Context, Definitions and Initial Findings." *Games and Culture* 6.2 (2011): 103–33.

———. "Narrative Structures in Computer and Video Games: Part 2: Emotions Structures, and Archetypes." *Games and Culture* 6.3 (2011): 203–44.

Järvinen, Aki, Satu Heliö, and Frans Mäyrä. *Communication and Community in Digital Entertainment Services: Prestudy Research Report.* Tampere, Finland: Tampere UP, 2002.

Jordan, Patrick. "Forward." *Funology: From Usability to Enjoyment.* Eds. Mark A. Blythe, Kees Overbeeke, Andrew F. Monk, and Peter C. Wright. Dordrecht, The Netherlands: Kluwer Academic P, 2004. xi–xiii.

Juul, Jesper. "A Clash Between Games and Narrative." *Digital Arts and Culture Conference.* Bergen, Finland: ACM, 1998.

———. *Half-Real: Video Games Between Real Rules and Fictional Worlds.* Cambridge, MA: MIT P, 2005.

Klabbers, Jan H. G. *The Magic Circle: Principles of Gaming and Simulation.* Rotterdam, The Netherlands: Sense, 2009.

Nacke, Lennart. "From Playability to a Hierarchical Game Usability Model." *Proceedings of the 2009 Conference on Future Play on@ GDC Canada.* ACM, 2009.

McCabe, Allyssa, and Carole Peterson. "What Makes a Good Story?" *Journal of Psycholinguistic Research* 13.6 (1984): 457–80.

Moberly, Kevin, and Ryan M. Moeller. "Working at Play: Modding, Revelation, and Transformation in the Technical Communication Classroom." *Computer Games and Technical Communication: Critical Methods and Applications at the Intersection.* Burlington, VT: Ashgate, 2014. 189–207.

Pagulayan, Randy, and Keith Steury. "Beyond Usability in Games." *Interactions* 11.5 (2004): 70–71.

Rehak, Bob. "Playing at Being: Psychoanalysis and the Avatar." *The Video Game Theory Reader.* Eds. Mark J. Wolf and Bernard Perron. London: Routledge, 2003. 103–27.

Rubin, Jeff and Dana Chisnell. *Handbook of Usability Testing: How to Plan, Design, and Conduct Effective Tests.* Hoboken, NJ: Wiley, 2008.

Sansone, Anthony. "Game Design Documents: Changing Production Models, Changing Demands." *Computer Games and Technical Communication: Critical Methods and Applications at the Intersection.* Burlington, VT: Ashgate, 2014. 109–23.

Schell, Jesse. *The Art of Game Design: A Book of Lenses.* Burlington, MA: Elsevier, 2008.

Segal, Erwin M. "Narrative Comprehension and the Role of Deictic Shift Theory." *Deixis in Narrative: A Cognitive Science Perspective* (1995): 3–17.

Silverman, Barry G., Michael Johns, Ransom Weaver, and Joshua Mosley. "Authoring Edutainment Stories for Online Players (AESOP): Introducing Gameplay into Interactive Dramas." *Lecture Notes in Computer Science* 2897 (2003): 65–73.

Zimmerman, Josh. "Psyche and Eros: Rhetorics of Secrecy and Disclosure in Game Developer–Fan Relations." *Computer Games and Technical Communication: Critical Methods and Applications at the Intersection.* Burlington, VT: Ashgate, 2014.141–56.

Chapter 8
Psyche and Eros:
Rhetorics of Secrecy and Disclosure in Game Developer–Fan Relations

Josh Zimmerman

According to legend, the god of love, Eros, was ordered by his mother Aphrodite to punish the beautiful Psyche by making her fall in love with an ugly mortal.[1] Instead, Eros fell in love with her. Eros became Psyche's lover, though she was unaware of his divine nature as he came to her only in the dark. Psyche was overcome by her desire to know her lover and looked at Eros's face as he slumbered. Eros fled, but Psyche was eventually able to earn her place as his wife by overcoming a series of challenges and earning the favor of the other gods. Psyche and Eros's story offers lessons on (1) how secrets create desire and (2) how desire structures relationships between the desired and the desiring. It shows how desire can both reward and punish, and how it motivates action. While they are products of the ancient world, these lessons offer valuable insight to modern readers, and not just in the context of personal romantic relationships.

Starting from the idea that secrets generate desire, I posit that Psyche and Eros's story serves as a metaphor for the relationship between producers and consumers of computer games, an industry heavily reliant on secrecy. Computer games emerge from both the entertainment and software industries, offering a unique opportunity to examine how technical communication artifacts, often considered dry and unemotional, are used to encourage and direct the intense passions of users in complex, conflicting ways. In this chapter, I show how fans become workers in the development process, a mobilization organized through technical communication artifacts unique to the computer game development process. I begin by framing the rhetorics of secrecy and disclosure that attempt to convert non-fans into fans. Next, I discuss the cycle of secrecy and disclosure, first showing how developers employ rhetorics of secrecy through teasers and non-disclosure agreements to create desire for their upcoming games. Then, I examine how rhetorics of secrecy are energized by complementary rhetorics of disclosure, instantiated through press releases, "previews," and community events. I will end this chapter by examining a model of computer game development that, on its surface, moves away from this

---

[1]   The story of Psyche and Eros has been retold and adapted repeatedly, using various combinations of Greek and Latin names. I will be using Greek appellations here.

cycle but that may have more similarities than differences with it. First, some basic terms need defined.

Developers, Users, and Players: Defining Terms

The development practices of game designers vary wildly between organizations. On one end, small indie developers operate on shoestring budgets and as literal family affairs. Large companies, meanwhile, fund development of AAA titles for millions of dollars with enormous staffs. Practices also change depending on the game's genre, the platform being developed for, and the market the game will be released in. Further, who counts as a "developer" is difficult to parse. Development teams include coders, writers, visual artists, QA testers, project managers, and so forth. Each of these individuals comes to the development project with their own perspective and skills, but operates as part of a larger organization and subject to what Linda Driskill calls internal and external sources of meaning that shape and regulate the individual's behaviors and communications (63). External sources of meaning include regulatory bodies, consumer groups, or competitors, whereas internal sources are influences that arise from within the organizational culture and structure (59, 64). Driskill's analysis is useful because development teams consist of many individual actors who are motivated by their own external and internal factors, making discussion of generalized "developer" behavior inherently reductionist. I argue, however, that individual actors are subject to powerful influences—both internal and external to the organization—that attempt to align their behaviors with the goals of the organization. For instance, information about a game's release date might be classified as secret. Individual actors then take steps to keep that information secret, regardless of their personal preferences, a behavior rationalized through the impact that keeping the secret will have on the future of the game. These behaviors are part of what David Boje calls "antenarrative," or "prospective sensemaking" that imagines the future as if it has already happened (8). The individual actor's behaviors are made sense of by relating them to the future release of the game and the harm a leak may have on the company's futures and thus his or her own. In this way, individual motivations are aligned with the goals of organization, resulting in more uniform behaviors that might be identified with a metonymic "developer." So when I refer to a developer, I am referring to the corporate organization, one that consists of many individual actors with possibly clashing motivations and goals whose personal motivations have been realigned, to at least some extent, with the larger goals of the organization of which they are a part.

Players and fans are also central to this discussion. This chapter is focused on computer games prior to release. That means the cycle of secrecy and disclosure includes subjects who are not yet players of the game and therefore cannot be fans based on an enjoyment and celebration of that experience. The cycle I describe is primarily intended, in fact, to convert these users (what I will call non-fans/

non-players) into fans and players—in particular, fans and players who have particular work to do in order to ensure a successful launch of the game. The technical communication artifacts under examination structure and regulate how that work is performed by players, granting them what Spinuzzi calls "functional empowerment" with the user being able to "perform their tasks in the prescribed manner" (13). The exact order of conversion, whether a non-player becomes a fan first or a player first, is murky. Regardless of whether the fandom or the playing comes first, each subjectivity requires the establishment of particular relationships between developer and user. Those subjectivities structure power dynamics between developers and users, establishing a hierarchy that regulates the cycle of secrecy and disclosure and the work of fans.

Finally, the artifacts under analysis need some definition. I am examining artifacts from a variety of modalities, each likely developed by separate parts of the development team or a team outside of the development organization. Some of these artifacts are legal documents while others are the products of marketing departments. What unites these artifacts is their status as technical communication, which is, as David Dobrin defines, "writing that accommodates technology to the user" with technology being defined broadly as "a way that people, machines, concepts, and relationships are organized" (119). Dobrin's definition posits that technical communication "accommodates" a new technology to a user by making "the strange, invasive, expensive, or inefficient into the familiar and useful" (121).[2] Accommodation does not mean, however, that the technology is modified but that the "user" is able to stop grappling with "the concrete abstract" and start to work with the "manipulable concept" (121).

In this chapter, the technology in question, the concept to be manipulated, is not the game, but a discursive structure that accommodates the user to itself (the user learns how the structure works, how to function within it). This process of accommodation is an inversion of what Sun calls "user localization," in which a user determines "how to make use of a technology in their life spheres" (459). This process is contrasted with "developer localization," a process in which an artifact is translated into different languages or the interface altered to fit a different cultural context. In contrast, user localization finds a technology adapted to the user as she discovers how it functions at both a material level ("How many characters are allowed in a text message?") and at a social-symbolic level ("How is a text message interpreted in my unique social context?") (466).

Sun invokes du Gay's "circuit of culture" wherein the technology moving through nodes of production, consumption, regulation, representation, and identity (464). She argues that, in most cases, developer localization only occurs in the production node and that all other nodes are dominated by user localization. In the cases I examine, these other nodes are colonized by the production node, the

---

[2] This is what Kocurek discusses in her chapter "Rendering Novelty Mundane," yet her argument focuses on the technical documentation that pertains to computer game hardware. I am focused primarily on software and Intellectual Property development.

end result of which is to bring user localization within the sphere of influence of the development team. This process occurs by reshaping the user context into one more beneficial to the developer, accommodating the user to the discursive structures of production, and requiring the user take on subjectivities and the power relations those subjectivities come with.

The Wheel Turning: The Cycle of Secrecy and Disclosure

Relying on Kenneth Burke's definition of rhetoric as "the use of language as a symbolic means of inducing cooperation in beings that by nature respond to symbols" (43), the rhetorics of secrecy and disclosure I examine produce a state of desire in the user, particularly a desire to know more. That desire generates increased interest in an upcoming release. At its most basic, the cycle of secrecy and disclosure resembles a seduction, with secrecy working to generate desire, an erotic charge, and disclosure representing a release of libido. The presence of desire and the intense affective response that attends it encourages the fannish performance that Matt Hills argues characterizes fan engagement, a performance that is "part of a cultural struggle over meaning and affect" (xi). The erotogenic nature of the cycle is a vital component in generating interest that will, hopefully, translate into strong sales for the game. The first step in this cycle is the deployment of a rhetoric of secrecy.

A rhetoric of secrecy is a discursive oxymoron. It communicates, but what it primarily communicates is that something has been left unsaid. In fact, these rhetorics instantiate Derrida's *différence*, the meaning of the communication becoming clear only when the term not present is acknowledged (5). A key characteristic of this rhetoric is that each utterance is separated from the one preceding it and the one following it by a carefully gauged amount of time. This allows the rhetoric of secrecy time to generate desire amongst users. When enough time has passed to work users into a heightened emotional state *vis-à-vis* the release, a state particularly associated with fandom: the developer discloses, meaning a release of the previously secret information, which then results in fannish disclosure (such as postings on social media sites, cosplay, fan art, and so forth). Through the practice of fannish disclosure, the user performs fandom and thus takes on the subjectivity of "fan."

These fannish disclosures sustain interest in the current release in addition to creating more demand for future releases from the developer. For example, computer game developer Arkane Studios released new content titled *The Knife of Dunwall* in April 2013 for their 2012 game *Dishonored*. Prior to the release, Arkane Studios posted concept art of new locales, characters, and weapons to the game's Facebook fan page. They then asked fans to weigh in on that content, posting polls with questions such as, "Will you use Daud's [the new content's main character] Arc Mine in the *Knife of Dunwall*?" Additionally, Arkane Studios posted fan-created tribute videos, drawings, and songs to their Facebook page. This process relied on the fans' already established enthusiasm for *Dishonored*, but it expanded upon that enthusiasm by offering small glimpses of new content before explicitly asking for and then valorizing particular types of fannish disclosure. In doing so, fans were trained to perform particular behaviors within the release structure.

As part of that training, rhetorics of secrecy establish an "inside" and "outside" to the release structure. The developer inhabits the inside space, where the game awaits release. On the outside, users wait for information, each utterance from the developer being followed by what amounts to meaningful silence. But not complete silence. Instead, the developer establishes that inside information *can* and *will* be shared but that only certain people may access that information and only under certain circumstances. That the secret can and will be shared is important because unshareable secrets becomes secrets to be stolen, whereas secrets than can be earned encourages users to accommodate themselves to the demands of the discursive structure in order to join the developer on the "inside."

Through the establishment of this structure, not only does the developer gain access to the business-sustaining support of fans, but they also establish power dynamics between themselves and the fan community, particularly in relation to who has the power to access and release information. Those dynamics inform the behaviors of both fan and developer, encouraging them to accommodate themselves to modes of communication and action that often serve the interests of the developer. It would be a mistake, however, to assume the relationship between developer and fan is necessarily exploitative of the fan. At its core, the relationship between developer and fans is transactional, with both the developer and the fans taking part in a subculture where access to the inside of the development structure is valued as a form of cultural capital. While the developer defines the terms of access, only the fan can grant the economic and cultural support necessary to sustain the developer's projects. These relationships are complex and often unequal, but not necessarily a directly adversarial "David vs Goliath" scenario. Instead, the relationship is better described in terms of Yin and Yang, with motivations and goals sometimes complementing, sometimes clashing, but with one always reliant on the other for existence and expression. To better illuminate this dynamic, I explore specific technical communication artifacts related to the rhetorics of secrecy.

Leave Them Wanting More: Teasers

One of the more popular instantiations of the rhetoric of secrecy is the "teaser." Teasers have been previously discussed in technical communication research in a number of forms: as a web link, a small snippet of text connecting to a larger, explanatory body of text; as part of a business development plan for a start-up companies website; and as a description of a paper abstract (Riley and Spartz; Fraiberg, Pierson and Pierson; Rodman). In each case, the teaser is characterized as a short, informative piece of information that points towards a more information-dense text. The teasers discussed here share that essential nature, but teasers in computer game development take a form that remain largely unexplored in the literature on technical communication. Game teasers are designed to generate interest in the developer's game before release. Material from the game, be it in-game footage, cinematics, concept art, or a playable demo, present just a bit of information to the user. But more important is the sense that more is around the corner. Through the teaser, developers communicate two things: first, the project exists, and second, there is more than a user can currently see. The user becomes Psyche, barred from seeing her lover's face but desiring him all the more for knowing he is so tantalizingly close.

Psyche and Eros's relationship is most directly instantiated in the "teaser trailer," such as the one released prior to Valve's *Portal 2*. In this video, a viewer sees the ruins of Aperture Science, the setting of the first game, and the "corpse" of the first game's villain, the evil computer GLaDOS. Suddenly, the user sees GLaDOS twitch and move. The scene shifts repeatedly, the viewer seeing brief glimpses of new game locales, enemies, and finally, the series protagonist Chell falling. And then the screen cuts to black; only GLaDOS' robotic voice remains. The trailer gives the viewer a vague sense of the game's shape but leaves many questions. In particular, the narrative connection between the first and second games is left mysterious. The user has only disconnected images whose larger meaning only becomes clear when more information is supplied by the developer.

Users who have become fans, however, often create their own scenarios until that time, investing their time and energy into the game on other forums. For instance, the teaser trailer for *LEGO Marvel Super Heroes* posted to YouTube on April 30, 2013 has been viewed 131,208 times at the time of this writing. The comments section is filled with comments such as, "HURRY UP AND RELEASE THIS GAME FOR CRYING OUT LOUD!!!!!!!!!" and, "I find it awesome that they will have Iron Man 3 suits! I wonder what else will be there" (Fmessi23; brightfamia). Many viewers comment multiple times, engaging in extended dialogues with other commenters. Even negative comments become a route for further investment in the property as commenters jump to the game's defense. Through their engagement with one another in the YouTube comments, these viewers labor for the developer, building interest in the game prior to its release through their commentary and also by increasing the social media penetration of the media by reposting, reblogging, or otherwise sharing the teaser.

The teaser trailer is only one form of the teaser. Another form can be seen on *Guild Wars 2* developer ArenaNet's website for the game. ArenaNet slowly doled out information about the available character classes for the game with highly stylized character silhouettes standing in for the unrevealed classes. As the months before release passed, ArenaNet filled in each silhouette, revealing the character class previously and literally cloaked in shadow. The efficacy of this strategy is evident in the amount of press that each revelation generated in games media such as Joystiq, Kotaku, or on sites such as Reddit. For instance, the May 19th, 2011 reveal of the Engineer class was heralded by stories on all of the previously mentioned gaming journalism sites as well as sites PCGamer, Massively.com, Tentonhammer.com, and MMORPG.Com (Augustine; Bayer; Ethec; "Guild Wars 2 Dev Journals").

The revelation of *Guild Wars 2* Engineer class routinely employed multiple modes of communication. The revelation coverage on Gamespot, for instance, included a text-based review, an image, and a video showcasing the new class's abilities (Park). Another example of such multi-modal communication can be found on the website for the 2013 reboot of *Tomb Raider*, which includes teaser videos, images, and press releases. Working across a variety of modes, teasers allowed developer Square Enix to generate interest for their release across various platforms, including games media, YouTube, and Twitter. It also established that Square Enix remained the source for canonical information about the release, regardless of the mode of communication.

This phenomenon is not a recent one. Examples of this multi-modal strategy can be found from the earliest days of commercial computer game history. *The Legend of Zelda* (1986) is a good example with both print and television commercials for a variety of national markets (Nintendo). What has changed since those early days is an explosion of modal options not the use of multiple modes itself. Regardless of mode, however, the teaser operates in a similar fashion. The developer is positioned as the source of knowledge on the inside of the structure. Users are outside, generating their own ideas, waiting for confirmation or denial of their theories.

Non-Disclosure Agreements

The teaser represents a rhetorical strategy wherein information moves from the inside of the release structure to the outside. But rhetorics of secrecy related to the movement of users from the outside of the structure to the inside, such as Non-Disclosure Agreements (NDAs), also play a role in the development cycle. That movement from outside to inside is a type of knowledge sharing, defined by Appleyard as "the transfer of useful know-how or information." As Appleyard notes, there are different categories of knowledge sharing based on whether and what type of restrictions exist on how and what knowledge is shared. In general, NDAs would be categorized as a private-restricted mode of knowledge sharing, meaning that the channels for knowledge transfer are not publicly available and that access to and use of the knowledge is restricted by legal agreement (138). In enforcing the NDA, the developer maintains control of what and how information is released. Control of that flow of information is important not only to avoid spoiling the excitement for fans, but also, as noted by Klee, because the NDA offers legal protections that even patents may fail to provide (120). Through the NDA, developers establish that both employees and users are subject to mechanisms that control the flow of information. The NDA, then, establishes the structure of the inside space before any player even knows the game exists by situating individual employees in relationships of power with one another and the organization.

The NDA can and should be considered a part of the games technical documentation. As Peterson notes, technical documentation provides "programmers and game coders . . . clearly articulated ideas that they can refer to while designing the game" (6). In this same vein, the NDA provides clearly articulated guidance regarding what and how information moves both inside and outside of the organization, guiding the development process as surely as any style guide. In particular, employee NDAs give developers access to legal remedies should an employee leak information or otherwise compromise the inside/outside structure of the release. For example, a Microsoft NDA states, "Confidential information means information that Microsoft designates as being confidential or which, under the circumstances surrounding disclosure out to be treated as confidential by Recipient" (Microsoft). In the case of unauthorized disclosure, the employee acknowledges that "monetary damages may not be a sufficient remedy for unauthorized disclosure of Confidential Information and that Microsoft shall be entitled, without waiving any other rights or remedies, to such injunctive or equitable relief as may be deemed proper by a court of competent jurisdiction" (Microsoft). What exactly "equitable relief" would be is not described.

What constitutes as an employee breach varies from company to company. An example submitted to the web comic *The Trenches*, for instance, details how one QA tester nearly lost his job: The tester's boss told him to ask friends and family to participate in the company's upcoming Beta test. The employee did so, but posting a Beta notice on Myspace was not the sort of "asking" the company imagined and the employee only narrowly escaped firing ("Big Brother's Watching"). The amount of scrutiny an employee faces also varies. Another submission to *The Trenches* describes a tester who was fired for discussing a bug with another tester in the company cafeteria ("Secrets"). The harshness of the response to even the possibility of a breach serves to underline just how vital the control of information is to the pre-release development process. And despite the seeming harshness of the above examples, NDAs for employees do provide remedies for real leaks, such as a QA tester who posted tester cheat codes online for his friends ("Yes, The NDA Applies to That Too, You Idiot").

In addition to the NDA, developers deploy any number of secrecy-maintaining techniques and technologies to manage the flow of information with actors outside of the organizational structure, such as physical building security and media blackouts. But while both security and media control are vital to maintaining secrecy, they remain industry focused. For players, the NDA is likely the only piece of this apparatus they will encounter, and even then, only in the context of an alpha or Beta test prior to the game's release. These player-focused NDAs explicitly establish what Markel calls the "five exclusive rights" held by copyright holders: reproduction, modification, distribution, public performance, and public display (200). The developer holds these rights regardless of whether an NDA is present or not. What the NDA does is inform the player that the developer holds those rights and that *they do not*. The NDA establishes that the relationship between the developer and the player is first a legal one, not a ludic one, a relationship based on the "rules of play" (Lawotska 385). The NDA, in fact, establishes that the user's relationship to the developer is one regulated by a legal framework to which they must consent before a ludic relationship—a relationship where the user may become a player—is even possible.

The most widespread use of the NDA for players is during closed Beta testing, a type of testing common to most computer software. Closed Beta in the computer game industry, however, is particularly important because it is the point where the developer exerts the most control over both the speech and silence of testers through the NDA. Prior to this state (alpha testing), the developer may have few gameplay secrets to hide as the game is in very early development. Closed Beta, in contrast, represents a point when large portions of the game have moved from concept to product and therefore must be guarded against theft or leak. But at this stage of testing the game may still have a large number of serious "game breaking" bugs or incomplete systems. The NDA allows the developer to keep word of their "broken game" off of news sites or forum communities as such stories could have serious implications for initial sales of the game. Yet they need to test at this "broken stage" because of the need for iterative game design and playtesting in creating a player-centered experience (Sansone; Sherlock; Tilley et al.).

But the demands of the player NDA may also be for speech. For example, when I participated in the Beta process for Trion World's MMORPG *Rift,* I was required to sign an NDA as part of the sign-up process for the Beta. In my agreement with Trion, I not only agreed to keep the information from the Beta test confidential, but also to pay Trion for the right to participate in the Beta if they demanded it (they never did) and:

> to test, evaluate and analyze the Beta Software and its operation, features and capabilities, and performance,
>
> to comply with the reasonable requests of Trion from time to time regarding testing, and
>
> (iii) to provide feedback and comments to Trion (including, but not limited to, bugs reports and test results).

All of the produced material "shall be the sole and exclusive property of Trion and/or its licensors shall have the perpetual right to use all . . . of Recipient's feedback or comments in any manner or media now known or hereafter devised" (*Rift* NDA 1.4). This NDA not only establishes that a Beta tester cannot share information without authorization but also that the player is consenting to be subject to the developer's control of the game. It formally establishes that the player is not gaining power over the developer or the release by being a tester. In a manner analogous to how Jenkins saw what he called a "brain trust" develop amongst *Survivor* spoilers, the NDA establishes that even the "inside" of the release structure has its own inside ("Spoiling Survivor" 38). Further, the NDA establishes that the player is not allowed to disclose information regarding the release without approval while at the same time they are required to disclose to the developer when it is asked of them. Here the complementary rhetoric of disclosure becomes evident, specific instantiations of which I examine next.

Rhetoric of Disclosure: Developer Disclosure

Disclosure, meaning a release of information previously held in secret, can operate as a rhetorical flourish, drawing on the excitement of fans as a new piece of information emerges. It can also, however, be a demand for speech, a requirement for disclosure, from the developer to the player, a games journalism site, or from a fan community. Disclosure is required from both the developer in the form of new information and from the player in the form of public displays of fandom. Developer disclosure, such as preview articles and preview trailers, moves information from the inside of the release structure to the outside. These disclosures take the form of press releases on major gaming websites, major site updates on the developer's own website, or the release of announcement videos (which I will differentiate from teaser trailers more fully below) on sites such as Gametrailers.com or YouTube. Through disclosure, the developer provides fodder for discussions and arguments on gaming news sites and blogs, which in turn stimulates fan discussion.

On the developer side, while disclosure is still selective, it is distinct from the rhetoric of secrecy in that it focuses on revelation—the sense that a world-changing secret is emerging—and not in the sense that something is being left unsaid. Disclosure often occurs through regular "updates" or "releases" from developers to news outlets. For example, on 1 February 2013, games journalism website *Kotaku* posted a "preview" of the upcoming release *God of War: Ascension*. Written by freelance games journalist Matt Cabral, the preview details the hands-on experience of its author, an experience overseen by members of the development team. The preview contains developer-provided pictures from the game, each one more beautiful and engaging than the last. Such a preview is as much sales pitch as actual journalism. It should be noted, however, that Cabral's access to the preview was likely predicated on his playing the *God of War* demo with the developer's "guidance" and using developer provided images. Therefore, disclosure in these cases should be understood as the carefully managed stage show, not unfettered speech. Returning to Sun's invocation of the "circle of culture," I see here the node of representation being subsumed into the node of production, with the journalist's textual output (the "preview") being accommodated to the discursive demands of modern computer game development, serving as a cog in the ever-expanding machine of computer game development.

What interest, however, does a developer have in so carefully controlling such a preview? Because in releasing carefully managed previews, the developer shapes future players' experience of the game by framing it for them ahead of time. For instance, Cabral describes his experience of playing the game as "busting out." He describes the *God of War* series protagonist attacks as "unleashing" and "opening more baddies from brains to balls." New game features are "thrilling" and "evolved." These descriptions may be Cabral's experience of play, but notice how the sensory and affective impact of the game is framed for future players. The game has already been judged to be exciting, bombastic, and impactful. Thus, the players find themselves already embedded in a discourse before they play the game. Should the player not hold a high opinion of the game, that opinion emerges already in disagreement with the status quo judgment about the game.

While the manipulation of games journalists acts to frame and promote the game with experiential description and high ratings, developers simultaneously control release information through announcement videos, complimenting the message and saturating the mediascape with promotional materials. These videos are distinct from teasers in that the announcement's focus is on what is being shared, not on creating the sense that something is left unsaid. An example of this is "*World of Warcraft*'s *Mists of Pandaria* Preview Trailer" (Blizzard Entertainment). The trailer offers a primer on the story of inter-faction warfare between the various races of *World of Warcraft* but also offers information regarding a new options and systems in the expansion. In the video, text flashes across the screen, telling players to expect a new class, new pet battle systems, a new race, and other improvements. The provided information helps the viewer to understand the contours of the new expansion and provides an opportunity for the players to prepare themselves for changes in the game technology. The trailer frames those changes in the terms of the players' past experiences ("For All the Challenges We Have Faced . . ."), but presents the new features of the expansion as a chance for the players to test the limits of the game world. To employ Dobrin's terminology, the player is being encouraged to accommodate their history of play to the new form it will take in the expansion.

Rhetoric of Disclosure: Player Disclosure

Each of these forms of developer disclosure relies on the notion that fans will actually see them. Considering how fractured the media landscape in general is and how niche the various gaming outlets are, that is far from certain. To increase their chance of reaching a large number of potential fans, developer disclosures must provide opportunities for viewers to generate their own discussion, hopefully in the form of fannish disclosure. Fan disclosure acts to shore up the developers own. Put simply, developers can claim they are developing a spectacular game with innovative systems and earth-shattering stories, but if they are the only one saying such things, the message is not terribly persuasive. Instead, the developer must work to develop an ever-expanding fan community that will support their assertions about the upcoming release. Notice, however, that developers cannot simply unleash fans and hope. Instead, developers must attempt to manage fan disclosures to keep discussion of the game on message. That means creating venues for fan disclosure with carefully moderated modes of expression such as community events, forums, and official channels on websites such as YouTube. These forums become a space for fans to engage in what Spinuzzi calls "distributed work": "the coordinative work that enables sociotechnical networks to hold together and form dense interconnections among and across work activities" ("Technical Communication in the Age of Distributed Work" 268). The work being distributed is the work of marketing the game, and of building a sustaining fan community for the developer's future projects. Fans are trained for that work, given "functional empowerment," through their interaction with the discursive structure established by the rhetorics of secrecy and disclosure; their output influenced and regulated by the technical communication artifacts I have discussed already, especially considering that fannish productions often incorporate materials from artifacts such as teaser trailers and concept art (Spinuzzi, *Tracing Genres Through Organizations* 13).

As a final example that encapsulates the entire cycle, Massively Multiplayer Online Role-Playing Game (MMORPG) developer Trion Worlds hosted contests on their Facebook page that offered a key to the Beta test of their game *Rift* as a prize. Contests including players writing about the part of the game they were most excited about or in demonstrating their knowledge of the game lore that had been released so far. Trion asked players to publicly disclose, sharing their excitement for an unreleased title in order to possibly gain a position as an unpaid tester. Some disclosures, however, were not met with the "reward" of a Beta key. Rhetorics of secrecy and disclosure, in fact, require that some players receive no answer because only through a combination of silence and selective disclosure with some people remaining outside can the inside/outside dichotomy of the release be maintained. Further, this practice creates a dynamic in which desire is established through lack. Some fans who disclose find themselves rewarded. Others do not. The final effect, however, is not to silence future disclosures but to encourage them. Each act of disclosure, as long as it takes place within the structures established by the developer, presents an opportunity for the discloser to be rewarded. Players' desires, then, are harnessed in furtherance of the developer's goals.

Alternative Models

Rhetorics of secrecy and disclosure are most powerful early in the Beta process. Prior to public testing, the developer shares only small snippets with approved games media outlets. Releases become more substantive as the game near release. But as the game nears release, more information passes from inside of the structure to the outside. This decreases the distinction between the two and makes the game less compelling. Like a balloon leaking air, the inside space collapses as there are fewer secrets to keep. Eventually, everything that is to be known about the release is available. At this point, secrecy becomes illogical. At the same moment, disclosure loses its appeal because nothing is left to disclose. Instead, developers must shift to the next thing, a new secret to be kept and eventually disclosed. This may be a new game, expansion, or downloadable content. Thus, the cycle of secret keeping and disclosure drives player excitement and investment in the developer's projects, hopefully converting them to fans, which leads to the new project.

There are, however, other approaches to the process. An example is *Pathfinder Online*, a Massively Multiplayer Online game (MMO) currently under development by Goblinworks, Inc. In May 2012, Goblinworks crowd-sourced funds for its technology demo through Kickstarter, an online, community-based funding source. In November of 2012, Goblinworks returned to Kickstarter to secure their entire development budget. Goblinworks proposal was straightforward: Backers who pledge $100 or more are identified as "Crowdforgers" and promised special access to the Beta process. Goblinworks promises that Crowdforgers will not only have access to the Beta but that they will work *with* the developer to establish games features and systems. The major thrust of Goblinworks pitch is that players can "buy-in" to the inside of the development structure. They write, "We want a very close symbiosis with our customers, getting their feedback on our design ideas and, once the game is launched, iteratively adding content to the game based on their feedback" ("*Pathfinder Online* Technology Demo").

This process seems, on its surface, to flatten the power disparity between developers and players by offering players greater influence in the development process. Notice, however, that while Goblinworks promises "symbiosis," symbiosis only occurs between different species. The customer and the developer are still separate classes with the power dynamic that class distinction implies still intact. There is still an inside/outside to the development process. Players are still accommodated to technologies of power through Kickstarter agreements and the inevitable testing agreements. Players who have not paid for the privilege of access still wait outside. While this approach does offer interesting possibilities for computer game development, I believe that it would be incautious to hail it as a new paradigm when it seems to share more similarities with current models than it has differences.

In the end, its largest innovation is that players are pre-paying for access to the inside space. So yes, the model has changed in that the developer is building enthusiasm for their release by selling influence and access to the game early in the development process. But what has changed for the player is the cost of admission, not the requirement that players take on particular subjectivities or that players accommodate themselves to structures of power and control, trained to those subjectivities through their interaction with a variety of technical communication artifacts. Consider that the *Rift* NDA proffered the possibility that I might be charged for participation in the Beta process. In this case, the company actually *is* charging for the Beta process. This new model is not Eros revealing his face to his beloved freely. Instead, Eros is sitting in a brightly lit room, charging admission for a peek.

Works Cited

Appleyard, Melissa. "How Does Knowledge Flow? Interfirm Patterns in the Semiconductor Industry." *Strategic Management Journal* 17 (1996): 137–54.

Arenanet. *Guild Wars 2*. NCSoft, 2012. Personal Computer.

Arkane Studios. *Dishonored.* Bethesda, 2012. Personal Computer.

———. *The Knife of Dunwall*. Bethesda, 2013. Personal Computer.

Augustine, Josh. "New Guild Wars 2 Profession Revealed: The Tinkering Engineer!" *PCGamer*. 19 May 2011. Web. 23 May 2013.

Bayer, Rubi. "Guild War 2's Explosive Seventh Class: The Engineer." *Massively. com*. 19 May 2011. Web. 20 May 2013.

"Big Brother's Watching." *The Trenches*. 05 Jan. 2012. Web. 4 Apr. 2013.

Blizzard Entertainment. "World of Warcraft: Mists of Pandaria Preview Trailer." *YouTube*. 20 Oct. 2011. Web. 17 March 2013.

Boje, David. "Expanded Book Proposal: Antenarrative and Storytelling Organizations Handbook." n.d. Web. 17 May 2013.

brightfamia. "LEGO Marvel Super Heroes Video Game." *YouTube*. 5 May 2013. Web. 8 May 2013.

Burke, Kenneth. *A Rhetoric of Motives*. New York: George Braziller, 1955.

Cabral, Matt. "God of War: Ascension Gives Kratos Even More Ways to Kill." *Kotaku*. Web. 1 Feb. 2012.

Crystal Dynamics. *Tomb Raider.* Square Enix, 2013. Xbox 360 .

Derrida, Jacques. *Margins of Philosophy*. Chicago: U of Chicago P, 1982.

Dobrin, David. "What's Technical About Technical Writing?" *Central Works in Technical Communication*. Eds. Johndan Johnson-Eilola and Stuart Selber. New York, NY: Oxford UP, 2005. 107–23.

Driskill, Linda. "Understanding the Writing Context in Organizations." *Central Works in Technical Communication*. Eds. Johndan Johnson-Eilola and Stuart Selber. New York, NY: Oxford UP, 2005. 55–69.

Ethec. "Guild War 2's Seventh Profession Revealed: The Engineer." *TenTonHammer.com*. 19 May 2011. Web. 23 May 2013.

Fmessi23. "LEGO Marvel Super Heroes Video Game." *YouTube*. 07 May 2013. Web. 8 May 2013.

Goblinworks, Inc. "Pathfinder Online: A Fantasy Sandbox MMO." *Kickstarter*. 27 Nov. 2012. Web. 10 February 2013.

———. "Pathfinder Online Technology Demo." *Kickstarter*. Web. 9 May 2012.

"Guild Wars 2 Dev Journals: Arena.Net Reveals the Engineer." *MMORPG. COM*. 19 May 2011. Web. 20 May 2013.

Hills, Matt. *Fan Cultures*. New York: Routledge, 2002.

Jenkins, Henry. "Spoiling *Survivor*: Anatomy of a Knowledge Community." *Convergence Culture: Where Old and New Media Collide*. New York: New York UP, 2006. 25–58.

Klee, M.M. "The Importance of Having a Non-Disclosure Agreement." *IEEE Engineering in Medicine and Biology Magazine* 19.3 (2000).

Kocurek, Carly A. "Between the Novel and the Mundane: Technical Writing and the Transition to Coin-Op Video Games." *Computer Games and Technical Communication: Critical Methods and Applications at the Intersection*. Burlington, VT: Ashgate, 2014. 56–67.

Lastowka, Greg. "Rules of Play." *Games and Culture* 4.4 (2009): 379–95. Web. 1 March 2012. "Lockdown with Golf." *The Trenches*. 16 Feb 2012. Web. 4 Apr. 2013.

Markel, Michael H. *Ethics in Technical Communication: A Critique and Synthesis*. Westport, CT: Ablex, 2001.

Microsoft "Microsoft Corporation Non-Disclosure Agreement" 09 Apr. 2002. Web. 8 May 2013.

Nintendo R&D 4. *Legend of Zelda*. Nintendo, 1987. Nintendo Entertainment System.

Park, Andrew. "Guild Wars 2 Preview—The Engineer Revealed." *Gamespot*. 19 May 2011. Web. 9 May 2013.

Peterson, Martin. "Why Game Documentation Is Essential to a Satisfying User Experience." *Society for Technical Communication Usability SIG Newsletter*. Oct. 2004. Web. 23 May 2013.

Rodman, Diane. "Single Sourcing Career Project for Research-Based Writing Classes." *The 2007 Proceedings*. Eds. Sherry Southard and Melissa Place. Springfield, MO: Missouri State U, Spring 2008.

Sansone, Anthony. "Game Design Documents: Changing Production Models, Changing Demands." *Computer Games and Technical Communication: Critical Methods and Applications at the Intersection*. Burlington, VT: Ashgate, 2014. 109–23.

"Secret Plans are Secret." *The Trenches*. 06 Nov. 2012. Web. 4 Apr. 2013.

"Secrets." *The Trenches*. 25 Aug. 2011. Web. 4 Apr. 2013.

Sherlock, Lee. "Patching as Design Rhetoric: Tracing the Framing and Delivery of Iterative Content Documentation in Online Games." *Computer Games and Technical Communication: Critical Methods and Applications at the Intersection*. Burlington, VT: Ashgate, 2014. 157–69.

Spinuzzi, Clay. *Tracing Genres Through Organizations: A Sociocultural Approach to Information Design*. Cambridge: MIT P, 2003. Internet Resource.

———. "Guest Editor's Introduction: Technical Communication in the Age of Distributed Work." *Technical Communication Quarterly* 16.3 (2007): 265–77.

Tilley, Alex, Carmen Blandino, and Jennifer deWinter. "User-Testing Narratives: Usability Testing, Playtesting, and the Liminality of Computer Games." *Computer Games and Technical Communication: Critical Methods and Applications at the Intersection*. Burlington, VT: Ashgate, 2014. 125–40.

Trion Worlds. "*Rift*–NDA Agreement (Non-disclosure agreement)." 3 Dec. 2010.

————. *Rift*. Trion Worlds, 2011. Personal computer.
Valve. "Portal 2 Teaser Trailer." *YouTube*. 15 June 2010. Web. 1 May 2013.

Chapter 9

Patching as Design Rhetoric: Tracing the Framing and Delivery of Iterative Content Documentation in Online Games

Lee Sherlock

Patch notes have historically served the function of technical documentation for online games that undergo iterative content development and for developers that continue to address technical and user experience issues post-release (for example, fixing bugs and hardware or driver conflicts). The notes accompanying patch versions represent the *official* documentation; they contain all the data that not only qualifies design changes but also quantifies exactly how things should be working mechanically. Although this documentation is published and made available to player audiences, it has typically not been featured as a way to understand what is happening in patches from inside a game developer's perspective or as a set of design-driven rationales. Rather, patch notes are a collection of all the technical language and data that players may dig through if they want to spend time gaining a more precise understanding of how game mechanics are being affected under the hood of the game. In this sense, patch notes have often been understood more as an archive than a presentation; they are made public to be accessed as needed but not given attention as a target for design resources in themselves.

As game developers have increasingly drawn on social media to create space for player communities and have used online platforms as multimodal spaces to preview and reflect on new game content, patching has developed into a more complex rhetorical situation. Patches have shifted away from being understood as version updates into player-developer negotiations over expected design changes and rationales for certain directions and decisions tied to the development of each patch. Patch documentation, too, has a more complex role; not only has its singularity as *the* text associated with a particular patch disappeared, but also it is increasingly seen as a rhetorical opportunity, a site in which one can enact persuasion. The rhetorical framing of patch documentation becomes critical as players bring their own histories, expectations, and interests to their readings of each patch.

In this chapter, I trace three approaches to the rhetorical framing and delivery of patch documentation by three different game development companies via their public communications to players: Riot Games, Blizzard Entertainment, and Grinding Gear Games. These three companies all manage online games that have active player communities, although audience concerns as well as the styles of gameplay represented influence the rhetorical paths they have chosen in documenting and presenting their patch development. The tension between documenting patch information in a comprehensive, neutral sense—via technical language, datasets, and precise description—and using patch documentation as a platform to express design rationales in context of what the patch changes represent is handled in different ways. This rhetorical tension characterizes what McAllister refers to as a "transformative locale" in the computer game complex. McAllister argues that transformative locales "mark the sites where personal, communal, and societal transformations occur in relation to the dialectic. They are points at which the assumptions, rules, and constraints of ideology are altered" (60). McAllister's analytical framework for computer game discourse emphasizes the articulations and exchanges of power that are at work in gaming culture and the dynamics of power that are central to how patching happens as a rhetorical activity and how it is received by players. In addition to the rhetorical and ideological work of patch documentation, I will trace some ways in which game development companies have begun to take advantage of multimodal communication platforms and social media in the service of framing patch documentation and public rationales for iterative design work. The affordances and constraints of these decisions hold implications for the public work of technical and support documentation, and though the contexts I focus on here are all tied to game development discourse, domains and systems such as software development, user support, and digital archival have stakes in their approaches to this public work.

League of Legends Patch Previews: Packaging Patch Information in Social Media Spaces

As a free-to-play game produced by a relatively lesser known but growing development studio (Riot Games), *League of Legends* has used social media platforms to its advantage in recruiting a player base. For players who are just getting introduced to the game, Riot offers access to two free champions—playable characters, each with their own ability set—by having players subscribe to their YouTube channel or like their Facebook page. *League of Legends*' gameplay focuses on a team-based variation of real-time strategy, commonly referred to as a Multiplayer Online Battle Arena (MOBA) scenario in which players control a single character rather than manage units and resources at a macro level. Due to how gameplay is framed, competitive balance is key, particularly with respect to champion design and the roles that players wish to focus on.

For *League of Legends*, patching as a rhetorical activity devotes much of its resources to addressing the power balance among champions and trying to tweak them in such a way to maintain a general level of fairness while opening or closing certain modes of play within the *League of Legends* metagame. The following levels of priority typically organize patch notes: revisions to individual champions are listed first, and general gameplay, UI, and item changes are pushed to the bottom. Additionally, the notes for individual champions contain developer annotations that explain the most recent changes in relation to overall power level and what roles and playstyles the champion is intended to fill from a design perspective. For example, on the Patch 3.03 notes page, the revisions made to the champion Taric's abilities are framed as such:

> These changes provide opponents with early lane counterplay to Taric by reducing the amount of passive Armor granted by Shatter. In return, Taric is gaining meaningful ways to potentially scale into the later game, new itemization options and better ability to engage his opponents at close range.

Without this explanatory piece to situate the data, players would get the raw information about Taric's armor value being reduced and the rest of this set of changes, but they would not necessarily make the connection with larger objectives centering on balance and player agency. These design changes are framed as a tradeoff; the designers acknowledge that they are making this champion weaker in a certain area but emphasize that in doing so, they improve Taric's late-game playability and introduce more chances to make meaningful gameplay decisions. The developer's *vision* for how individual champions should play as compared to the reality of their practical use is a common trope in *League of Legends'* patch documentation. In discussing a change to the champion Rumble, the patch notes explain a complete reworking of his ultimate ability:

> Rumble's ultimate was intended to be an area control effect but, with the large upfront damage it deals, it tends to be used more as a long-range nuke instead. With this patch, we're adjusting The Equalizer to better match its original intent. (Morello. "Patch 3.5 Notes." *League of Legends.*)

Whatever the original design intent, however, players bring to the game histories playing certain champions and personal expectations tied to them. The forum on champion feedback hosted on Riot's site is a testament to the investments that players have in particular champions and play experiences. Player "DaSpartan Legacy" offers an entire redesign of the champion LeBlanc's ability set, reflecting that he used to play LeBlanc often but the experience has become tedious due to a lack of distinct interactions among skills. In his forum thread, the author summarizes these suggested changes by presenting a metagame rationale, echoing the design language that Riot Games representatives employ: "In general, [LeBlanc's] ultimate mimicking Distortion and Ethereal Chain should focus on the utility rather than damage to allow smart plays on Leblanc as well as improve her contributions to the team in team fights" ("A really fun, feasible and innovative rework"). Introducing patch changes, especially ones that are more than just data-driven tweaks and represent substantial design overhauls, is an instance of community management as much as a refinement of developer intentionality. Framing a rationale for champion design changes in broader terms has an added effect, ideally, of softening the blow when a player's favorite champion suddenly becomes less powerful. Ethos and identity work are at play in patch documentation, too; it is not only a neutral site of information gathering.

Along with the full patch documentation on the official *League of Legends* website, Riot Games has used its social media channels to package its patch changes into more bite-sized highlight reels. The RiotGamesInc YouTube channel features a regular patch preview series, which map out a few significant themes in the patch—typically, any major gameplay or UI elements along with the social infrastructure of the game (like the competitive matchmaking system and ranked play) are emphasized alongside key champion revisions. The videos are framed to offer a glimpse into Riot's design rationale: They are typically guided by a voiceover dialogue in which members of Riot's design staff are prompted to comment on the patch changes, not just to summarize them for a general audience but to answer the "so what?" question. Clips from *League of Legends* gameplay are synced with this dialogue to help illustrate, visually and aurally, the implications of the changes being introduced in a particular patch. For example, in the Patch 3.03 preview video, the developers are asked what the new Smart Ping system is "all about." In his response, designer "Brackhar" leads with a user experience rationale before explaining how players use it on a technical level:

> With Smart Ping, we wanted to give players more ways to communicate with their teammates – especially in situations where there isn't enough time to type. ("League of Legends – 3.03 Patch Preview." *Riot Games*)

As it turns out, Smart Ping is an option added to the user interface designed to enrich the technical communication affordances available to players, especially under the pressure and time constraints of competitive gameplay. Smart Ping offers a kind of shorthand to communicate the urgent, 'just in time' messages that can make or break the tactical and social cohesion of a *League of Legends* team (Gee 142; see, also, deWinter's discussion of just in time in this volume). Brackhar emphasizes the iconic significance and multimodality of the Smart Ping system:

> In addition to providing normal visual and audio cues, these new pings will also place an easily identifiable waypoint on the ground. ("League of Legends—3.03 Patch Preview." *Riot Games)*

The Smart Ping system is positioned as an opportunity for "adaptive" players to communicate key information and track other champions' movements more intuitively, but the Riot developers claim that they do not want to replace or interfere with current communication mechanisms in the game that carry out similar objectives, such as text-based chat and the default ping system. Clay

Spinuzzi argues that from this perspective, the designers express sensitivity to player habits and the innovations that users of designed systems engineer to manage their everyday needs. He identifies the trope in user-centered design research of closing off user workarounds in the effort to construct a central design solution: "[R]esearchers working within these approaches tend to take such innovations as rough solutions to common underlying problems, solutions that should be officially refined and consolidated by a trained designer if these underlying problems are to be truly solved" (3). Riot resists the impulse to implement Smart Ping as a standardized communication system in the place of existing player innovations, recognizing that forcing players to use Smart Ping as the sole channel of alert communication could result in negative play experiences, particularly for players who have developed and practiced their existing communication habits for a long time.

From Customer Support to Developer Interviews: Framing Design Changes in *World of Warcraft*

Out of the three approaches to documenting patch information that I trace in this chapter, Blizzard is the most high-profile development company and manages one of the most popular online game franchises in *World of Warcraft*. The text-based patch notes and hotfixes are hosted on Blizzard's official site, along with built-in threaded comment functionality in which players can use their accounts to log in and discuss patch changes. Increasingly, Blizzard has moved to integrating textual patch notes in a general news and multimedia developer commentary space. For example, the 5.2 patch notes document is part of a much larger textual ecology that features design feature previews and commentary, organized thematically to address particular player interests such as end-game raiding, player vs. player modes, and changes local to specific character classes ("Patch 5.2: The Thunder King Now Live"). Along with this "round-up" of content posts, developer interviews on third-party sites are thumbnailed and linked to provide more insight into the rationale behind specific patch features. On the patch round-up page, Blizzard embeds a YouTube trailer for the 5.2 patch, but the framing and purpose of this video differ from how Riot Games sets up their YouTube channel with respect to patch content. For Blizzard, the patch trailer fills the narrative gap that patch documentation alone cannot fully articulate: It showcases scenes from the game and presents a narrative introduction to key events and story arcs contained in the patch. The patch trailer is a purely "in-character" cinematic device; it focuses on major characters from the in-game *World of Warcraft* universe, deciding to leave the fourth wall intact rather than establish a public platform to articulate a rationale for patch changes. Blizzard has opted instead to let the patch round-up page carry out much of this rhetorical work. In addition to the developer blogs that preview, synthesize, and comment on various bits of patch information, there are links to no fewer than fifteen developer interviews directly tied to Patch 5.2, hosted on various gaming sites and *World of Warcraft* community spaces.

To a certain degree, the popularity of *World of Warcraft* as a gaming franchise and the diversity of online community spaces tied to *World of Warcraft* allow for the rhetorical framing of the patch to be a bit more distributed and specialized. For example, players who mainly want to hear about Player versus Player (PvP) changes and rationales can check out the 5.2 developer interview hosted on Arena Junkies, a site specializing in PvP combat and arena matches in particular. The wealth of developer interview content offers the interested player a better sense of the transitions between patches as well; developers take the opportunity to walk through patch content in terms of short- and long-term design strategies, reflecting on what has worked so far, for whom, and what they prioritize as being the most important targets for revision. In the Wowhead interview for 5.2 on raid content and gearing for raids, *World of Warcraft* developer Ion Hazzikostas describes the intended balance in difficulty for the new raid bosses in the context of current player progression:

> The first couple of bosses of the new raid tier are intentionally tuned to be somewhat more accessible for players who haven't necessarily completely finished Heart of Fear and/or Terrace of Endless Spring on normal mode. [. . .] At the same time, we have reduced the difficulty of the 5.0 raids when 5.2 comes out—there's a 10% reduction to health and damage across the board in all those zones. (perculia. "Wowhead's Patch 5.2 Interview with Lead Encounter Designer Ion 'Watcher' Hazzikostas." *Wowhead*)

In this response, the patch change is situated as an effort to help boost the progression of player groups that have not cleared old raiding content and prepare them to have a meaningful stake in clearing the new raid content. The difficulty of designing raid content across audiences remains a tricky balancing act, as much of the commentary focuses on making the upcoming raid accessible but not too simple while tracking how various player bases have fared with respect to the content represented in the last few patches. The design changes framed in patch discussions are thus tied to evidence drawn from analytics, which can be used as points of reference to articulate why features and refinements are being introduced in new content iterations.

Although Blizzard has not taken the same path as Riot Games in creating regular video content to function as patch previews, they have experimented with using their Customer Support YouTube channel for this purpose. Upon releasing the 5.0.4 patch, Blizzard released a video that walks through major design changes and drawing on in-game captured video to showcase their associated UI interactions. Unlike the Riot Games patch previews, Blizzard uses explicit storytelling conventions in this video to thematically sort design changes: The features covered in the video are broken down into numbered chapters. Additionally, the approach taken to describing design features is a procedural walkthrough with careful attention paid to noting each action-based step via the new interface. The voiceover narration in the video starts by guiding the player through the new talent system using this method:

> The first thing we notice is that we have unspent talent points. We open the Specialization and Talents window, where a help overlay displays tooltips about the new interface. Seems pretty clear. We toggle the help system off so we can choose our specialization. ("New talents and account wide systems in World of Warcraft (WoW 5.0.4)" *Blizzard Entertainment*)

The language and procedural style narrate an explicit walkthrough of the new patch interface, highlighting the most significant changes and anticipating what will be most salient to users upon loading their freshly patched clients. The use of "the first thing we notice" draws attention to the talent point system, creating a prompt for players to address their allocation of talents as a priority before moving on. The first person plural voice is used consistently in the video, establishing a shared task of exploring the new interface rather than being *told* what to do by developers. The voiceover narration uses technical language to describe the interface elements, naming each window and pointing out embedded help features that annotate the new interface elements. The rhetoric of this video suggests a customer support stance, but a certain disconnect is at work because the video is still presented as a patch showcase and not a video targeted at solving a specific technical issue as with most of the videos in the Blizzard Customer Support channel. Since Blizzard has not continued to produce these patch walkthrough videos regularly, it suggests that they interpreted Patch 5.0.4 as more complex from a technical standpoint and saw an opportunity to produce a video that served the dual purposes of anticipating potential user experience issues and showcasing new design features. For Blizzard, the ecology of design preview blogs and interview media that circulate around official patch documentation are more suited to articulating a public design rationale while emphasizing a story-driven approach to presenting patch content as expressed in the cinematic preview trailer.

Beta Development in *Path of Exile*: Leveraging Forums for Design Conversations

Path of Exile represents a higher-stakes environment for patching as a rhetorical activity. It is an action-RPG game made by a relatively small development studio, Grinding Gear Games, and is their first major game development project. *Path of Exile* entered public open beta in January 2013, so the cycles of design changes and community feedback articulated through patching do not only affect iterative changes to a *stable* product—(such as an already released and commercially successful game)—but also will influence in substantial ways the design strategy for the game and its success and popularity down the line as an anticipated release.

Evaluating modes of delivery, Grinding Gear Games' strategy for publishing patch notes is more mono-modal; patch notes are written via text in a conventional documentation form, using themes and bulleted technical language to archive specific design changes and bug fixes. At least in this stage of *Path of Exile*'s development, the designers have not drawn on video as Blizzard and Riot Games have done to express a design rationale for patch notes and foreground particular design changes as the most relevant and high priority.

The forum space on *Path of Exile*'s official website serves as the central hub for patch documentation; each set of patch notes has its own forum thread dedicated to it, resulting in a long list of threads ordered chronologically that trace the development of the beta and date back to August 2011. All of the threads are created by user "Chris" (Chris Wilson), who identifies himself in his signature as the lead developer of the game. In this sense, there is more transparency in audience as to what effect player feedback might actually have on game development; rather than creating a forum post in the hopes that a design team member or community manager might eventually find it and comment on its content, players can comment in threads dedicated to specific patches. In some instances, Wilson frames patch documentation posts with questions or notes that invite player response. For example, in the 0.10.3c patch thread, Wilson notes that item display and looting changes "are the result of a lot of internal testing and discussion of player feedback." He then poses two questions about user experience that players are invited to comment on:

> Was it easier to read what items drop now that fewer are allocated and the size of the item hovers doesn't change? Does the increased allocation duration help enough in terms of being able to grab items in time assuming you react quickly? (Chris [Chris Wilson]. "0.10.3c Patch Notes." *Path of Exile*)

The patch notes serve the traditional generic role of documenting design changes in a central, comprehensive text, but Wilson also makes a move to acknowledge that player feedback has directly influenced the direction of user experience design and creates a targeted prompt to elicit more feedback on specific issues. As technical communicators, we should pay attention to how these dialogic exchanges are negotiated by game developers and community managers, especially in social media spaces, which are more hybridized in terms of rhetorical agency than a traditional set of patch notes. Focusing on online game guides, Luce notes in this collection that "the shift from corporate guides to online gaming forums has altered the conditions and nature of authority and agency within guides and walkthroughs" (4). Luce's chapter points to the ethical and ideological issues that can emerge when game documentation moves outside of organizational governance into player-driven online spaces. For community managers whose job is to publicly manage and frame player feedback, accounting for how players-as-agents can publicly articulate a range of positions and values can help articulate a strategy for response in line with organizational ethos.

In another thread, Wilson prefaces the patch notes with a reference to an explanatory post made by a different member of the development team in the General Discussion forum, emphasizing that they should be read *together*: "we strongly urge you to read [the explanation of balance changes] alongside these patch notes" ("0.10.0 Patch Notes"). Like the *League of Legends* patch preview videos, Wilson pairs the documentation work of patch notes with the purpose of articulating design rationales directly from a developer's perspective. In the explanation post that Wilson references, user "Qarl" (Carl de Visser) parses the difference in purpose between the posts, though they both reference the 0.10.0 design changes as a common object. The post in the General Discussion forum serves as "a more broad, high level explanation of what sort of balance changes were made, and why we made them," while emphasizing that the post does not set out to address *all* design changes ("Open Beta—Design Changes"). In de Visser's post, he also establishes a thematic link between content from the patch notes, creating a narrative around the decision to deliberately weaken, or "nerf," skills that are perceived to be too powerful. He highlights several skill changes listed in the patch notes that are tied to this purpose, and he presents a rationale arguing that overpowered skills undermine the relationship between players' agency as problem solvers and the challenge presented by the game:

> We also want to make players earn their power. If there is something that allows a player to succeed with no effort, and without working hard to ensure all their passive choices, gear choices, and play choices line up with it, then that game element will be changed. (Qarl [Carl de Visser]. "Open Beta—Design Changes." *Path of Exile*)

For players who want to be on the more competitive end of the spectrum, the work of filtering and digging through the technical side of patch notes is positioned as rewarding; simply consuming information from other players about the most efficient play practices will not be as successful in the long term. From a technical communication practitioner's standpoint, understanding this dynamic can help in the planning stages as content developers anticipate how users will respond to existing documentation and generate their own documentation. Antonio Ceraso argues that this evaluation can be performed strategically as a kind of "responsiveness management," offering a set of heuristic questions to assess how and when users engage with *official* technical documents and for what purposes they write their own documentation (250–52). Encouraging users to be active problem solvers and creating a motivated context for reading documentation critically can also help troubleshoot where existing documentation might not be carrying out its intended work.

For *Path of Exile*'s development, the developers of Grinding Gear Games value the dialogic affordances of online forums as a platform to deliver and archive their patch documentation. Although the patch notes are posted in separate threads and mostly as stand-alone texts that may limit the ways players can interact with them rhetorically, the developers do prioritize specific issues for player feedback and explicitly link rationales from various developers' perspectives to the information contained in patch notes. Members of the development team are also active in these forum threads, which suggests a desire to frame conversations around specific changes represented in patching. Like the official forums hosted by Blizzard and Riot Games, there are mechanisms in place to make developer postings more visible; Grinding Gear Games has its own website dedicated to developer post tracking with a note that it enables players to more easily 'stalk the devs.' Within the textual ecology of the forums, the developers work with and against the affordances of using individual forum threads as a historical method for archiving patch notes. While this decision serves a useful organizing function, it also limits the ways that links between design rationales communicated via developers and the hard data of patch notes can be constructed.

Conclusion

In all three of the approaches to patch documentation that developers for Riot Games, Blizzard Entertainment, and Grinding Gear Games have taken, they have exercised an awareness that patch notes are a site where adaptive rhetorical work can and should be carried out. Beyond just reporting, organizing, and archiving information, releasing patch notes represents an opportunity to frame specific arguments to specific audiences and is a pivotal moment in ethos construction. Players hold expectations not only for the content of patches as bundles of iterative design changes but also for the genre standards that patch documentation should be held accountable to. As Josh Zimmerman argues in this collection on the rhetorics of secrecy and disclosure negotiated by fans and game developers, "At its core, the relationship between developer and fans is transactional, with both the developer and the fan taking part in a subculture where access to the inside of the development structure is valued as a form of cultural capital" (p. 145). Game developers rely on social media channels such as YouTube to manage the construction of image around iterative content design, as in the patch preview videos designed by Riot Games staff to showcase new features. From a player's perspective, patch documentation has taken on an expected genre function of fulfilling players' desires for disclosure, not only in the sense of presenting hard data but offering a glimpse into what the developers were thinking as they put the patch together. For instance, a post on the collaborative blog *Kill Ten Rats*, which focuses on critiquing MMO design culture, outlines from a player perspective what the best way to compose patch notes consists of. First, the precision and completeness of data is emphasized; Zubon argues that quantification is an important measure for testing "as you want people to test if the numbers actually come out that way, especially since some of the notes are correcting ability numbers or text so that they match (ditto for graphic effect and area of effect)." This is the classical imperative that patch notes have typically answered to, but the post goes on to note the importance of an explicit framing of developer intent. Zubon cites a set of *City of Heroes* patch notes as evidence, claiming that, "one thing they do well is pointing to themes. Some of that is the advertising copy for, 'Come try our new stuff! It's awesome!' but the valuable part is expressing the developer intent in the patch notes." Players have started to recognize and argue for explicit developer rationales as an expected genre function of patch documentation, and associated textual platforms like developer interviews, podcasts, blogs, and forums have expanded the options and capacities for developers to choose how and when to release such information publicly.

These cases also show what Stolley calls the various 'integrations' that game development companies have engineered with respect to how they use social media in the service of patch documentation. Some of these strategies appear to be more central and deliberate; Riot Games, for instance, has incentivized the use of Facebook and YouTube to engage players in their social media streams, while using their YouTube channel as a hub for patch documentation, news, commentary on fan culture, and other episodic kinds of content. The links in Riot Games' textual network lead players to explore this space—for example, the splash interface when first loading the game client and Riot's official website frame and embed this YouTube content. The leveraging of these spaces as a transmedia-driven game development and marketing strategy points to a broader rhetorical crafting of experiences. This strategy recalls the possibility space that Jennifer deWinter and Ryan Moeller point to in the introduction to this collection as an implication of studying technical communication and computer gaming alongside one another: "Here, we see an opportunity for technical communication to be transformed: we can imagine technologies, not as systematized approaches to defined problems, but rather as systems of human expression" (8). Given the investments that players have in negotiating the content and expectations of gaming experiences in online spaces, we might look to patching as a model of "expressive" problem solving. In other words, patching and its associated documentation practices maintains a dialogue between game developers and players that is founded in technical practice but also reveals the emotional and ideological stakes of computer games as designed experiences that accumulate their own histories.

For technical communicators, the mediations represented by these companies' documentation practices can be instructive, not because they represent a more idealized set of strategies per se, but for the decision tree they help illustrate. When and how should documentation draw on social media and online multimedia composing spaces, and to what ends? In what cases is a central *archiving* function effective, and when is a more distributed strategy called for? What are the affordances of making designer intentionality transparent in public documentation? What are the implications of revealing internal or not-yet-released information? By carefully thinking through these kinds of questions and continuing to pay attention to what users say patch documentation *should do*, technical communicators can map out design solutions that match how they wish to engage (or not) with social media. Liza Potts and Dave Jones outline four characteristics of a well-designed technical communication strategy that leverages social media: From a user experience perspective, its content should be locatable, navigable, discoverable, and retrievable. Potts and Jones's design heuristics emphasize movement through multiple spaces, and for a site like Blizzard Entertainment's patch release hub for 5.2, they have designed to encourage movement across textual networks and zones of affiliation. As user documentation and other forms of technical communication are opened to increasingly layered techniques for framing via social media and multimodal and interactive forms of writing, being able to articulate the rhetorical grounds on which these instances of communication are built becomes all the more critical.

Works Cited

Ceraso, Antonio. "How Can Technical Communicators Plan for Users?" *Solving Problems in Technical Communication*. Eds. Johndan Johnson-Eilola and Stuart A. Selber. Chicago: U of Chicago P, 2013. 237–61.

Chris [Chris Wilson]. "0.10.0 Patch Notes." *Path of Exile*. Grinding Gear Games, 23 Jan. 2013. Web. 28 Mar. 2013.

———. "0.10.3c Patch Notes." *Path of Exile*. Grinding Gear Games, 18 Mar. 2013. Web. 28 Mar. 2013.

DaSpartan Legacy. "A Really Fun, Feasible and Innovative Rework Suggestion on LeBlanc." *League of Legends Community*. Riot Games, 26 May 2013. Web. 28 May 2013.

deWinter, Jennifer. "Just Playing Around: From Procedural Manuals to In-Game Training." *Computer Games and Technical Communication: Critical Methods and Applications at the Intersection*. Eds. Jennifer deWinter and Ryan M. Moeller. Burlington: Ashgate, 2014. 69–85.

deWinter, Jennifer, and Ryan M. Moeller. "Intoduction: Playing the Field: Technical Communication for Technical Games." *Computer Games and Technical Communication: Critical Methods and Applications at the Intersection*. Eds. Jennifer deWinter and Ryan M. Moeller. Burlington: Ashgate, 2014. 1–13.

Gee, James Paul. *What Video Games Have to Teach Us About Learning and Literacy*. 2nd ed. New York: Palgrave Macmillan, 2007.

"League of Legends—3.03 Patch Preview." *Riot Games*. YouTube, 28 Feb. 2013. Web. 28 Mar. 2013.

Luce, A. V. "'It Wasn't Intended to Be an Instruction Manual': Revisiting Ethics of 'Objective' Technical Communication in Gaming Manuals." *Computer Games and Technical Communication: Critical Methods and Applications at the Intersection*. Eds. Jennifer deWinter and Ryan M. Moeller. Burlington: Ashgate, 2014. 87–106.

McAllister, Ken S. *Game Work: Language, Power, and Computer Game Culture*. Tuscaloosa, AL: U of Alabama P, 2004.

Morello. "Patch 3.03 Notes." *League of Legends*. Riot Games, 28 Feb. 2013. Web. 28 Mar. 2013.

———. "Patch 3.5 Notes." *League of Legends*. Riot Games, 27 Mar. 2013. Web. 28 Mar. 2013.

"New Talents and Account wide Systems in *World of Warcraft* (*WoW* 5.0.4)." *Blizzard Entertainment*. *YouTube*, 27 Aug. 2012. Web. 28 Mar. 2013.

perculia. "Wowhead's Patch 5.2 Interview with Lead Encounter Designer Ion 'Watcher' Hazzikostas." *Wowhead*. ZAM Network, 28 Feb. 2013. Web. 28 Mar. 2013.

Potts, Liza, and Dave Jones. "Contextualizing Experiences: Tracing the Relationships Between People and Technologies in the Social Web." *Journal of Business and Technical Communication* 25.3 (2011): 338–58.

Qarl [Carl de Visser]. "Open Beta—Design Changes." *Path of Exile*. Grinding Gear Games, 23 Jan. 2013. Web. 28 Mar. 2013.

Rygarius. "Patch 5.2: The Thunder King Now Live." *World of Warcraft*. Blizzard Entertainment, 7 Mar. 2013. Web. 28 Mar. 2013.

Spinuzzi, Clay. *Tracing Genres Through Organizations: A Sociocultural Approach to Information Design*. Cambridge, MA: MIT P, 2003.

Stolley, Karl. "Integrating Social Media Into Existing Work Environments: The Case of Delicious." *Journal of Business and Technical Communication* 23.3 (2009): 350–71.

Zimmerman, Josh. "Psyche and Eros: Rhetorics of Secrecy and Disclosure in Game Developer–Fan Relations." *Computer Games and Technical Communication: Critical Methods and Applications at the Intersection*. Eds. Jennifer deWinter and Ryan M. Moeller. Burlington: Ashgate, 2014. 141–56.

Zubon. "How to Write Patch Notes." *Kill Ten Rats*. 19 Nov. 2009. Web. 28 Mar. 2013.

Chapter 10

"You Are How You Play": Privacy Policies and Data Mining in Social Networking Games

Stephanie Vie

Though online social networking sites like Facebook, MySpace, Google+, and LinkedIn have collectively affected communicative acts for nearly two decades, it is only recently that academic attention has been paid to these sites. The explosive growth of social networking coupled with its impact on twenty-first century communication has encouraged technical communication scholars to critically examine these spaces. Today, online social networking sites are firmly entrenched in the lives of many average everyday Americans, including a growing number of older adults. Older adults' social networking site use has grown significantly: From 2009 to 2011, the participation of those aged 65 and older in social networking sites grew 150 percent while 72 percent of adults between 30 and 49 used social networking sites overall (Zickuhr and Madden 2–9). Such statistics combat clichéd assumptions of social networking as an activity enjoyed mainly by teenagers. For example, while a stereotypical view of Facebook is of a space heavily populated by teens and young adults, the site's statistics show that Facebook has a more balanced user population. Other social networking sites like Google+ have experienced similar growth among older participants, while professional networking spaces like LinkedIn have always targeted adult professionals as their main audience. And, as such, they are having a growing impact on the communicative habits and literacy practices across a considerable population of the United States.

Along with explosive growth among all users but predominantly among adults, Facebook and Google+ in particular have experienced a surge in users' participation in social networking games such as *Words with Friends*, *CityVille*, and *Happy Street*. Facebook has estimated that more than 250 million people monthly play games on the site, and of the approximately two hundred social games on Facebook, there are more than a million monthly active users for each (Tam). As participation in these games has grown, the games themselves have grown more sophisticated, and their designers, marketers, and distributors have helped delineate social networking games as a distinct category of their own. For instance, social networking games have more clearly defined themselves in relation to other games media like Massively Multiplayer Online Games (MMOGs), console games, and personal computer games. Thus social networking games can be defined as any commercially sponsored or designed games embedded within a social networking site that are playable by users only within that site and that encourage or require sociality with networked connections. Unlike console or personal computer games, then, social networking games rely on both the game medium (the social networking site itself) and the social structure of the game (users are encouraged or required by the game to interact with members of their social network). While MMOGs also include sociality (such as requiring groups of players to collaboratively complete quests), they differ from social networking games in that they are playable outside of a social networking medium. Jesper Juul notes that:

> such games . . . are *socially embeddable*: games for which much of the interesting experience is not explicitly *in* the game, but is something that the players add to the game. . . . [T]he game takes on meaning from the existing relation between the players. . . . Furthermore, people playing [social networking games] are often themselves a spectacle, making these games more interesting even for those who are not playing. (20, emphasis in original)

Juul's depiction showcases the importance of embedded sociality in setting these games apart from others. Finally, many social networking games are also casual games; while a definitive description of casual games is difficult given their variance, they are generally easy to play, require no special gaming background, are simple to start and stop, and are playable in short increments (Russoniello et al. 53). Much like how social networking sites themselves have gone through a period of definition (particularly in setting them apart from earlier established media like blogs and dating sites) and growth, social networking games have—albeit more recently—moved through a similar period of establishment and growth.

The establishment and growth of social networking sites has prompted academic attention to their impact on literacy and communication. However, little discussion of the impact of gaming in social networking sites has yet occurred. Game studies scholars have attended particularly to MMOGs, console games, and personal computer games but have not yet focused in depth on social networking games. Much of the work on gaming in technical communication has focused on the relationships between game players and game spaces (Vie, "Tech Writing"; Araki and Carliner), including an examination of games' procedural rhetorics (Eyman; Mason). Within writing studies more broadly, researchers have attended to the intersections of computer gaming and student literacy (Gee; Hawisher and Selfe; Moberly; Alexander) and the impact of game design on the construction of players' avatars (deWinter and Vie; Hoag and Schell; Waggoner), while scholarly monographs such as McAllister's *Game Work* have studied multiple aspects of the computer game complex as a whole. The previous literature on rhetorical, social, ethical, and procedural aspects of games provides a strong basis for further research on social networking games, an area ripe for further study.

Social networking games, particularly within Facebook, provide a rich space for technical communication scholars to examine not only the impact of these game spaces on the user's experience—considering their impact on rhetorical and technological literacy, for example—but also the creation, marketing, and circulation of these spaces within a game development framework. While technical communicators have long been interested in examining data as they are circulated through an information economy, the ethical ramifications of privacy policies and data mining in social networking games are of particular importance given the dearth of analysis in this area. This chapter examines the latter, an undertheorized aspect of game studies within the space of social networking sites and within the field of technical communication. This chapter pays particular attention to the clarity of privacy policies in social networking sites and games as well as the process of data mining and recursive shaping of the games based on data-mined user behaviors. Drawing on actor-network theory as its theoretical framework, this chapter examines the actors in game development and marketing and illuminates how the developers of social media games, the players, and the game spaces themselves (including privacy policies) work together as actants within a framework that relies on data and databases, thereby evoking questions of the ethical responsibilities of game developers.

My aim in this chapter is, therefore, to argue that social gaming spaces are fruitful sites for analyzing how these games have been designed and are maintained to stimulate a particular kind of communication: how the players' data is elicited to create a user-friendly gaming space on the surface and to segment and categorize players behind the scenes. While game analytics is nothing new, the integration of social ties with the game play space is of importance for scholars of technical communication and rhetoric. Given that data mining in social games affects not only the players, but the players' social connections—their Facebook or Google+ friends—as well, it is crucial that technical communication scholars articulate potential ethical issues brought up through data mining in social games played in social networking spaces. Privacy policies in social networking games are of particular importance given their connections with the data mined from players. Understanding privacy policies and social networking games as rhetorically purposeful actants within a network allows players to better understand the implications of the communicative choices offered to them (or sometimes imposed upon them) within these spaces.

A critically aware stance toward the technologies we use allows us to better articulate the kinds of relationships we would like to have with technologies: If those technologies are ones we choose to use ourselves, then understanding their political, ethical, social, and rhetorical dimensions affords us the opportunity to make more informed choices that align closely with our personal values. But in some cases, technologies are imposed upon us; for example, a technical communicator might be employed in a workplace that mandates the use of Adobe or Microsoft Office products (see Moberly and Moeller's chapter in this collection for a critique of individual resistance against dominant ideologies). Even in such instances, critical awareness of the human-technological interface and its effects are necessary: Many workplaces regularly refresh or update technologies and ask for employee input on those choices. Employees who are aware of the implications of the technologies they are asked to use are better able to educate others about those implications and possibly affect policy changes as a result. As Gurak has argued, most people do not operate on a conscious level that allows them to examine technologies as artifacts with backgrounds, politics, and agendas, instead preferring to view them as things that are "invented, advertised, packaged up, and sold to you . . . and do not, in and of themselves, make you do things" (2). Similarly, Moberly points to the multiple intersections between capitalism and games, arguing that games have the potential to make users aware of the "insidious, violent discourse of consumerism that is disseminated through works of popular culture like computer games" (296). Rhetorically aware individuals are therefore better able to assess the construction, dissemination, and marketing of social games and decide for themselves in what ways they are comfortable participating in them (if at all). They are more aware of how data mining and privacy policies in social networking sites operate in the service of capitalism, allowing companies to "understand" users better in order to target them with ads and enhance their user experience. And finally, they are better able to understand the myriad ways technologies are not just designed, but have designs on us.

Social Networking Sites, Connectivity, and Privacy

The increasing use of social networking sites among American adults means that today, it is easier than ever to visualize how individuals are connected to others; similarly, it is simple to look up a person's social networking profile, to connect with him or her, and to discover a great deal of information about that person through the user profile. Social networking sites have become nearly ubiquitous, and, as a result, are significantly impacting how we think about privacy and connectivity. Social networking games, too, wreak their own specific changes on the public and private sphere. Within the space of social networking games, Losh points out how egalitarian mechanisms for making new connections in social networks can butt up against the sometimes hierarchical systems of ranking on leaderboards, creating a challenging environment for sustained and synergistic game play (345). In this example, the harmonious collaboration privileged by social networks' reliance on personal relationships clashes with the competitive nature of some game spaces. Too, social networking games can, by virtue of their embedded sociality, become frustrating for users—asking a social networking "friend" who is really an acquaintance to add the application, play the game, or assist the user in acquiring an item or finishing a challenge can overstep the bounds of appropriate behavior in social networking spaces. Both social networking sites and the games played within these sites are continually affecting change in how we think about connections and privacy.

Along with the changes in connectivity and privacy wrought by social networking sites, users must contend with the sheer number of privacy options, terms of service documents, and end-user licensing agreements for the social networking sites and games in which they participate. A 2008 study by McDonald and Cranor attempted to estimate how much time would be spent if users were to read the privacy policy for each site they visit yearly; they estimated that the average user would have to spend approximately forty minutes per day reading through their privacy policies and that "if all American Internet users were to annually read the online privacy policies word-for-word each time they visited a new site, the nation would spend about 54 billion hours reading privacy policies" (560). While it is difficult to accurately measure the time it takes to read privacy policies, end-user license agreements, and other terms of service documents, McDonald and Cranor's research points to the considerable burden placed on users of social networking sites and games to keep up with policies that affect their rights—including whether or not their personal data may be shared with, or stored and used by, others.

Of course, we should not simply assume that only uneducated or lazy users are at fault for not reading terms of service documents, or that those users who fail to keep up with privacy policies and terms of use documents are unconcerned about how their information will be used and shared. Many terms of service documents are couched in legalese, difficult to read and understand for the average user. The case of musician Billy Bragg, a British protest singer who fought the social networking site MySpace in 2006 over its terms of use, is illustrative of this issue: Bragg uploaded his music to MySpace to promote his work to a broader audience. A friend pointed out that MySpace's terms and conditions seemed to imply that the site had "a nonexclusive, fully paid and royalty-free worldwide license" to any uploaded songs; Bragg withdrew his entire catalogue of music in protest and repeatedly complained until, finally, MySpace changed its terms and conditions to assure users that they continued to own the rights to their materials, including music, uploaded to the site (Vie, "I Gave" 108). As a professional musician concerned about intellectual property rights who unknowingly nearly signed the rights to his music away, Bragg is a perfect example of the impact that well-written and clearly disclosed terms of service documents (or the lack thereof) can have on users of social networking sites.

This impact is based in part on the idea that technical documents like privacy policies are themselves actors within the social network. Within actor-network theory, technologies can have equal agency alongside human actants in a given communicative situation; within the social networking game setting, the applications themselves along with the privacy policies and terms of service documents associated with those applications should be considered actors given their influence on the players' communicative choices. Sidorova and Sarker describe actors as rhetorical agents with an interest in persuasion; they can be human or nonhuman and are enmeshed in a collective network wherein each actor can be defined and understood only in relation to other actors (53). Nonhuman artifacts have interests inasmuch as those interests are embedded as part of their design, or as Gurak asserts, "technologies are invented by people and imbued with design choices that give those devices certain trajectories" (2). As participants within social networks, the individuals who play social networking games are in a constant process of translation, which involves problematization, or the moment when an actor determines the identities and interests of other actors that are consistent with its own interests (Sidorova and Sarker 54). Problematization can be difficult for players of social networking games as often the privacy policies—and, by extension, the game developers who have composed those privacy policies—demonstrate interests that are not necessarily aligned with those of the players. Privacy policies and terms of service documents are unfortunately frequently designed not to be read; their interests as actors within the networked system are in fact to be seen as little as possible. They are often difficult to find, difficult to access, and difficult to understand, all in a deliberate effort to convince other actors in the system (through the omission of documents describing privacy policies) that the technology—in this case, the social networking game—has the users' best interests in mind and supports their concerns about privacy, too. In this way, the composition of privacy policies often incorporates elements of rhetorical misdirection (Markel 198).

Even in privacy policies and terms of service documents that are clear and accessible, the information may be presented within a binary system that allows for little (if any) user control over their own data. For example, the Facebook game *Candy Crush Saga* hosts a privacy policy that allows the user little choice in determining how their data will be shared and with whom; the privacy policy and terms of service rely on binaries such as the following (emphasis added in italics):

- 3.1 By playing our Games, you give your consent to the way we may collect, process and use your personal data. Any personal information that we may collect is also subject to the policy of this social network. By playing our Games you are giving the social network permission to share your email address and other information that will allow us to personally identify you. This is intended to make our Games more enjoyable for you and others that play our Games on the social network. *If you do not agree to our privacy policy you shouldn't play our Games.*
- 9.2 Your only right with respect to any problems or dissatisfaction with any of our Games is *to discontinue your use of that Game* and we are not responsible or liable for any interruptions or errors that you may experience while playing our Games.
- 10.3 We grant you a limited licence to access and play our Games subject to these terms, including a limited licence to use an image of any avatar (if any) that you may create using our Games (an Avatar) and/or any screenshot of anything that you may create using our Games (a Screenshot), *providing it is not used to say anything negative about any of our Games* and such use complies with these terms.

- We reserve the right to update these terms from time to time. If you do not wish to be governed by any updated version of the terms, *your only remedy is to stop playing our Games.*

This terms of service document relies strongly on a binary, either/or system of helping users understand how their data will be collected and used. Essentially, King.com (creator of *Candy Crush Saga*) states that either you will allow your information to be shared or you will stop playing the game. No options in between are offered, such as consenting to certain types of sharing or emailing to request that your data be deleted. In addition, the phrasing of the terms of service is mostly negative; for example, users are allowed to share screenshots of avatars they create within the game "providing it is not used to say anything negative about any of our Games." These terms of service, while clear and mainly easy to understand, are written in such a way to be unwelcoming to the average player should he or she actually read the document.

Certainly technical communicators have a responsibility to compose end-user license agreements and privacy policies in ways that help, not hinder, users to understand them. Applying principles drawn from technical communication studies, such as providing relevant hierarchical headings, chunking information, and using call-out boxes to allow users to skim policies for greater understanding is one step to address this issue. Similarly, using the social media platform itself to disseminate easy-to-read policy changes—rather than burying lengthy screeds regarding changes deep within the site—is another means of reaching users. In other words, better alignment of nonhuman actors within the social networking system with the privacy concerns of human actors would allow for greater trust to be built among the members of the network. The following examples from one popular social networking game, *Words with Friends*, illustrate the tensions between technological actors (privacy policies) and human actors (game players) within the social networking space.

In Figure 10.1 and Figure 10.2 below, the privacy policies as technological actors are designed with a rhetoric of misdirection or obfuscation at their core. The privacy policies are not equally presented to players before gameplay is offered; depending on a player's mode of entry into the game, he may or may not be presented with the full privacy policies. Like many other social networking games, *Words with Friends* posts on a user's timeline when she plays; these posts encourage other users to participate as well. In this case, when a user clicks "Play now!" in *Words with Friends* after seeing the link on another user's timeline, the game appears within Facebook, but the privacy policy is simply listed as a link at the bottom in gray text on a white background that is difficult to see. The privacy policy is nearly impossible to discern to the right of the anthropomorphized letter tile, which in fact partially obscures the link to the terms of service (see Figure 10.1).

However, if users access the game from the Facebook App Center (a repository of all available applications, including games), then those users are presented with

Figure 10.1   *Words with Friends* Accessed from a User's Timeline

a clearer link to the privacy policy (see Figure 10.2 below). Given that sociality is prioritized in social networking games, users are more likely to see and participate in games based on seeing their friends doing so; as a result, users may be less likely to see and understand the privacy policies for those games.

The above figures show how the user's understanding of privacy policies in social networking sites and games frequently depends on how he or she accesses applications. Indeed, accessing applications that are suggested by one's friends may mean that a user has to work even harder to find, access, and understand the privacy policies for that application.

Similarly, these examples demonstrate how technological actors in social networking games can be designed to confuse or obfuscate information crucial to human actors' needs and desires. In *Words with Friends* as shown above, the privacy policy is hosted offline (on Zynga.com) and is slightly over 5,500 words long, which McDonald and Cranor's research demonstrates is an overly lengthy policy (552). The privacy policy is separate from the terms of service document, which is on yet another page and is 7,640 words long; combined, the two policy

Figure 10.2   *Words with Friends* Accessed from the Facebook App Center

documents are over 13,000 words long—over fifty pages of information for a consumer to read before agreeing to play a game with friends. Yet privacy in social networking sites is a major concern of most users; according to a 2012 PEW Internet & American Life research project on privacy management in social networking sites, almost two thirds of users restrict access to their profile, prune their friends list of people they don't know, and delete comments and photo tags they don't want to share (Madden). Thus a tension exists between the desires for privacy of most human actors and the embedded "desires" coded into the nonhuman actors in this system: the privacy policies, terms of service documents, and even the game systems themselves encourage the greatest amount of sharing and openness possible, which opposes most social media users' desires to share in limited ways within carefully defined networks.

Technical communicators can play a significant role in mediating the user experience for participants in social networking sites in terms of helping them understand how privacy is handled in that space. Markel's analysis of corporate privacy policies articulates a framework derived from the Federal Trade Commission; technical communicators can use this framework to assess these policies based on four categories: notice, choice, access, and security (203). The examples from *Words with Friends* shows how one of the largest social networking game developers, Zynga, fails to meet many of the suggested means of presenting privacy policies in ways that are usable for players. While the site does have a privacy policy statement, it is not equally easy to find and accessible from all pages. The statement is written clearly, but is overly lengthy and presents a burden for an interested reader. The user is not offered a choice of options for the use of the data; Zynga only allows a user to opt in fully or otherwise delete the account. As the popularity of social networking games increases, technical communicators have the ability to help users better understand the privacy options and terms of use for participation in those games, a responsibility that may be addressed through more open communication with game developers. This communication could take the form of reflective analysis of game development assisted by technical communicators (Daer) or public writing in gaming spaces that encourages collaboration between players and developers (Johnson). As Greene and Palmer point out, however, while calls have been made to make technical communicators part of the game development cycle, few have answered (p. 31). This lack will likely remain a tension point for the industry but may also become an exciting challenge for technical communicators in years to come.

"You Are How You Play": Data Mining and Player Analytics

Social networking games also offer an intriguing space for technical communicators to explore the intersections of data mining and analytics. While other games, particularly MMOGs, involve connectivity and privacy, social networking games differ in an interesting way. The nature of social networking sites like Facebook (one of the largest United States social networks with the greatest number of social networking games in heavy use) relies on accurate user information and therefore the accumulation of accurate personal data. This means that game players in Facebook often share a great deal of personal information with game developers. That is, Facebook's "real name" policy requires that users are not allowed by the site's terms of service to use a pseudonym or nickname; while of course users can and do get around this policy through clever tricks, the majority of users abides by the real name policy and showcase truthful information about themselves.

   Additionally, social networking sites rely on users' connectivity and sharing behaviors; after all, what good is a social networking site where all of the users have locked their profiles down as private? Or where it is impossible to find a long-lost classmate or friend because they failed to list their actual name? True networking is difficult to perform in the face of rigid privacy settings or user deception. Social networking sites, therefore, encourage users to both share broadly and to share true information with others. For this reason, social networking games have different implications for users than console or personal computer games, or even MMOGs, as these spaces do not regularly require (and, in fact, for safety reasons, often advise against this kind of sharing) that users list their full name and encourage sharing personal information like friends, location, schools attended, workplaces, and so on.

Kristin Arola has argued that in social networking sites, "You are what you post and what others post about you" (9). When gaming in social networking sites, this argument is extended: you are also how you play. The combination of the two implies that social networking games rely not only on who you are (based on what you post and what your connections post about you) and on how you play (based on analysis of your gaming behaviors, scores, and other patterns), but also—and perhaps most concerning for privacy overall—based on the preferences and user data of your connections. Data mining in social games attempts to predict user preferences and by extension the preferences of the users' friends as well; its analysis of distribution, retention, and monetization showcases how games in social networking spaces are not simply fun and entertaining diversions but highly sophisticated tools for behavioral analysis of and marketing to large groups of people (see deWinter's chapter in this collection for a discussion of the persuasive power of adaptive in-game messaging). Much like how social networking sites themselves rely on users making connections by sharing news, pictures, comments, and other elements on the users' personal profile, games in these spaces encourage players to share with their friends and get them to play too. For example, many social networking games automatically post status updates to a user's Facebook timeline that display the user's current score, invite friends to play, or show the user's status in a competition on a leaderboard. These social posts are an important means of recruiting new players to the game; Figure 10.3

Figure 10.3   Friend's Social Gaming Activity on the Author's Facebook Timeline

shows how myVEGAS slots, a social networking game, posts on behalf of a player on the author's Facebook timeline.

Other games rely on cooperative play; for instance, a user might be required to send an item to another player or receive an item from a friend to be able to move on in the game. Returning to actor-network theory once more to analyze how communicative acts are shaped in social networking games, it is clear that the games themselves are programmed in ways that mimic human actors' communicative patterns in social networking sites. Participants in social networking sites regularly post comments on each other's profiles, share images, links, and pictures, and otherwise engage in networking (broadly defined). The games themselves have been designed to mimic the communication patterns of social networking site users and encourage higher numbers of users to participate in them; this mimicry is unlike other forms of gaming, like MMOGs and console games, and is therefore of particular interest for those who study the relationship between human and technological actants in closed networked systems like social networking sites.

What is intriguing about this relationship is the tensions that often exist between the goals of the technological system—in this case, the social networking game—and the goals of many users—here, the game players. Social networking games are programmed to elicit a high level of sharing practices: They encourage users to post game play statistics on their Facebook Timelines, for example, and push players to invite all of their Facebook friends to also begin playing the game. Indeed, many game designers have programmed automatic invitation systems triggered when a user signs up and begins playing; when players sign up, if they doesn't carefully examine the screens presented to them, they may unwittingly spam hundreds of Facebook friends with invitations to play the game as well. Yet many social networking site users are concerned about privacy as well as maintaining relationship boundaries; in other words, many users prefer not to needlessly spam their friends with information they feel will not be interesting or useful to them. For example, the player in Figure 10.3 above described to me that "whenever a game gives me the Facebook share option, I tend to just say no, not wanting to flood timelines. [However,] Vegas Slots snuck past me a few times" (Cadle).

Given that "you are how you play" in social networking games, the games themselves are altered based on how you play. Jacobs and Sihvonen are careful to point out that developers altering games based on gameplay patterns and user feedback is not new; what is new, however, is the rapidity with which social networking games can implement changes based on user performance and feedback. Much like Billy Bragg convinced MySpace in a short period of time to change its user policies, players in social networking games can quickly see, or ask to see, changes in the game based on their experience. Jacobs and Sihvonen recount how *FrontierVille* adapted its gameplay based both on user feedback and play patterns: "Players gave feedback concerning the balancing of a special food item they could buy to receive additional energy. In . . . a few days, the item had been modified as requested by the players. . . . Zynga also announced changes to the energy balancing . . . and leveling . . . based on the result of the game play as opposed to player request" (4). The authors label the former mode of influence over game play *direct participatory design*, while the latter (where the game developers changed the mode of play based on patterns they saw) is termed *silent participatory design*. Unlike in many console or computer games, social networking games are in a state of near-constant or "perpetual beta" existence while the game changes to adapt to the players. That is, traditional games marketing and development focuses heavily on the formative creation of those games; a game like *Call of Duty* or *BioShock* would involve market analyses, game design, user testing, and finally production and dissemination. Based on player feedback and sales data, other editions of the game might eventually be released as either standalone sequels or expansion packs. Ultimately, though, the bulk of the design and development work would occur prior to the game's release. In contrast, social networking games and massively multiplayer online games have the advantage of near-constant game player tracking. Vast numbers of data are gathered each time a player logs in and interacts with the system. Behind the scenes, the design of the game—its look and feel, its game environments, its controls, and so on—can be adapted in real time in response to data gathered. Social games rely on both formative and summative analysis of player data—sometimes without the players' awareness (or informed consent) that such data are being gathered, stored, analyzed, and used.

Playnomics is one company that mines user data in social games, analyzes this data to segment users by behavior, employs predictive algorithms to determine which players are likely to enact particular behaviors, and targets new game players based on the connections of analyzed users that are displayed in social networking sites. Chethan Ramachandran, CEO of Playnomics, notes that "Our predictive scoring system reveals hidden traits about players. . . . Just like a credit score, our scores are portable across games, and predict how a player will perform in any game environment. . . . Our platform algorithmically determines the best type of player for your game and then matches that profile to our databank of over 20M players to bring you new, high quality customers who will love your game" (quoted, in Takahashi). Ramachandran's description of the active role of the gaming system highlights its importance within the system: it *reveals* hidden traits; it *determines* the best type of player. The active role that the game itself takes again showcases how social networking games are not simply technologies to be used by players, but are active players within the game system itself. The data mining and algorithmic profiling that social networking games engage in are hallmarks of nonhuman actors in networked systems.

Conclusion

Ian Bogost has argued that games are

> not just stages that facilitate cultural, social, or political practices; they are also media where cultural values themselves can be represented—for critique, satire, education, or commentary. When understood in this way, we can learn to read games as deliberate expressions of particular perspectives. In other words, video games make claims about the world, which players can understand, evaluate, and deliberate. Game developers can learn to create games that make deliberate expressions about the world. Players can learn to read and critique these models, deliberating the implications of such claims. (119–20)

As technological actors in networked systems, social networking games are designed and continually reshaped to provide a more engaging and fun product for players. But as games researcher Malaby argues, too often we limit ourselves to the idea that games are entirely about fun and entertainment. When we assume that games are simply programs designed to create a fun experience, we fail to consider games as technological actors with designs of their own. Technical communicators have long been interested in attending to ethical issues that emerge from corporate communications such as privacy policies and terms of service, as well as the ethical issues that emerge from the large-scale collection and dissemination of user data in social spaces. Games study scholars and rhetoricians have investigated from a critical rhetorical standpoint the procedural rhetorics of games, the formation of player relationships and user avatars, and the game development and production cycle (indeed, many of the chapters in this volume touch on these themes, such as Ouelette's work on ethics and queer theory in games and professional communication, Moberly and Moeller's work on capitalist ideology and the opportunities presented in modding culture, and even Luce's work on the ethics of procedural manuals for games that have offensive content). Given the significant overlap of these two spheres of study and given the lack of sustained attention to the ethics of online social networking games in the scholarly literature, it is imperative that future research on social networking games involves analysis from technical communicators and games study scholars.

In his articulation of a "grammar of gameworks," McAllister argues that games work in five integral areas of power: *agents*, who have power to effect change in a game system; *functions*, or the purposes of those effects; *influences* and external forces that impinge on agents and functions; *manifestations* of the effects; and *transformative locales*, the places and instances that ideologies have specific transformative effects (1). Applying this five-pointed framework to social networking games alongside actor-network theory illustrates more clearly how these kinds of games are themselves agents alongside the players; the games have indeed been programmed to analyze player data, to respond to players' concerns and needs, and to shape and be shaped in return by the players in the system. As a result, the transformative locale of social networking sites is a space where certain ideologies are privileged: Certain attitudes toward sharing, particularly sharing of one's personal information, is reified while other attitudes, such as controlling one's private data and thoroughly reading privacy policies, are frequently discouraged and thus made invisible. Social networking games—as technologies of influence—encourage us to elide concerns about privacy by making awareness of privacy settings, policies, and implications frustrating to access, parse, and understand. The games and their associated privacy policies and terms of service work as agents in a reciprocal relationship with the individuals who play those games. As such, while these games can and do have many positive effects—such as bringing people together via collaborative gameplay, relieving the pressure of daily life through the fun of playing games, and teaching individuals critical thinking skills—I have demonstrated in this chapter that they also document a lack of awareness about privacy and the implications of data mining in the United States.

Works Cited

Alexander, Jonathan. "Gaming, Student Literacies, and the Composition Classroom: Some Possibilities for Transformation." *College Composition and Communication* 61.1 (2009): 35–63.

Araki, Marci, and Saul Carliner. "What the Literature Says About Using Game Worlds and Social Worlds in Cyberspace for Communicating Technical and Educational Content." *Technical Communication* 55 (2008): 251–60.

Arola, Kristin L. "The Design of Web 2.0: The Rise of the Template, the Fall of Design." *Computers and Composition* 27 (2010): 4–14.

Bogost, Ian. "The Rhetoric of Video Games." *The Ecology of Games: Connecting Youth, Games, and Learning.* Ed. Katie Salen. Cambridge, MA: MIT P, 2008. 117–40.

Cadle, Lanette. "Re: Question re: permission to use an image." Message to the author. 20 May 2013. Email.

Candy Crush Saga. King.com. Video game.

CityVille. Zynga. Video game.

Daer, Alice J. "This is How We Do It: A Glimpse at Gamelab's Design Process." *e-Learning and Digital Media* 7.1 (2010): 108–19.

deWinter, Jennifer. "Just Playing Around: From Procedural Manuals to In-Game Training." *Computer Games and Technical Communication: Critical Methods and Applications at the Intersection.* Burlington, VT: Ashgate, 2014. 69–85.

deWinter, Jennifer, and Stephanie Vie. "Press Enter to 'Say': Using Second Life to Teach Critical Media Literacy." *Computers and Composition* 25 (2008): 313–22.

Eyman, Douglas. "Computer Gaming and Technical Communication." *Technical Communication* 55.3 (Aug. 2008): 242–50.

Gee, James Paul. *What Video Games Have to Teach Us About Learning and Literacy.* New York, NY: Palgrave, 2003.

Greene, Jeff, and Laura Palmer. "It's All Fun and Games Until Someone Pulls Out a Manual: Finding a Role for Technical Communicators in the Game Industry." *Computer Games and Technical Communication: Critical Methods and Applications at the Intersection.* Eds. Jennifer deWinter and Ryan Moeller. Burlington, VT: Ashgate, 2014. 17–33.

Gurak, Laura J. *Cyberliteracy: Navigating the Internet with Awareness.* New Haven, CT: Yale UP, 2001.

Happy Street. GodziLab. Video game.

Hawisher, Gail, and Cynthia Selfe, eds. *Gaming Lives in the Twenty-first Century: Literate Connections.* New York, NY: Palgrave, 2007.

Hoag, Trevor, and Tekla Schell. "The Avatar that Therefore I Am (Following)." *Currents in Electronic Literacy*, 2010. Web. 20 Mar. 2013.

Jacobs, Melinda, and Tanja Sihvonen. "In Perpetual Beta? On the Participatory Design of Facebook Games." *Proceedings of DiGRA 2011 Conference: Think Design Play* (2011): 1–8. Web. 30 Mar. 2013.

Johnson, Matthew S. S. "Public Writing in Gaming Spaces." *Computers and Composition* 25 (2008): 270–83.

Juul, Jesper. *A Casual Revolution: Reinventing Video Games and Their Players.* Cambridge, MA: MIT P, 2010.

Losh, Elizabeth. "In Polite Company: Rules of Play in Five Facebook Games." *ACE '08 Proceedings of the 2008 International Conference on Advances in Computer Entertainment Technology* (2008): 345–51.

Luce, A. V. "'It Wasn't Intended to Be an Instruction Manual': Revisiting Ethics of 'Objective' Technical Communication in Gaming Manuals." *Computer Games and Technical Communication: Critical Methods and Applications at the Intersection.* Burlington, VT: Ashgate, 2014. Pages.

Madden, Mary. "Privacy Management on Social Media Sites." Pew Research Center's Internet & American Life Project. 24 Feb. 2012. Web. 30 Mar. 2013.

Malaby, Thomas M. "Beyond Play: A New Approach to Games." *Games and Culture* 2.2 (2007): 95–113.

Markel, Mike. "The Rhetoric of Misdirection in Corporate Privacy Policy Statements." *Technical Communication Quarterly* 14.2 (2005): 197–214.

Mason, Julia. "Video Games as Technical Communication Ecology." *Technical Communication Quarterly* 22.3 (2013): 219–36.

McAllister, Ken S. *Game Work: Language, Power, and Computer Game Culture.* Tuscaloosa: U of Alabama P, 2004.

McDonald, Aleecia M., and Lorrie Faith Cranor. "The Cost of Reading Privacy Policies." *I/S: A Journal of Law and Policy for the Information Society* 4.3 (2008): 540–65.

Moberly, Kevin. "Composition, Computer Games, and the Absence of Writing." *Computers and Composition*, 25.3 (2008): 284–99.

Moberly, Kevin, and Ryan M. Moeller. "Working at Play: Modding, Revelation, and Transformation in Technical Communication." *Computer Games and Technical Communication: Critical Methods and Applications at the Intersection.* Burlington, VT: Ashgate, 2014. 189–207.

Ouellette, Marc. "Come out Playing: Gender, Sexuality, and Constrained Agency in Computer Games and Technical Communication." *Computer Games* and Technical Communication: Critical Methods and Applications at the Intersection.* Burlington, VT: Ashgate, 2014. 35–51.

Russoniello, Carmen V., Kevin O'Brien, and Jennifer M. Parks. "The Effectiveness of Casual Video Games in Improving Mood and Decreasing Stress." *Journal of CyberTherapy & Rehabilitation* 2.1 (2009): 53–66.

Sidorova, Anna, and Suprateek Sarker. "Unearthing Some Causes of BPR Failure: An Actor-Network Theory Perspective." AMCIS 2000 Proceedings (2000). Web. 30 Mar. 2013.

Takahashi, Dean. "Playnomics Figures out How Game Players Rate When it Comes to Potential Purchases." 1 Mar. 2012. Web. 30 Mar. 2013. <http://venturebeat.com/2012/03/01/playnomics-figures-out-how-game-players-rate-when-it-comes-to-potential-purchases-exclusive/>.

Tam, Donna. "Facebook Game Developers Generated $2.8 Billion in 2012." CNet News.com. 26 Mar. 2013. Web. 30 Mar. 2013.

Vie, Stephanie. "'I Gave My Rights Away for a Song': How Billy Bragg Persuaded MySpace to Change its Tune on Ownership." *The Business of Entertainment: Popular Music.* Ed. Robert C. Sickels. Westport, CT: Praeger, 2009. 107–19.

———. "Tech Writing, Meet *Tomb Raider*: Video and Computer Games in the Technical Communication Classroom." *E-Learning* 5.2 (2008): 157–66.

Waggoner, Zachary. "Life in Morrowind: Identity, Video Games, and First-Year Composition." *Currents in Electronic Literacy*, 2010. Web. 20 Mar. 2013. <http://currents.cwrl.utexas.edu/2010/waggoner_life-in-morrowind>.

Words With Friends. Zynga with Friends. Video game.

Zickuhr, Kathryn, and Mary Madden. "Older Adults and Internet Use." Pew Research Center's Internet & American Life Project. 6 June 2012. Web. 30 Mar. 2013.

Chapter 11

Working at Play:
Modding, Revelation, and Transformation in the Technical Communication Classroom

Kevin Moberly and Ryan M. Moeller

At first glance, technical communication seems especially appropriate to the procedural rhetorics that Ian Bogost and a number of other computer game scholars have popularized. Concerned with forms and outcomes and preoccupied with the rhetorical relationship between rules and discourse, technical communication seeks to instill in students many of the same values that James Gee celebrates as "good" in gamers: a fundamentally neoliberal, marketplace-oriented subjectivity in which earning power (or, in Gee's case, learning power) is synonymous with self-surveillance and self-regulation. Understood in this sense, it is perhaps not surprising that ideological critiques of the types usually associated with cultural studies occupy an uneasy position in many technical communication pedagogies. Dismissed as impractical and counterproductive to the realities of teaching writing in the workplace, such approaches are often reduced to a cursory recognition that the economic disparities between workers and managers can result in power struggles that disrupt normally harmonious labor relations. Arguing that it is imperative to teach students a more nuanced understanding of how ideology "works," this chapter describes how computer game modding, or modifying commercial games, can serve as the basis for what Dan Ding describes as a "revelation pedagogy" (156)—a pedagogy that is designed to help students become more conscious not only of the ideological assumptions upon which many of the practices that technical communication valorizes as natural and inevitable are rooted but also of how they can affect change by working within and against these assumptions. After addressing the critical exigencies that justify this project, this chapter describes how such a pedagogy might be realized by adapting the five-part "grammar of gameworks" that Ken S. McAllister proposes in his 2004 work, *Game Work*: *Language, Power, and Computer Game Culture*. It concludes by offering a brief sketch of how this pedagogy might be implemented in a semester-long technical writing class.

Proceduralism, Ideology, and Technical Communication

In his aptly titled 2011 essay "Against Procedurality," Miguel Sicart critiques what is, arguably, one of the dominant critical paradigms in contemporary computer game studies: the proceduralism championed by Ian Bogost and others who seek to understand how games produce meaning through their underlying processes and systems of rules. While Sicart recognizes the influence of these approaches, he argues that they are ultimately problematic not only because they construct game designers as the sole arbitrators of what games mean, but more significantly, because they represent complex behaviors such as play as inherently rational, mechanical processes. Proceduralism, he contends, promotes an ultimately disempowering, unidirectional, and instrumentalist understanding of how games work, one that implicitly constructs play as work and in doing so, reduces players to passive recipients of content that is produced by a privileged class of authors or artists.

Recognizing that the meaning of games (and thus their value) is not produced exclusively by following their rules but through what he describes as a fundamentally dialogical "process of appropriation," Sicart proposes an alternative model of game studies, one that understands that the "meaning of a game, its essence, is not determined by the rules, but by the way players engage with those rules, by the way players play." Sicart thus constructs play as both an answer and an antidote to the implicitly dehumanizing tendencies of proceduralism. Citing the work of Johan Huizinga, Roger Caillois, and others, he argues that play endows players with an expressive power that must be considered when trying to understand how games produce meaning. He writes:

> Play is not only a performance. Play does not only include the logics of the game —it also includes the values of the player. Her politics. Her body. Her social being. Play is a part of her expression, guided through rules, but still free, productive, creative. Without the openness of play, the player cannot express or explore their ethics, their politics. (n.p.)

To Sicart, then, players are the primary authors and producers of the games they play: interlocutors who, in attempting to work within and against the constraints of the rules, often produce meanings that challenge or transcend those which the game designers intended.

Emphasizing reflection, interpretation, and dialog, Sicart's response to proceduralism recalls some of the most common ways that technical communication scholars raise about respond to the dominant ideologies of technical and scientific writing. As Ding writes in his 1998 article, "Marxism, Ideology, Power and Scientific and Technical Writing," technical communication does not interpellate technical communicators as individuals but as rationalized subjects: cogs or automatons who "do not have the autonomy in deciding what to write about in the workplace" and must therefore efface themselves to the demands of the larger, formal systems of production that define the workplace (36). According to Ding, technical communication scholars have developed two primary though antithetical pedagogies in response: 1) a functionalist approach that attempts to make students aware of but does not challenge the dominant ideology, and 2) a critical interprevist approach that seeks to foreground the role that students play in interpreting, reflecting, and thereby producing the formal systems that comprise the dominant ideology. Quoting Blyler, Ding writes that interprevists attempt to both empower students and disrupt the dominant ideological discourses of the workplace by teaching students to recognize and "expose 'the process by which a particular organizational ideology produces and reproduces communication practices of social actors'" (137). As with the model of critical play that Sicart advocates, critical interpretivism thus constructs the individual as the primary site of resistance against the otherwise opaque and dehumanizing processes that are imposed upon the subject by a variety of external forces.

Ding's critique of resistance pedagogies thus speaks to many of the shortcomings of the player-centered approach that Sicart advocates. Sicart explicitly describes proceduralism as a form of scientific management, ideologically imbricated in capitalist control. From this, he advocates what is, arguably, a model of resistant play, one that also privileges interpretation and reflection as an antidote to the otherwise rationalizing and disempowering tendencies of proceduralism. Sicart, however, does not substantially challenge one of the primary ideological tenets that makes proceduralism so appealing as a discourse: the trope of the designer as author or artist who, through the sheer force of her individual ability, is able to transcend the constraints imposed by her material circumstances. Instead, he reinscribes this trope. Constructing the player in the negative image of the designer, Sicart reduces the complex question of how games produce meaning to a struggle between two versions of the same thing: two idealized individuals who, through procedure or play, fight to assert dominance over each other. As he writes, "Games structure play, facilitate it by means of rules. This is not to say that rules determine play: they focus it, they frame it, but they are still subject to the very act of play. Play, again, is an act of appropriation of the game by players." The result is often that the complex sociopolitical relationships that define contemporary texts are reduced to a simple author-audience model of production, one which, as Ding writes about resistance pedagogies, does not acknowledge that the ruling power constitutes a hidden audience that, through ideology, "looms large in every step of writing, restricting or even coercing the communicators" (156). Thus, by having technical communication students modifying or modding computer games, we can complicate the modes of production that are made available to players; rather than just receiving the rules and playing the rules of the game, modding asks players to be co-constructors of meaning.

Modding as a Revelation Pedagogy

Conscious of the shortcomings of resistance pedagogies, Ding instead calls for a radical expansion of the types of skill-based pedagogies that are traditionally privileged in teaching technical communication—a "revelation pedagogy" that, in his words, not only "serves to reveal to students that they are always restricted by ideological factors" but more significantly, helps them recognize how the types of performance that they encounter in the contemporary workplace function to maintain and reproduce the dominant discourse (156–7). Building on the work of social constructivists such as Herndl and Trimbur, Ding writes that the overall goal of this pedagogy is to make students conscious of how, in policing dissent and difference, ideology paradoxically functions to produce the types of collaboration and consensus that technical communication values. Ding argues, however, that the best place to stage such a pedagogy is not the workplace but the classroom, which, as he points out, often presents students with simpler and more familiar versions of the ideologies that they will encounter in the workplace, ideologies that are both "intended to transmit [the] ideology of the ruling force and to restrict writer's writing to the prescribed format and content." As he explains, "Once students become aware of the restrictive nature of the ideological properties of the school, teachers may begin to introduce the more complicated ideological properties in the workplace and how they affect technical communication" (157). While Ding acknowledges that such a pedagogy will require instructors to adopt techniques more commonly employed in the liberal humanist classroom than in the technical communication classroom, he argues that such a departure is justified not only because it will teach "technical communicators to contextualize themselves and their writing among the workplace ideological properties" but because it will make technical communication more relevant to the exigencies of the contemporary workplace. As he writes, "By representing technical communication as an ideological and social instrument to solve problems, we have to stress the importance of being rhetorical technical communicators, who understand the determining nature of the ideological and social issues and who know ways to deal with them aptly" (158).

What is required, then, is an intermediary location—a site that, located between the classroom and the workplace, can function as what McAllister describes as a "transformative locale"—a site at which traditional paradigms can no longer be maintained and whose contradictions thus provide the impetus for "transformative experiences" (59). The practice of "modding," or modifying commercially produced computer games, can provide such a site. As McAllister writes about the struggles surrounding technologies such as the lightbulb, phonograph, and sewing machine, "technological innovation . . . is one of the most common sources of locale boundary crossing" (60). This is very much the case with modding. Modding is made possible not only through digital high technologies and through the various communities that have coalesced around these technologies, but through the vast, decentered networks of production required to sustain both these communities and technologies. Modding, as such, is a site of struggle. As with many aspects of computer games, it marks a liminal space whose boundaries are still very much in question as a variety of agents and institutions attempt to both come to terms with the performances that characterize gaming as an emerging genre, and to appropriate and repurpose these performances for their own ends. Since modding requires students to confront and work within these oftentimes fraught boundaries, it can help them become more conscious of the much more established and, therefore, opaque, constraints that define the various discourses that intersect in the technical communication classroom. Modding can thus enable students to make the transition between the forms of production that are privileged by consumerism as a discourse and those that technical communication privileges.

Although the term modding is used to describe a wide variety of activities, some of which are much more complex than others, the practice ultimately depends on one of the unique characteristics of computer games as a medium: the fact that, as Andrew Galloway points out, a game's engine is distinct from the data files that define its graphics, sounds, narrative, and gameplay[1]. As he explains,

> A single game engine may facilitate a wide variety of individual games. The game engine is a type of abstract core technology that, while it may exert its own personality through telltale traces of its own various abilities and features . . . is mostly unlinked from the gameplay layered within it. The game, like all other digital objects, is but a vast clustering of variables, ready to be altered and modified. (112)

Thus, while modding is often celebrated as a form of counterculture in which players co-opt or reappropriate the tools of the gaming industry, modding nevertheless depends on this industry to a degree that, according to Galloway, is "not seen in previous avant-garde movements." As he argues, "game modders benefit from, and, in fact, require commercial games, game engines, and hardware to make their work. Few new-media artists build their game engines from the ground up, and practically none of them build their own computers" (113). Modding, as such, provides an excellent metaphor for what, to Ding, is one of the practical realities that defines the material relationship between technical communicators and the companies that employ them: Although the texts that technical communicators produce are rarely the primary products of the companies that employ them, their

---

[1] Many scholars recognize three primary, though often overlapping categories of mods. The first type, total conversion mods such as *Counterstrike* not only replace the graphics, story, sounds and other artistic elements of the parent game, but also oftentimes radically alter its gameplay. Partial conversion mods, by comparison, only replace specific aspects of the parent game—its story, for instance, its maps, sounds, graphics—but otherwise leave the underlying game unchanged. User-interface mods, or add-ons, are often designed to supplement the way that players interact with networked games like *Halo* or massively multi-player games such as *World of Warcraft*.

work nevertheless shapes the production of the company, affecting its products in much of the same way that the various data files that modders produce affect the output of the engines at the core of the games that they modify.

Producers, Players, and the New Knowledge Economy

One of the primary paradigms that modding challenges is that which occupies the center of both Sicart's response to proceduralism and many of the resistance pedagogies that Ding critiques: namely, the notion that it is possible and desirable to distinguish between two privileged, though antithetical subject positions—between the designer and the player, the author and the reader, and the manager and the worker. Indeed, many game scholars assert that modding is a primarily liberating, meaning-making activity, unencumbered by author-reader or producer-consumer relationships. Postigo, for example, writes:

> Fan-programmers form knowledge communities whose actions are informed by participatory culture and that at times are in opposition to the commodity-driven proprietary nature of the cultural industries. These dynamics are no longer only part of the fan culture but have also become part of mass culture so that in the closing days of 2006, consumers were collectively named person of the year by Time Magazine because of our participation in blogs, YouTube, MySpace, and other social networking and production venues. (301)

Sotamaa makes a similar argument in the unpublished 2004 paper "Computer Game Modding, Intermediality and Participatory Culture." Noting that mods are "celebrated as a new medium for artistic innovation and simultaneously successfully used as a marketing strategy for new retail titles," Sotamaa cites modding as an example of larger changes that are taking place in the way media is produced and consumed—changes that, as he writes, go "beyond the simple oppositions of cooptation and resistance." To Sotamaa, then, modding embodies the promise of new media. Citing Jenkins and Manovich, he writes, "by acting as the avant-garde of the culture industry, new media industries and cultures can pioneer new types of authorship, new distribution models and new relationships between producers and consumers."

Gee also celebrates modding in his 2003 book *What Video Games have to Teach us About Learning and Literacy*. Citing the practice as an example of how "video games incorporate a powerful learning principle that fits well with inquiry-based classrooms and with workplaces that encourage workers to think proactively and critically to build new knowledge in practice for the business," he argues that modding allows players to "not just be passive consumers but also active producers who can customize their own learning experience" (208). We see these claims as problematic in that they reveal the degree to which Gee's work is grounded in (and functions to reproduce) what Dyer-Witheford and other scholars have identified as a larger belief in an ongoing "information revolution." As Dyer-Witheford writes in his book *Cyber-Marx: Cycles and Circuits of Struggle in High-Technology Capitalism*, this belief is predicated on a "vision of the future in which the capitalist development of technology leads to social salvation, whether through the perfection of the marketplace or its transcendence" (30). He explains:

> Along with a number of synonymous or associated terms . . . the phrase "information revolution" has come to define contemporary anxieties and hopes about the future. For, according to the theorists of this revolution, the technoscientific knowledge crystallized in computers, telecommunications, and biotechnologies is now unleashing an ongoing and irresistible transformation of civilization, dramatic in its consequences, unavoidably traumatic in the short term, but opening onto new horizons nothing short of utopian. (15)

To Dyer-Witheford, then, the information revolution represents an ultimately disempowering discourse. Preoccupied with the promise of high technology, it not only constructs the problems of the present tense as temporary, though necessary, prerequisites of progress, but it also constructs the individual subject as inherently incapable of addressing these problems. The information revolution thus reinforces the view that, aside from blind faith in the power of the marketplace and the potential of digital high technology, the only thing that is possible, viable, or valuable is the status quo.

Understood in this sense, it becomes clear that what Postigo, Sotamaa, and Gee celebrate about modding is its potential, as a technology, to not only induct students into the emerging knowledge class but in doing so, to induct them into the proper relationship as subjects to the various high technologies of salvation. Gee makes this point explicitly in his discussion of how modding teaches students what he calls the "Insider Principle" (197), or a new subject position that, emerges at the intersection of the traditional subject positions valorized as natural and immutable by industrial capitalism. Although modding promises to interpellate participants into the privileges associated with the knowledge class, it requires them to construct themselves as subjects within what, to use Huizanga's term, is a magic circle whose boundaries are defined in the master image of the high technology that enables it: in this case, computer games. The result is quite literally that the possibility of an outside or alternative modes of subjectivity are rendered irrelevant and, therefore, invisible. Yet as Gee makes clear in his critique of "left-wingers" (203) in the conclusion of his book, this outside also includes materialist approaches that are critical of the transformative power of technology and of the so-called "free market" upon which much of this technological production is beholden, approaches that specifically address issues that theorists of the information revolution say should no longer matter or be obsolete: class conflict, labor, inequity, and exploitation.[2]

---

[2]   This tendency to use the promise future as a pretense to ignore the problem of the present-tense can also be seen in Gee's dismissal of the issue of sexism and racism in

Gee's celebration of modding thus foregrounds the degree to which modding relies upon the promise of a privileged position to convince players to construct themselves in subject positions that are severely limiting, if not outright exploitative—in other words, to convince them to construct themselves as workers rather than as authors, artists, or designers. Indeed, as Kücklich writes in his 2005 article, "Precarious Playbour: Modders and the Digital Games Industry," modding is extremely beneficial to the mainstream gaming industry. It not only builds brand loyalty, increases name recognition, and extends the shelf-life of commercial games, but it also provides the industry with a significant source of innovation and labor, all at a fraction of what it would cost to hire employees to perform similar tasks. For more on how the game industry exploits players as free laborers, see Zimmerman's chapter in this collection. Kücklich argues that this lopsided economic arrangement is due, in large part, to the fact that modding is associated with play rather than work and, as such, is not seen as serious enough that modders should be recognized much less remunerated for their work. Comparing modding to similar forms of digital collaboration such as open source software development, he writes,

> the development of "free" software has come to be seen as a valid, if slightly eccentric, form of work. Modding, on the other hand, still has to struggle to free itself from the negative connotations of play: idleness, non-productiveness and escapism. And while the digital game industry increasingly acknowledges the contribution of modders, they have no incentive to contest this view: the perception of modding as play is the basis of the exploitative relationship between modders and the games industry. (n.p.)

To Kücklich, then, modding is a "precarious" form of labor. Constructed at the intersection of work and leisure, play and production, he argues that it is symptomatic of what Deleuze calls "deregulation," or the displacement of the regulation of power from the institution to the individual, who, through self regulation, is simultaneously constructed as both the subject and instrument of coercion. As he writes, "the solitary player is archetype of the individual who upholds the rules simply for the sake of the pleasure she derives from submitting

---

games. Defending his decision not to address the issue of gender in his book, he writes, "As to gender: I have no doubt that video games, like most other popular cultural forms, overstress young, buxom, and beautiful women in their content. Furthermore, with several major exceptions, these women are often not the main characters in games. However, as more girls and women play games, this will change" (11). Yet as we know from Ouellette's chapter, "resistance to alternative readings or constructions indicates that these unofficial texts do constitute a threat and an intervention in the complacency of an industry that is marked by the constrained agency that is (re)produced in and through . . . normalizing discursive practices" (p. 40).

to them, since, paradoxically, her freedom results from her submission to the rules of the game."

Modding as Gamework

Understood in this sense, modding is perhaps not as liberatory nor as empowering many claim. Although the practice undoubtedly has the potential to grant participants access to otherwise privileged subject positions, this promise is often deployed strategically by the gaming industry and other interests as a means as a means of securing otherwise cost-prohibitive forms of labor and inducting subjects into coercive relationships. Zimmerman documents several of these coercive relationships in his chapter, "Psyche and Eros: Rhetorics of Secrecy and Disclosure in Game Developer–Fan Relations." Modding is thus implicated in what Dyer-Witheford describes as a larger, ongoing capitalist strategy of appropriation in which technology is deployed to devalue the work (and therefore disenfranchise) populations of otherwise skilled workers in the name of progress. Yet as Dyer-Witheford points out, this is a double-edged sword: while technology can be deployed to negate the skills and disrupt the cultural practices in which the political power of targeted groups is manifested, it can also be (and is often) used by these groups to gain advantage. To Dyer-Witheford, this dual and ostensibly contradictory potentiality is possible not because technology is inherently neutral but because it is shaped as much by the desires of those who are in power as by those who are not. As he writes, "automating machinery can be understood as imprinted *both* with the capitalist's drive to deskill and control workers, and *also* with labour's desire for freedom from work—to which capital must respond by technological advance" (72). This is certainly the case with modding, which is imprinted both with a desire on the part of the mainstream culture industry to produce the types of subject positions that are valued by the contemporary neoliberal marketplace and with a desire on the part of players to either acquire to the status associated with these subject positions or to resist or otherwise escape such coercion. This is, arguably, also the case with the technologies and discourses that intersect in the technical communication workplace—technologies and discourses that, though naturalized by ideology, nevertheless exist at the intersection of a number of critical struggles.

Modding can help technical communication students become more cognizant of these intersections when taught in conjunction with the "grammar of gameworks" that Ken Mcallister proposes in his 2004 work *Game Work: Language, Power, and Computer Game Culture* (1). As McAllister writes, computer games are complex artifacts whose meaning is produced not only through the dialogical struggles between designers and players but also by a number of influences that exist outside yet nevertheless impact this ostensibly self-contained and rarefied relationship—influences that include, but are not limited to the hardware and software on which the games run, the infrastructure required to produce and maintain this hardware and software, the marketing and reviewing practices that promote and categorize games, and the various critical and aesthetic traditions that inform what designers and players regard as beautiful, compelling, or worthwhile game play.

Recognizing the need for a critical framework to address this complexity, McAllister proposes a "grammar of gameworks" that, like Burke's pentad, is designed to help scholars identify critical struggles within the computer game complex and to understand how these struggles intersect and are manifested in specific games. As he explains,

> The grammar of gameworks takes into five integral areas of power: agents (who have the power to catalyze transformative effects; functions (the purported and actual purposes of those effects); influences (the external forces that impinge upon agents and functions and that inevitable change the transformative effects of historically situated artifacts); manifestations (the ways that transformative efforts are realized in particular contexts); and transformative locales (the spatio-temporal instances in which ideologies—individual, communal, or societal—have specific transformative effects). (64)

Such a grammar, McAllister argues, is beneficial because it offers scholars what Kellner describes as a "multiperspectival" approach to games, an approach that recognizes that because of the complex, interdependent, and often global nature of much contemporary media production "isolated analyses of means of production, texts and artifacts, and audience reception of the products of the culture industry are no longer sufficient." (41). In doing so, this grammar can also help scholars identify possible sites of intervention, intersections at the struggles that comprise the computer game complex that afford the opportunity to influence the shape of the computer game complex itself through "critique-driven action" (65). McAllister's grammar thus represents a preferable approach to the revelation pedagogy Ding envisions, one that avoids the positivist and ultimately disempowering implications of other approaches. Recognizing that scholars must focus on more than simply privileged subject positions in order to understand complex cultural productions such as computer games, he understands that "computer games are comprised of rhetorical events that work to make meaning in players" and that these events are themselves expressions of large dialectical struggles at play within the computer game complex (31). At the same time, he uses the constructed subject positions as a starting point from which scholars can develop more nuanced analyses of games. Used in conjunction with modding, McAllister's grammar can be used to train students to analyze the sometimes opaque rhetorical practices that characterize technical communication through the five "areas of power" McAllister summarizes above: agents, functions, influences, manifestations, and transformative locales (64).

Modding, for example, asks students to play at being workers. A manifestation of the contradictions inherent in many of the subject positions that characterize work in the so-called knowledge economy, modding interpellates subjects as agents primarily through what Sutton-Smith understands as "rhetorics of identity." In his work *The Ambiguity of Play*, he explains that although rhetorics of identity often appear similar to those involving power, they "focus on the use of play forms as forms of bonding, including the exhibition and validation or parody of membership or traditions in a community" (91). Modding requires students to construct themselves and perform in the image of both privileged and nonprivileged agents—not only as designers, workers, and players, but as what Mcallister refers to as "virtual agents," or avatars who "serve as mediums (in the spiritualist sense) between the real-world will of the player and the game world's response to that will" (46–7). Since students must occupy all of these roles by turns (and sometimes simultaneously), modding serves as an excellent site to help them understand how their ability to express themselves and act as agents is determined by the various subject positions that they assume.

Teaching modding as a form of playing with identity can also help students become more conscious of what McAllister understands as the "functions" or forms of agency that specific subject positions allow (47). Bay and Blackmon, for example, discuss some possibilities for allowing students to play with their "professional" identities by building avatars and objects in *Second Life*. For example, assuming the role of game designer affords students a wide range of functionality, as Ritter shows in his chapter on team-based game design in his technical communication class. Articulated through design documents, storyboards, and other forms of conceptual documentation, this subject position allows them to manipulate and arrange the aesthetic elements of the game, define rules and behaviors, and engage in other high-level tasks that are traditionally the purview of the author or artist. Yet to implement their designs, students must work within much more constraining forms of agency—the scripting language that the game engine recognizes, for example, or the interface-driven controls of *Photoshop*, Microsoft *Word*, or other third-party software. Finally, validating their designs through usability testing requires students to function as players, often through the virtual agents they create and program. Although such subject positions ostensibly offer students the least amount of agency, they foreground an important aspect of functionality that is often not apparent in more privileged forms of subject positions: the fact that, as McAllister points out, agency is as much about what subjects might do with the tools on hand as it is about what they can or cannot do (49). By asking students to approach functionality in this manner, as the source of a range of possibilities that may or may not be sanctioned, instructors can make two important points: First, that even the most restrictive subject positions afford opportunities to cheat or challenge; and second, that much of the work of authoring, designing, or managing involves anticipating and limiting such behaviors. The different roles that modding recognizes can thus function as a metaphorical framework to help students become more conscious of the struggles between various hierarchical though often overlapping classes of workers that characterize the technical communication workplace.

Modding, however, also requires students to come to terms with what McAllister describes as "influences" or the larger cultural, material, and historical conditions that exist externally to the game, yet impact the way the game is constructed. As McAllister points out, computer games are not an original medium by any stretch of the imagination, but instead

> draw heavily on preexisting media concepts and models, partially because mass media such as TV and newspapers have become naturalized to developers . . ., but also because they know that many people will feel more comfortable working with a game—building, marketing, and playing in it—if it is like other media with which they are already familiar. (51–2)

Computer games are also implicated in a complex system of economic production that, as McAllister writes, "extends far beyond the cost of games themselves." As he explains, "Thousands of attendant expenditures support any given computer games: hardware that stores, runs, and displays it; software that controls the interface between the game and the hardware; peripherals that allow players to improve their experiences with the game" (53). While students need not be completely aware of these or any of the other myriad of influences that impact the computer game complex, modding can nevertheless serve as the basis for a number of analytic assignments that require them to quantify the ways that their performances as subjects are constructed by external material circumstances.

Modding provides two obvious locations for such a pedagogy. The first is, of course, the game itself. By asking students not only to modify the various graphics, sound, and map files that are a game includes, but also to document and evaluate their attempts through reports and similar assignments, instructors can make them aware of how their ability to alter the meaning of a game is dependent on their access to hardware and software as well as their comprehension of the sometimes esoteric skill sets and genre conventions that comprise game design. The second location is the engine at the core of the game. As Galloway points out, many of the assumptions about the way that particular games operate are hard coded into their engines (112). These include assumptions about hardware and software, as well as assumptions about the underlying physics through which the game represents reality. Although many of these assumptions are external to the game itself, they nevertheless take on concrete, material manifestations inside the game. As such, they provide an excellent starting point for a larger discussion about the way that Althusser conceives of ideology—that is, as "the imaginary relationship of individuals to their real conditions of existence" (162). Indeed, by making students aware of how their ability to play and modify games is shaped by often unstated preconceptions about what is natural, permissible, and inevitable, instructors can help them understand the degree to which, as technical communicators, their performances are dictated by what Ding refers to as a "hidden audience": ideological assumptions about how they should conduct themselves as workers, writers, or any number of the other subject positions that the field valorizes (158). For example, Vie explicitly explores how many of the social games that characterize *Facebook* construct players as agents through their Terms of Service and similar instances of technical communication.

Such an awareness can, in turn, be leveraged to help students become conscious of what McAllister describes as the "manifestations" or "meaning making events" that distinguish genres of texts and performances from each other. Building on a schema that Chris Crawford introduces in his 1994 work *The Art of Computer Game Design*, McAllister explains that the meaning of games is manifested through four key strategies, "representation, interaction, conflict, and safety" (55). By studying the way that a particular game represents reality, scholars can thus "begin to see how a computer game's developers make their rhetoric—their attempts to manage meaning—manifest for players" (56). McAllister makes much of the same point about conflict, writing that it "provides an especially good opportunity for understanding how broader dialectical struggles are uniquely dramatized in the computer game complex" (57). While McAllister makes it clear that these manifestations are unique to computer games, his analysis is nevertheless useful in that, used in conjunction with modding, it can help students develop a more sophisticated understanding of how textual production works—a model that recognizes that although texts often appear unified, they are comprised of a number of distinct textual strategies, all of which represent an attempt to exert rhetorical influence by manipulating the distinctive characteristics of texts. Modding, as such, can be used to facilitate a broader discussion about how the organizational or formatting characteristics of, say, a report or memo constructs readers as subjects. In doing so, it can help students become more conscious of the degree to which their ability to express themselves is determined by the unique manifestations of the genres and technologies in which they are working.

This is particularly the case with new media, which as Anne Wysocki writes, requires composers to be aware of the unique materialities of digital media. As she explains:

> I think we should call "new media texts" those that have been made by composers who are aware of the range of materialities of texts and who then highlight the materiality; such composers design texts that help readers/consumers/viewers stay alert to how any text—like its composers and readers—doesn't function independently of how it is made and in what contexts. Such composers design texts that make as overtly visible as possible the values they embody. (15)

In letting students experiment with the ways that games make meaning through manifestations such as representation and conflict, modding provides students with hands-on training in the types of visual, aural, spatial, and procedural strategies that have come to characterize new media as a form of production. Modding, as such, can provide an important supplement to the predominantly text-centered pedagogy that Ding advocates. It can not only help students become more attuned to the types of multi-modal performances that are becoming increasingly valuable in the technical communication workplace, but in doing so, it can make them more conscious of how these technologies impact their status as workers.

Modding thus offers students a relatively low-stakes site at which to both experience and experiment with many of the complex dialectical struggles that intersect in the texts and performances that define technical communication. Deployed as a site of critical production, it can ultimately help students identify what McAllister describes as "transformative locales"—the locations within texts at which "transformative experiences take place" (59). Since modding appears "new" and unfamiliar, it can foreground struggles that, as Kline et al. argue, might otherwise appear natural or inevitable in more established fields such as technical communication: "For it is in a materialist history of a new medium that we can uncover the dimensions of intentionality and conflict that ground both critical evaluation and progressive advocacy with regard to culture and technology" (49). By exploiting this ambiguity, instructors can position modding as a middle ground—a medium—between work and play, production and consumption, and many of the other binaries that are deployed metonymically in the technical communication classroom. In doing so, they can help students become more conscious of what McAllister describes as the complex "nexus of forces" that intersect and are expressed in the otherwise opaque texts and performances that characterize technical communication (9). This awareness can, in turn, help students recognize that subjectivity is never immutable nor static but is constructed, maintained, and policed by a staggering variety of socioeconomic, political, and cultural influences, all of which ultimately manifest themselves in the subject's ability (or inability) to perform. By asking students to use modding as the medium through which they compose themselves as technical communicators, instructors can thus make the point that although these intersections often appear oppressive, they also represent opportunities, transformative locales, that can be exploited to bring about the sort of transformations in which, according to McAllister, all change is rooted.

Practical Considerations

As with any attempt to construct a pedagogy around digital technology—especially a technology as fraught with sometimes negative connotations as computer games—instructors must be conscious of a number of practical considerations that concern not only how to integrate modding into the technical communication classroom, but also how to integrate such a course into a larger program of study. This problem, which is analogous to the way that Galloway and others describe modding, requires instructors to adapt traditional pedagogical elements in a manner that simultaneously takes advantage of the potentials of modding yet maintains the integrity of the larger discipline. Perhaps the best place to begin is with the fraught question of what game (or games) are best suited for such a pedagogy. As discussed earlier, the gaming industry has embraced modding to such a degree that instructors have a staggering number of choices. For example, many of the games in popular franchises are published with toolkits that are designed to facilitate modding. These include games in the *Civilization, Crysis, Dungeon Siege, Elder Scrolls, Far Cry, Neverwinter Nights*, and *Warcraft* franchises. Still other games such as *Little Big Planet, Minecraft,* and *ModNation Racers* incorporate modding as a central element of their gameplay. Finally, many of the games in the *Half-life, Halo*, and *Grand Theft Auto* franchises can also be modded, through doing so requires a variety of open source third-party software applications. Assigned singly or in combination, any of these games (and many others) can be used with the pedagogy described in this chapter.[3] However, constructing the course around a single game has a number of advantages, namely that instructors only have to design a single set of assignments and provide support for a particular game. Accordingly, instructors can choose a game that is as accessible as possible, a game that, at minimum, includes a modding toolkit, is available cross-platform, and does not require extravagant hardware or is otherwise cost prohibitive to purchase. Instructors must also consider other factors, such the size and the quality of the modding communities that surround the game, which can provide an invaluable source of tutorials and other supplementary materials.

Finally, instructors should consider the content of the game itself. Despite Gee's claim that with time, games will become less sexualized, racialized, and violent, it is important to recognize that, like many other forms of mass culture, computer games are implicated in the ideological project of the culture industry. They not only encode stereotypes about race, gender, and sexuality, but they also ask players to respond violently to these stereotypes, oftentimes in an attempt to restore a sense of order and normalcy to the otherwise unstable worlds of the games. Instructors, as such, must carefully consider the content of the games they bring into the classroom lest they present this content as normal or natural and, in doing so, alienate students. This is not to say, however, that instructors must necessarily shy away from games that deal with race, gender, or sexuality. As Ouellette points out in his chapter in this book, such games present an opportunity to broach a subject that is extremely relevant to technical communication but one that is rarely addressed in the literature: the subject of how race, gender, and sexuality are simultaneously constructed and policed through the workplace. Modding can be an especially fertile means of exploring this issue in that it explicitly provides students with the tools through which to "queer" or intervene in commercial computer games.

---

[3]   As Jennifer L. Bay and Samantha Blackmon argue in their chapter in this book, *Second Life* also gives participants the opportunity to engage in world building, object creation, scripting and a number of other modding-like activities. It is important to note, however, that although *Second Life* promotes itself as a "free" virtual environment, much of the creation that occurs in the space is monetized. Building, for example, requires players to rent virtual land from Linden Labs, the cost of which can be cost-prohibitive for individual users and even for smaller institutions.

Instructors must also carefully consider how they construct the course. Although contemporary students are often portrayed as digital natives to whom activities such as gaming come naturally, not all of the students who enroll in the course may be comfortable with gaming; further, even those who do identify themselves as gamers may approach the prospect of modding with trepidation.[4] Instructors can help alleviate student anxiety by structuring the course around a scaffolded pedagogical approach such as that which Barton and Moberly describe in their article "Quests and Achievements in the Classroom" and Grouling et al. discuss in this collection. Articulated through a number of parallel, layered continuums, such a pedagogy can help students make the transition not only from relatively simple to complex modes of performance, but ultimately from familiar to unfamiliar subject positions. For example, instructors might begin by simply asking students to play the game they have selected. As the focus of an informal series of memos or other low-stakes assignments that require students to reflect on their experience, this activity serves a dual purpose. On one hand, it introduces students to the conventions of the game at the center of the course and, to some degree, of gaming in general. On the other hand, it offers instructors a starting point for a larger discussion of many of the issues surrounding agents and agency that McAllister identifies in the first two elements of his grammar. Once students have successfully completed the game, instructors can ask them to play a number of third-party mods that have been created for it and write formal reports evaluating these mods based on criteria that established game scholars have developed. Since this assignment requires students to master the practical tasks of installing and running mods for the game, as well as to research and integrate viewpoints outside of their immediate expertise, it can prepare students to begin modding, as well as serve as a starting point for a larger discussion of what McAllister understands as influences.

Instructors can introduce modding in much the same way—through a series of initially simple, small-scale tasks that are not only designed to teach students the basic proficiencies that more complex forms of modding require, but which also serve as the impetus for a variety of reflective, evaluative, and analytical writing assignments that require them to apply concepts from McAllister's grammar. For example, to teach students the basic functions of the game's modding toolkit, instructors can construct a series of short, tutorial-like exercises designed to lead students through the process of creating a simple scene by adding player-characters, non-player characters (NPCs), props, and other elements. Once students have successfully completed these exercises, instructors can ask them to demonstrate competency by employing these skills to implement a scene of their own design. Used as the basis for a series of progress reports or self-evaluations, the recursive nature of this assignment can help students become more conscious

---

[4]   To some degree, instructors can address this concern by being careful to use the word "modding" in the course title and making sure that the course description published in the university catalog explicitly states that the class will include a modding component.

of the different types of agency that modding affords and also help them better understand how these types of agency are constructed through assumptions encoded into the game and its toolkit. Instructors can use a similar strategy to teach McAllister's concept of manifestations. By asking students to first revise and then gradually expand the scenes they have created to tell a simple story, instructors can foreground the degree to which computer games and similar forms of digital media challenge the traditional, linear modes of communication that technical communication often privileges. Moreover, this assignment can serve as the inspiration for a number of nontraditional writing assignments that provide students with practical experience with multi-modal composing, assignments such as story boards, design documents, video presentations and tutorials, and other materials produced through digital media.[5]

These documents, in turn, can become the foundation for a collaborative final project in which, working in small groups, students produce argumentative games that are designed to explicitly inspire political, social, or cultural transformations. Coupled with portfolios, presentations, or perhaps even assigned as part of a public gaming exposition, this project requires students to leverage the transformations that they have experienced during the semester to achieve an outcome that, in many ways, contradicts ideological assumptions about what should be possible through play and through the workplace. This project, as such, presents students with a tangible example of what, to Ding, is both the goal and the challenge of revelation pedagogies: not only how to recognize the material and ideological forces that shape discourses such as gaming and technical communication but how to work within and against these forces to affect change. Constructed at the intersection of production and consumption, of work and play, and of any number of the other contradictory potentialities that modding embodies, such projects can thus foregrounds a question that is always present, though not often acknowledged in traditional technical communication pedagogies: the inherently fraught question of how to translate critique into action.

Works Cited

Althusser, Louis. "Ideology and Ideological State Apparatuses." *Lenin and Philosophy.* Trans. Ben Brewster. New York: Monthly Review, 1971. 127–87.
Barton, Matt and Moberly, Kevin. "Quests and Achievements in the Classroom." *Design and Implementation of Educational Games: Theoretical and Practical*

---

[5] As Jeff Greene, Laura Palmer, Anthony T. Sansone, Jennifer deWinter, and Lee Sherlock detail in their chapters in this book, computer games and technical communication intersect explicitly in game manuals, tutorial materials, design documents, and patch notes. Accordingly, such nontraditional assignments might include exercises such as producing parts of a game manual or requiring students to produce weekly or biweekly patch notes that document their modding activities.

Perspectives. Ed. Pavel Zemliansky and Diane Wilcox. Hershey: IGI Global, 2010. 206–25.

Bay, Jennifer, and Samantha Blackmon. "Inhabiting Professional Writing: Exploring Rhetoric, Play, and Community in *Second Life.*" *Computer Games and Technical Communication: Critical Methods and Applications at the Intersection.* Burlington, VT: Ashgate, 2014. 211–31.

Baudrillard, Jean. *The System of Objects.* Trans. James Benedict. New York: Verso, 1996.

deWinter, Jennifer. "Just Playing Around: From Procedural Manuals to In-Game Training." *Computer Games and Technical Communication: Critical Methods and Applications at the Intersection.* Burlington, VT: Ashgate, 2014. 69–85.

Ding, Dan. "Marxism, Ideology, Power and Scientific and Technical Writing." *Journal of Technical Writing and Communication* 28.2 (1998): 133–61.

Dyer-Witheford, Nick. *Cyber-Marx: Cycles and Circuits of Struggle in High-Technology Capitalism.* Chicago: U of Illinois P, 1999.

Galloway, Andrew. *Gaming: Essays on Algorithmic Culture.* Minneapolis: U of Minnesota P, 2006.

Gee, James Paul. *What Video Games Have to Teach Us About Learning and Literacy.* New York: Palgrave McMillan, 2003.

Greene, Jeff, and Laura Palmer. "It's All Fun and Games Until Someone Pulls Out a Manual: Finding a Role for Technical Communicators in the Game Industry." *Computer Games and Technical Communication: Critical Methods and Applications at the Intersection.* Burlington, VT: Ashgate, 2014. 17–33.

Grouling, Jennifer, Stephanie Hedge, Aly Schweigert, and Eva Grouling Snider. "Questing through Class: Gamification in the Professional Writing Classroom." *Computer Games and Technical Communication: Critical Methods and Applications at the Intersection.* Burlington, VT: Ashgate, 2014. 265–82.

Kline, Stephan, Nick Dyer-Witheford, and Greg de Peuter. *Digital Play: The Interaction of Technology, Culture, and Marketing.* Montreal: McGill-Queen's UP, 2003.

Kücklich, Julian. "Precarious Playbour: Modders and the Digital Games Industry." *The Fibreculture Journal* 5 (2005): n.p. Web. 13 March 2013.

McAllister, Ken S. *Game Work: Language, Power, and Computer Game Culture.* Tuscaloosa: U of Alabama P, 2004.

Ouellette, Marc. "Come out Playing: Computer Games and the Discursive Practices of Gender, Sex, and Sexuality." *Computer Games and Technical Communication: Critical Methods and Applications at the Intersection.* Burlington, VT: Ashgate, 2014. 35–51.

Postigo, Hector. "Of Mods and Modders: Chasing Down the Value of Fan-Based Digital Game Modifications." *Games and Culture* 2.4 (2007): 300–13.

Ritter, Christopher, Sameer Ansari, Scott Daner, Sean Murray, and Ryan Reeves. "From Realism to Reality: A Postmortem of a Game Design Project in a Client-Based Technical Communication Course." *Computer Games and Technical*

Communication: Critical Methods and Applications at the Intersection. Burlington, VT: Ashgate, 2014. 283–306.

Sansone, Anthony. "Game Design Documents: Changing Production Models, Changing Demands." *Computer Games and Technical Communication: Critical Methods and Applications at the Intersection.* Burlington, VT: Ashgate, 2014. 109–23.

Sherlock, Lee. "Patching as Design Rhetoric: Tracing the Framing and Delivery of Iterative Content Documentation in Online Games." *Computer Games and Technical Communication: Critical Methods and Applications at the Intersection.* Burlington, VT: Ashgate, 2014. 159–69.

Sicart, Miguel. "Against Procedurality." *Game Studies: The International Journal of Computer Game Research* 11.3 (2011): n.p. Web. 10 March 2013.

Slaughter, Sheila, and Gary Rhoades. *Academic Capitalism and the New Economy: Markets, State, and Higher Education,* Baltimore: The Johns Hopkins UP, 2004.

Sotamaa, Olli. "Computer Game Modding, Intermediality and Participatory Culture." *Olli Sotamaa.* University of Tampere, n.d. Web. 13 March 2013.

Sutton-Smith, Brian. *The Ambiguity of Play.* Cambridge, MA: Harvard UP, 2001.

Vie, Stephanie. "'You Are How You Play': Data Mining and Behavioral Analysis in Social Networking Games." *Computer Games and Technical Communication: Critical Methods and Applications at the Intersection.* Burlington, VT: Ashgate, 2014. 171–87.

Wysocki, Anne Francis. "Opening New Media to Writing: Openings and Justifications." *Writing New Media: Theory and Applications for Expanding the Teaching of Composition.* Logan: Utah State UP, 2004. 1–42.

Zimmerman, Josh. "Psyche and Eros: Rhetorics of Secrecy and Disclosure in Game Developer–Fan Relations." *Computer Games and Technical Communication: Critical Methods and Applications at the Intersection.* Burlington, VT: Ashgate, 2014. 141–56.

PART IV
Games in the Professional and Technical Communication Classroom

Chapter 12

Inhabiting Professional Writing: Exploring Rhetoric, Play, and Community in *Second Life*

Jennifer L. Bay and Samantha Blackmon

Virtual worlds are often touted in the popular press as the new way to communicate globally and efficiently, making virtual world literacy a key skill for success in the global economy. In 2011 virtual worlds gained 214 million new users (Korolov). But while adults are more likely to participate in virtual worlds such as *Second Life*, less evidence exists on how educators should best approach such online simulations to teach Business and Technical communication. Despite this lack of discussion, virtual worlds are still rhetorically rich sites for exploring what it means to communicate and participate in a workplace community.

In this chapter, we argue that virtual worlds such as *Second Life* offer productive possibilities for professional writing classroom contexts. While *Second Life* is not a game *per se*, it contains ludic (or game-like) elements and can be productively examined using game theory and pedagogy. We suggest that there are particular abilities that participjating in virtual worlds requires and fosters; such abilities are coterminous with the writing and communication skills that college students need to succeed in the workplace. Seminal work on professional writing literacies has differentiated among rhetorical, visual, information, and computer, to name a few (Nagelhout, 1999; Cargile Cook, 2002; and Selber, 2004), but such distinctions are more difficult to parse in virtual worlds due to the blurring of material and virtual spaces. Thus we need to rely on a different vocabulary to come to an understanding of what is happening in virtual worlds. That vocabulary hinges on two concepts that don't often get discussed in professional and technical communication: play and identity. These two theoretical concepts define the motivations behind and the activities that largely constitute participation in virtual worlds. The desire fueling these two concepts is so strong that they can sometimes overcome initial obstacles of access and usability in online spaces such as *Second Life*.

We chart the following trajectory in developing our argument. First, we discuss the concept of literacy or "multiliteracies" in professional and technical communication, demonstrating that such definitions ignore spatial experiences of the workplace. Such spatial dimensions are exactly those that are being touted by virtual world companies as useful for business contexts. Next, we discuss virtual worlds and their attraction for businesses, especially the concepts of play and professional identity and how they fit into workplace contexts. We consider some of the abilities that virtual worlds like *Second Life* foster and that are useful for understanding how to operate in workplace contexts. Finally, we conclude with pedagogical implications for using Second Life in professional writing classroom contexts. Along the way, we challenge the notion of 'literacy' as a concept useful for understanding how humans operate in the digital age and instead posit that we need to start thinking about inhabiting a world or a way of being in the world. In this model, teaching, then, becomes cultivating inhabitance in a world.[1]

Rethinking Literacy

Technical Communication research in the first decade of the twenty-first century investigates how we might conceptualize the skills that Technical and Professional communicators might need on the job. Nagelhout's essay "Pre-Professional Practices in the Technical Communication Classroom: Promoting Multiple Literacies through Research," an early precursor to this research, attempts to parse out the specific literacies that are required for workplace success. Nagelhout delineates the following four primary literacies that instructors should actively promote: rhetorical, information, visual, and computer. Such literacies "help students meet the demands of the post-industrial age of information" (289). Nagelhout goes on to outline these four literacies and discuss assignments that will encourage them in technical and business communication service courses.

Three years later, Cargile Cook extended these four literacies in "Layered Literacies: A Theoretical Frame for Technical Communication Pedagogies." She explains that while technical communication pedagogy is historically grounded in basic literacy skills for engineers, "today, technical communicators need to be multiliterate, possessing a variety of literacies that encompass the multiple ways people use language in producing information, solving problems, and critiquing practice" (5–6). She outlines six key literacies for technical communicators: basic, rhetorical, social, technological, ethical, and critical. According to Cargile Cook, these literacies can be layered; that is to say, rather than each of these literacies being discrete formations, they can be combined, integrated, and situated in programs, courses, and class activities in multiple ways (6). Custer, in his chapter, "The Three Ds of Procedural Literacy: Developing, Demonstrating, and Documenting Layered Literacies with Valve's Steam for Schools," provides an example of such layering using procedural literacy as an umbrella. Not insignificantly, Cargile Cook argues that such literacies should not be taught in isolation nor can any one course cover all of them successfully; instead, these literacies are complexly interrelated.

---

[1]   We are consciously using the term inhabitance as a way of being in a world. Let us be clear that although there are linguistic similarities, we are in no way invoking Bourdieu's concept of *habitus*. In contradistinction to Bourdieu, inhabitance allows us to consider that we can be in multiple worlds and may have varying modes of inhabitance for each.

Likewise, Selber's *Multiliteracies for the Digital Age* provides a useful conceptual framework for thinking about the skills fostered via technology. Selber provides a structure for understanding what might be called digital multiliteracies, or a literate landscape that involves, functional, critical, and rhetorical literacies. Like Selber, we believe that "teachers should emphasize different kinds of computer literacies and help students become skilled at moving among them in strategic ways" (24).

Each of these three models are worthwhile attempts to understand the skills necessary for professional writers in the workplace, but virtual environments complicate how we conceptualize these skills. While all three of these writers emphasize the interrelatedness of these literacies, they are still divided into discrete blocks of skills that can be combined and recombined in a variety of ways. Moreover, the terms 'reading' and 'writing' are still central to how we think of literacy. A case in point is Pearce's "Spatial Literacy: Reading (and Writing) Game Space." Pearce argues that games struggle "with the representation of space on the two-dimensional, albeit dynamic plane of the screen, requiring players to develop a sense of spatial literacy, that is, a mode of conventions for 'reading' game space" (1). Notice that gamers still 'read' gaming spaces, and, as some research in composition has noted, gamers produce an extraordinary amount of writing in association with games. But does reading and writing capture how individuals interact with games and other virtual environments? That is, how do we account for interaction that goes beyond discrete literacies—literacies that are more environmental or even spatial? While technological literacy is its own category in many of the traditional paradigms, in today's digital landscape, we cannot separate out technology from other types of literacies; it is ubiquitous, so to speak. Similarly, the idea of layering these literacies is predicated on a two-dimensional model (layering as one on top of another), not on a more immersive, 3-D model in which literacies might be situated in experiential or embodied ways. In short, the work we've done in professional writing has not conceptualized how such literacies can be structured spatially and technologically. What's missing in these essays and what Wysocki and Johnson-Eilola hinted at in 1999 is an environmental or spatial literacy—an ability to understand and inhabit a particular space, in this case a virtual environment.

In their essay, "Blinded by the Letter. Why Are We Using Literacy as a Metaphor for Everything Else?" Wysocki and Johnson-Eilola move toward something like a spatial or environmental literacy when they try to "analyze and reconstruct new approaches to communication that prioritize ways of knowing other than those dependent on 'literacy.'" They eventually abandon the term literacy because of the limits it places on pushing the boundaries of how we understand the digital realm: "Why aren't we instead working to come up with other terms and understandings—other more complex expressions—of our relationship with and within technologies?" they ask (360). Information can now be conceived "as something we move (and hence think) within" (363). In this sense, the people's relationship with information and the technologies associated with it becomes spatial rather than time or skill based; time and space collapse into each other. Understanding information spaces, then, involves "figuring out how we all are where we are, and about how we all participate in making these spaces and the various selves we find there" (366). Wysocki and Johnson-Eilola's invocation of the self here is not incidental because is implies that what we call literacy involves identity; moving through and with information involves a certain sense of self or a self-involvement.

We don't mean to get into an interrogation of literacy here, but merely to point out that virtual worlds such as *Second Life* explode traditional notions of literacy, as well as attempts at more nuanced understandings of technological literacy. Following Wysocki and Johnson-Eilola, we think of literacy as involving the ability to move through information. In their words, "Literacy can be seen not as a skill but a process of situating and resituating representations in social spaces" (367). That process of situating and resituating representations is what we might refer to as rhetoric, as a kind of rhetorical living, a way of being in the world and an attunement to one's environment. This kind of attunement is very similar to how technical and professional communicators function in professional workplace settings and especially how they might be trained to enter such settings. It is more than a skill, although like a skill, it can be cultivated. What we're talking about here is creating a self in a world, an approach that professional writing might draw from phenomenological research methods.

In "Researching Literacy as a Tool, Place, and Way of Being," Steinkuehler, Black, and Clinton investigate possible methods for analyzing new digital literacies. They pose three particular approaches that can inform methodological considerations of new digital literacies: activity theory, distributed cognition, and phenomenology. While professional writing research has discussed activity theory and distributed cognition in various contexts,[2] less attention has been paid to phenomenology. According to Steinkuehler, Black, and Clinton, a phenomenological approach would conceive of a literacy experience as "the outcome of a dynamic interaction between a subject (person using literacy) and an object (the literacy technology being used). These coordinations between the person and the literacy technology are inscribed in the subject-body as sense-movement configurations, which provide a material base upon which consensual meanings can rely" (97). In this way, literacy can be seen less as a skill set or approach and more as a way of being, and more particularly, a way of being that involves the body. In short, literacy is experiential: "To define literacies as 'ways of being' makes salient how using literacy requires gaining a familiarity with experiencing it" (97). Steinkuehler, Black, and Clinton go on to apply Markham's metaphors of user's experiences with information technologies to literacy as tool, place, and way of being. And while their example of literacy as a way of being is

---

[2]   For more on activity theory in technical communication, see David Russell; for a good example of the work on technical communication and distributed cognition, see Dorothy Winsor.

single-player video games,[3] we can see something like *Second Life* as perhaps a stronger example of literacy as a way of being.[4]

Virtual Worlds and the Potential for Business Contexts

Examining Multi-User Virtual Environments (MUVEs) like *Second Life* requires us to rethink the ways in which we conceptualize the kind of paradigm invoked by the term "multiliteracies." As one of the more popular virtual worlds available to the public but also used in business settings, *Second Life* illustrates the kinds of spatial and rhetorical inhabitance that MUVEs foster. We consciously want to move away from the term *literacy* for the same reasons as Wysocki and Johnson-Eilola have outlined. As Sullivan and Porter define in *Opening Spaces*, "As a productive art, rhetoric is concerned with how a discourse can be constructed to achieve a certain effect" (27). Inhabiting virtual spaces requires us to consider rhetoric as an inhabitance. But first, we outline some key terms that guide how we will think about the spaces we discuss.

Various terms can be used to define the concept of a virtual world. Bell defines the term "virtual world" as "a synchronous, persistent network of people, represented as avatars, facilitated by networked computers" (2). Beyond this basic definition, Bessiere, Ellis, and Kellogg distinguish between two common understandings of virtual worlds: Multi-User Virtual Environments (MUVEs) like *Second Life* and Massively Multiplayer Online Role Playing Games (MMORPGs) like *World of Warcraft*. This second type of world is game oriented as opposed to the open-ended orientation of MUVEs. The authors further explain that MUVEs like *Second Life* "provide a more open-ended experience. The power of MUVEs derives from their extensive affordances for user interaction, but that greater range also makes them more daunting for new users." Another distinction of importance here is that "In a MMORPG the game's producer provides nearly all in-world content. A MUVE, on the other hand, features content almost entirely crafted

---

[3] Steinkuehler, Black, and Clinton use Massively Multiplayer Online Games (MMOGs) as examples of literacy-as-place, which makes sense because they do not include "role playing" in the acronym. Role-playing would involve identity construction and embodiment, which would move further into literacy as a way of being.

[4] While Steinkuehler, Black, and Clinton write about games in general and MMOGs in particular, it is important to note that Linden Labs does not consider *Second Life* a game but rather a virtual world where one can live an alternate existence. Linden Labs stresses that *Second Life* is "a virtual world [that] provides almost unlimited freedom to its Residents. This world really is whatever you make it. If you want to hang out with your friends in a garden or nightclub, you can. If you want to go shopping or fight dragons, you can. If you want to start a business, create a game or build a skyscraper you can. It's up to you" ("Second Life | FAQs"). Rather than being quest driven or being regulated by a set of rules, *Second Life* sees its freedom and creativity as being the center of its existence and the main thing that keeps it from being a game.

by users. This leads to a more diverse and typically less coherent experience, reflecting the diversity of creators and less high-level coordination" (2885). In short, MMORPGs are built for users whereas MUVEs are also built *by* users. This distinction is significant in that MUVEs like *Second Life* provide users with the opportunity to engage in building the world or in producing content. This focus on producing content as opposed to consuming or interpreting content means that the user embodies an inherently rhetorical position within the world.

But this focus on building is also coupled with the notion of play, an issue that is common to both MMORPGs and MUVEs. Dutch philosopher Johan Huizinga identifies five characteristics of play in his book, *Homo Ludens*, which he summarizes as:

> a free activity standing quite consciously outside 'ordinary' life as being 'not serious', but at the same time absorbing the player intensely and utterly. It is an activity connected with no material interest, and no profit can be gained by it. It proceeds within its own proper boundaries of time and space according to fixed rules and in an orderly manner. It promotes the formation of social groupings which tend to surround themselves with secrecy and to stress their difference from the common world by disguise or other means. (13)

Of importance here is the stress on the distinction between the 'real' world and the world of play, as well as the focus on no material interest or profit. Bessiere, Ellis, and Kellogg identify play as a significant barrier to integrating virtual worlds into professional contexts because they are perceived as "identified primarily with socializing and playing, rather than working" (2887). But as Cory Ondrejka, one of the creators of *Second Life*, notes, the boundaries between play and work are continuously blurred in virtual worlds.[5] He provides an example of clothing design in *Second Life*: "When a resident of *Second Life* decides to explore clothing design and eventually converts that skill into real world income by taking her in-world earnings and trading them with other residents for US dollars, it is unclear what parts of the activity were play and what parts work" ("Collapsing" 33). This trend of monetary interactions crossing between virtual worlds and real life is not new and is becoming more common across virtual environments; *World of Warcraft*, for instance, also allows users to charge for their in-world creations.[6] Yet monetary considerations are not just what define work in virtual worlds; as Ruggill and

---

[5]   In many forms of games, the lines between work and play are blurred. See, for instance, professional sports in which players are paid to play.

[6]   The distinction between MUVEs and MMORPGs is not an easy one to parse. We believe that the concept of play is inherent to both, which is what makes *Second Life* game-like. Similarly, we're not quite sure that students don't already encounter and experience the space as a game. Thus, while we distinguish between these two concepts in this section, we believe that *Second Life* can be approached and analyzed as a game because of its allowance for play.

McAllister note, there is an incredible amount of work that goes on behind the scenes in game development, from employees programming the game to users mastering the environment. They ultimately argue that the computer game is better understood in terms of work than play (83–4). While Ruggill and McAllister make a compelling argument, we believe that the distinction is not so clear, and it is especially not so clear for business and technical writing students, who are learning what the world of work might entail.

Play, then, in this context is not clearly demarcated from professional work; it requires skill, expertise, and can offer monetary rewards. A key characteristic, though, if we take Huizinga's characteristics into consideration, is that MUVEs provide a certain freedom to explore and learn without the same level of consequence. That is, users can explore virtual space, learn rhetorical production, and fail miserably at it without the same consequences that might occur in real life. One argument we can make, then, is that virtual worlds not only offer us the opportunity, not just the cliché, to "build new worlds" but also the opportunity to build new rhetorical engagements through inhabitance.

This is crucial for professional and technical writing students because part of what we're doing in the classroom is introducing them to rhetorical engagements common in the workplace. Becoming a professional in a workplace environment is not just about entering a pre-established environment; it's about building that workplace through research, observation, interaction, and more. Once a newcomer enters the workplace, the dynamics inevitably change; one's presence alters that workplace, so it must be continually rebuilt by inhabitants as well as built anew by the newcomer. This is why theories such as Lave and Wenger's legitimate peripheral participation do not completely capture what happens when a newcomer enters the workplace because it assumes a static work environment that does not change with a newcomer's presence or interaction. The newcomer does not just enter a community of practice, but his or her presence also changes that community of practice, making it into a different—and new—world.[7]

Lave and Wenger describe legitimate peripheral participation as "learners inevitably participate in communities of practitioners and that the mastery of knowledge and skill requires newcomers to move toward full participation in the sociocultural practices of a community" (29). Their definition seems to be in line with what we might see happening in virtual worlds yet on what we might argue is a much more material level. That is to say, mastery and skill in MUVEs involves building—of self, of objects, of community—so that it is not enough to say that newcomers 'read' the environment, learn how to operate within it, and integrate themselves in that established community. Rather, newcomers become part of that community by literally building rather than adapting; this is a different spatial

---

[7]   An obvious move here would be to go to activity theory as a way to understand what happens with the introduction of a new agent into a workplace environment. If we had more time, we would explore this possibility. For now, though, we would like to concentrate on the spatial dimensions of workplace literacy, which is what best relates to *Second Life*.

experience of being in the workplace than we have seen discussed in professional writing. If we see building as a critical component to being in MUVEs, then sites like *Second Life* can open up broader meanings for what it means to work, to be a professional, and to engage in business and industry.

Virtual worlds such as *Second Life* offer us a material embodiment of a kind of world building. It does not just introduce students to a technology that they might encounter in the workplace; it allows them to participate in building a working self, a workspace, and a working community. In short, this kind of building is a material form of invention.

Background on *Second Life*

In order to understand a bit more about the professional possibilities within *Second Life,* we need to provide more background on the world. Linden Labs launched its first beta version of *Second Life* in 2002. It emerged as an idea from founder Philip Rosedale, "who wanted to create a 3D virtual world with user generated content, where they could interact with each other in real time" ("History of *Second Life*"). The *Second Life* website describes itself as "a free 3D virtual world where users can socialize, connect and create using free voice and text chat." Statistically, "Eighteen million people have registered in *Second Life* from over 150 countries." *Second Life* has its own separate work solutions site, describing itself as "the leader of virtual meeting, event, training, prototyping, and simulation solutions that catalyze innovation while reducing the cost and environmental impact of travel." There is a page listing advantages to working in the world, as well as another page describing what *Second Life* is and why a company might choose *Second Life.*

Many companies use *Second Life* for employee training, networking, and mentoring. IBM, for instance, "has more than 5,000 employees using *Second Life* for purposes such as sales training or collaborating across different geographic regions." IBM is partnering with Linden Labs, the creator of *Second Life*, to create an enterprise version of *Second Life* that can be used behind a corporate firewall (Takahashi). Moreover, Kaplan and Haenlein lay out five corporate opportunities available within virtual social worlds like *Second Life*: advertising through virtual stores, sponsorship, or advertising spaces; virtual product sales, or selling digital versions of existing products; using virtual social worlds to conduct market research on participants; human resources recruiting; and organizing internal meetings and knowledge exchange (566–7). It is this last opportunity—virtual meetings—that seems to be much more widely discussed in media accounts of *Second Life* in business contexts. Early on, Linden Labs targeted some businesses to perform market research in *Second Life*, but that approach did not seem to work. What has been more successful is highlighting the world's strength as a setting for virtual conferences, meetings, and trainings. IBM has led the way with this initiative, "hosting an annual gathering of its leading thinkers in *Second*

Life" in 2008. They are quoted as saying that they saved $350,000 by hosting the conference virtually (Morrison). *Second Life*'s work site provides quite a few case studies, including IBM, of businesses that have chosen *Second Life* as a place for business. IBM is also partnering with Linden research to create enterprise-safe virtual worlds (Takahashi).

One important observation we would make here is the distinction between *Second Life* and this emerging 'enterprise *Second Life*,' which is isolated from the main *Second Life* environment, provides limited avatars and extremely limited collaboration tools. In terms of cultivating world building, this is not the kind of limiting environment that we might want to introduce students to. The openness of *Second Life*, while it may seem disruptive, is also its strength. It exposes students to a wider variety of people, places, and events to which they can play, experiment, and ply their emerging rhetorical skills. Thus, while students as future professionals may end up using the enterprise *Second Life*, they will be more rhetorically astute from their experiences with the larger and more expansive *Second Life*.

Inhabiting *Second Life*

Second Life is defined, like most MUVEs, as a digital space that one inhabits. In fact, users are referred to as residents, indicating that they "live" in that space. But that space is not one that is predetermined for residents; rather, users are expected to create themselves and their world (see Figure 12.1). First and foremost, inhabiting the space requires an intuitive ability to figure out and even master the interface fairly quickly, as well as an ability to figure out who you are and how to move your body in the space. Once participants are in the environment, there are other abilities that develop from interactions with the software and with other

Figure 12.1   Screenshot of Purdue Island in *Second Life*

residents in the world. In constructing and presenting an avatar, users develop an understanding of how to build identity through material and communicative means. As users develop their online personae, they are forced to learn more about ethos building, project management, managerial skills, networking, and other abilities. Clearly, such skills have the possibility for cultivation in educational environments such as professional writing courses.

We see four types of rhetorical engagement essential for inhabiting *Second Life* that could have direct application to professional writing courses: building a self, building objects, building with others, and finally, dealing with disruption and failure. All four of these rhetorical engagements are necessary to participate in a MUVE and a professional setting. The remainder of this chapter will outline these four engagements and will conclude with some caveats for teaching with MUVEs.

Building a Self

Digital environments have strongly encouraged students to learn how to create and maintain online personae. The Pew Research Center's report "Reputation Management and Social Media" depicts young adults as very active in managing their online reputations, taking steps to restrict personal content on social media sites. And with good reason, Madden and Smith explain, since,

> online reputation matters; 44% of online adults have searched for information about someone whose services or advice they seek in a professional capacity. People are now more likely to work for an employer that has policies about how they present themselves online and co-workers and business competitors now keep closer tabs on one another.

Businesses care about how employees and associates present themselves online, causing young adults to be more vigilant about creating an online self that is appropriate and professional in appearance and demeanor, a point that Vie reiterates in her chapter on social media games. With the rise in online job applications and video interviews, an online persona may be the first point of contact between an employer and potential employee. As such, professional presentation through online portfolios, emails, and interviews has become a standard area of teaching in professional and technical writing classrooms.

Virtual environments like *Second Life* offer students another opportunity to engage in the rhetorical act of building a professional identity online and perhaps "practice" some of the theories and strategies they have learned about persona building in asynchronous settings. As Brown and Duguin stated many years ago, "in learning to be, in becoming a member of a community of practice, an individual is developing a social identity. In turn, the identity under development shapes what that person comes to know, how he or she assimilates knowledge and information." In becoming a professional, students need to learn that ethos and credibility can be actively built. That is, one can construct his or her professional identity, and nowhere is this more apparent than in the material space of MUVEs.

When people first enter the *Second Life* space, they choose a physical identity from a predetermined list. From there, they can customize their personal avatar by creating or buying clothing and other physical accoutrements. Despite the problems with stereotypes in these avatars, the construction and development of a *Second Life* persona can become an important opportunity for invention. Questions arise, such as: How do you want to invent and present yourself in this space? And, if virtual spaces like *Second Life* are used in business contexts, how do you see yourself as a professional in this context?

Many professionals who work with social media see their online selves as part of their professional personae and as demonstrations of their technical expertise. One example is Sarah Robbins, or 'Intellagirl' as she is known online. Figure 12.2 shows a popular image of Robbins in which she is shown back to back with her *Second Life* avatar. From this image, it is clear that Robbins sees herself and her *Second Life* avatar as two components or two sides of her professional identity. This image is, in a sense, building ethos for Robbins as a *Second Life* expert.

We can think of many ways in which students can benefit from thinking about how they would build their professional personae in MUVEs like *Second Life*, from how they might play around with constructing their avatars—working on how they want to see themselves and how others see them as professionals—to how they might leverage their virtual identity in real life work situations. One important

Figure 12.2   Image of Sarah Robbins, aka "Intellagirl"

distinction we would make here is that we are not talking about using MUVEs as opportunities for analysis or for hermeneutics. There has been some discussion in composition studies about using *Second Life* as a site for the exploration of online subjectivity. deWinter and Vie, for instance, outline heuristics that can be used in composition classrooms to critically examine digital subjectivities. They write, "because avatars both reflect and deviate from players' offline identities, students can consider the appearance of their own avatars and how those representations connect to their identifications with race, class, age, gender, sexuality, and other personal markers" (316–17). Similar discussions might occur in professional writing classrooms and for important reasons, but it seems that here the goal of building an identity in *Second Life* is to analyze and interrogate the cultural assumptions surrounding it, the very call that Ouellette makes in chapter two of this volume. We would like to focus on building and playing as goals then on analyzing the professional implications of such identities in workplace contexts.

Building Objects

One of the most spatial elements of inhabiting *Second Life* is building objects, whether those are physical objects, buildings, clothing, or other items. There is a thriving entrepreneurial economy in *Second Life* based on building and creating for others. As Mennecke et al. note, "Business activity is thriving and growing with residents retaining intellectual property rights to the items they create. A resident can build a virtual object like a chair, sell it to other residents, and invest the earnings in a new accessory for her avatar." They then explain that because Linden dollars, the currency of *Second Life*, can be converted to US dollars, residents can make a profit from their building. In sum, building can provide entrepreneurial opportunities for residents of *Second Life* while also creating the material conditions for community and collaboration.

   We see at least two opportunities for professional writing students building in *Second Life*: learning the building interface and enacting user-centered design. The left frame of Figure 12.3 shows the interface for building an object in *Second Life*. While this interface looks similar to other graphic manipulation interfaces like Adobe Photoshop, it distinguishes itself as an interface designed for users to build from scratch. That is, most students have experience using a program like Photoshop as an image manipulation or text creation tool. Building in *Second Life* starts with inventing the object. Sometimes, of course, residents model their creations after real-world objects, but other times, such creations can push the limits of possibility. An example can be found in the right frame of Figure 12.3, which depicts several objects suspended over the island. Building is a critical engagement here because there are fewer opportunities to merely use or modify existing models. Thus, residents figure out how to construct dimensions for objects, placement, and other components that work within the 3-D environment.

Figure 12.3   Screenshot of Building Interface Viewer in *Second Life* (left) and
Screenshot of Purdue Island in *Second Life* with Objects
Suspended in the Air (right)

Because building in *Second Life* occurs primarily for others, whether those others
are one's avatar or for entrepreneurship, there are rhetorical implications of that
building. In building an island, business, or other structure/artifact, participants
must consider principles of user-centered design. They must consider the uses of
the building/artifact and the possible residents who might want to use it. As Michael
Salvo outlines in his important article on user-centered design, "collaborative
design methods challenge technical communicators to invent and design new roles
for themselves in new collaborative design methods" (274). User-centered design
in an environment like *Second Life,* then, forces professional writers to think
about their roles as experts in understanding what residents need in an emerging
world. Moreover, because *Second Life* is an open environment, residents can build
both models of real world structures, as well as innovate and rethink traditional
spaces. In this case, user-centered design takes a different turn as residents must
consider the wide variety of uses possible in a MUVE like *Second Life* and adapt
to those possibilities.

While Linden Labs ties building in *Second Life* directly to entrepreneurship
and commerce (see http://secondlife.com/whatis/create.php), we think that the
potential for play and inhabitance also allows for different kinds of purposes
outside of commerce. For instance, Ondrejka reports that in 2007, the American
Cancer Society hosted their Relay for Life in *Second Life* and raised over
$120,000 ("Collapsing" 28). This is a powerful testament for thinking about
how building in MUVEs involves more than just objects; it also allows for the
possibility of building more equitable social worlds. In part, this is due to the fact

that building in MUVEs allows for forms of collaboration that are specific to the building environment.

Building with Others

Neither building a professional identity nor building objects happens in isolation. Thus, working with others in community is a critical component in *Second Life* and can be adapted to the professional writing classroom in many forms, such as collaboration, project management, and decision-making in teams. As we mentioned earlier, one of the more prominent uses of *Second Life* in business contexts has been online meetings and conferences, which both reduce costs and allows participants from all over the world to converge in the same space. Ondrejka posits that this ability for embodied, placed, and simultaneous collaboration distinguishes MUVEs like *Second Life* from other interactions on the web (33). Moreover, he claims that embodied and place-based interactions in MUVEs can engender trust more readily because people are more likely to trust avatars than asynchronous exchanges ("Collapsing" 40). Ondrejka, as one of the creators of *Second Life*, has rather grand ideas about the potential of his virtual world for collapsing geographic boundaries and enhancing models of citizenship. But his observations about the rise of virtual collaboration in MUVEs mirror research on the importance of distributed teams in professional writing and even push further toward what Ondrejka calls "amateur to amateur education." He explains that residents spend a great deal of time in *Second Life* educating one another and demonstrating skills to newcomers: "Rather than redirecting the questioner to the solo experience of reading a Web site or learning a new piece of software, the demonstration is a social and collaborative experience, creating context and social bonds" ("Education" 240). In this context residents collaborate with one another in real time not only to build but also to teach one another. This kind of work gives a new perspective on the model for workplace training, especially in an age of distributed work.

As companies outsource, downsize, and distribute themselves across the globe, virtual teams have becomes important models for work. In many instances, workers may never meet in person with their coworkers or supervisors. As this shift has occurred, professional writing scholars have responded with discussions on the importance of crosscultural and interdisciplinary collaboration. Paretti et al., for instance, identify three knowledge domains that professional writing students need to understand in working with distributed teams: communication in distributed teams; crosscultural issues, and the mediation of professional identity (329). MUVEs like *Second Life* are environments in which these three domains can be addressed in pedagogical situations dealing with virtual teams. Because *Second Life* lacks the geographic boundaries of traditional space, residents login from all over the world, making such a space perfect for global classroom collaborations. More importantly, as mentioned earlier, the user-centered nature of designing and building in *Second Life* is an opportunity for professional writers to rethink traditional roles in designing and communicating information. It is the culture of *Second Life* that allows for this possible innovation, "a culture of shared creativity as Ondrejka describes it, which "allows residents to learn from the examples of others, to situate their goals and desires within the contexts created by others" ("Collapsing" 28). Identifying common goals and working with them, whether they are user centered or team coordinated, are key to the success of virtual teams. Additionally, as Thomas Malaby observes, the world of *Second Life* allows for the cultivation of social bonds "because of the broad range of small to large acts of coordination (of bodies, of avatars), any of which may succeed or fail" (64). Small disruptions or failures are part of building teams, but they also provide opportunities for how to assess and deal with such instances.

Dealing with disruption and failure

Learning how to deal with disruptions is an essential skill for success in any workplace. All professionals will be faced, at some point or another, with situations or conflicts that they must negotiate, often without any rules or guidance. The very playful nature of MUVEs like *Second Life* coupled with the freedoms that users have in creating often give rise to unique disruptions to the environment itself, as well as demonstrations against companies, people, or causes. In 2006, a CNET interview with *Second Life* estate mogul and virtual millionaire Ailin Graef (aka Anshe Chung) was disrupted by an attack of flying penises, which not only ended the interview but eventually crashed the Linden Labs *Second Life* server (see Figure 12.4).

Figure 12.4   Screenshot of Flying Penis Attack in *Second Life* (Video of the attack is also available online.)

This instance has received widespread attention in the media as a humorous example of what is called 'griefing' in *Second Life*.[8] According to Dibbell, a griefer is "an online version of the spoilsport—someone who takes pleasure in shattering the world of play itself." Griefers attempt to disrupt the world of play, and those disruptions are nothing new to the online realm. Similar disruptions have occurred in MMORPGs, such as the 2006 incident at the *World of Warcraft* funeral of a popular character who died in real life; in this incident, the guild Serenity Now crashed the event and attacked all of the attendees.

While role-playing a funeral in *World of Warcraft* is a grand gesture to both the avatar and the woman being behind the character, the difference here is that *World of Warcraft* is still seen as a game space that is being appropriated for a real world tribute. In contrast, the flying penis attack in *Second Life* is less acceptable since it is often used as a professional (and educational) space; in short, it is meant to be the users' "second life" and thus more realistic (and dare we say, serious). Thus, disruptions such as griefing have become more and more significant. As Dibbell reminds us: "Amid the complex alchemy of seriousness and play that makes online games so uniquely compelling, the griefer is the one player whose fun depends on finding that elusive edge where online levity starts to take on real-life weight—and the fight against serious business has finally made it seem as though griefers' fun might have something like a point." Dibbell goes on to provide an example of Prokofy Neva, a *Second Life* real estate entrepreneur who earns a small income renting out her properties. Griefing attacks have cost her hundred of US dollars in lost revenue. But the flying penis attack is also a good example of how virtual worlds can provide us with opportunities to practice responses to disruptive situations and to understand the real world implications to such entrepreneurial situations.

In addition to disruption, failure in MUVEs serves as another opportunity for students to learn from their mistakes without extreme consequence. Failures may be perceived (at least now) to have less impact on one's professional status than in other places. As Cory Ondrejka jokingly notes, failure is a requirement in entrepreneurial situations, and *Second Life* is no exception. But more importantly for students is the fact that exploration, play, and failure can take place in *Second Life* with fewer consequences than in real life situations.

A Cautionary Tale: Things That We Need to Be Aware of When Teaching in MUVEs

Despite the lack of real life consequences, there are downsides to teaching in MUVEs such as *Second Life*. Moore and Pflugfelder outline two dominant responses from students to classes in environments such as *Second Life:* bored and lost. In their article, they explain that their own experiences as bored and

---

[8] For more on the issue of griefing and spoil sporting, see Moeller et al. and Wark.

lost graduate students in MUVEs prompt them to encourage instructors to contextualize assignments and outline the specific purposes of being in MUVEs. Because MUVEs are not goal oriented as we might see in MMORPGs, there can be a perceived lack of interactivity and engagement, which instructors must struggle to get over. Moreover, the potential for play in such a world can be stifled with assignments that are too constrictive or with problems with hardware or software. Because of the graphics intensive nature of MUVEs like *Second Life*, running the program requires fairly robust processors, new graphics cards, and a stable broadband connection to the Internet that is sufficiently fast without being too fast.[9]

Other potential problems are outlined in Jeffrey Young's *Chronicle* article in which he presents the reasons why some colleges have moved away from using *Second Life* to building their own virtual learning places. Young writes, "moving around in *Second Life* can be so clunky that some professors and students have decided that it's just not worth the hassle." This difficulty in moving around and mastering the interface reflects the steep learning curve that some users face with *Second Life.* In their study of teaching a graduate course in *Second Life,* Mennecke et al. report that students felt "overwhelmed with the complexity of the SL viewer." Related to the complexity of the interface is the even more difficult learning curve for programming and world building. If understanding basic movement and communication are difficult, being able to operate in the economy to build, buy, or sell items is even more so.

In addition to the clunky movement and the building interface in *Second Life,* other aspects of the user interface (UI) are just as clunky and impossible to navigate for the new user. The inventory menu is reminiscent of the file system of early versions of the Windows operating system or current versions of Unix, both of which are foreign to most contemporary students (see Figure 12.5).

A final caveat that Young notes is that Linden Labs is a private firm, and teaching in that space is vulnerable to all kinds of changes in corporate structure, from shifts in privacy practices to elimination of the world all together. It is for this reason among the others that colleges have decided to create their own virtual worlds rather than rely on *Second Life*. Still, we feel that *Second Life* will still be a model for corporate sponsorship and meeting spaces, and thus experience in any virtual world will be useful for professional writing students.

In this chapter, we've tried to demonstrate that MUVEs like *Second Life* can prove to be rhetorically rich sites for professional writing students to learn about the spatial dynamics of professional development and interaction. While MUVEs may not last in the long run, no doubt there will be other new virtual spaces in

---

[9]   According to the *Second Life* wiki, a connection speed of at least 500 kilobits per seconds is necessary to run *Second Life*, but a connection speed that is too high can also cause problems by causing packet loss (http://wiki.secondlife.com/wiki/Help:Lag). *Second Life* is also not compatible with dial-up Internet, satellite internet, and some wireless internet services.

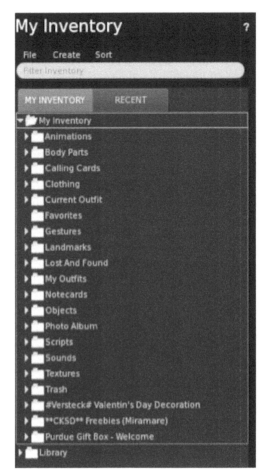

Figure 12.5   Screenshot of the Inventory Interface in *Second Life*

which users construct digital versions of themselves. In building these selves and spaces, we will need to continue to think about how professional writers physically and spatially construct their professional identities and work with others. An exploration of this kind of building might shift the ways in which we think of literacy as something we inhabit rather than something we learn.

Works Cited

Bell, Mark W. "Toward a Definition of 'Virtual Worlds.'" *Journal of Virtual Worlds Research* 1.1 (July 2008): 1–5.

Bessiere, Katherine, Jason B. Ellis, and Wendy A. Kellogg. "Acquiring a Professional 'Second Life:' Problems and Prospects for the Use of Virtual Worlds in Business." CHI 2009 Case Studies Specific User Populations. April 4–9, 2009. Boston, MA. 2883–98. Web. 13 June 2010.

Bourdieu, Pierre. *Outline of a Theory of Practice*. Trans. Richard Nice. Cambridge: Cambridge UP, 1977.

Brown John Seely and Paul Duguin. *The Social Life of Information*. Cambridge, MA: Harvard Business P, 2000.

Cargile Cook, Kelli. "Layered Literacies: A Theoretical Frame for Technical Communication Pedagogies." *Technical Communication Quarterly* 11.1 (2002): 5–29.

Custer, Jason. "The Three D's of Procedural Literacy: Developing, Demonstrating, and Documenting Layered Literacies with Valve's Steam for Schools." *Computer Games and Technical Communication: Critical Methods and Applications at the Intersection*. Burlington, VT: Ashgate, 2014. 247–63.

deWinter, Jennifer, and Stephanie Vie. "Press Enter to 'Say': Using *Second Life* to Teach Media Literacy." *Computers and Composition* 25 (2008): 313–22. Web. 8 June 2010.

Dibbell, Julian. "Mutilated Furries, Flying Phalluses: Put the Blame on Griefers, the Sociopaths of the Virtual World." *Wired* 16.02. 18 Jan. 2008. Web. 10 June 2010.

"History of Second Life." n.d. Web. 19 Feb. 2010. <http://wiki.secondlife.com/ wiki/History_of_Second_Life>

Huizinga, Johan. *Homo Ludens: A Study of the Play-Element in Culture*. London: Routledge, 1949.

Kaplan, Andreas M., and Michael Haenlein. "The Fairyland of *Second Life*: Virtual Social Worlds and How to Use Them." *Business Horizons* 52 (2009): 563–72. Web. 15 June 2010.

Korolov, Maria. "Virtual World Usage Accelerates." *Hypergrid Business*. 28 July 2011. Web. 10 June 2013.

Lave, Jean, and Etienne Wenger. *Situated Learning: Legitimate Peripheral Participation*. Cambridge: Cambridge UP, 1991.

Linden Labs. "*Second Life* FAQs." 2010. n.d. Web. 8 June 2010.

Madden, Mary, and Aaron Smith. "Reputation Management and Social Media." *Pew Research Center's Internet and American Life Project*. 26 May 2010. Web. 2 June 2010.

Malaby, Thomas M. "Contriving Constraints: The Gameness of *Second Life* and the Persistence of Scarcity." *innovations* (Summer 2007): 62–7. Web. 10 June 2010.

Mennecke, Brian, Lesya M. Hassall, and Janea Triplett. "The Mean Business of *Second Life*: Teaching Entrepreneurship, Technology, and e-Commerce in Immersive Environments." *Journal of Online Learning and Teaching* 4.3 (2008). Web. 8 June 2010.

Moeller, Ryan M., Esplin, Bruce, and Conway, Steven. "Cheesers, pullers, and glitchers: The rhetoric of sportsmanship and the discourse of online sports gamers." *Game Studies: The international Journal of Computer Game Research* 9.2 (2009). Web. 2 February 2014.

Moore, Kristen, and Ehren Pflugfelder. "On Being Bored and Lost (in Virtuality)." *Learning, Media, and Technology* 35.2 (2010): 249–53.

Morrison, Scott. "A Second Chance for Second Life; Northrop, IBM Use Virtual World as Setting for Training, Employee Meetings." *Wall Street Journal* A27. 10 Oct 2009. Web. 15 June 2010.

Nagelhout, Ed. "Pre-Professional Practices in the Technical Communication Classroom: Promoting Multiple Literacies through Research." *Technical Communication Quarterly* 8 (Summer 1999): 285–99.

Ondrejka, Cory. "Collapsing Geography: *Second Life*, Innovation, and the Future of National Power." *innovations* (Summer 2007): 27–54. Web. 18 May 2010.

———. "Education Unleashed: Participatory Culture, Education, and Innovation in *Second Life*." *The Ecology of Games: Connecting Youth, Games, and Learning*. Ed. Katie Salen. Cambridge, MA: MIT P, 2008. 229–52.

Ouellette, Marc. "Come out Playing: Computer Games and the Discursive Practices of Gender, Sex, and Sexuality." *Computer Games and Technical Communication: Critical Methods and Applications at the Intersection*. Burlington, VT: Ashgate, 2014. 35–51.

Paretti, Marie, Lisa McNair, and Lissa Holloway-Attaway. "Teaching Technical Communication in an Era of Distributed Work: A Case Study of Collaboration Between U.S. and Swedish Students." *Technical Communication Quarterly* 16.3 (2007): 327–52.

Pearce, Celia. "Spatial Literacy: Reading (and Writing) Game Space." Proceedings: Future and Reality of Gaming Conference. Vienna, Austria. October 17–19, 2008. 1–19. Web. 18 May 2010.

Ruggill, Judd Allen and Ken S. McAllister. *Gaming Matters: Art, Science, Magic, and the Computer Game Medium*. Tuscaloosa: U of Alabama P, 2011.

Russell, David. "Rethinking Genre in School and Society: An Activity Theory Analysis." *Written Communication* 14.4 (1997): 504–54.

Salvo, Michael. "Ethics of Engagement: User-Centered Design and Rhetorical Methodology." *Technical Communication Quarterly* 10.3 (2001): 273–90.

Selber, Stuart. *Multiliteracies for a Digital Age*. Carbondale: Southern Illinois UP, 2004.

Steinkuehler, Constance A., Rebecca W. Black, and Katherine A. Clinton. "Researching Literacy as a Tool, Place, and Way of Being." *Reading Research Quarterly* 40.1 (2005): 95–100.

Sullivan, Patricia and James Porter. *Opening Spaces: Writing Technologies and Critical Research Practices*. Greenwich, CT: Ablex, 1997.

Takahashi, Dean. "IBM and Linden Lab to Create Enterprise-Safe Virtual Worlds." DigitalBeat. 2 April 2008. Web. 29 May 2010.

Wark, McKenzie. *Gamer Theory*. Cambridge, MA: Harvard UP, 2007.

Winsor, Dorothy. "Learning to Do Knowledge Work in Systems of Distributed Cognition." *Journal of Business and Technical Communication* 15.1 (2001): 5–28.

Wysocki, Anne, and Johndan Johnson-Eilola. "Blinded by the Letter. Why Are We Using Literacy as a Metaphor for Everything Else?" *Passions, Pedagogies, and 21st Century Technologies*. Eds. Gail E. Hawisher and Cynthia L. Selfe. Logan, UT: Utah State UP, 1999. 349–68.

Vie, Stephanie. "'You Are How You Play': Privacy Policies and Data Mining in Social Networking Games." *Computer Games and Technical Communication: Critical Methods and Applications at the Intersection*. Burlington, VT: Ashgate, 2014. 171–87.

Young, Jeffrey. "After Frustrations in *Second Life*, Colleges Look to New Virtual Worlds." *Chronicle of Higher Education*. 14 Feb. 2010. Web. 23 Feb. 2010.

Chapter 13

How *World of Warcraft* Could Save Your Classroom: Teaching Technical Communication through the Social Practices of MMORPGs

Melissa Bianchi and Kyle Bohunicky

In a 2012 interview with Internet forum *Big Think,* John Seely Brown, drawing on the work of Huizinga and Juul, stirred up controversy across gaming communities and business publications by claiming that *World of Warcraft* (*WoW*) players were preferable job candidates to many professionals who possess Masters degrees in Business Administration. "I would rather hire a high-level *World of Warcraft* player than an MBA from Harvard," announced Brown, who suggests that *WoW*'s advantages for professionalization emerge from its gameplay and organizational structure. Despite the surprise of business and gaming communities alike, Brown's comments are not entirely novel. At a South by Southwest (SXSW) Interactive panel earlier in 2012, Bing Gordon, Electronic Arts' chief creative advisor, argued that "If you're going to build a company, you have to do it like a *World of Warcraft* guild leader builds guilds" (quoted in McElroy). Both Brown and Gordon similarly note that *WoW*'s design rewards coordination and cooperation over competition, offering an organizational model that they suggest many companies should learn from and adopt. Moreover, both Brown and Gordon emphasize the skills and abilities that *WoW* players (especially dedicated players and guild masters) can offer corporate culture because they commonly juggle managerial responsibilities, act as mediators, and assess situational risks during collaborative gameplay.

Central to both Brown and Gordon's claims yet relatively understated by each is how inter-player communication in the game directs, guides, critiques, and supports cooperative gameplay. Instead of seeing players' communications as a point of mediation that hinders collaboration, Gordon and Brown gesture towards writing in *WoW* as being a usable medium through which players can achieve common goals. Our essay demonstrates that Massively Multiplayer Online Role-Playing Games (MMORPGs) like *WoW* encourage writing practices that are applicable to professional workspaces, and we explore the possibilities of using *WoW* as a space for reimagining and supplementing traditional technical and professional writing pedagogy.

Huizinga's opening chapter to *Homo Ludens: A Study of the Play-Element in Culture*, explores some of the crucial implications of play for communication and discourse formation. Huizinga observes that play functions as either "a contest *for* something or a representation *of* something" (13, emphasis in original), providing players with a means of stepping outside common reality. Play features activities that participants engage with as *actual reproductions* of events (rather than as purely figurative imaginings). Because play is both outside of and a significant part of reality, it is ideal for studies of the development, acquisition, and transformation of discourses as they are governed by the formal qualities of games. Of these formal qualities, Huizinga observes that play "Proceeds within its own proper boundaries of time and space according to fixed rules and in an orderly manner" (13). This point has remained a consistent element in discussions about how rules as well as spatial and temporal boundaries promote the formation of social groups and their distinct discourses. Huizinga's suggestion that the formal elements of play shape the expression and meaning of game content (20) is perhaps best summarized by Juul, who notes that "[r]ules themselves create fictions" (13). This can also be said of discourse.

Because games inhabit a liminal space between reality and fiction, players who are immersed in game-related discourses can learn communication skills that are applicable to situations and events beyond the confines of the game's design. Squire, a computer game designer and researcher on computer games and education, has demonstrated that computer games can effectively supplement traditional education models with situated learning environments. In *Video Games and Learning*, Squire recounts several successful case studies in which he used computer games as pedagogical tools in the classroom. For his research, he has high school classes playing *Civilization 3* to facilitate world history education for marginalized students in Boston (109–39) and *Citizen Science*, an adventure game of his own design, to teach students about limnology and environmental policy. Squire suggests that playing computer games provides students with two important educational qualities not found in traditional classroom pedagogies:

> (1) the learning cycle of a player developing goals, reading the game space for information, taking action in the game world, and then reading games for feedback; and (2) the social experience of participating in particular game communities, which is where much of the reflection, interpretation, and media production occurs as interpretations are debated and legitimized. (30)

The first quality identifies play as a feedback loop between players and the gamespace in which the player reads, acts, reviews, and then re-acts to the computer's response. According to Squire's definition, we theorize play as a systematized approach for addressing a specific problem or event defined by the game's designers and the computer. Because play is a repetitive practice that aims at resolving and responding to events defined by a computer, play within game structures is itself a technology. Squire's second quality addresses how players seek out game-related communities to debate and refine their approaches to play, the play of others, and the computer's responses to their play within the affordances of gamic rules. Technical writing is an analogous practice that seeks to elucidate alien or obtuse technologies. Technical communication and in-game/online writing are both motivated by and respond to the problems or ambiguities within complex systems composed of human (designers, end-users, distributors, writers) and nonhuman (organizations, machinery, economics, space) actors and agents. Play and the practice of writing about play are forms of technical communication that players frequently produce in computer games and on the Internet. In-game writing is especially invested in technical writing practices as players will often dialogue to address, critique, praise, or direct the flow of play while elucidating how play and players may resolve a problem or address an event defined by the computer. Our own research suggests that players and students who practice technical writing through play and writing about play in the context of computer games like *WoW* develop an understanding of technical writing as *problem*-driven discourse, giving them a means to contextualize the relationship between technology and technical writing through application.

Before examining how playing *WoW* acculturates students in these technical writing outcomes and expectations specifically, there must be a distinction between Multi-User Virtual Environments (MUVEs) and Massively Multiplayer Online Role-Playing Games (MMORPGs). The former category describes worlds such as Sony's *PlayStation Home*, *Second Life*, and some Multi-User Dungeons (MUDs) and MUD Object Oriented (MOOs) that emphasize open-ended creative play and have less clearly defined rules and objectives. As Bay and Blackmon observe in "Inhabiting Professional Writing: Exploring Rhetoric, Play, and Community in Second Life," MMORPGs such as *WoW*, *Guild Wars*, and *EverQuest* feature strongly rule-governed gameplay motivated by specific rewards that help incentivize and direct players' interactions within the digital environment. Unlike MUVEs, *WoW* guides players towards explicit ends that include end-game raiding, guild management, and high-level group player-versus-player combat (PVP) which provide contexts in which players must develop what Bay and Blackmon describe as a professional identity from which they can "perhaps 'practice' some of the theories and strategies they have learned about persona building in asynchronous settings" (p. 220). Players professionalize or prepare for these activities by acquiring and developing communicative and collaborative skills that are necessary for successful participation in the game.

The goal-oriented, reward-driven, and collaborative conditions of MMORPGs like *WoW* teach students compositional practices that mirror academic and professional expectations and outcomes for technical writing. Recent work in technical writing theory (Selfe, 2007; Bridgeford, 2007; Cooper, 2007) asks that technical communication instructors and students reconceive of workplace communications as a problem-solving activity. These theorists underscore the notion that instructors and students should analyze and understand the role of both interpersonal exchanges and the organizational culture as technologies operating within larger systems. Similar to Bay and Blackmon, we also claim that through participating in virtual worlds' writing communities like *WoW*, students learn how institutional, social, economic, and cultural factors help shape the spaces in which they create, revise, design and exchange texts. The knowledge that students acquire in these digital spaces can be implemented within and among other communities of practice, demonstrating students' understanding of how these communities use, adapt, and transform rhetoric. As students join guilds and pick-up groups in games like *WoW*, they observe the rhetorical processes through which communities determine membership and agree on rules for negotiating meaning. Bay and Blackmon note that this type of participation occurs because "[i]dentifying common goals and working with them, whether they are user-centered or team-coordinated, are key to the success of virtual teams" (p. 225). Game chat can be used to demonstrate how usability is not inherent to a document but instead is situated within specific contexts, which teaches students how to construct solutions around social complexity. Finally, raid and trade culture emphasize how the clear communication of information depends on both evoking the contexts in which documents are used and also engaging the needs of the reader(s) they address.

To generate productive encounters with these technical communication practices using *WoW* in the classroom, we had students create a game character, choose a class and a profession, and play with other social groups in the game with a special focus on dungeon and questing parties and guilds. In addition to embedding students in a diverse set of compositional protocol, we also had students shadow high-level players who occupy a position of leadership within *WoW*'s community. While instructors played alongside students, we also encouraged inter-player learning to disrupt the relational structures between students, the instructor, and the classroom space that often prohibit situated learning. Technical communication classes should be sites in which students encounter organizational writing practices such as those experienced in MMORPGs like *WoW* because game players regularly deploy technical writing to collaborate with others, to reflect and guide responses to problems, and to buy and sell goods and services. Students playing and writing in MMORPGs quickly learn how the production of *effective* and *usable* communication is shaped by and shapes human and nonhuman agents.

Chat Windows: Writing Technologies and Ecologies in *WoW*

With a subscription base of over ten million players, Blizzard Entertainment's *WoW* is one of the largest and longest running MMORPGs on the market (Blizzard Entertainment). While the game has been periodically updated with game patches since its debut in 2004, *WoW* has also seen four major expansion packs: *The Burning Crusade*, *Wrath of the Lich King*, *Cataclysm*, and most recently, *Mists of Pandaria*. The game's narrative is set in the fictional world of Azeroth, where players must join one of two warring factions: the Alliance or the Horde. To manage the game's large subscriber base, players must first select a server, or realm, to join before entering the game world. This system of servers ensures that the game runs smoothly while simultaneously maintaining several separately populated though equally designed versions of Azeroth. As a result, *WoW*'s player population is separated across these servers with very limited areas for cross-realm interaction. Currently, there are 241 servers to choose from in North America alone, each capable of hosting roughly tens of thousands of players at any given time (Blizzard Entertainment). Servers are divided into three different types:

- Player-versus-Environment (PvE) in which players cannot kill players of the opposing faction;
- Player-versus-Player (PvP), where players can attack one another; and
- Role-playing (RP) servers for players who choose to adopt their avatar as a fictional character and act out its own specific storyline during gameplay.

RP servers are further divided into two subcategories: RP-PvE and RP-PvP. While previous versions of *WoW* did not completely facilitate cross-server or cross-realm communication, recent patches to the game have made such exchanges possible via Blizzard's Real ID system.

Players entering *WoW* for the first time will quickly encounter a complex and oftentimes overwhelming ecology of writing genres when switching between the various chat channels in the game's chat window (Figure 13.1). In these channels, players can communicate using text, forward slash commands (often accompanied by matching avatar gestures and noises), and hyperlinks to in-game items and game-related information.

The forms of communication that players deploy and encounter depend on a number of factors, including the channel they choose to participate in, the previous conversations that have recently occurred in that channel, where the player is located in the game space, who they are currently sharing the game space with, and whether they are participating in quests, dungeons, or raids. The chat window itself

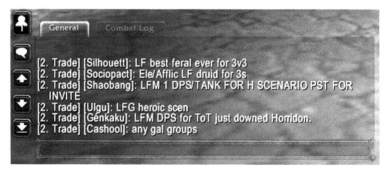

Figure 13.1   Trade Chat Window from Orgrimmar on the Kil'jaeden
                Server (*WoW*)

allows players to type their communications into a text bar that filters messages into specific channels, which include: 'whispers' or 'tells' (private player-to-player messaging), group chat, raid chat, guild chat, 'spatial' chat (messages visible to players within a certain range of the writer's avatar), and 'zone' chat (which is further subdivided into several channels based on communication content including: general, trade, local defense, looking for group, and so on). Through *WoW*'s chat function, players can not only speak to other players but can also send links to quests, achievements, class abilities, in-game items, and so on. Additionally, the game offers players the option to block messages from specific individuals by selecting the "Ignore" function.

Given the complexity of genres and writing practices in *WoW*, it is difficult for many nonplayers to conceive of *WoW* and other MMORPG spaces as productive writing communities. Insiders and players who are members of the MMORPG community have constructed effective genres of communication in context, which means that outsiders will find it difficult to understand the rhetorical action performed by these genres beyond the circumstances of their inception. Figure 13.2 illustrates how *WoW*'s discourses are both specific to their rhetorical situation and at the same time can be exclusionary to nonmembers of the community.

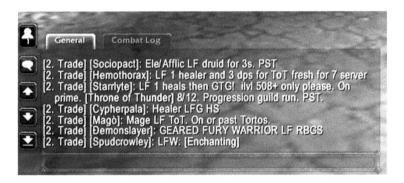

Figure 13.2   Screen Capture of Trade Chat in Orgrimmar on the Kil'jaeden Server from *WoW*

The "[2. Trade]" designation in the chat log indicates that this specific chat channel was designed by the game's developers to provide players with a space for conducting the sale and trade of in-game goods and services. The name of the player writing follows the chat title and also appears in brackets. For individuals who are unfamiliar with the conventions of online chat rooms or the processes of MMORPG digital economies, 'Trade' chat may prove difficult to decipher given its reliance on writing conventions and user actions that are unique to this community and similar online environments. For example, the discourse of trade chat relies on acronyms for phrases like 'looking for group' (LFG), 'please send tell' (PST), and 'good to go' (GTG); abbreviations for dungeon and raid names, class skills, and in-game events; hyperlinks to achievements, items, quests, and professions; finally, MMORPG specific terms like 'progression,' 'guild run,' and 'geared.' While these writing conventions may be inscrutable to nonplayers or students unfamiliar with the game's discourse, they are quickly acquired through immersion and participation in the game's community. Through playing *WoW* and engaging with the community, students can experience firsthand the process of immersion as articulated by Luzón in "Genre Analysis in Technical Communication." Luzón suggests that students gain greater insight into organizational culture and its expectations when placed within the social context in which the technical writing is situated. Luzón argues that learning through immersion raises students' awareness of the work that technical writing performs within various, interconnected discourse communities (290). Practicing immersion through *WoW* enables students to engage genres as complex, generative clusters of communication artifacts and activities that modify and are modified by the player community.[1]

For example, *WoW*'s chat window illustrates how players not only use the channels programmed into the game as they are labeled—such as using Trade chat to sell and exchange goods and services—but they also adapt or create other channels to fill specific needs or address new problems. General chat in the game's less populated major cities, like Silvermoon, are often used by role players to play out narratives because the game does not provide an Role Player-specific chat. Or similarly, the Oldschool chat channel was created so players could discuss and form parties for tackling older content in the game without having to compete with players in general and trade chat looking for groups to play through the game's newest content. These in-game avenues for communication inform how players interact with other genres of writing linked to *WoW* including game-related wikis, forums, and guild websites, often using the former to determine how interactions between players proceed in the latter and vice versa. Groups or guilds often organize through forums and websites, so that once they have logged into the game, chat can be devoted to "business" or group communications necessary for strategizing towards reaching a particular common objective such as instructions and plans for raiding, for group PVP combat, for tackling achievements, and so on. The creation of these genres and their interactions with one another perform specific functions for players so that gameplay communication and processes are structured towards the players' satisfaction of specific in-game goals.

Taken as a whole, *WoW*'s chat channels form what Spinuzzi describes as "genre ecology" or clusters of communication artifacts and activities. As Spinuzzi's theoretical model would suggest, these color-coded channels are

---

[1] For more on the complexity of player modifications, please see Moberly and Moeller's chapter in this collection. There is also a rich history of using genre analysis in technical communication, please see Spinuzzi and Moeller and Christensen, as well.

simultaneously accessible and in dialogue with one another as players act as a bridge between multiple channels, thus connecting several separate actors and events simultaneously. Figure 13.3 depicts *WoW*'s color-coded chat channels, and how they, despite being distinctly labeled, can sustain multiple forms of discourse.

Figure 13.3   Guild Chat and Trade Chat from Orgrimmar's Chat Log on the Kil'jaeden Server

In this example, trade chat is not only being used by players to advertise the sale and exchange of goods and services, but it also serves as a social forum where players can express their opinions and ideas (in this case, about Gamon, one of the game's non-player characters). Guild chat here is also being appropriated for similar ends rather than for discussing guild-related endeavors. While communication in these genres typically reflects the problem for which they were designed, writing in these spaces is fluid and can take on the characteristics of other types of chat channels, such as personal tells or general chat.

As we will demonstrate, players adopt an *open-system approach* to their entanglement in *WoW*'s genre ecology, which Spinuzzi describes as an approach that recognizes "human interactions with complex technologies are inevitably mediated by dynamic and unpredictable clusters of communication artifacts and activities" (170–71). Given the complexity of *WoW*'s communication systems, contemporary technical communication theory is well equipped to examine the intersections between technical writing, systems theory, MMORPG discourses, and genre analysis. Specifically, work by Spinuzzi et al., Moeller and Christensen, and Mara and Hawk has laid the groundwork for addressing these intersections by reconceptualizing technical writing through posthumanism. For Mara and Hawk, "even when the profession of technical communication was imagined in terms of isolated forms or end-of-the-process editing, technical writers were still operating in interconnected, complex rhetorical systems." Technical communication here is conceived of as a system that interweaves human and nonhuman agents rather than as a singular, privileged, and often isolated compositional practice. This approach to technical communication, however, is commonly ignored by administrative pedagogies that treat students as an end user or product, often obviating the entanglement experienced by technical communicators: "Precisely because technical communicators have always been writing and living in organizational systems, we have had an emerging awareness of the gaps in understanding between the fabricators of such systems and the end users who may not be aware of the intricacy of some of these systems." The design of *WoW*'s social structures is analogous to the knotted organizational networks that technical writers inhabit insofar as these systems feature specific gaps or challenges, either intentionally or unintentionally implemented by their fabricators or the game's designers. Players must find solutions to address these challenges through their gameplay, which is shaped by and shaping inter-player communication. Mara and Hawk observe that "many of the theories technical communicators use to explain and anticipate right action still fail to fully account for the implications of operating between and within interconnected and often unaccommodating systems" (2), but MMORPGs can illustrate this for students because of the transparency of the system's artifice. MMORPGs support a dynamic pedagogy that moves between social context immersion and a removed examination of genres specifically because of the degree to which its environments are constructed.

Play and Praxis: Teaching Technical Communication through *WoW*

Like Spinuzzi, we have students explore genres as "messy," contingent groups of decentralized systems by immersing them in the discourse practices and activities of a genre ecology. To help familiarize students with how genre ecologies operate with regard to technical communication, we used *WoW* as an organizational model. We divided the class in half and each group was assigned two avatars and one of two lower level dungeons to participate in. Once in a dungeon group with nonstudent players, each group needed to request instructions for defeating the dungeon's bosses from other players in their party. We emphasized that students record these conversations, specifically those that directly addressed their play and that elucidated ways they could play that were not originally apparent. We also asked them to note in what ways nonstudent players addressed the apparent gaps in their knowledge about the game and how to play, as well as how receptive were nonstudent players to these questions about play and participation. In many ways, we were asking students to document the ways that procedural information is passed to students through mentoring, something that deWinter touches on in an earlier chapter of this collection. After completing the dungeon successfully, students were asked to review their conversations in these dungeons and make observations about the discourse used during the community activity. Next, some of the students were asked to switch groups while their classmates prepared to enter the second of the two dungeons. The students switching groups were asked to write instructions to their peers explaining how to defeat the game's bosses before entering the dungeon. Once the students complete the dungeon, the class was asked to compare and contrast the writing style, tone, and practices of writing in the game to those outside of it. For students unfamiliar with the game's writing genre, the first part of the exercise was challenging as they had to pick up on many of the game's specific writing practices, such as abbreviations, acronyms, terms.

Many of *WoW*'s high-end raiding guilds demand that players applying for guild membership submit a form of documentation similar in structure and design to a professional job application packet. In a second exercise designed to teach resume writing, students were assigned the task of constructing a guild application for a high-level player character provided by the instructor. Guilds make up the backbone of *WoW*'s social structure, varying in size from as little as ten players to as large as one thousand members. Players who belong to a guild are distinguished from nonaffiliated members by a "guild tag" that appears below their avatar's name. According to most *WoW* players, guild membership shapes and frames a large part of players' social experiences of the game, including their most important in-game relationships (Williams et al.). Not only do members of the same guild communicate with one another, but they can also share in their experiences of the game including leveling together, trading goods, completing achievements, raiding, and participating in PvP battles. Some guilds are much more goal oriented than others, whereas some are casual social groups, and these different contexts require players to learn and use specific types of discourse. The goals of a guild and its ethos shape the tone, structure, and style of writing that participating players produce. Casual guilds composed primarily of close friends who play together will typically have a much less informal communication style than more committed guilds that are highly invested in performing successfully in raids or PvP battlegrounds. Moreover, guild documents like mission statements, recruitment and expulsion policies, and external websites take on specific types of rhetoric that parallel in-game writing genres.

To familiarize students with resume writing and the contingency of genres, we tasked students with creating, among other things, a resume directed toward the leaders of a specific guild that not only exhibited the skills and accomplishments of the in-game character but also was persuasive in its request for entry into the guild. In order to identify what information would be most useful and important to provide these guild leaders as well as to highlight the contingency of genres like resume writing, students had to interact with members of the *WoW* community through chat, game forums, and guild websites. For students unfamiliar with the game's discourses and its genres, this exercise proved to be difficult as they had to learn a vocabulary for player-character skills and abilities in the process. From the assignment, students derived an ecological framework for thinking about writing genres as variable mediators that shape players' activities. Whereas the classroom orients writing around the demands of the instructor, *WoW* distributes it in relation to a complex social environment, and students became sensitive to how players actively respond to and succeed (and fail) to achieve their goals because of communication. Players need to learn how to evaluate communities and the discursive practices associated with them. Students immersed in *WoW* quickly pick up reading and writing practices that enable them to communicate effectively in a technical or professional work environment.

Participating in raids can also be a productive pedagogical experience because when players face difficult boss battles they engage in what Squire calls "recursive play" (116). Under such circumstances, players must collaborate to devise an attack strategy, observe the results of its implementation, and then, should they fail, collaborate to devise a different plan. In this manner, players learn the properties of the game's model as they play, and as Squire notes, "This process is a form of hypothesis testing in which players observe a phenomena, analyze their causes, and implement solutions" (116). In tandem with learning to think critically and collaboratively about problems through recursive play, students can also benefit from playing *WoW* and other MMOs by reflecting on the communicative processes—namely reading and writing—that are involved in gameplay.

Finally, we wanted to investigate whether *WoW* could provide a space that would encourage students to think critically about the role of bodily communication in technical writing. Our assignment was influenced by the observations of McNair et al. in "Towards a Pedagogy of Relational Space and Trust," and we played with their suggestion that language use becomes the predominant if not the only mode through which individuals can form a working knowledge of one another and the common goals they share within virtual environments. As McNair et al. suggest, because physical cues are absent from these mediated spaces, language is often conceived as determining how social exchanges are received and interpreted (235). What this means for *WoW* and other MMORPGs that do not rely primarily on voice-over-internet protocol (VoIP) for player-to-player communication is that language takes the form of players' writing practices.[2] Aside from the chat box, however, player communication in the game relies secondarily on avatar gestures. Players can make their avatar perform certain gestures by typing in a /command into the chat box. For example, if a player targets someone else in the game and types "/ wave" into chat, the chat entry will read "You wave at [target player's name]" and the player's avatar will raise its arm in salutation. The representation of gestures in the game world vary, however, with some only producing the textual component of the exchange—the result of coding limitations—while others maintain both the textual and kinesthetic aspect of the gesture. This illustrates for students the links between technical writing and physical communication, which models McNair et al.'s observation that "the absence of physical and social contexts and the presence of mediating technologies can severely hamper knowledge sharing in distributed teams by disrupting the necessary social networks and interpersonal trust that

---

[2]   *WoW* has offered players a VOIP option since as early as 2009, and many players who use *WoW* to engage in the kinds of activity we describe in this chapter use third party VOIP applications like TeamSpeak, Vent, or Mumble to communicate with one another. For more on how players use these applications, see Moberly. However, for the purposes of this chapter, we intentionally downplayed the VOIP capabilities of *WoW* in order to encourage students to focus on communication via chat boxes and character gestures.

underpin successful collaboration" (236). Students can therefore use *WoW* as a context to experiment with action and language as deeply connected concepts, exposing how breakdowns in one form or the other must be compensated for. Because the game's design does not allow players to see or read each others' real body language and gestures, players rely on coded avatar animations and writing to express their responses to in-game occurrences and each other. Conversely, in raids where time for discussion is often limited, students observed how advanced *WoW* players rely less on verbal cues and more on visual, gestural ones produced by the avatars of their fellow party members. For example, players watched for animations signifying that characters are changing positions, dying, and casting attacking and healing spells in order to assess the activities and progress of the raid party, as well as to indicate what the individual player needs to accomplish during the raid encounter.

McNair et al.'s research shows the significance and value of moving from just talking about physical bodies to also incorporating discussions of the digital body in the multimodal technical writing classroom. Their claims return us to Brown and Gordon's initial visions of learning professional practices in computer games. If the future of businesses and corporations is envisioned such that these professional spaces possess a social and collaborative structure similar to *WoW*, then classrooms need to adapt their curriculums to address these changes. MMO players regularly interact with issues related to enculturation, regularized discourse, and genre; and further research might also investigate how they develop their own rhetorical techniques that could inform the pedagogical praxis of technical communication curriculums. As Gordon suggests, "I think that every Fortune 500 company should have a gamer in the executive suite . . . game design is the new MBA" (McElroy).

Works Cited

Bay, Jennifer, and Samantha Blackmon. "Inhabiting Professional Writing: Exploring Rhetoric, Play, and Community in *Second Life*." *Computer Games and Technical Communication: Critical Methods and Applications at the Intersection*. Burlington, VT: Ashgate, 2014. 211–31.

Berkenkotter, Carol, and Thomas N. Huckin. *Genre Knowledge in Disciplinary Communication*. Mahwah, NJ: Lawrence Erlbaum, 1995.

Blizzard Entertainment. "Alliance and Horde Armies Grow with Launch of *Mists of Pandaria*™." *Business Wire*. Blizzard Entertainment, 4 Oct. 2012. Web. 2 Feb. 2013.

Bridgeford, Tracy. "Communities of Practice: The Shop Floor of Human Capital." *Resources in Technical Communication: Outcomes and Approaches*. Ed. Cynthia Selfe. Amityville, NY: Baywood, 2007. 161–78.

Brown, John Seely. "How *World of Warcraft* Could Save Your Business and The Economy." *Big Think*. Floating University, 2012. Video.

Cooper, Marilyn M. "Exploding the Myth of Transparent Communication." *Resources in Technical Communication: Outcomes and Approaches.* Ed. Cynthia Selfe. Amityville, NY: Baywood, 2007. 309–30.

deWinter, Jennifer. "Just Playing Around: From Procedural Manuals to In-Game Training." *Computer Games and Technical Communication: Critical Methods and Applications at the Intersection.* Burlington, VT: Ashgate, 2014. 69–85.

Huizinga, Johan. *Homo Ludens: A Study of the Play-Element in Culture.* London: Routledge, 1949.

Juul, Jesper. *Half-Real: Video Games Between Real Rules and Fictional Worlds.* Cambridge: MIT P, 2011.

Luzón, María. "Genre Analysis in Technical Communication." *IEEE Transactions on Professional Communication* 48.3 (2005): 285–95.

Mara, Andrew and Byron Hawk. "Posthuman Rhetorics and Technical Communication." *Technical Communication Quarterly.* 19.1 (2010): 1–10.

McElroy, Griffin. "You're Hired, Now Let's Kill Onyxia—Bing Gordon on Structuring Your Business Like a *WoW* Guild." *Polygon.* Vox, 12 Mar. 2012. Web. 2 February 2013.

McNair, Lisa, Marie Paretti, and Marcia Davitt. "Towards and Pedagogy of Relational Space and Trust: Analyzing Distributed Collaboration Using Discourse and Speech Act Analysis." *IEEE Transactions on Professional Communication.* 53.3 (2010): 233–48.

Moberly, Kevin. "Composition, Computer Games, and the Absence of Writing." *Computers and Composition* 25.3 (2008): 284–99. PDF file.

Moberly, Kevin, and Ryan M. Moeller. "Working at Play: Modding, Revelation, and Transformation in Technical Communication." *Computer Games and Technical Communication: Critical Methods and Applications at the Intersection.* Burlington, VT: Ashgate, 2014. 189–207.

Moeller, Ryan M. and Christensen, David M. "System mapping: A genre field analysis of the National Science Foundation's grant proposal and funding process." *Technical Communication Quarterly* 19.1 (2010): 69–89.

Orlikowski, Wanda J., and JoAnne Yates. "Genre Repertoire: Norms and Forms for Work Interaction." MIT Sloan School, 1994. 3671–94. Working Paper.

Selfe, Cynthia L. "Introduction." *Resources in Technical Communication: Outcomes and Approaches.* Ed. Cynthia L. Selfe. Amityville, NY: Baywood, 2007. 1–4.

Spinuzzi, Clay. "Genre Ecologies: An Open-System Approach to Understanding and Constructing Documentation." *ACM Journal of Computer Documentation.* 24.3 (2000): 169–81.

———. *Tracing Genres Through Organizations: A Sociocultural Approach to Information Design.* Cambridge, MA: MIT P, 2003.

———, William Hart-Davidson, and Mark Zachry. (2003). "Chains and Ecologies: Methodological Notes Toward a Communicative-Mediational Model of Technologically Mediated Writing." *Proceedings of the International*

Conference on Design of Communication, 24, New York, NY: ACM, 2006. 43–50.

Squire, Kurt. *Video Games and Learning: Teaching and Participatory Culture in the Digital Age*. New York, NY: Teachers College P, 2011.

Williams, Dmitri, Nicolas Ducheneaut, Li Xiong, Yuanyuan Zhang, Nick Yee and Eric Nickell. "From Tree House to Barracks: The Social Life of Guilds in *World of Warcraft*." *Games and Culture* 1.4 (2006): 338–61.

World of Warcraft. Irvine, CA: Blizzard Entertainment, 2012. PC game.

Chapter 14

The Three D's of Procedural Literacy: Developing, Demonstrating, and Documenting Layered Literacies with Valve's Steam for Schools

Jason Custer

Initially serving as a compilation of the acclaimed game *Half Life 2* and its subsequent expansions *Half Life 2: Episode 1* and *Half Life 2: Episode 2*, Valve's *Orange Box* also introduced players to *Team Fortress 2* and *Portal*. The impact of these latter releases continues in a variety of contexts, including the massive success of *Team Fortress 2*'s switch to a free-to-play model that yields reports of students paying for portions of their college tuition using in-game objects (Hernandez). *Portal,* meanwhile, earned several game of the year awards for its unique physics puzzle-based twist on the classic first-person shooting formula. Valve later introduced the sequel *Portal 2* to nearly universal acclaim, netting even more critics' game of the year awards. In the time since *Portal 2*'s launch, developer Valve released more of their titles for free in much the same vein as *Team Fortress 2*. In the case of *Portal 2*, however, this free release came in the form of Valve's Steam for Schools in 2012. Through Valve's website, Teach with Portals, educators can apply for keys to download Steam for Schools, which includes *Portal 2*, the *Portal 2 Puzzle Maker*, and other software like *Universe Sandbox*. These freely available tools shift the potential of Valve's products from entertainment to helping enterprising students to pay for tuition by selling in-game objects and other tangible benefits for technical communication students in our classrooms. In other words, Steam for Schools presents a unique opportunity to foster a range of technical communication literacies in our students.

In this chapter, I focus on the ways that utilizing *Portal 2* and the *Portal 2 Puzzle Maker* enacts the approach to technical communication discussed by Cargile Cook in her piece "Layered Literacies: A Theoretical Frame for Technical Communication Pedagogy." I demonstrate how using Steam for Schools can help technical communication instructors map Cargile Cook's literacies to the development of procedural literacy via gameplay and level design. Cargile Cook asserts that, although "historical frames progressively complicate technical communication instruction, none of them fully articulate the multiple literacies necessary to succeed in the twenty-first century workplace. ... The layered literacy frame . . . synthesizes these components into six key literacies (8). The literacies defined in Cargile Cook's text include basic, rhetorical, social, technological, ethical, and critical literacies. These literacies easily transfer to the use of computer games in the classroom, and when matched with activities and assignments focused on content creation within the context of computer games, collaborative design, procedural documentation tasks, and reflection, students demonstrate core competencies in technical communication.

Students engage with the layered literacies described by Cargile Cook through what I call the three D's of procedural literacy: developing procedural literacy, demonstrating procedural literacy, and documenting procedural literacy. First, *developing* procedural literacy or understanding how games present procedures in the form of interactions within rule-based systems comes in the form of gameplay itself. I will discuss procedural literacy in terms of Bogost's work later in this chapter. After becoming familiar with the processes of a computer game through interactive gameplay, students must then *demonstrate* their awareness of processes in games. In my study, students did this using *Portal 2* for composing within the game itself using the *Portal 2 Puzzle Maker*. Finally, students *document* procedural literacy by creating procedural documentation for their designs: in my case, students designed puzzle chambers and crafted reflections that focused on the process of creating a test chamber with a partner, using someone else's instructions to duplicate a test chamber, and solving the chamber itself.

The combination of content creation tools and gameplay included with many game releases allows instructors to teach these three aspects of procedural literacy in the classroom with a relatively low threshold to entry, helping students to develop critical literacy and communication skills. In the following section, I will further discuss Bogost's notion of procedurality while elaborating on the classroom context of my experiences with Steam for Schools. In sum, this chapter brings together Ian Bogost's work with procedurality and Stephanie Vie's application of computer games to the technical communication classroom to illustrate how students can develop, demonstrate, and document procedural literacy with Steam for Schools through the lens of Cargile Cook's "Layered Literacies" approach to teaching technical communication.

Defining Procedural Literacy

Research and evidence from several fields hint at the potential benefits for students. Not only do computer games provide ample opportunities to engage with new literacies (Hsu and Wang, 2009; Gee, 2003; Yancey, 2004; the New London Group, 1996; Bogost, 2008), but also a lengthy history of empirical research links computer games to positive learning behaviors (Egenfeldt-Nielson 188). The question of why to use games has thus been explored and discussed at length by several others to reach several different ends, including fostering new literacy skills or more explicitly didactic content, which suggests that computer games provide effective pedagogical tools. In the spring of 2013, I used my course to focus on exploring the ways that computer games inform writing, argument, and communications skills in students to foster procedural literacy skills in particular. Before outlining the context of this course and unit on procedural documentation, I first turn my attention to defining procedural literacy.

Bogost, a game designer and scholar, focuses on procedurality in both his book *Persuasive Games: The Expressive Power of Videogames* and his preceding article "The Rhetoric of Video Games." In his discussion of procedurality, Bogost focuses on two things specifically: procedural literacy and procedural rhetoric. By playing computer games, students begin to understand an advanced form of argument in the procedural rhetorics, and they can become procedurally literate through gameplay itself (*Persuasive* 260). Bogost traces the term procedurality back to Janet Murray's *Hamlet on the Holodeck*. In it, she "defines the four essential properties of digital artifacts: procedurality, participation, spatiality, and encyclopedic scope" (quoted in "Rhetoric" 122). Bogost calls procedural literacy "interacting with procedural systems that make strong ties between the processes in a model and a representational goal—those with strongly argued procedural rhetorics. Otherwise said, we can become procedurally literate through play itself" (*Persuasive* 255). Put simply, procedural literacy as discussed in this chapter is an understanding of how complex, system-wide processes work both in gameplay situations and communication with other players or users.

One of the foremost goals of my course is to foster the development of procedural literacy and an understanding of how complex processes function in games through a combination of gameplay and analysis throughout the semester, culminating in a project that asked students to develop procedural literacy in a specific context through play and demonstrate that procedural literacy through documentation and design. With this in mind, I designed a course at Florida State University entitled "It's Dangerous to go Alone: Take This! Writing About the Rhetoric of Videogames," a course designed to fulfill the requirement for the second half of FSU's Composition requirement focusing on research. My goal in designing this course was to define and explore what I have come to call "videogame-infused pedagogy" that focuses on the following goals:

1. Teaching procedural and professional writing by actively using games inside the classroom.
2. Bringing the research of James Gee and Ian Bogost together with the Framework for Success in Postsecondary Writing, a guideline for writing instruction developed by the Council of Writing Program Administrators, National Council of Teachers of English, and National Writing Project to target specific learning goals and outcomes across a wide range of pedagogical practices.

To accomplish this, I focused on freely available games and those that do not require advanced computers. My work to define a videogame-infused pedagogy hinges strongly on the Framework for Success in Postsecondary writing. According to the agencies affiliated, the Framework "describes the rhetorical and twenty-first-century skills as well as habits of mind and experiences that are critical for college success" ("Framework for Success in Postsecondary Writing"). The Framework breaks down these skills and experiences into a series of Habits of Mind and Outcomes instructors can target with their pedagogical practices, such as creativity, openness, engagement, persistence, responsibility, curiosity, metacognition, rhetorical knowledge, critical thinking, writing processes, knowledge of conventions, and the ability to compose in multiple environments. As a baseline model for informing my approach to videogame-infused pedagogy in the writing classroom, the Framework gave shape to the units of my course and allowed each unit to target set preliminary goals and outcomes.

Following the design informed by the Framework, I divided the course into four units, the first, Seeing Yourself in the Game World, asked students to design an avatar and explain how this avatar and the world it occupied reflected their experiences with games and/or the world around them. For a more in-depth look at these activities within a professional context, please see Bay and Blackmon's chapter in this collection. Also, for ways to challenge students' perceptions of gender, sexuality, and culture in game worlds, please see Ouellette's chapter. The second unit, Seeing the Game World Procedurally, tasked students with performing a procedural analysis of a computer game and considering it from the perspective of Bogost's procedural rhetoric. DeWinter's chapter in this collection shows how computer game manuals and in-game training teach players this procedurality as they play games. Unit three, Creating a Game World of Your Own, focused on designing computer games using Twine, a text-based game creation tool, and using programs like Photoshop to design advertisements for the games in question and target a specific audience. Sherlock's chapter in this collection demonstrates the complex relationship between developers and players, complicating students' notions of audience as a general concept. The final unit, and the subject of this chapter, served as a capstone for the previous units. Becoming the Test Subject: Participating in the Game World asked students to utilize Steam for Schools to play computer games in class, create puzzle chambers in *Portal 2* and document their processes and reflect on them. Each unit focused on targeting different Outcomes and Habits of Mind from the Framework for Success for Postsecondary Writing as well as Cargile Cook's layered literacies, and the final unit targeted all of the Outcomes in the Framework and focused on gameplay first and foremost as the place where student composition, design, and communication took place, transitioning from a more traditional composition context for writing to one focused on skills and processes emphasized in technical communication.

Specifically, this final unit of my course placed students in groups of two to play *Portal 2* in class for two 50-minute class periods, create and document the creation of a puzzle chamber for two 50-minute class periods (as well as outside of class), and use two more 50-minute class periods to attempt to duplicate another group's instructions to recreate and solve the puzzle as well. Students were required to create a puzzle chamber, instructions of at least 250 words (with or without images of their choosing), and a reflection of at least 500 words describing experiences playing, designing, writing documentation for, and working with someone else's documentation of a puzzle chamber. This assignment targeted all five of the Outcomes outlined in the Framework for Success: Rhetorical Knowledge, Critical Thinking, Writing Processes, Knowledge of Conventions, and the Ability to Compose in Multiple Environments. My initial choice to target these outcomes through procedural literacy, however, segues directly back into my ambition with this course to explore computer games and procedural literacy through the lens of technical communication and Cargile Cook's layered literacies specifically.

Developing Procedural Literacy

With a concrete definition of procedural literacy established, I would like to build on Bogost's work to show the ways that playing computer games in the classroom space and composing within the gamespace itself helped my students develop procedural literacy. To reiterate what Bogost says in his texts: "procedural literacy means more than writing computer code; it also comes from interacting with procedural systems themselves" (*Persuasive* 255). This happens when players engage with a procedural system repeatedly through gameplay. Steam for Schools provided me with a concrete approach for engaging students with systems and processes within a set context (*Portal 2*) and with a specific goal in mind (solving the puzzle chamber).

Portal 2's gameplay takes place primarily in a series of puzzle chambers that were designed in the game's fictional universe to test its subjects—in this case, the game's mute female protagonist, Chell—for scientific research. While *Portal 2* literally and figuratively breaks the walls of the game apart by having players navigate through a series of connecting corridors behind the scenes of the fictional company, Aperture Science, the bulk of the gameplay takes place in tightly structured spaces designed to have one precise solution. This solution tests the subject's wits and skill with the portal gun obtained at the game's beginning. The portal gun twists time and space; the player can fire the entrance at one wall and the exit portal at another wall and then use the portal to move multi-dimensionally to solve space-based puzzles. Throughout this gameplay process, then, students become procedurally literate within the context of a piece of software (*Portal 2*) through experience and experimentation.

In the final unit of this course, students began by playing the game for two days in class, using the basic story mode to become familiar with the way the game's rules and systems work. In many cases, students asked peers for help with solving certain puzzles, or waited until I walked by to ask for assistance. As time passed, however, students asked fewer questions, and based on their experiences with playing *Portal 2*, they became increasingly able to solve puzzles on their own. This process of becoming procedurally literate through play sets a precedent for the rest of the unit and serves as a foundational component of developing procedural literacy itself. In a more traditional, non-gaming technical communication course, procedural literacy may be taught by immersing students in any procedural system (like instruction sets, for example) and allowing them to experiment with the rules of the system and understand the best practices for interacting in the system.

Cargile Cook's "Layered Literacies" intersects with students' gameplay experiences in this context to link Steam for Schools to the larger picture discussions about the application of computer games to the technical communication classroom. Among the literacies outlined by Cargile Cook in this piece, technological and social literacy are critical for students beginning to develop procedural literacy. "Technological literacy," Cargile Cook notes, "has only recently begun to appear in technical communication pedagogical frames, yet it has become an integral component of most technical communication instruction" (13). She goes on to write, "by its earliest and most basic definition, technological literacy means that communicators must know how to use computer applications" (13). In this first subsection of this unit, students are both developing procedural and technological literacy by becoming literate in gameplay processes and how they work within a specific context. Puzzle games serve this purpose especially well, as following the rules of games and puzzles is essential to successfully progressing. Whereas it is possible to proceed in many gameplay types and programs without an understanding of how to complete a set of processes, *Portal 2* encourages player exploration while requiring a set approach to succeeding in a given context. Assigning students to work in small groups also encouraged students to develop what Cargile Cook calls social literacy. Cargile Cook states that "for success, among the most important of these social skills is the ability to collaborate and work well with others" (11). Asking students to collaborate on a single-player game and single-player task of creating a puzzle in groups encourages communication and collaboration between the authors to help foster social literacy.

Many students in the classroom had never played *Portal 2* when we began this final unit of the course and thus took advantage of the initial first few days of exploring and experimentation to learn how the game itself functioned with a partner, developing their procedural literacy, technological literacy, and social literacy simultaneously. In the introduction to their reflective writing, one student noted the following:

> Overall designing and building a test chamber was a fun and creative process that I had expected to be far more limiting. Most games don't allow as much of the full game as the *Portal 2* test chamber creator does, I didn't feel limited in how or which elements I could use which was nice. Full disclosure, I have never played through *Portal 2* so getting to try out new elements without knowing how the folks at Valve originally used them made for plenty of science.

"Science" here refers to the strong themes of science and experimentation that permeate sterile white walls of *Portal 2*'s fictional setting in the Aperture Science laboratories while also serving as a fitting metaphor for the process of experimenting with writing and creating inside the game itself. The process of creating content within the game is what I asked students to focus on in the reflective component of the project, yet this student specifically discussed gaining and elaborating on their procedural literacy skills by taking part in "plenty of science" while designing a puzzle. This part of the project and the student's reflection above also clearly focuses on the development what Cargile Cook names technological literacy: The student learned how processes and elements of the game itself he had yet to experience were used through gameplay. As this reflection was individualized, many students did not reflect with any length on their experience working with the partners but in many cases referred to the decisions being made by the group as a whole, writing things like: "My group started out with the generic open space room, but we couldn't decide how to make it both fun and challenging. The group decided on making our puzzle into a narrow hallway filled with gun turrets." These pieces were absent of criticism of group work as a whole, suggesting in many cases that decisions were carried out harmoniously within the groups, but nonetheless providing no evidence to suggest this specifically. Future versions of this project and offshoots of it will likely revolve around designing a component that focuses on asking students to generate group reports and reflect on the element of the process specifically, which is in line with what Cargile Cook suggests (12).

Based upon the student example above, my students used Steam for Schools to develop procedural, social, and technological literacy. Gameplay encourages them to develop procedural and technological literacy by learning the rules and processes of a game and how they function. The story campaign and level creation suite in Steam for Schools provides students with powerful, streamlined ways to learn the rules of a piece of software and then take that knowledge and create something with it in the same software they learned it from. This form of technological literacy sets a worthy precedent for technical communicators well beyond a computer game context. Furthermore, students develop social literacy in this group context by effectively communicating with their partners and solving puzzles and gaining procedural literacy skills together, be it as a single player moves through a puzzle or another who observes this process. Through experience, observation, and collaboration, gameplay in the context of developing levels and documenting procedural gameplay can encourage students to develop social literacy and work together in achieving these goals.

Demonstrating Procedural Literacy

Playing *Portal 2* in the classroom is only the beginning of developing layered and procedural literacies. As students designed puzzle chambers in my class using Steam for Schools, they took the procedural literacy developed through gameplay and have a chance to demonstrate it using the content creation tools in the *Portal 2 Puzzle Maker*. Demonstrating procedural literacy is made available in the package of software provided by Steam for Schools as the means of *creating* content within the same gamespace as students learn procedural literacy skills. This is akin to the close relationship between reading and writing in linguistic literacies. In taking advantage of these tools, students demonstrate their procedural literacy skills using content creation tools, but they also further demonstrate the social literacy as well as rhetorical literacy identified by Cargile Cook. In her discussion of rhetorical literacy, Cargile Cook notes that it "can also be identified when students demonstrate other literacies, such as schemas, basic literacy, and graphical by choosing displays appropriate or by making genres, reasoned organizational stylistic or graphic choices for their specific audiences or writing contexts" (10). Without wishing to say too much about how this connects to the process of students creating documentation and reflecting on their experiences creating levels in the *Portal 2 Puzzle Maker*, I discuss content creation systems in games and how Steam for Schools allows ways to shift from simply asking students to play games and write about them to developing rhetorical and social literacies while demonstrating the procedural literacy developed from gameplay.

As Moberly and Moeller discuss in "Working at Play: Modding, Revelation, and Transformation in Technical Communication," content creation systems have become popular in computer games like *LittleBigPlanet*, *Neverwinter Nights*, and *Skyrim*, enabling players to create their own content for use within game worlds. These types of content creation tools date back to 1985's *Lode Runner* software, which allowed users to generate content and edit levels. More recent games such as *LittleBigPlanet* made great strides in encouraging and soliciting the creation of content from users and as a result influenced other modern game developers to do the same on a larger scale. *LittleBigPlanet* garnered attention for its ease of use, powerful content creation tools, and the booming community surrounding it (Jones, 2012; Westecott, 2011; Boyce et al., 2012). In many ways, titles like *LittleBigPlanet* and its sequel *LittleBigPlanet 2* are examples *par excellence* of developers engaging users with content creation software, as seen in the whopping six million levels created and posted online by players (Boyce et al. 10). Moberly and Moeller problematize this aspect of the computer game industry in their chapter in this collection; however, Valve's introduction of the *Portal 2 Puzzle Maker* provides players with all of the tools required to make a level of any type with many of the available objects in the game. Players begin with an empty rectangular room and a toolbar displaying all of the available items (see Figure 14.1). From here, designers can do whatever they choose to alter the shape, layout, and obstacles in the way of a player's progress. By the same accord, players can also create a puzzle chamber without a plausible solution, meaning that players have full access to all the tools used to create levels in *Portal 2* with virtually no limitations on their use. This availability and ease of use led to the development of over 270,000 publicly available levels in the Steam Workshop.

The increasing scope and ease of use for content creation tools in computer games make them ideal candidates for encouraging students to demonstrate the

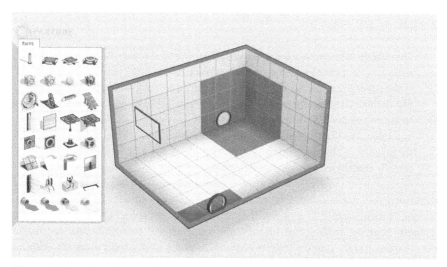

Figure 14.1   *Portal 2 Puzzle Maker* Interface with Toolbar

procedural literacy skills developed by playing the main game and doing so with software that is easy to use and instructors can access for free in Steam for Schools.

For one third of the unit on demonstrating, students worked in groups to take the experiences from playing the game and create their own puzzle chambers while documenting the process of creating it. I divided the students into groups of four, and within those groups, I asked students to pair up. These peer review groups worked together all semester to provide feedback on each other's writing in the units discussed earlier. In this final unit, students needed to design a chamber and instructions for the other pair in the four-person group. Students had to duplicate and solve the puzzle chamber using the instructions crafted throughout the gameplay and documentation processes. These tasks could be divided however the students saw fit, and working in pairs allowed students to collaboratively design puzzles, create the level inside of the game, and articulate how this was done using images and/or text. The student quoted earlier said this of his experience creating the puzzle chamber itself:

> After making a test chamber and accidentally forgetting to use lights I decided to use the darkness as one of the challenges in a test chamber, that is where the dizzy array of light bridges came from. It was meant to be a distraction and to make the player act like a fly attracted to a light in the night. In testing with a few classmates, that portion worked beautifully. The second half of the chamber and perhaps the most well planned traps were the speed goo and turret holes. The first one had less goo so that it was more obvious what to do and to teach the player how to accomplish the second one with a bit of faith. I then realized how troublesome it was and created the abridged version of the chamber for the instructions.

Another student added that:

> Our puzzle starts out with the player looking down the narrow hallway with
> multiple gun turrets looking right back at them. To start, the player must make
> a portal anywhere on the map in order to get rid of the gun turrets. Once the
> player shoots a portal under each turret to get rid of it, the player then must walk
> to the end of the path, where they will see the finishing point. Although, there
> is a catch, the finishing point is midway up the wall. So, here the player sees
> the puddles of blue and orange goo and wonders if this will aid them or if they
> actually need to incorporate it in their plan.

Returning to Cargile Cook's layered literacies and the student reflections above,
we see students exhibiting social literacy and rhetorical literacy in these puzzle
designs. Starting with social literacy, the requirement to collaborate on puzzle
designs and jointly demonstrate procedural literacy skills tasks students with an
understanding of how to complete a single-player task as a group, reconfiguring
the standard approach to gameplay seen here and encouraging communication in
the design and articulation of how the puzzle functions. Students must carefully
consider the design of the puzzle itself as well as how the puzzle exists spatially,
and how this design and solution can be articulated for an audience of someone
else with somewhat limited knowledge of *Portal 2* (given that playing the game
in class on two occasions was all that was required of students). Cargile Cook's
discussion of social literacy suggests that it is related most closely to collaborative
skills (12). By asking students to collaborate in spaces requiring a single user
(much like the process for some users of procedural documentation) students
consistently create, revise, reconsider, and document with social literacy skills at
the forefront.

Similarly, in designing the puzzle chamber, students exhibit rhetorical literacy.
In her discussion of social literacy, Cargile Cook notes that "collaboration, as
a component of the writing process, first appeared in Aristotle's work when he
defined dialectic rhetoric as a collaboration or interchange between rhetors and
their audiences" (11). This interplay between audiences and rhetors, creators and
audience, comes across strongly in the student reflections quoted above. The first
student discusses the labyrinthine chamber he designed with a partner and the
process of testing it with other students.[1] Despite the fact that this process seemed
to be successful, he made an interesting choice: "I then realized how troublesome
it was and created the abridged version of the chamber for the instructions." The
second student noted that in the chamber his group designed, "there is a catch,

---

[1]   It may be of interest to note that testing their levels was something my students did
entirely of their own choosing as I did not require students to test chambers with their peers.
Given its success in this class, I will likely require students to playtest their levels in future
adaptations of this project because, as Tilley et al. note in this volume, playtesting asks
creators to be user- or audience-centered in their creations.

the finishing point is midway up the wall. So, here the player sees the puddles of blue and orange goo and wonders if this will aid them or if they actually need to incorporate it in their plan." These choices are interesting in light of Cargile Cook's discussion of rhetorical literacy, since "rhetorical literacy can also be identified when students demonstrate other literacies, such as schemas, basic literacy, and graphical by choosing displays appropriate or by making genres, reasoned organizational stylistic or graphic choices for their specific audiences or writing contexts" (10). Thus, choices made in design may demonstrate rhetorical literacy, and in the examples above, we see such literacies in practice with students giving specific consideration to the approaches of designing their chambers and how this would affect the player.

By designing chambers and demonstrating procedural literacy, students also demonstrate rhetorical literacy when they consider players' needs in their designs. The first student completely altered the shape of the original design to ensure it was possible to clearly articulate its design to an unknowing audience, while the second student's group specifically used visual cues to mislead the intended audience. The second student's group, by including deliberate decoy items like the blue gel (which allows players and objects to bounce off of it) and orange gel (which allows players and objects to move quickly across it), created a design that calls attention to and subverts the designer and the end user's procedural and rhetorical literacy skills. Through gameplay, this group of students knew that the orange and blue gel served as critical components of solving puzzles in a specific way. They laid them out for the end user in an attempt to trick them into using these items to solve a puzzle that does not require them at all, an interesting design and rhetorical move in this space and evidencing the playful nature of game design.

Not only does this demonstration of procedural literacy indicate a clear and advanced knowledge of what these items mean but also what they symbolize to anyone who might encounter them. Placing the blue and orange gel as decoys demonstrates procedural literacy in action as they know what these items can do. Simultaneously, this move also subverts the audience's expectations for this design; this ties directly into how the student designers expected the player to encounter this chamber and anticipated her to think, "if blue and orange gel are here, they must do *something*, but what?" Whether the player inevitably found this to be a trick on the part of the creators, this design decisions nonetheless serves as a compelling example of students demonstrating procedural literacy and rhetorical literacy as they showed their knowledge of these items in the context of the game and immediately subverted them for the purpose of affecting their audience in a specific way and anticipating the procedural literacy of the audience as well. Without a knowledge of what these two gels entailed, both the creators and their intended audience could easily bypass them and solve or create a puzzle without them; however, these students successfully demonstrated advanced procedural literacy as well as audience awareness that hinges on the procedural literacy of the player. This playful attempt to subvert the knowledge of the audience demonstrates and hinges on procedural knowledge in both the designers and the audience as well as a strong sense of play in the two groups.

Documenting Procedural Literacy

In the final component of this unit, I asked students to create two types of documentation: 1) a procedural walkthrough to illustrate the puzzles they designed; and 2) a reflective essay to discuss the overall experience itself, what they learned from creating puzzle chambers, and what they learned when trying to work with someone else's documentation to reproduce and solve a puzzle chamber. At its core, asking students to develop procedural documentation for software requires knowledge of how processes operate within the context of that software. I designed these components initially to serve as ways to assess the background processes and experiences students had creating puzzles; the process of documenting the chambers themselves was left deliberately open ended, allowing students to use images, text, and any combination thereof to create a guide that explained how to recreate the chamber each group collaborated to design. Here, in the final days of this unit where students documented, tested, and reflected on the process of designing and duplicating puzzle chambers, the literacies discussed in the previous sections come together and coalesce in what Cargile Cook's terms basic literacy.

In designing this assignment and unit, my main goal was to depart from the relatively traditional approaches I took in teaching this course. I wanted to introduce students to technical writing in an effort to encourage composing practices within *Portal 2* and explore a facet of writing many introductory writing courses at FSU ignore. As a culmination of the tasks students do to develop and demonstrate procedural literacy in this context of this course, asking students to document procedural literacy practices asks students to further demonstrate Habits of Mind from the Framework for Success, such as metacognition or "the ability to reflect on one's own thinking as well as on the individual and cultural processes used to structure knowledge" ("Framework"). Beyond this, documenting procedural literacy in reflective writing and actual procedural documentation can help students to become conscious of the related technical communications literacies throughout the gameplay and design phases, such as basic, social, and rhetorical literacies seen in the student pairings.

Located specifically within the technical communication pedagogy, Vie advocates for using games in the context of the technical writing classroom in her piece, "Tech Writing, Meet *Tomb Raider*: Video and Computer Games in the Technical Communication Classroom." She states that "incorporating video games into the classroom is an ideal means of capturing students' attention and indulging their creativity while at the same time teaching them important aspects of technical writing" (2). One of these aspects is procedural documentation. Playing *Portal 2* coupled with activities focused on procedurality fosters procedural literacy in students as well as an increased awareness of how processes work in the software documented and critical understandings of procedural documentation. Vie's research encourages students to learn communication practices using games like *Tomb Raider* and *The Legend of Zelda: Twilight Princess* to present additional rhetorical situations players can write from:

> walkthroughs available for the Wii game *The Legend of Zelda: Twilight Princess* range from all-purpose guides to completing the game to more targeted guides to completing Link's mini-games, capturing all of the available Poe Souls, finding all of the heart containers, and even a "minimalist challenge" for completing the Cave of Ordeals under a particular set of restrictions (3).

Vie further notes that instructors can use assignments and computer games to teach usability testing as well. Thus, Vie provides a solid foundation for exploring computer games, technical communication pedagogy, and procedural documentation. Bringing this together with the elements of the unit discussed previously—like group work, reflections, and designing content with the games—allow instructors to target a wider range of possibilities for students in the classroom than using computer games solely as a source of documentation. Thus, this final section of the unit marries the practical approach forwarded in Vie's work with the theoretical approach outlined in Cargile Cook's "Layered Literacies."

Early in her article, Cargile Cook advocates the development of "basic literacy," and how "early textbooks reflected this focus and frequently taught the 5C's—completeness, consideration, clarity, courtesy, and correctness" (8). She goes on to add that "to assess whether students possess basic literacy, instructors will need to do and more than evaluate students' writing for correct usage, grammar and spelling" and suggests that "discussions such as these might take place in a variety of ways from assignment post-mortem sessions to short memos attached to assignments" (9). Here, asking students to reflect on the process of creating documentation and reflecting on it serves a dual purpose; instructors can assess and consider the thought process behind student designs and documents and encourage the development of "basic literacy" skills. Process memos like these serve a functional purpose in that they allow students to reflect on and articulate the process of creating something for course objectives, be it an essay, image, or computer game. Taken a step further, however, these process memos also encourage critical awareness and critical reflection from students. As Cargile Cook notes, "discussions or post-production memos allow students to situate or reflect upon their writing within its social, political, technological, and ethical landscapes" (17). The process memo assignment allowed students to articulate and reflect on the processes contained within the unit and assignment, and in writing these, students both intentionally and unintentionally show signs of rhetorical awareness and literacy as well as commented on the social experience of working with a group member affected the final project. Recall how the first student's reflections even taught me something about how I create assignments and has encouraged me to include a testing requirement for puzzles created in future courses or how the second student's reflections demonstrated a procedural literacy beyond what her inclusion of gels might have indicated on its own.

Considerations and Conclusions for Using Steam for Schools

Steam for Schools demonstrates potential for helping students to develop, demonstrate, and document procedural literacy skills and engage with a host of other literacy practices, but before attempting to bring computer games into the classroom, several considerations should be addressed, as noted by deWinter et al. in their piece "Computer Games Across the Curriculum: A Critical Review of an Emerging Techno-Pedagogy." These include questions of funding, access, assessment, resistance, and ethics. Purchasing game licenses for an entire classroom of computers personally or through a university structure may prove difficult if not impossible and would undoubtedly be costly. Perhaps more importantly, "it is at the point of access where the rubber meets the road in computer game-based pedagogies. There simply is no possibility of such pedagogies if students, teachers, and institutions cannot easily and indeed pleasurably play" (deWinter et al. n.p.). Choosing games that can run on university computers and knowing who to contact to install and maintain games on university computers is essential. Similarly, instructors should prepare for the possibility of both student and peer resistance. While students may question the value of computer games as a pedagogical tool—a topic explored by Snider et al. in this collection—the first wave of resistance may come from administrators and fellow teachers: "Administrators' and teachers' concerns, by contrast, lie in a different direction, one marked with a legitimate anxiety about litigation ('how dare you expose my children to that kind of garbage?') and pedagogical quality ('what happened to teaching reading, writing, and recitation?')" (deWinter et al. n.p.). These are noteworthy concerns for any instructor interested in bringing computer games into the classroom.

I developed my course with Steam for Schools it was a free, educationally sanctioned software program capable of running on a vast majority of available PC and Mac hardware on campus. Most classroom computers[2] will be able to run *Portal 2* and the *Portal 2 Puzzle Maker* software with very few issues so long as the university allows administrative access to the network. Similarly, the relatively easy to use nature of the source engine Valve uses to build its games provides a great deal of flexibility for a range of hardware configurations that titles like *LittleBigPlanet* simply cannot match. In many contexts, using educational software can serve as a deterrent as it conjures images of games such as *Math*

---

[2]   The minimum requirements for running Portal 2 include Windows 7 / Vista / XP or Mac OSX 10.6.7 or higher, a 3.0 GHz Pentium processor or dual core 2.0 GHz processor, 1GB of RAM for Windows XP or 2GB Vista or OSX, 7.6 GB of hard drive space, a video card with at least 128 MB of memory and DirectX 9 with support for Pixel Shader 2.0b and audio output that is DirectX 9.0c compatible ("Teach with Portals").

Blaster and other "edutainment" titles. Steam for Schools, however, provides a helpful balance of highly regarded software with a broad appeal, a lack of the overt violence prevalent in many modern games, and designated "educational editions" of games like *Portal 2*. Thus, Valve's Steam for Schools may prove a more palatable option for bringing computer games into the classroom than other potential approaches using otherwise critically regarded series like *BioShock* or *Tomb Raider*, which engage more obviously and often with concerns of violence and gender roles.

There are real drawbacks on relying on third-party online software for educational purposes. For example, the class did have issues with the Valve servers going offline for maintenance during this unit, which derailed the progress of some students on certain computers for a class period. Bay and Blackmon speak to this challenge in their chapter of this book, noting that some educators are opting to build their own virtual environments rather than relying on *Second Life* for their classroom. And in the cases that they present, these educators have good reason to do so. However, Bay and Blackmon note that there are still a number of benefits to using *Second Life* to teach students professional skills, and likewise, I would echo this: Using Steam for Schools, while sometimes problematic in terms of ownership and access, is an excellent medium through which to teach procedural and layered literacy with a ubiquitous medium.

Considerations aside, this chapter highlights the potential for Steam for Schools to help students to develop, demonstrate, and document procedural literacy, and how doing so ties into the approaches to teaching technical communication pedagogy outlined by Cargile Cook and Vie. In concluding her piece on the layered literacies approach to technical communication pedagogy, Cargile Cook's calls on us to incorporate new literacy practices in the classroom: "[T]o be applied most effectively in assignments, courses, and programs, [layered literacies] will most likely not be considered solely as independent instructional objectives. Rather, they should be viewed as extremely fluid, complicating technical communication instructional activities and goals rather than simplifying them" (23). Steam for Schools provides a set of powerful, free tools applicable to a wide range of classroom settings, while highlighting many technical communication practices including advanced documentation techniques and engagement with several crucial literacies. In the context of this course, this served simultaneously as a departure from the norm and an introduction to a new form of writing with a videogame-infused pedagogy. The process of developing, demonstrating, and documenting procedural literacy with computer games branches out well beyond the classroom, however, as connections to technical communication pedagogy show. A wide range of possibilities for developing procedural, social, rhetorical, basic, and critical literacies (among others) can result from using tools like Steam for Schools in the classroom, yet I should be clear that such results hinge on the goals of a given course and instructor. Yet by targeting student collaboration and reflection, instructors can facilitate students' literacies beyond what may seem to onlookers as simply playing games.

Works Cited

Bay, Jennifer L., and Samantha Blackmon. "Inhabiting Professional Writing: Exploring Rhetoric, Play, and Community in *Second Life*." *Computer Games and Technical Communication: Critical Methods and Applications at the Intersection*. Burlington, VT: Ashgate, 2014. 211–31.

Bogost, Ian. *Persuasive Games: The Expressive Power of Videogames*. Cambridge, MA: MIT P, 2010.

———. "The Rhetoric of Video Games." *The Ecology of Games: Connecting Youth, Games, and Learning*. Ed. Katie Salen. Cambridge, MA: MIT P, 2008. 117–40. Web. 10 Oct. 2011.

Boyce, Acey, Antoine Campbell, Shaun Pickford, Dustin Culler, and Tiffany Barnes. "Maximizing Learning and Guiding Behavior in Free Play User Generated Content Environments." *Proceedings of the 17th ACM Annual Conference on Innovation and Technology in Computer Science Education*. ACM, 2012.

Cargile Cook, Kelli. "Layered Literacies: A Theoretical Frame for Technical Communication Pedagogy." *Technical Communication Quarterly* 11.1 (2002): 5–29.

deWinter, Jennifer. "Just Playing Around: From Procedural Manuals to In-Game Training." *Computer Games and Technical Communication: Critical Methods and Applications at the Intersection*. Burlington, VT: Ashgate, 2014. 69–85.

deWinter, Jennifer, Daniel Griffin, Ken S. McAllister, Ryan M. Moeller, and Judd Ethan Ruggill. "Computer Games Across the Curriculum: A Critical Review of an Emerging Techno-Pedagogy." *Currents in Electronic Literacy* (2010): n.p. Web. 29 Jan. 2013. http://currents.dwrl.utexas.edu/2010/dewinter_et_al_computer-games-across-the-curriculum.

Egenfeldt-Nielsen, Simon. "Overview of Research on the Educational Use of Video Games." *Digital Kompetance* 3.1 (2006): 184–213. Web.

"Framework for Success in Postsecondary Writing," n.d. Web. 10 Oct. 2012. 10 Jan. 2014.

Gee, James Paul. *What Video Games Have to Teach Us About Learning and Literacy*, revised Edition. New York: Palgrave Macmillan, 2007.

Grouling, Jennifer, Stephanie Hedge, Aly Schweigert, and Eva Grouling Snider. "Questing through Class: Gamification in the Professional Writing Classroom." *Computer Games and Technical Communication: Critical Methods and Applications at the Intersection*. Burlington, VT: Ashgate, 2014. 265–82.

Hsu, Hui-Yin, and Shiang-Kwei Wang. "Using Gaming Literacies to Cultivate New Literacies." *Simulation & Gaming* 41.3 (2010): 400–417.

Jones, Dave. "Black Boxes and Co-Creation in *LittleBigPlanet 2*." *Selected Papers of Internet Research* 0.12.0 (2011): n. pag. Web. 1 Jun. 2013.

Moberly, Kevin, and Ryan M. Moeller. "Working at Play: Modding, Revelation, and Transformation in the Technical Communication Classroom." *Computer*

Games and Technical Communication: Critical Methods and Applications at the Intersection. Burlington, VT: Ashgate, 2014. 189–207.

Ouellette, Marc. "Come out Playing: Computer Games and the Discursive Practices of Gender, Sex, and Sexuality." *Computer Games and Technical Communication: Critical Methods and Applications at the Intersection.* Burlington, VT: Ashgate, 2014. 35–51.

Portal 2. Windows, Mac, Playstation 3, Xbox 360. Developed by Valve. Published by Valve, 2011.

Sherlock, Lee. "Patching as Design Rhetoric: Tracing the Framing and Delivery of Iterative Content Documentation in Online Games." *Computer Games and Technical Communication: Critical Methods and Applications at the Intersection.* Burlington, VT: Ashgate, 2014. 157–69.

The New London Group. "A Pedagogy of Multiliteracies: Designing Social Futures." *Harvard Educational Review* Spring (1996): 60–92.

Tilley, Alex, Carmen Blandino, and Jennifer deWinter. "User-Testing Narratives: Usability Testing, Playtesting, and the Liminality of Computer Games." *Computer Games and Technical Communication: Critical Methods and Applications at the Intersection.* Burlington, VT: Ashgate, 2014. 125–40.

Valve. *Teach with Portals.* Valve Corporation, n.d. Web. 1 June 2013.

Vie, Stephanie. "Tech Writing, Meet Tomb Raider: Video and Computer Games in the Technical Communication Classroom." *E-Learning and Digital Media* 5.2 (2008): 157–66.

Westecott, Emma. "Crafting Play: Little Big Planet." *Loading ...* 5.8 (2011): 90–100. Web. 1 June 2013.

Yancey, Kathleen Blake. "Made Not Only in Words: Composition in a New Key." *College Composition and Communication* 56.2 (2004): 297–328.

Chapter 15

Questing through Class: Gamification in the Professional Writing Classroom

Jennifer Grouling, Stephanie Hedge,
Alyssa Schweigert, and Eva Grouling Snider

It's the first week of class, and several confused students wander the halls of our English department. These wayward students haven't been looking for their classrooms or the nearest restroom. Instead, they've been looking for their professional writing instructor's office. Why? To earn a badge. For us, this moment represents a success, a moment where we saw tangible results from gamifying our courses.

Gamification, the process of applying game principles to non-game settings in order to increase engagement, has been utilized in business settings, in social media, and recently in education (Landers and Callan 399; Li et al. 72; Muntean 323; Kapp 10; Sierra and Stedman "Ode"). Although a trend, the evidence that gamification in education does indeed increase student engagement is limited. Often gamification is discussed theoretically, and the few existing qualitative studies have not yet focused on writing classes. When it comes to games and writing, the field has talked about the connection between games and literacy (Gee; Selfe and Hawisher) and the use of games within the writing classroom (for example, see 25.3 special edition of *Computers and Composition,* as well as the accompanying texts in this volume). Yet gamification as a pedagogical practice in technical and professional writing classrooms offers a rich opportunity for continued study.

In this chapter, we report on our practice of gamifying three sections of a professional writing course. Using survey and interview data as well as artifacts from participants, we discuss the effectiveness of gamification for increasing student engagement and meeting course goals. As might be expected, our results are mixed. Our participants included both students who embraced and struggled with the gamification of the class. Before we present our findings, we examine the literature on gamification in education and delineate our methods, including our data collection and analysis. We then divide our findings into themes drawn from common course goals in technical and professional writing classes: collaboration, professionalism, and project management. We conclude by suggesting specific pedagogical practices and discussing additional considerations based on our findings and experiences.

Gamification and a Pedagogy of Engagement

In "Videogames and the Future of Education," Ian Bogost states that videogames can play "a deliberate and disruptive role as agents of educational reform" (123) and deWinter et al. agree that games can disrupt our expectations for education. This disruption is both valuable and potentially uncomfortable. Teachers, administrators, parents, and even students may be resistant to the use of games in educational contexts because of their "radical" potential for reform (deWinter et al.). But is the use of games in education always radical? Lee and Hammer point out that educational structures already have similarities to games; grades function much like badges and students "level up" when they complete a year (147). When we talk about the potential of games within education, then, we need to talk about *how* and *why* we are using games.

Within writing classrooms, games have been used to help students understand writing in communities beyond the university (Moberly; Bianchi and Bohunicky), to challenge students' notions of authority and authorship (Alberti), and to engage students in public writing (Johnson; Moberly and Moeller). Writing instructors have used existing games, such as *World of Warcraft* (Shultz, Colby and Colby), and have created games to teach writing (Sheridan and Hart-Davidson 324). However, whether or not these efforts qualify as "gamification" is debatable.

While most scholars agree that gamification involves applying "game-like structures in non-game environments" (Sierra and Stedman "Ode"), whether those structures are game mechanics or something more is debatable. Gamification can involve such practices as using leaderboards, point rewards, achievements, and badges. However, Kapp argues that adding badges and rewards is not real gamification (12), and Ian Bogost calls achievements-based gamification "bullshit" ("Gamification"). For Kapp, gamification must involve "game thinking." He defines game thinking as converting the way we consider an activity to include "competition, cooperation, exploration, and storytelling" (11). Rewarding our students for the work they do is not enough; gamification must change the way they conceptualize that work. For Kapp, the relationship between serious games and gamification is complex, and we should not limit our definition of gamification to the application of game mechanics within a classroom (17).

Landers and Callan also see "the creation of casual social games to support (but not replace) courses" as gamification (405). However, they also argue that offering rewards for multiple learning activities is more powerful than using a serious game, which is often defined by only one set of learning objectives (421). Games that aren't designed specifically for classrooms often carry additional agendas and may even reinforce cultural and societal norms contrary to the educational reform we strive for. Bogost laments that "the future of educational games starts with an industry that, by and large, is not really interested in figuring out how, when, why and to what end videogames might serve the ends of educators" (120). We could, instead, create our own games for our own classrooms, but such games would still be limited in scope and flexibility. For us, part of the value of gamification is in expanding the self-efficacy of our students by encouraging them to make more of their own educational choices.

We believe that achievement-based gamification can be successful, as do others. Sierra and Stedman acknowledge Bogost's concerns, agreeing that simply "renaming grades as points and changing extra credit activities to achievements" may not cause significant change ("Ode"). Nevertheless, they do think gamification *can* enhance engagement and experience in certain situations. Similarly, Lee and Hammer argue that gamification should not be used haphazardly, but that we must "know what problems we are trying to fix, design systems to fix those specific problems, develop ways of evaluating whether those fixes work, and sustain those fixes over time" (148). Drawing on this scholarship, we set out to gamify our classrooms by using achievements (badges, side quests, and points-based attendance) because we identified problems that we felt gamification could address. Like Muntean, we used gamification to encourage desirable behaviors, to correct negative behaviors, and to increase social engagement and collaboration (325, 328).

When we refer to gamification in this article, then, we mean structures such as points, rewards, and achievements, not the creation or use of serious games. While this particular definition of gamification has met with some resistance, it has not been adequately tested in practice through qualitative research methods such as the ones engaged with in this study. Li et al. tested the use of gamification, including the use of casual games, participation points, and leaderboards, in an online computer science course (74). Similarly, Landers and Callan conducted a mixed method study of 600 students who were a part of a psychology class that incorporated game elements into an online social network (400). Li et al. found that the gamified class posted triple the amount of content and concluded that gamified practices may lead to more engaged, collaborative learning (76). Landers and Callan also champion positive results, noting that communication and motivation generally increased among their participants (416). Initial qualitative evidence on gamification is positive. We aim to add to a general discourse about gamification with experiential qualitative data.

To further define gamification, it is important to consider its purpose. Scholars agree that the use of game mechanics in non-game situations is designed to increase *engagement* and *motivation* (Kapp 10; Landers and Callan 399; Lee and Hammer 146; Muntean 323). In professional contexts, this may mean persuading customers to buy more products or visit more vendors. In education, it means encouraging our students to participate more actively in our courses. In the context of professional writing, we saw engagement as behaviors that demonstrated professionalism, collaboration, and good project management skills—behaviors encouraged in our course objectives.

Methods

In order to conduct this study, two members of our research team gamified their classes, and the entire research team worked to collect and analyze the research data. The findings we focus on are from three sections of English 231: Professional Writing, which is part of the core requirements for the Professional Writing minor at Ball State University. The class is required of Professional Writing minors but is also cross-listed as an elective for Telecommunications majors. As such, students are usually a mixture of English majors, Telecommunications majors, and Professional Writing minors from diverse majors across campus. The class is listed as a sophomore-level class, but students often take it during their junior year. Students in the class conduct rigorous qualitative research in a knowledge work model (in this, we enact theories and practices proposed by scholars in technical communication, such as Spinuzzi and Winsor). In particular, the students' research focuses on communicative technologies, ranging from social media to entertainment technologies to learning technologies.

As the instructor of English 231, Eva gamified the class in Fall 2012. She focused on three particular areas: badges, quests/side quests, and attendance. Throughout the semester, students could earn up to twenty-four different badges, which were recorded on a badge "sheet." Eva also implemented a gamified assignment structure, calling main assignments "quests" that were graded as Excellent, Good, Fair, and Poor (language drawn from quest-style games). Smaller assignments called "side quests" were graded for completion. Finally, she implemented point-based attendance inspired by social games where players receive cumulative rewards for logging in on consecutive days. These practices emerged from areas of the course where we wanted performance to improve: such as participation and attendance. However, they also worked to forward the goals of the course, particularly the course objective of managing complex collaborative and individual projects. Depending on which side quests and badges they chose, students also would further the course goals of responding appropriately to different rhetorical situations, effectively using technological tools, and understanding and navigating common professional genres. Side quests and badges often were scaffolded to give students more experience with skills and resources that they would use on larger projects.

Research Methods

As our research questions were focused on student engagement and perceptions of gamification practices, the thick description provided by qualitative methods proved to be an appropriate approach for our study. As Stake points out, qualitative methods and methodology are focused on getting at "how things work," gaining insider perspectives and individual experiences to make sense of different phenomena. Too often, as we noted in our literature review, discussions of gamification practices leave out student perspectives and opinions. In order to access this student perspective, we utilized three different methods of data collection:

- entrance and exit surveys,
- semi-structured interviews, and
- artifact collection.

We administered entrance and exit surveys to students; these surveys were instrumental in accessing a broad range of student voices. The surveys were a mix of yes/no, Likert scale, and open-ended questions. The entrance survey asked questions about gaming habits and practices, motivation, and attitudes towards course work and collaboration. The exit surveys were primarily Likert scale and open-ended questions that invited students to reflect on their experiences in a gamified classroom. Students were asked to rate their experiences with collaboration and motivation during the course, as well as being asked specifically about their enjoyment of the course, and whether or not they thought the gamification techniques were useful. Surveys were administered digitally via Qualtrics, and students were given a unique ID number to preserve confidentiality, particularly during the period when they were still in the course.

Semi-structured interviews were conducted near the end of the semester by two researchers not involved with teaching the course to help eliminate bias and ensure anonymity. Interviews were between twenty and forty minutes long and asked questions focusing on the student experience in class: what they liked, what was working, and how students described and engaged with the gamification techniques.

We also collected a number of student artifacts throughout the semester, including student projects and their final course evaluations. The course evaluations were particularly important for hearing student voices as many students were more open about perceived shortcomings in the evaluations than they had been in the surveys.

Method of Analysis

Our findings were coded using six different initial codes, which were loosely grouped into two themes: classroom practices and professional writing goals. Our three "classroom practices" codes focused on the three key methods we implemented in the classroom: attendance points, badges, and side quests. Our three professional writing goals were collaboration, professionalism, and project management, and these starter codes were generated from the course goals in the syllabus. From these initial starter codes, second- and third-pass coding revealed more emergent themes stemming from student perspectives. This chapter focuses specifically on professional writing goals, but these goals were influenced and shaped by the thoughts and observations students had regarding classroom practices.

Findings and Discussion

In this section, we simultaneously present the findings and discuss the significance of those findings as they pertain to the main goals and objects of the class and instructor. After describing the general profile of our student participants, we consider the effects of gamification on collaboration, professionalism, and project management.

Students, Gamers, and Student Gamers: Participant Profile

While our entrance survey was intended to serve as a baseline for comparisons with exit survey data, it also served to paint a picture of who our participants were both as gamers and as students. We asked a significant number of questions about participants' gaming habits and perceptions of themselves as students. In this section we present our relevant findings about our participants' overall habits as gamers and students.

First, our participants were primarily casual gamers. Nineteen of our twenty-six respondents played games for four or fewer hours per week, with the majority (eleven) of those playing one or two hours each week. Most participants played analog games (board and card games) casually, and a significant number (eleven) of participants reported playing casual mobile games like *Angry Birds* and *Words with Friends*. This runs counter to narratives in the field about students: namely that they are avid gamers who value constant play. For example, Stephanie Vie talks about "Generation M" where students have constant access to media, including computer games (12). Likewise, even students who game regularly do not necessarily see it the same way that Lacasa, Mendez, and Martinez do, that is, as "a meaningful and natural role in everyday life" (342). Students who self-identified as avid gamers consistently mentioned they did not have time to play games because of their busy schedules. Students anecdotally reported playing games significantly more often in the summer months. This finding was further complicated by the research location, as a significant number of students reported not having their preferred gaming devices or consoles with them at school.

Our participants were fairly social in their game playing. A majority of respondents (seventeen out of twenty-six) played games with friends at least once a month, and most of those (nine respondents) played at least once a week with friends. We also saw this reflected in their reasons for playing games. When asked what motivated them to play, and while games, gameplay, story, competition, challenge, and graphics were important factors, more participants reported friendship as the dominant motivating factor. Analog games were particularly popular with participants who reported playing games with friends regularly.

As students, our participants reported being very motivated in their classes, particularly in-major and upper-division classes. We asked our participants what motivated them in these classes, and they reported that career goals, grades, and graduation were particularly strong motivators. Interestingly, grades and career goals were closely linked for our participants; of the six participants who mentioned being motivated by career goals, five mentioned grades in the same sentence. It seems, then, that intrinsic motivation (such as interest in a particular career) and extrinsic motivation (such as good grades) are intertwined for our students. A few students reported being motivated by personal interest in course content, in-class activities, a desire to learn, and passionate/engaging teachers, though these were far less common responses.

"Like Teammates in a Game": The Effect of Gamification on Collaboration

As mentioned above, we identified three themes in our data: collaboration, professionalism, and project management. The first of these, collaboration, is a significant goal in English 231 and a common objective in many technical and professional writing courses. Students in these classes can expect to learn teamwork through drafting and revising collaborative documents. As one of our participants put it, "there was just so much of learning how to work with others. And that has to be vital for the workplace, that you have to know how to work with others." In particular, English 231 featured a semester-long collaborative project that focused on students' collaborative relationships with their research team members. Some teams will be more successful at managing that collaboration, and we sought to help mitigate the difficulties of teamwork through gamification practices.

Many of the badges and side quests that students in English 231 could earn were collaborative in nature. Some tasks rewarded entire teams for successful work; for instance, the first group to receive IRB approval earned a badge. We identified badges like these as a way to motivate students to develop successful collaboration techniques. Additionally, several of the side quests required teamwork. One in particular asked teams to develop a fictional organization and an identity package for that organization, including a logo, masthead, and organizational profile. We designed this side quest to bring teams together, promoting a sense of unity among members. Given this deliberate attempt to increase collaboration, we analyzed our data to see what affect our gamification practices had on collaboration.

The answer to that question is mixed. We found that gamifying the class helped increase students' overall reported enjoyment of collaboration. At the beginning of the semester, our participants reported feeling conflicted in regards to collaboration. Most enjoyed sharing ideas and workload but lamented the loss of control, the inevitable imbalances and inequalities between team members, and the difficulties of juggling schedules. In our exit surveys, however, our participants reported that their overall enjoyment of collaboration increased from a reported 4.5 (on an 8-point scale) in non-gamified courses to 5.5 in the gamified class.

That result, however, was complicated when we examined individual perspectives. In general, we found that the gamification framework aided collaboration *when students were in groups with strong collaborative dynamics already*. Several of our participants were members of teams with successful collaborative dynamics. Those participants highlighted the gamification practices as bringing their teams closer together. For instance, one of the badges students could earn involved attending a presentation or workshop in the library. Notably, this badge did not explicitly encourage collaboration. One of our participants, Elise, seized the opportunity to get to know one of her group members better, asking him to come with her to a presentation to earn the badge: "[I was] like hey, let's do this together, even though I don't know you myself. [We] built a little bit of a friendship," she said. "Because of the badges, we meet a lot more . . . and do things together and plan . . . . I've made friends because of [the badges]." Similarly, when discussing the side quest that asked groups to develop an identity package, Elise said: "we came up with our own little hashtag: it's called #wepinninbro, and that's going to be our little logo that we put on everything, 'cause you get a badge for that, too, and we all have kind of adopted . . . the same system and built a little bit of a friendship." For Elise, whose group was already collaborating successfully, the badges added to their sense of camaraderie and improved teamwork.

Unfortunately, gamification did not have a positive effect on the groups whose dynamics were less successful. One participant, Brad, identified his group as struggling, saying: "I am a super senior. My two partners are . . . first-semester sophomores. And so this . . . seems to be a little overwhelming for them, and we're, as a group, having some trouble keeping up with it." He later acknowledged that his group had not completed any collaborative badges and side quests because of their difficulties with "both time and scheduling." Another participant, Grace, highlighted the positive aspects of being rewarded for teamwork, saying, "it's kind of nice to know, okay, I can do this with my team and we can all kind of get the reward for it." But as much as Grace liked the *idea* of collaborative badges and side quests, she also indicated that her group's plans to complete some of the collaborative side quests fell short because her group did not "mix so well."

Clearly, this is a mixed result. On the one hand, any increase in enjoyment of and engagement with collaboration could be viewed as positive. Students like Grace did see the value in opportunities for collaboration within a professional writing course. Another participant, Rick, said of gamification, "I feel like it suited the style of the class in that it was like a whole group project, pretty much the whole class." Our students saw gamification and collaboration as a natural fit, even if they did not see a direct increase in their group's collaborative success as a result of gamification.

On the other hand, we hoped gamification would smooth out discrepancies between groups: Groups with strong dynamics and grades could ignore the extra work of collaborative badges and sidequests and groups with weaker dynamics and grades could seek out those aspects. In practice, gamification actually *increased* the gap between the most successful groups and the least successful groups as the most successful groups used the gamified elements to strengthen their collaborative relationships and the least successful groups (in terms of collaboration) did not.

One reason increasing collaboration through gamification proved difficult involves the balancing of different students' priorities and motivations. One of the advantages of individual badges and side quests is that students have the option to choose tasks that fit their motivations; competitive students might choose to complete badges that have a public element, while students invested in social media might choose to complete badges that involve those social media. Several of our participants identified this flexibility and customization as a positive aspect of badges and side quests. For collaborative badges and side quests, though, students with diverse motivations and priorities have to come together and agree to complete what is, at its core, *optional* or *extra* work. Additionally, some students were confused about which badges and side quests were individual and which were collaborative, and this confusion also hindered collaborative efforts. Overall, very few teams actually completed collaborative badges or side quests, which we would attribute to these differences.

"We're Adults, Not Pre-teens": Professionalism, Fun, and Games

Many professional writing instructors ask students to consider their professional conduct and be accountable to one another and the instructor. This emphasis on professionalism—and its attendant practices and behaviors—may be complicated by gamification. Although games can be serious business on a cultural level, they are seen as something to enjoy, something to poke fun at and bond over, and something to entertain. Presumably, most instructors gamify their classes because games are engaging, but in reality, games are perceived to *entertain* far more than they engage. Western culture is one in which *work*—and its itinerant values, including professionalism—seems to be at odds with *play* (see Huizinga and Caillois for further discussion of the concept of play). By linking games and professionalism, gamification has the potential to problematize the culturally constructed binary between work and play.

Students in English 231 spend the first week of class discussing what it means to be a professional and a professional writer, a question posed most clearly in Faber's article "Professional Identities: What Is Professional about Professional Communication?" This view of professionalism is particularly antithetical to the cultural perceptions surrounding "playing games." Perhaps this cultural perception led to one of the comments on English 231's course evaluations: "the whole class was like a *World of Warcraft*-ish theme, and the syllabus had pictures of swords on it. We're adults, not pre-teens . . . [the] material is childish."

Comments like this are directed specifically at our rhetorical approach to gamification, something that should be a major consideration for any instructor interested in gamifying classes. For example, we carefully modeled our syllabi on computer game instruction manuals. After all, computer game manuals are examples of professional writing, so this move seemed logical. Like professional computer game manuals, the syllabus for English 231 contained some jokes about the quests and the class, and it emphasized the campiness and irreverent, self-referential humor of many adventure games and RPGs. This design was mirrored in quest information sheets.

However, there are many potential rhetorical approaches to gamification. Our badges and badge lists, for instance, were more closely modeled on social media gamification, borrowing heavily from badges used in *Foursquare, 750 Words*, and *Fitocracy*. Our participants generally reported that they appreciated and connected with this approach, unsurprising considering that most of our students have experience with social media and social games but not with adventure games and role-playing games (RPGs). While much of the written and visual rhetorical approach to gamification could be considered superficial—the skin over underlying pedagogical principles and practices—it clearly has an effect on students' perceptions of the class.

Our most successful attempts to connect gamification and professionalism came in the form of badges and side quests that encouraged students' professional development outside of class. We noted before that Elise used a badge asking her to attend a presentation in the library to form bonds of friendship, but she also noted that similar badges, what she called "academic badges" (in opposition to "fun badges"), helped her in terms of professional development: "So it's like pursuing my passion for the workforce, for whatever I'm going to do, because obviously I wanna do what I want to do." Grace also characterized the library badge in terms of professional development, saying "it's kind of like . . . helping yourself out, to kind of be more resourceful and to see what else is out there." Our participants also observed that achievements asking them to add professional elements to documents helped them become better professional writers. Barry noted that the branding side quests helped him "in thinking critically about professional writing" and in "building professional looking or professional sounding" documents.

A significant number of students drew a line between professional and "fun" badges and side quests, though they were often mixed on which they preferred. Several did mention "fun" badges, such as the badge that asked students to come to class in costume on Halloween, seemed "tacked on" or unnecessary to a class on *professional* writing. Fun is good, they suggested, but only when it is in the service of professional development. In many ways, these students echoed the observation made by deWinter and Moeller in the introduction to this collection: "play denies the seriousness of the workplace, while at the same time being deadly serious itself" (p. 7). Students in the gamified courses struggled with this tension between play and serious work.

Our participants specifically *wanted* the class to be productive for their careers, and they realized that the achievements were structured to be less essential to professional development than the main work of the course. When discussing the main project, Elise said, "I know there might be a job that I get which requires this kind of research, so I want to get experience . . . to put on my resume." She viewed the main work of the class as something she could showcase and that would have direct applications for her career, while she viewed the gamified elements as fun but more peripheral.

As a whole, the gamification actually *hurt* the professionalism of the class. In the entrance survey, our participants rated their classes as extremely valuable, with a median rating of seven out of eight. The value of the gamified class dropped from a seven to a five on the exit survey, and several students commented that the class was less "valuable" or "applicable" than they wanted, at least in part because the class was too focused on fun and games.

None of this, however, addresses one of the essential components of professional conduct: the ability to show up on time and prepared, a factor students also readily viewed as professional behavior. When we set out on this research project, one of our goals was to increase attendance in our classes. English 231's gamified attendance policy was based on social games. On the first day of class, students who were present earned one attendance point. Every day that students were present, they added a larger number to their attendance point total: on the second day, they added two for a total of three; on the third day, they added three; and so on. The policy punished students who were absent on consecutive days, resetting their rolling count to one.

Participants noted that the gamified attendance policy worked to increase attendance. In the exit survey, almost all students reported being present every day. Grace mentioned that her perfect attendance came about in part because of the attendance policy. Many students, though, found the system mystifying and confusing: not a single interviewee could tell us the attendance policy without referencing course materials. We believe this is in part a function of the fact that the instructor kept track of these records herself and did not make them publicly available to students. We see a clash between game mechanics and the execution of a gamified class: social games give us immediate rewards for logging in, but students in the gamified class did not see their rewards for showing up to class until the end of the semester. Direct and immediate feedback is a major part of that as is providing students feedback and reward for things they are already doing.

Classes Are Not Open World Games: Deadlines, Project Management, and Achievements

In addition to collaboration and professionalism, project management is central to technical and professional writing classes. According to Kampf, professionals in the contemporary workplace are often asked to juggle numerous cross-functional projects with varying deadlines and deliverables. One of the student objectives of English 231 is to manage complex projects, both collaborative and individual. However, our data showed that students had difficulty handling the open deadlines that were a part of our gamification strategies.

In English 231, the quests (such as major assignments) mostly had specific due dates, though some of those dates (such as the IRB protocol) were set by individual research teams based on their team's timeline for the semester. To encourage proactive behavior, several badges were awarded to teams who completed work before other teams. With a few exceptions, though, achievements could be earned at any point in the semester. We believed this flexibility would allow students to spread out the work of badges and side quests in a way that worked for their schedules. In practice, though, it resulted in a chaotic scramble in the final weeks of the semester.

Our students were also extremely protective of their time, and achievements required time that they were often unwilling to give. Rick mentioned he had planned to complete several professional development badges, "but things just got really busy." He liked badges he could earn early in the semester, when he was less busy, "but in the middle of the semester . . . I would highly doubt I would be as motivated to go do things like that, because . . . as the semester goes on it just gets so much busier." A majority of students expressed a desire to complete more achievements but the lack of time held them back.

Another factor was that some of the gamified elements, particularly the side quests, were "time consuming" and "difficult" enough that students tended to put them off. There was a clear line between badges and side quests that they weren't willing to cross: Badges that took a few minutes or even an hour out of their day were acceptable to complete throughout the semester, but side quests that asked for two to three hours of work were not. This was particularly pronounced because nothing was due until the end of the semester. Several participants pointed out that they barely managed work with specific due dates; as Barry put it, "[I won't] go out of my way to do things that aren't due until forever away as far as I'm concerned." Barry was also adamant that the ability to handle open deadlines was simply too much for a sophomore-level class. He said, "I feel like that's a little bit of a high expectation for a 200 level course to have students . . . actually balance that workload all on their own."

Second, because students had to remember to "check" documents for the available achievements, they had a tendency to forget what they were or even that they were possibilities for them. When faced with entirely open deadlines and a long list of potential options, our students generally felt overwhelmed. Perhaps the most common refrain in our research data regarding badges and side quests (particularly side quests) was: "I'm honestly really not that familiar with them . . . . I'm saving it till the last minute" (Elise). One of our participants told us, "I think I've done one, and I don't remember what it was."

Despite these difficulties, students consistently expressed liking the flexibility of open deadlines. Rick said, "I've enjoyed that those can be done and turned in anytime that you want . . . that has been helpful . . . . I like the ideas of rolling due dates with small assignments." Grace agreed, saying, "if other classes were actually laid out that way, I think it would be beneficial for the teacher and for the students because the students will be more involved." In practice, however, students almost universally waited until the end of the semester to earn achievements, if they did at all.

Postmortem and Pedagogical Tips

Although our study was limited to one semester of professional writing classes at one university, the combination of our qualitative data and our own observation lead us to some important implications for gamification in professional writing courses. In this section, we reflect on those implications and offer suggestions for other professional writing teachers. Specifically we offer the following tips:

- Design achievements to allow for students' different motivations;
- Make terminology simple and clear and condense related mechanics as much as possible;
- Provide an opening letter or guide to gamification for students;
- Base gamification on social media rather than on traditional analog games and computer games;
- Carefully consider the rhetoric of (and behind) gamification;
- Structure achievements so that they can only be earned at specific points and so that they don't take more than 30–45 minutes to earn;
- Create achievements that reward students for things they are already doing; and
- Manage instructor expectations.

One of the biggest advantages of gamifying a course is that it creates multiple tracks for student success. Thus, we suggest that instructors *design achievements to allow for students' different motivations.* Just as games allow for different approaches and play styles, a gamified class gives students the flexibility to succeed in a number of different ways. Having achievements for students who value collaboration and camaraderie are just as important as having achievements for students who are individually competitive. Also, ensure that the course structure and point allocations actually allow for branching paths to student success; in general, required achievements destroy the benefits of flexibility.

Participants in our study almost universally expressed confusion at terminology, including the subtle differences in our achievement system (such as badges and sidequests). It's important to *make terminology simple and clear and condense related mechanics as much as possible.* Although we did not have any international students participating in our study, our own observations from other classrooms indicate that terminology can be particularly problematic for international students. As much as online gaming has the potential to connect people globally, gaming norms are culturally dependent and gaming literacies vary across cultural lines. Through practice and repetition, international students acquire—to varying extents—the literacies necessary to complete college classes at an U.S. research university. In other words, it is a game they have learned to play. However, when we alter these literacies through gamification, we often add to the difficulties international students already face. The simpler the terminology and the course structure, the less difficulty students will have engaging with gamification.

We believe that another way to mitigate confusion is to *provide an opening letter or guide to gamification for students*. Students in professional writing classes are typically sophomore-level or higher, and those students have developed ingrained classroom literacies and formed habits surrounding their classes. By creating a syllabus modeled after a game manual, we departed from students' syllabi genre knowledge, and this led to confusion. While there are advantages to breaking with traditional genres, students may need help in reading documents written in less traditional formats. An opening letter may help them navigate these new genres and can also serve as a model of professional correspondence.

Several of our participants considered the gamified elements we based on computer or traditional analog games to be childish. None, however, felt that way about the gamified elements based on social media. Thus, we suggest that instructors *base their gamification on social media rather than on traditional analog games and computer games*. Additionally, many students come to class with social media literacy, but many do not come in with gaming literacies. Badges are a natural fit for a technical or professional writing class, but quests, side quests, and leaderboards may be less intuitive. This corroborates previous research; authors such as Li et al. were particularly successful in implementing gamification as a part of a larger push for social networking in the classroom.

As members of the professional writing field are particularly aware, teaching is a rhetorical act, and the documents associated with teaching are inherently rhetorical. It's important to *carefully consider the rhetoric of (and behind) gamification*. Although we think basing gamification on social media rather than computer games can be helpful for students, that's not to say that quests, side quests, and leaderboards *can't* work in a technical or professional writing class. It just might be a harder sell for upper level students. We built a rhetorical framework positioning the class as an adventure that students would embark upon, and that framework was less successful than we had hoped it would be. A rhetorical framework that emphasizes gamification in business is likely to be much more successful. In addition, we need to consider the way our gamification practices are viewed within the larger institutional structure. Teachers who gamify their classes need to be aware of the institutional context and how to talk about such practices within documents such as tenure and promotion files. Linking our teaching practice to our research helped us show that we were approaching gamification in a pedagogically sound manner.

One of the biggest problems we encountered with gamification was that students almost universally did not manage open deadlines with achievements effectively, waiting until the end of the semester to earn achievements. Landers and Callan also noted some difficulty in getting students to do optional work (417). We thus suggest that instructors *structure achievements so that they can only be earned at specific points and so that they don't take more than 30–45 minutes to earn*. Tying achievements to units or even specific due dates may help prevent a mad dash at the end of the semester to catch up (and help instructors avoid a mountain of grading). This also allows for gamification to be used for scaffolding and for encouraging good student practice throughout the semester. In addition, students were more likely to engage in optional work when that work took 30–45 minutes rather than several hours to complete.

Another problem we encountered with students completing achievements was that students often did not realize what achievements were available to them. While some achievements are meant to encourage new behaviors, it's also important to *create achievements that reward students for things they are already doing.* In both gamified social media and in computer games, people earn achievements as a part of a natural progression. If you want everyone in your class to work to earn achievements, one way to do so is to ensure that students will earn achievements naturally throughout the class. A way to ensure this is to implement hidden badges, the earning criteria for which are revealed *after* students earn them, a concept similar to unlockable achievements. These badges reward students for class participation and reinforce good student behavior, such as asking questions of a guest speaker.

Lastly, we found that gamifying our classes resulted in adjusting our own expectations of the role games play in the classroom. Games may be significantly changing our culture, but they will not revolutionize a classroom overnight. In other words, *manage instructor expectations.* We found that students generally enjoyed the gamified elements of the class. Gamification increased attendance and encouraged collaboration for some. It did not, however, universally increase collaboration. Nor did it turn students into ideal or perfect students. With well-managed expectations, instructors can focus their gamification on one or two specific, moderate goals so that gamification has a greater chance of being successful.

Conclusion

Ultimately, institutional context is a key factor in the decision to gamify a technical or professional writing class. Is the class a service course? Are other faculty already gamifying their classes? This last point is easy to overlook, but it is important. Developing a community of practice strengthens members of that community and allows for dialogues about best practices that can only result in positive changes. These factors are all important in the success of gamification. Our study is limited as we only studied gamification within one particular institutional context.

Further exploration is necessary and vital. Currently, qualitative research on gamification is limited, and most studies that do report on gamification, like ours, do so upon initial implementation. In other words, we still need to study gamification after the kinks have been worked out. We were deliberate in our development of gamification, designing it to answer problems we saw in our classrooms. However, one thing we found was that the problems weren't always as they seemed. While motivation is often heralded as an issue in education, professional writing courses exist within majors and minors, unlike first-year composition courses. As our survey showed, students were already motivated in their coursework so, to an extent, we were addressing a problem that was less severe than we thought. In fact, because of their advanced standing, some students resisted gamification on the grounds that it was too childish. They sought to be treated as professionals, and they did not see gamification as doing so.

Even so, we believe there is a significant argument to be made for incorporating gamification in technical and professional writing courses that goes beyond engaging our students. Gamification is a growing practice in business, and as such, it is something that our students will likely encounter and may even be asked to create themselves. Kapp reports that "more than 50 percent of organizations that manage innovation processes will gamify those processes within the next decade" (19). Anderson and Rainie also predict that "50% of corporate innovation will be 'gamified' by 2015." When we present gamification, then, to our professional writing students, we suggest presenting it within this larger professional context. Games may eventually revolutionize education, but they are more quickly revolutionizing business, and this trend is important for technical and professional writing instructors and students to be aware of and even critical of.

We believe that adding a layer of metanarrative about gamification practices (ie. discussion of the ways these practices are growing more popular and prevalent in larger professional contexts) can help mitigate student resistance and situations where students are simply gaming the instructor by faking interest in the course structure and activities. Building in places for students to be self-reflexive about the efficacy of gamification techniques within the classroom—a practice which our study participants informally engaged in as we questioned them—allows students the space to explore their own positive and negative reactions while providing an exploration and critique of emergent gamification practices. Combining such reflection with examples of gamification from external professional contexts provides students the opportunity to see the professional value of gaming activities while still legitimizing negative reactions and constructive critique of these practices.

Beyond the professional sphere, we must further investigate and critique gamification in the classroom to better understand *how* these practices work and *if* we should adopt these practices into our pedagogy. We must also consider which practices are sustainable over time. While we do not see gamification as just a passing fad, we recognize that types of gamification may come and go. Lee and Hammer argue that gamification in education should "sustain fixes over time" (148). Ultimately, we found that the way we gamified our classes initially was not sustainable. We have since modified our approach to more limited use of gamification, mostly the use of badges to reward students for natural classroom behaviors that we want to encourage. Gamification does not necessarily mean turning a class into a game or making it an adventure as we originally presented it to our students. We believe gamification that works, gamification that is sustainable, is supplemental. It supports, rather than replaces, our already existing pedagogies.

Works Cited

Alberti, John. "The Game of Reading and Writing: How Video Games Reframe Our Understanding of Literacy." *Computers and Composition* 25.3 (2008): 258–69. PDF file.

Anderson, Janna Quitney, and Lee Rainie. "Gamification: Experts Expect 'Game Layers' to Expand in the Future, with Positive and Negative Results." *Pew Research Centre.* Pew Research Centre's Internet & American Life Project, 18 May 2012. Web. 1 May 2013.

Bianchi, Melissa, and Kyle Bohunicky. "How *World of Warcraft* Could Save Your Classroom: Teaching Technical Communication Through the Social Practices of MMORPGs." *Computer Games and Technical Communication: Critical Methods and Applications at the Intersection.* Burlington, VT: Ashgate, 2014. 233–46.

Bogost, Ian. "Gamification Is Bullshit." *Bogost.com.* 8 Aug. 2011. Web. 1 May 2013.

———. "Videogames and the Future of Education." *On the Horizon* 13.2 (2005): 119–25.

Caillois, Roger. *Man, Play, and Games.* Champaign U of Illinois P, 2001.

deWinter, Jennifer, Daniel Griffin, Ken S. McAllister, Ryan M. Moeller, and Judd Ethan Ruggill. "Computer Games Across the Curriculum: A Critical Review of an Emerging Techno-Pedagogy." *Currents in Electronic Literacy* (2010): n.pag. Web. 1 May 2013.

deWinter, Jennifer, and Ryan M. Moeller. "Introduction: Playing the Field: Technical Communication for Technical Games." *Computer Games and Technical Communication: Critical Methods and Applications at the Intersection.* Burlington, VT: Ashgate, 2014. 1–13.

Faber, Brenton. "Professional Identities: What Is Professional about Professional Communication?" *Journal of Business and Technical Communication* 16.3 (2002): 306–37.

Gee, James Paul. *What Video Games Have to Teach Us About Learning and Literacy.* 2nd ed. New York: Palgrave Macmillan, 2007.

Huizinga, Johan. *Homo Ludens: A Study of the Play Element in Culture.* New York: Harper and Row, 1970.

Johnson, Matthew S.S. "Public Writing in Gaming Spaces." *Computers and Composition* 25.3 (2008): 270–83.

Kampf, Constance. "The Future of Project Management in Technical Communication: Incorporating a Communications Approach." IEEE International Professional Communication Conference Proceedings. Saratoga, New York. Oct. 2006.

Kapp, Karl M. *The Gamification of Learning and Instruction: Game-based Methods and Strategies for Training and Education.* San Francisco: Pfeiffer, 2012.

Lacasa, Pilar, Laura Méndez, and Rut Martínez. "Bringing Commercial Games into the Classroom." *Computers and Composition* 25.3 (2008): 341–58.

Landers, Richard N., and Rachel C. Callan. "Casual Games as Serious Games: The Psychology of Gamification in Undergraduate Education and Employee Training." *Serious Games and Edutainment Applications*. Ed. Minhua Ma, Andreas Oikonomou, and Lakhmi C. Jain. London: Springer, 2011. 399–423.

Lee, Joey J., and Jessica Hammer. "Gamification in Education: What, How, Why Bother?" *Academic Exchange Quarterly* 15.2 (2011): 146–51.

Li, Cen, Zhijiang Dong, Roland H. Untch, and Michael Chasteen. "Engaging Computer Science Students through Gamification in an Online Social Network Based Collaborative Learning Environment." *International Journal of Information and Education Technology* 3.1 (2013): 72–7. PDF file.

Moberly, Kevin. "Composition, Computer Games, and the Absence of Writing." *Computers and Composition* 25.3 (2008): 284–99. PDF file.

Moberly, Kevin, and Ryan M. Moeller. "Working at Play: Modding, Revelation, and Transformation in Technical Communication." *Computer Games and Technical Communication: Critical Methods and Applications at the Intersection*. Burlington, VT: Ashgate, 2014. 189–207.

Muntean, Cristina Ioana. "Raising Engagement in E-Learning Through Gamification." *Proc. 6th International Conference on Virtual Learning ICVL*. 2011. PDF file.

Selfe, Cynthia L., and Gail E. Hawisher, eds. *Gaming Lives In The Twenty-first Century: Literate Connections*. New York: Palgrave Macmillan, 2007.

Sheridan, David Michael, and William Hart-Davidson. "Just For Fun: Writing and Literacy Learning as Forms of Play." *Computers and Composition* 25.3 (2008): 323–40. PDF file.

Shultz Colby, Rebekah, and Richard Colby. "A Pedagogy of Play: Integrating Computer Games into the Writing Classroom." *Computers and Composition* 25.3 (2008): 300–12. PDF file.

Sierra, Wendi, and Kyle D. Stedman. "Ode to Sparklepony: Gamification in Action." *Kairos: A Journal of Rhetoric, Technology, and Pedagogy* 16.2 (2012): n.p. *Kairos*. Web. 1 May 2013.

Spinuzzi, Clay. "What Do We Need to Teach About Knowledge Work?" Austin, TX: University of Austin, Texas P, 2006. *Computer Writing and Research Lab White Paper Series #060925-1*. PDF file.

———. *Network: Theorizing Knowledge Work in Telecommunications*. New York: Cambridge UP, 2008.

Stake, Robert. *Qualitative Research: Studying How Things Work*. New York: Guilford, 2010.

Vie, Stephanie. "Digital Divide 2.0: 'Generation M' and Online Social Networking Sites in the Composition Classroom." *Computers and Composition* 25.3 (2008): 9–23. PDF file.

Winsor, Dorothy A. "Learning to Do Knowledge Work in Systems of Distributed Cognition." *Journal of Business and Technical Communication* 15.1 (2001): 5–28. PDF file.

Chapter 16

From Realism to Reality: A Postmortem of a Game Design Project in a Client-Based Technical Communication Course

Christopher Ritter, Sameer Ansari, Scott Daner,
Sean Murray, and Ryan Reeves

On the surface, technical communication and computer games seem to be at odds with each other. There is, of course, the fun versus serious dichotomy: Gameplay is supposed to be fun whereas technical communication is supposed to be serious because its artifacts are typically from and related to the workplace. Which brings up the second apparent dichotomy: technical communication seems to be about practicality, work, and productivity while games seem to be about just the opposite. According to foundational ludologist Caillois, play is antithetical to work because, by its very nature, it is unproductive.

Like so many of life's dichotomies, these ones break down quickly under scrutiny. Any college- or pro-level sports player will point out that the games they're playing are hardly fun anymore. And to even casually examine the political economies of college and pro-level sports is to see that while the games themselves don't produce anything, they are encased within enormous machines of training, marketing, sales, and consumption. Humans are not only symbol-making animals, as Burke writes in *Language as Symbolic Action* (16); we're also game-making animals, and a great many of our games are played with and for serious material and social stakes. The distinction between games and technical communication really breaks down when one makes a game for others to play. Bogost argues that games are series of procedures—actions and consequences—and that a well-made game whose procedural and representational elements are aligned meaningfully can teach the player about the meaning of those actions (5). This is procedural rhetoric. In many ways, this chapter echoes Custer's, but where Custer walks through the pedagogic application of a course to teach layered literacies, this chapter is a postmortem, a reflection of sorts, that ruminates on the process of making a game. We strongly posit the following: To make a game is to be composer of procedural rhetoric; in other words, a communicator of techniques, a technical communicator.

What follows is a reflection of our process and product of game-building in a technical communications course. In this chapter then, four of the members of a student team that took on a project to gamify[1] a cardiac rehabilitation center's diabetes education program present a postmortem of the development of this game, which was entitled *New Me*. The work is multivocal, with each student sharing his perspective. Chris Ritter provides a discussion of the overall context and perspective as the instructor of the course.[2] Throughout, unless otherwise specified, Ritter will discuss the course and use the first-person position for writing.

Ultimately, I argue that the project's success is attributable to two factors: One is the students. Technical communications at Georgia Tech is required by a handy variety of majors, from Business Administration to Computer Science to Industrial Design, and as a 3000-level course, technical communication is populated by juniors and seniors. Therefore, courses almost always contain students who are functionally literate in, for instance, web programming. The second factor behind the project's success was the class' focus on documentation—teaching the students to assess their technical capabilities, propose no more than they could deliver, report clearly on their progress, and leave a paper trail for future teams to follow. As Douglas Eyman argues in "Computer Gaming and Technical Communication: An Ecological Framework," "Documentation and usability represent the two most immediate avenues for bringing technical communication into game design processes" (243). Further, as Greene and Palmer note in the first chapter of this book, Eyman's claim is true largely because professional game designers rely on documentation in every stage of game development, from inventing and programming, to playtesting and writing the postmortem. I argue here that it doesn't take a great deal of specialized training in game design to teach technical communication students to design a game. Before turning to the postmortem, however, I first provide some background to the process of creating this class.

Background

When I started teaching technical communication in graduate school, my class was built on the following premise based on Gee's call for assignments that simulated real rhetorical situations in *Situated Language and Learning*: I presented the class as a simulated game development company. The students would each pitch game concepts, which I would winnow down to a handful of the best ideas. Working in teams, the students would write short high concept documents, then more detailed treatments, and finally, they would build prototypes of the games complete with instructions sheets.

---

[1]   Gamification is the process of adding game elements to something that is not a game, typically in order to make that thing more fun or engaging for users. For more on gamification in the technical communication course, please see Grouling et al.'s chapter in this collection.

[2]   For a high-level visual overview of this course from beginning to end, see this Prezi: http://goo.gl/XUlukN.

In the end and somewhat ironically, what ruined this class for me was coming to the Georgia Institute of Technology in fall 2010. At Georgia Tech, it seemed like half the professors and students were already professional game developers. The documents I had my students make were realistic, but the process wasn't. It was too compressed, for one thing; it was impossible to call any of the games "shippable" after only a couple months of part-time development. Worse, the students, many of whom were developing (or had developed) their own computer games for competitions and sale, had little interest in busting their asses on a prototype that wouldn't get developed further because the design team was going to disband after four months. Realism no longer cut it; I needed to find the *real*. I realized that I shouldn't be inventing rhetorical situations like so many games for my students to solve; they should be addressing real rhetorical situations.

The best route to the real that I could see was the service learning model. I had been thinking about trying a service learning class in order to get out of the cloister of the university and in touch with the communities around me, but I was unsure about how to begin. Fortunately, my university had an Office of Community Service (OCS), which had a huge database of local nonprofits, and I found a model syllabus for a client-based technical communication course that had been developed by Daniel Vollaro. In November, my OCS sent an email asking its partner organizations if they had any communication problems they didn't know how to or didn't have time to solve. I offered my technical communication class as a sort of consulting firm, which would put teams of students on the task of solving those problems. At that time, I didn't have a resource like Auburn's Service Learning Opportunities in Technical Communication (SLOT-C) Database,[3] so I had to define the project parameters fairly broadly. Projects had to:

- involve the creation of a single large workplace artifact (such as a website, an app, or a manual), or a group of closely related small artifacts (such as business cards and pamphlets);
- take a team of 6–10 approximately 150 person-hours to complete; and
- undergo composition and revision in four iterative stages, with feedback from an organization representative at each stage.

Representatives of six organizations met with me about a month before the spring 2011 semester began, and they brought real problems. An assistance center for the working poor needed to attract more donors and wanted to update its 90s-era website. A community art center lost its space because of a dishonest landlord and had to raise money for a new one. A summer camp for diabetic children needed to

---

[3] SLOT-C is designed to let instructors of service-based technical communication classes select organizations whose project needs perfectly match the instructors' assignment sequences. The SLOT-C's authors describe this as the ideal situation (Young and Mackiewicz, 265).

convey its policies to its campers and their parents and wanted brochures and info sheets to do so.

Suddenly, I saw my realism problem evaporate. I could never have invented projects like this. Now I didn't have to nor did I have to invent the solutions. The students took their projects seriously, and those that stuck it out found tremendous reward in helping their clients. Bonuses to students' civic engagement and self-esteem are well documented in the scholarship on service learning (see, for example, Huckin; Giles and Eyler; and Matthews and Zimmerman), and I saw evidence of these benefits over and over. More importantly, I relied on the students to invent creative solutions to the problems before them and to develop the technical capabilities to effect their proposals.

And in fall 2012, game-making returned in the form of a "serious" game aimed at improving the health of diabetes sufferers. The client, New Heart Center for Wellness, Fitness, and Cardiac Rehabilitation, gave us the following task:

> Participants will create a game that will be used to help individuals with diabetes become more engaged in the management of their disease . . . . In theory, game-based disease management should create more optimism, confidence, social cohesion, and skill development in participants.

Project Exigency

New Heart Center for Wellness, Fitness, and Cardiac Rehabilitation was founded in 1973 by Dr. Richard Lueker, a cardiologist in Albuquerque, New Mexico. Originally meeting in the gymnasium of an Albuquerque junior high school, the organization treated cardiac-event victims by having them walk rather than lay in hospital beds. This was a revolutionary idea at the time. The organization eventually gained a physical center with a few treadmills and has continuously grown in size and scope over the last forty years. It now approaches prevention holistically, monitoring diet, exercise, mental health, and social connections for each of its patients. In 2005, with a donation from a local philanthropist, New Heart built a facility of its own, which is part doctor's office, part gym, and part community center.

Just as New Heart has continuously pushed the boundaries of heart-disease prevention and rehabilitation over the last forty years, it has also sought out technologies that expand its reach beyond its physical center. In the early 2000s, it used broadband teleconferencing to conduct rehab sessions with patients in Gallup, NM, and training sessions with physicians in rural areas. When I met Dr. Lueker in 2011, he was looking for a way to get more people than New Heart's current patients to follow the Diabetes Self-Management Training program they had devised. When I suggested a web- or mobile-based game, he immediately saw its potential not only to spread New Heart's life-enhancing practices but also to make those practices fun and socially engaging. Beth McCormick, New Heart's

Director of Business Development, was equally excited by the project, and she pitched it to my fall 2012 class.

Team Formation (Weeks 1–4)

The first four weeks of the course were devoted to applying for and forming teams. On the second day of class, the clients came in (or in the case of New Heart, Skyped in) and introduced themselves to the students. The second and third weeks covered the rhetorics of résumés and cover letters, as the students applied for their teams. In the fourth week, I handpicked Project Managers, and they and I held a "draft" for the rest of the class, sorting them into teams consisting of Managing Editors, Writers, Graphic Designers, and Programmers.

Conducting an application assignment at the beginning of a technical and professional communication class immediately piqued the students' interests because most of them were either on or about to be on the job market. They all wanted to work on their résumés. The challenge was teaching them to think of every distinct application as a distinct rhetorical situation, with a customized résumé and cover letter. Class activities, therefore, focused on brainstorming the skills and experiences that would be useful for each project.

In the next section, one of the *New Me* team's Project Managers, Sameer Ansari, discusses the specific skills he looked for as he reviewed applications.

Sameer

After Scott and I were selected as Project Managers for the course, we independently reviewed the résumés of the team members of the course. A vital part of making this project successful was being able to develop a common vision in the team of the outcomes of this project. To do this we looked in the résumés for a specific range of skills in the team, including software design, graphic design, and prior video game development experience. One of the skills I personally looked for in the team was web design experience. Based on the skills of the available students in the course, we were able to make a strong focus on the research and design aspects of the project.

I would have liked to see portfolios showcasing work done by applicants, as this would have helped me get a feel for what languages we would design the final product in.

There are several interesting things to note about Sameer's comment. One is that as Project Manager, he had already begun thinking seriously about the skills that would be useful for the project, and based on the skills he saw in the set of applications, he calibrated his sense of what was possible. In other words, there weren't many students with technical expertise in computer game design and production, so Sameer focused more broadly on "research and design." His last sentence shows more evidence of his ownership of the project: He's telling me indirectly that the Track Application assignment would be more useful if it required portfolios of past work instead of only a résumé and cover letter.

A secondary challenge at the beginning of this course is persuading students to apply for the more complex projects, like *New Me*. This is where it's important to emphasize that the projects don't have to be "shippable" at the end of the semester for the students to be considered successful (and earn the coveted A grade); the teams simply have to articulate the goals they *can* achieve realistically. I repeat this point once teams have formed and are composing their proposals, but in the case of this project, I had to bring it up early.

Scott Daner, *New Me's* second Project Manager, recalls this speech:

Scott

At the beginning of the semester, when there were three projects to choose from, surprisingly, the game was the one that seemed to scare most of the students because it seemed like a very large undertaking. The company seemed like they had a lot of great ideas for a very interactive and engaging game, and it seemed trying to complete those goals in one semester would be a setup for failure. However, after seeing that there was very little interest in the game, even though there were many computer science majors and programmers in our class, Chris spoke with us more about what could realistically be done in a semester. He said that one major part of the communication between the team and client for this particular project would be conveying what is and isn't possible, and setting goals for the semester that allowed the next team to pick up where we left off without much struggle.

Ultimately, the number of applicants for the *New Me* project grew from three to nine, so my pep talk worked.

Proposal Stage (Weeks 5–7)

Weeks 5–7 of the course are devoted to the first project milestone: a proposal, in which each team identifies the problems their client is facing, the end objectives the team intends to reach, and the procedures they will undertake to get there. I faced two challenges at this point: to keep emphasizing realistic goal-setting and to get the students to articulate those goals clearly in their proposals. Because Georgia Tech is a highly competitive school, my teams tend to over-promise how much they can get done. This tendency is the biggest factor behind the handful of projects that have been considered failures, and I show the students examples of proposals that have over-reached. The following proposal is the *New Me* team's attempt after this lesson about scoping.

Problem

New Heart has expressed the impact diabetes is currently having on the modem world. This game is being developed to address the following problems:

1. People with diabetes can have difficulty in becoming and staying motivated to track and manage their illness.
2. Patients may not know how to effectively manage their illness.
3. People with the disease may feel isolated or need emotional support.

Objective

Our team plans to help solve these problems by creating the concept and framework for a web-based game that achieves the following goals:

The game will entertain and reward players for engaging in healthy behaviors to manage their diabetes.

These behaviors will follow the seven healthy behaviors defined by the American Association of Diabetes Educators (AADE):

- Healthy eating
- Physical activity
- Monitoring of blood glucose
- Regular medication intake
- Problem solving
- Health risk reduction
- Coping with diabetes
- Players will be taught healthy habits and practices through playing the game.
- A strong social element will be incorporated to connect players.

As can be seen from the snippets of the *New Me* proposal above, this team erred too conservatively, hedging their objectives to "the concept and framework" for the game. I failed to push them to define concrete deliverables, which made it harder to evaluate their project at the end.

Alpha Stage (Weeks 8–10)

Active development of the project began in the second half of the semester, and the project evolved in three iterative stages for which we used the software development terms *Alpha, Beta,* and *Release Candidate.* The students' goal in the Alpha Stage was to produce sketches and mockups—very rough drafts of the project's deliverables. My goal was to teach them how to present initial ideas, give and receive peer feedback, and report on their progress to their clients and me. However, as one reads the *New Me* team's accounts of their work in this period, they were also teaching themselves a great deal about audience analysis, procedural rhetoric, collaborative design, feedback solicitation, and interpersonal communication.

Scott: Audience Analysis

Our deliverable for the Alpha Stage was a High Concept Document (HCD), which included some amazing sketches, very clear descriptions of the general reward system, and navigation of the game.

The demographics for the game were a concern for us during the writing of the HCD. New Heart's patient demographics were almost exclusively seniors, a demographic that is rarely targeted by video game developers. To compound this difficulty, the team members were all of the Millennial generation. This made it difficult for us to understand the perspective of our target audience in terms of technical proficiency, aesthetics, and ideology. We ultimately created the following high concept document:

High Concept

In New Me you are a Superhero Living in a new world with many adventures to be had and villainous henchmen to defeat. You and other superheroes explore a fascinating story playing mini-game adventures together or even against each other! Study healthy lifestyle choices to power up your character with biotechnology. As your superhero gets more powerful, the better your superhero can compete, and the further you and your friends can explore!

The "superhero" theme the team envisioned for the game's setting evinces their assumption that the kinds of stories that appeal to their age group would also appeal to older players.

Scott: Procedural Rhetoric

The Alpha Stage of the project was probably the most difficult phase of the semester. Because there was no clear vision for what the game would actually be [outside] of the proposal, most of the work went into flushing out the game concepts. What would keep users interested in playing the game? How could we get patients to use it every day? Since the game is supposed to help patients develop habits, solutions to these problems were probably the most important aspect in developing a successful game concept.

The team drew on the role-playing game genre for inspiration, imagining that players would have avatars with character attributes like "constitution" and "strength," which would increase as players practiced the behaviors listed in the left column (see Table 16.1).

Table 16.1   Chart of Behavior Attributes for *New Me*

Behavior	Attribute
Healthy eating	Constitution
Physical activity	Strength
Blood glucose monitoring	Dedication
Regular medication intake	Constitution
Problem solving	Intelligence
Health risk reduction	Intelligence
Coping with diabetes	Dedication

Collaborative Design

As mentioned above, each student team was organized into five "tracks," or roles, that the students applied for and performed according to their expertise levels in management, writing, design, and programming. In what follows, programmer Ryan Reeves discusses the collaboration between graphic designers and programmers as they conceived the first interface mockups for game characters and the game map.

Ryan

During the early design phase, we always came back to what could be implemented in a clean and portable way. Programmers were dependent upon in this aspect; technological limitations ultimately altered how we could design the game and shaped what we wanted to deliver to New Heart. This was present in every aspect of the design process: every graphics mockup was carefully discussed between the graphic designers and programmers to ensure each mockup did not show impossible features. See Figure 16.1 for example of mockups.

Feedback Solicitation

An essential element of the documentation process is asking for feedback from the client. In the reports that accompany each of the project drafts, I required a "Recommendations" section in which the teams address their clients with specific questions about their deliverables. I stressed the importance of asking targeted questions since clients don't necessarily share the students' technical expertise or knowledge about the project. Below, Sean Murray, *New Me*'s Managing Editor, discusses the questions his team put to New Heart.

Sean

The Alpha Stage was the team's first opportunity to show and assess its capabilities. To this end, the team had assembled a progress report discussing the work that had been done and what was expected to come during the next

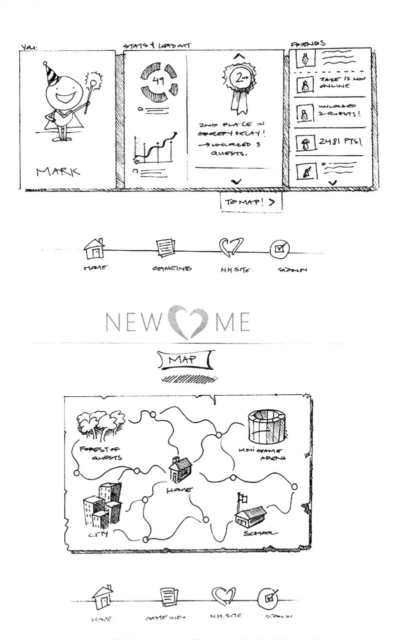

Figure 16.1   Mockups of Character Attributes and World Map Screens

stage. The team used this opportunity to request specific, targeted feedback from New Heart as well as establish a well-defined timetable for future stages. At this point in the design, the team wanted to leave as many options as possible for Ms. McCormick and New Heart to choose from in the concept of the game. We tried to ask questions regarding the theme of the game, as well as which features she would like to see and what we should plan to add to the game to best suit the user base. Here, we provide the recommendations section from the teams' Alpha Report:

Recommendations

We would like New Heart to review the game structures and High Concept Document we have designed and give us feedback for the questions described in the following list:

- Do you feel that the current setup of the game will attract players?
- What changes should be made to increase the game's attractiveness?
- What things are you most excited to see in our game?
- Do you agree with our decision on what platform to use?
- What kind of educational content do we need to include to best help the players?
- Will the theme of the game attract the desired audience?

Teaching Team Collaboration

In the discussion that follows, Scott and Sameer's accounts of managing their team illustrate how important a team's internal communication is to its functionality and success. Team communication is therefore a topic that my classes consciously attend to.[4]

Scott and Sameer: Managing Team Collaboration

Scott

Throughout the semester, there were ups and downs with how engaged everyone was in the project. In particular, we had one issue with a student who did not seem to be engaged in the project at all. Because of his schedule, he found it

---

[4] Every college student has worked on group projects, and everyone has had some kind of negative experience with them. My sense of my students' attitudes about group projects is that they see them as a necessary evil: a reality of their working world but one that brings a lot of pressure and stress. It became clear to me that the purview of our attention to communication needed to include the communication of the teams themselves. Consequently, around mid-term, we hold a "Team Health Summit" during which teammates evaluate one another's performance, analyze their team's communication, and state communicative policies they will then follow. They compose a memo that summarizes all of this.

difficult to make it to meetings. In turn, it was difficult to keep him engaged in the project. We also found it difficult to get in touch with him through other means of communication such as email or class time. For a good bit of the semester, we tried assigning work and seeing if he would get done, but we had no such luck. As communication lessened, Sam and I thought something needed to be done. We sent an email together expressing our concern that he had not been contributing to the project, but also expressing that there was still time to make up for not contributing, as well as valuable work still to be completed before the final deliverable. Unfortunately, not much changed, and as managers, we had to figure out a way to move forward with the project without the extra help. Luckily, we had many team members that did care and it was not difficult, as we saw throughout the semester to work around the problem.

Sameer

It was interesting to note how the dynamics of project management change when we transitioned from small groups (three to five people) to larger groups such as the nine we had. The biggest differences include the difficulty of group synergy with that many different influences, and the best solutions involved separating tasks into temporary weekly sub-groups with specific tasks. This worked extremely well after a few mishaps early on, and we were able to get some good work done.

Our organization needed some development. Due to scheduling conflicts, the inability to meet for long enough periods would make dissemination of tasks difficult, so we decided on virtual meetings through Google+ Hangouts, which was extremely helpful in getting our project off the ground. We set a goal of meeting at least twice per deliverable and working together to delegate tasks to the group. In so doing, we were able to meet in smaller groups for shorter periods as the project progressed. As we got more comfortable in our roles, we divided sections of work up to specific people or subgroups, including having subgroup leads to handle their group responsibilities.

Scott and Sameer also reveal one of the many lessons this course has taught me: Strong student leaders are crucial. Scott and Sameer were extremely capable Project Managers, handling team motivation, task division, and scheduling with little help from me.

Beta Stage (Weeks 10–13)

The general goal of the Beta Stage is to present working drafts of the project deliverables to the client. My task at this stage of the semester was to keep each of my nine teams accountable for meeting the objectives they had set by primarily reporting their progress. Project managers gave oral reports to me each week, and each team wrote a progress report to their client that accompanied their Beta deliverables. In class, the teams primarily workshopped one another's drafts.

As they delved deeper into their projects, the teams' interactions with me, one another, and their clients became increasingly challenging translations of technical content. As Slack, Miller, and Doak argue, translation is inherent in most conceptions of technical communication, but conceiving of technical communication as articulation (both in the sense of "saying" and in the sense of "joining") "allows us to move beyond a conception of communication as the polar contributions of sender and receiver to a conception of an ongoing process of articulation constituted in (and constituting) the relations of meaning and power operating in the entire context within which messages move" (90). In other words, as these projects evolve, students also find themselves in shifting relationships with one another, their clients, and me as well as with the technologies with which they are designing and the media with which they are communicating. As the *New Me* team's accounts of this stage show, they were getting more deeply entrenched in engaging the game's target audience while simultaneously negotiating shifting conceptions of who that audience was and what they could do.

Ryan: Programming

After completion of the Alpha Milestone, the team had a much more concrete idea of the direction the project would be headed. Since most of the brainstorming was complete, it was now important to begin deciding how the target audience could expect to interact with the game. Ultimately, accessibility became the main concern in deciding upon a platform for the game. The diversity of patients catered to by New Heart made deciding on a concrete platform a daunting task. Would the patients be accessing the software on mobile devices, tablets, or traditional computers? Since the answer could be all of these devices, we had to choose the most widely supported and flexible framework.

The main frameworks shared by personal computers that could be utilized for our game are those supported by modern web browsers. With the stable support of HTML5, we would have access to a hardware-accelerated drawing surface provided by the "canvas" element. This would provide us an abstraction for JavaScript on which we could render two-dimensional graphics on any device with an up-to-date web browser. It is worth mentioning that, despite not being used in our design due to stability, WebGL can be utilized to draw three-dimensional graphics on the canvas element. The introduction of WebGL is an important feature, since it could be used with our design to make three-dimensional games in the future.

Upon making a concrete decision of the design platform and graphical dimension, the programmers and graphics designers began working together to create design mockups. The designs created from this combined effort allowed the group, for the first time, to visualize the final product we were all working hard to create. This was a key moment for the group; through cooperative efforts, we were able to create tangible results.

With the evolution of modern technology away from standard one-use devices, most modern personal computers are accompanied by a comprehensive web browser. This gave us an advantage in that we knew the web browsers also supported multifarious standards necessary to properly render the wide gamut of website designs. This revelation dramatically altered how we thought about the design of the game; consequently, the Graphic Designers immediately began working with the Programmers to design mockups for the conceptualized webpage. What began as a search for how to best interact with New Heart's patients, and vice versa, soon became one of the key moments for the group as a whole; it was the first time through the design process in which everyone began to see a concrete product form. See Figure 16.2.

The newly decided platform did, however, introduce new problems for the group to solve. Internally, there were different ideas of what type of game we should be making, how the patients could interact with it, and what would be expected of them. These problems also seemed to arise concurrently with an issue stemming from future expandability: How would future teams continue using our

Figure 16.2   Webpage Mockup of the Character Stats Screen

framework to design and implement the game? During a Programmers' meeting we decided to design the entire game based around mini-games. Analogous to the Olympics, each game could have its own constraints, rewards, and player expectations. This also allowed future teams to create mini-games and insert them into the overarching webpage for patients to access.

Sean: Research

Developing concepts for the mini-game and quest system involved researching existing games. Our main researcher in the project, Kaili An, studied the core processes for developing mini-games on the Internet, and provided the team with background information on the motivations of these games. One of the key concepts in mini-games is providing a compulsion to continue playing the game through a sense of iterative success providing a constant sense of achievement.

We then fleshed out the execution of a mini-game concept including the game logic and start/end conditions. See Figure 16.3.

Sean: Writing

The in game avatar has an initial stamina/energy and speed which are functions of the player's constitution and fitness attributes, as well as an initial position. The win condition is when the game avatar's position in game passes the finish line.

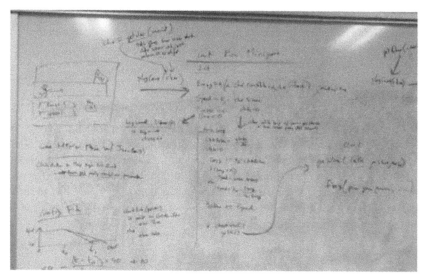

The logic of the game is as follows: Energy, Speed, Position, Time, and Clicks are initialized. Then, the game loop repeats every time step, checking the clicks per second of the player and updating the energy

Figure 16.3   Foot Race Mini-Game Concept

When writing the Beta Report and building the Beta Deliverables, the team had to take into account a change in demographics. After meeting with the client for feedback on the Alpha Stage, we were told that her hope was that the scope of the game would extend to all sufferers of diabetes, not just patients at New Heart. This broadened demographic presented challenges in terms of theming, gameplay, and our choice of medium. The team approached this change with both excitement at the prospect of our game one day being played by people worldwide and trepidation at the challenge that this would present.

The Beta Stage of the game concept also marked the beginning of the inclusion of technical documentation into the deliverables. This documentation included a mechanics document that detailed how the user interacted with the game as well as how the game used that information. Mockups of the main screens of the game were also drawn to illustrate what we expected the user to see while playing.

The Mechanics Document began as an extension of the High Concept Document, discussing high-level features and operations. From there, the document began to discuss how the game dealt with these features and how they affected the player. Our goal in this was to explain clearly and succinctly how we expected the game would be played and what role the player and system played in the design. To this end, the document provided examples of mini-games, map navigation, and quests; and it discussed at length how the player would be affected. It was imperative that this document be clear and understandable for the next team so they would have clear direction in how they should approach the creation of the game and the gameplay mechanics. See Figure 16.4.

Release Candidate Stage (Weeks 14–15)

As the semester's end approached, the projects needed to transition from the creation of new content to the polishing and presentation of that content. There was only about a week from when the students turned their "Release Candidates" in until they turned in their "Final Releases." I told the students that their Release Candidate should show the project at 99% completion, so they only had to make minor tweaks to it for the final version. However, readers might note that this team couldn't help but keep composing new ideas.

Scott: Managing
By this point in the project, there was one major piece of work left to be done: the first website design for the game. Sam put most of this together in just under a day, giving the team a great place to start from. Although there was no data backing any of the pages, and none of the information typed into the text fields was actually used for anything in the background, it still provided the first feeling that there really could be a game built off of the concepts we spent so much time

As players gain more experience, they unlock new choices for games and quests, as seen in Figure 2. In these areas, competition is fiercer and the quests become more difficult and long-term. For example, in the school, a mini game could be to simply choose the healthiest foods first out of a given set of items, but in the game arena, players would be racing against each other.

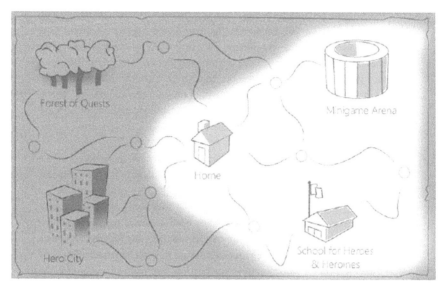

Figure 2. As the player advances, their world opens up, allowing them to do more without being overwhelmed.

Mini Games

When the player clicks the link to go to the mini game area, he or she is presented with a map of an imaginary world where one can travel to different locales. Each location contains one or more mini games for the player to play. The player can start different mini games depending on which location on the map is clicked. Clicking on a mini game will allow the player to start playing that game.

Figure 16.4   Part of the Team's Mechanics Document

developing. Also, this was the first time we could see how the graphics would actually fit into the game.

Ryan: Programming

Immediately following the Beta Milestone, the entire group met with the client in order to discuss the future plan. Everything we delivered up until this point covered the basic facets New Heart wanted for their game; however, we did not have the entire user experience mapped out. While our concept work was solid and we had a good foundation to build from, we did not have a clear cut design for the final product. This became increasingly apparent as we reviewed the documentation we delivered in the Beta Milestone.

To rectify this shortcoming, we immediately began altering the "Mechanics Document." The first iteration we completed for the Beta Milestone was lacking critical details needed to fully encapsulate user experience. Through the creation of the new version of this document, the team came together to discuss our visions for the game after completion. We discussed the critical pieces for implementation: functionality of the avatars, navigation throughout the game, and mini games. Unconventionally, the Mechanics Document was written to target non-technical audiences. We wanted not only for the client to be able to fully understand everything we were proposing, but anyone in the future groups, no matter their skill set.

Since the Release Candidate was our last major milestone, the group centered around polishing the design and making alterations to provide an enjoyable experience for New Heart's patients. That was the purpose of the game design from the beginning, and it was the core of the team's thought process throughout the whole project. Although it may not have been a central theme in the first few iterations, where conceptualization was harmonized, the Release Candidate was focused on providing a comprehensive design that implemented all of New Heart's ideals. From a programmer's perspective, this meant making sure the designs were in sync and implementation could be done in a cohesive manner.

In order to have a complete and sound design for the Release Candidate, the programmers became harsh critics of prior design iterations. We went through every screen in the game design and decided what was possible and what had to be removed. In order for our idea to be truly implementable by future teams, we couldn't produce an extravagant design that would take even the most highly skilled programmers years to implement. This mindset coupled with the desire to provide New Heart with the best game we could deliver is what ultimately lead us into the final Release Candidate design.

Sean: Writing

Writing for the Release Candidate consisted primarily of polishing and updating previous deliverables and preparing for the Final Release. This phase is where all of our past work and ideas were brought together into what would become our final deliverable to New Heart.

With our time working on this project nearing its end, we began to focus on effectively communicating our concepts and framework to the team that would take over. To minimize confusion, we looked over past documents to check for consistent tone and format. Our goal was to leave the project with a polished, clean package from which the next team could quickly and easily pick up and build.

Final Release Stage (Week 16)

In the last week of class, the students made minor adjustments to their "Project Deliverables" and presented them to their clients with a "Final Report." My goal at this point was to help them present their work so that their clients were excited about what they were getting.

Scott: Managing

This was surprisingly the easiest phase of development in the whole project. Because most of the work was already finished, the majority if not all of the time in the Final Stage of the project was spent polishing things up, and tying up the loose ends. This meant providing the code for the website, game mechanics, game graphics, and suggestions for where the game should go. Also, resolving any questions that arose towards the end of the semester was a major part in finishing the project. We made a few changes to the mechanics and design for the game, but the material we could not change, we talked about in the report so the next team would know where to go.

Ryan: Programming

Upon reaching the Final Release Stage, the group was almost entirely done with the game design. The client was impressed with our Release Candidate, and we only had to make a few minor tweaks to create a polished final product. Despite this, the Programmers wanted to complete one last major deliverable to show the client how the game would ultimately come together.

For the Final Deliverable, Sam and I decided to complete a small website to present an extremely basic walk through of how the game would look and function based off of our final proposal. The creation of this website, no matter how minimalistic, was important to us. We wanted the client to be able to tour through a live website in order to experience small parts of the design our team worked so hard to complete. Despite only having a few days to complete the website, we were able to create a minimalist view of how the game could function. In the end, we felt it was the best way we, as Programmers, could convey our design to New Heart.

By the Final Deliverable, the programmers were satisfied with all of the work we put into the project. Although some of us wanted to continue working on its completion, we were able to work with our group to provide a flexible and expandable design that covered every aspect presented to us by New Heart. In the end, for me, this was a memorable experience. I was proud of the work we all were able to accomplish throughout the design process. The end product was a solid design for a good cause, and I am glad I was a part of the team.

Sean: Writing

The Final Release was delivered only a few days after the Release Candidate. This marked the end of our project and our time working with New Heart. The writing work outside the final report for this stage was minimal, as there was not much time to update anything in a major way. The majority of our efforts were spent toward polishing past work and improving the reader's understanding in the same manner as the Release Candidate.

In preparing the Final Report, we wanted to leave Ms. McCormick feeling confident in what we accomplished. To this end, the Final Report looked over all that we had done since the beginning of the semester. We wanted to show New Heart everything we had achieved and all of the time and effort that had gone into this project. In addition, we wanted to address the future of the project so Ms. McCormick would walk away with the knowledge that we had planned for this to continue moving forward.

The final send-off with New Heart was met with feelings of excitement, anxiety, and relief. We were excited to see the project come as far as it had, and we were proud of what we had done in such a short time. Ms. McCormick seemed very pleased with our work, and it felt like the game could really become something bigger than what we had originally planned. This was a relief to us, as the team was constantly pushing to deliver better content to New Heart.

Conclusions

While this chapter has been in the review and revision process, *New Me* has gone through a second semester of development. The second team refined the game concepts even further, most notably abandoning the superhero motif. They also built working prototypes of a character builder and a mini-game. New Heart's Beth McCormick was satisfied with both teams' work, but she and I concluded after the second semester that *New Me* had gone as far as two temporary teams could develop it; it needed full-time development by a team that would last longer than a semester. Over the summer, I started gathering the most committed members of these two temporary teams into one persistent team, intending to obtain funding and develop *New Me* to completion.

But at the beginning of the fall 2013 semester, I learned something that made me want to go back to the drawing board: we needed to understand our audience better. In my new technical communication class, I had invited a guest lecture from Dr. Merrick Furst, Founder and Director of Flashpoint, a startup incubator at

Georgia Tech that practices "Startup Engineering," an extremely rigorous process of testing new products with their target audiences:

> Startup Engineering is a program and framework for finding genuine unmet demand and building scalable companies to satisfy it. Startup engineers take a "problem first" approach to identify inadequately addressed pain in their customer's personal or professional lives. They generate theories about customer improvement goals and the constraints that prevent existing solutions from meeting them. They work toward actionable truth by testing to disconfirm their theories, modifying them, and retesting. They prioritize and gauge progress through a framework of understanding, bounding, and reducing the risks that all early stage companies face. ("Startup Engineering")

Backed by the ethos of a career making, researching, and coaching startups, Furst spent a fascinating hour debunking the myth that someone can imagine a new technology, talk to their ideal audience once or twice, and make something people will actually use. He convinced me that the *New Me* game—if indeed a game was its best format—would only work if the patients at New Heart found it *too compelling not to use.* The only way to achieve that would be to test every single gameplay idea with those patients. That was something my students had never been able to do both because of physical distance and time constraints. It remains to be seen whether I can pull together a team with the mobility and persistence *New Me* will need. It also remains to be seen whether this class has made me Geppetto or Frankenstein (if they were *real,* of course); either way, they've made a new me.

There are five takeaways I hope to impart to technical communication teachers by helping my students tell their story about this project:

The students can really take ownership of these projects

I made initial contact with the client, brought the students together, and guided their progress, but they took over from there. They analyzed (and reanalyzed) their audience, assessed (and reassessed) their technical competences, managed their workflows, and composed and revised numerous documents multiple times. The class' structure prompted them to go through these steps, but much of their work came from their own sense of responsibility to the client, the target audience, and future development teams. As their teacher, I mostly found myself in the role of coach, helping them stay motivated and hone their communication towards more and more brilliance and clarity.

The upside of this situation is engagement; the students are committed to and enthusiastic about their work. In the game of education, the stakes are always real for the students, but they often forget that fact when the subject matter is fictional and the products of their labor are "just for a class." When their work actually mattered to someone besides themselves, they almost all abandoned their cynicism for undisappointed idealism, and they did truly good work. The downside of the students' engagement with the project is that the structure of school cuts it off: the semester ends and the project team disbands. With 100% turnover of the design team, the game's design was bound to change as new people brought new ideas. The design documents did offer some anchoring to the game's direction but not as much as a consistent team working from the beginning to the end of development would have done.

The game probably won't get finished during the class, but that's probably okay

The other potential drawback to undertaking a game project in a service learning technical communication course is that, at a certain point, the game has to actually get built, a feat of art and programming that exceeds the skillset of most technical communication students (even those at Georgia Tech). Further, this is often outside of the purview of most technical communication classes. As chapter one of this collection demonstrates, documentation is essential to computer game development, but more so at the beginning and end of the process. Indeed, as Sansone argues, spending time making design documents perfect during active development doesn't reflect what the games industry is coming to discover as the best practice of game development.

As a technical communication teacher, I'm not particularly bothered by that. My course outcomes (which have been established for all Georgia Tech technical communications courses by the School of Literature, Media, and Communication's Writing and Communication Program) revolve around strategies for rhetorical analysis and composition, which include: crafting artifacts that address the exigencies of various professional contexts, exhibiting effective and appropriate persuasive strategies; addressing diverse audiences with tact and sensitivity to cultural, theoretical, ethical, and legal concerns; collecting, shaping, and presenting technical information in ways that convey a clear purpose; and selecting and using genres according to the interplay of context, audience, and purpose within a given rhetorical situation. In addition to these rhetorical outcomes, we also have process-based outcomes and outcomes that require students to move across multiple modes and media. The way my course is structured, it meets all of these outcomes—the students can demonstrate success in their projects and in the course, even if their projects aren't "ready-to-ship done."

You may feel compelled to finish the project yourself

Prepare to think both like a teacher and like an account manager. While I've found that running a service learning class is no harder than running a self-contained class, it does have a larger scope because the clients comprise a new set of stakeholders. It's impossible not to care about the clients (indeed, caring about the clients is one of the points of service learning)—we want to do right by them, to see their projects succeed. If a project doesn't go well, I feel bad, not only for the students but also for the clients. If a project isn't finished at the end of a semester, I offer the client the option to continue with a new team in the next semester. In the case of New Heart, I could see that their project was larger than two semesters and in fact larger than a college class could accommodate. I feel obligated to see it through now, which is expanding and complicating my notions of my professional capabilities and duties. I wonder if being a game designer or communication consultant will help or hinder my progress towards indefinite employment and tenure. I'm mostly excited about this new direction in my career, but I'd be lying if I said I wasn't nervous.

The students will need a lot of access to their target players

Merrick Furst—not to mention my coauthors in this collection—has cemented a conviction I already held about the importance of playtesting. Audience feedback is essential to any service learning project's success, but it's especially important for a game project. Unfortunately, in this case, iterative design and testing were impossible because of the distance between my students and their audience. In retrospect, I probably wouldn't begin a project like this with a client that wasn't local. However, I wouldn't hesitate to undertake another game project if my students had access to playtesters. Which brings me to my final point.

It doesn't take a great deal of special technical knowledge to teach game design in a technical communication class

Because the class focuses on documentation, it mainly requires the teacher to help students learn good rhetorical analysis and composition practices. It helps to know a little bit about what makes a good game, but it helps more to model how savvy rhetors teach themselves the rhetorics of new media and new genres. Other than that, ensuring success on any particular project requires pushing the students to accurately and honestly assess what they are capable of building, especially with large, highly technical projects, so they don't get in over their heads. This has happened a few times—I don't want to suggest that every project goes as swimmingly as New Me—but flopped projects and unhappy clients are the exception to the rule. The rule is that reality beats realism, even in the magic circle of the classroom.

Works Cited

Anderson, Paul V. *Technical Communication: A Reader-Centered Approach.* 7th ed. Boston: Wadsworth, 2011.
Bogost, Ian. *Persuasive Games: The Expressive Power of Videogames.* Cambridge, MA: MIT P, 2007.

Burke, Kenneth. *Language as Symbolic Action: Essays on Life, Literature, and Method*. Berkeley: U of California P, 1966.

Caillois, Roger. *Man, Play, and Games*. Trans. Meyer Barash. Urbana, IL: U of Illinois P, 2001.

Custer, Jason. "The Three D's of Procedural Literacy: Developing, Demonstrating, and Documenting Layered Literacies with Valve's Steam for Schools." *Computer Games and Technical Communication: Critical Methods and Applications at the Intersection*. Burlington, VT: Ashgate, 2014. 247–63.

Eyman, Douglas. "Computer Gaming and Technical Communication: An Applied Framework." *Technical Communication* 55.3 (2008): 242–50.

Gee, James Paul. *Situated Language and Learning: A Critique of Traditional Schooling*. New York: Routledge, 2004.

Giles, Dwight E., Jr., and Janet Eyler. "The Theoretical Roots of Service-Learning in John Dewey: Toward a Theory of Service-Learning." *Michigan Journal of Community Service Learning* 1 (1994): 77–85.

Greene, Jeff, and Laura Palmer. "It's All Fun and Games Until Someone Pulls Out a Manual: Finding a Role for Technical Communicators in the Game Industry." *Computer Games and Technical Communication: Critical Methods and Applications at the Intersection*. Burlington, VT: Ashgate, 2014. 17–33.

Grouling, Jennifer, Stephanie Hedge, Aly Schweigert, and Eva Grouling Snider. "Questing through Class: Gamification in the Professional Writing Classroom." *Computer Games and Technical Communication: Critical Methods and Applications at the Intersection*. Burlington, VT: Ashgate, 2014. 265–82.

Huckin, Thomas N. "Technical Writing and Community Service." *Journal of Business and Technical Communication* 11.1 (1997): 49–59.

Matthews, Catherine, and Beverly B. Zimmerman. "Integrating Service Learning and Technical Communication: Benefits and Challenges." *Technical Communication Quarterly* 8.4 (1999): 383–404.

Sansone, Anthony. "Game Design Documents: Changing Production Models, Changing Demands." *Computer Games and Technical Communication: Critical Methods and Applications at the Intersection*. Burlington, VT: Ashgate, 2014. 109–23.

Slack, Jennifer Daryl, David James Miller, and Jeffrey Doak. "The Technical Communicator as Author: Meaning, Power, Authority." *Professional Writing and Rhetoric*. Ed. Tim Peeples. New York: Longman, 2003. 80–98.

"Startup Engineering." *Flashpoint @ Georgia Tech*. Web 7 January 2014.

Youngblood, Susan A., and Jo Mackiewicz. "Lessons in Service Learning: Developing the Service Learning Opportunities in Technical Communication (SLOT-C) Database." *Technical Communication Quarterly* 22.3 (2013): 260–83.

Index

Games Index